The Political Economy of Adjustment Throughout and Beyond the Eurozone Crisis

This volume focuses on the aftermath of the euro crisis and whether the reforms have brought about lasting changes to the economic and political structures of the crisis countries, or if the changes were short-term and easily abandoned post-bailout and post-recovery.

Starting with an analysis of the state of euro area governance at the onset of the crisis and the ensuing reforms, the book considers structural conditions as well as those specific to the domestic political economy of most of the countries affected by the crisis, including Greece, Ireland, Portugal, Spain and Italy. It presents up-to-date and incisive analysis of the aftermath of the crisis and suggests how we can situate it within our understanding of different national growth models in Europe.

This book will be of key interest to scholars, students and practitioners interested in the euro crisis, Economic and Monetary Union, European Union and European Politics, and more broadly in Comparative Politics, Political Economy, International Relations, Economics, Finance, Business and Industry.

Michele Chang is Professor of European Political and Governance Studies at the College of Europe.

Federico Steinberg is Senior Analyst at the Elcano Royal Institute and Lecturer of Political Economy at Madrid's Universidad Autónoma.

Francisco Torres is Visiting Professor of European Political Economy at Católica Lisbon School of Business and Economics and has been a Visiting Senior Fellow at the LSE since 2014 and PEFM Associate at St Antony's College, Oxford University, since 2012.

Routledge/UACES Contemporary European Studies

The primary objective of the new Contemporary European Studies series is to provide a research outlet for scholars of European Studies from all disciplines. The series publishes important scholarly works and aims to forge for itself an international reputation.

Competitiveness and Solidarity in the European Union
Interdisciplinary Perspectives
Edited by Paolo Chiocchetti and Frédéric Allemand

Changing Borders in Europe
Exploring the Dynamics of Integration, Differentiation and Self-Determination in the European Union
Edited by Jacint Jordana, Michael Keating, Axel Marx and Jan Wouters

Citizenship, Nation-building and Identity in the EU
The Contribution of Erasmus Student Mobility
Cherry James

The Informal Construction of Europe
Edited by Lennaert van Heumen and Mechthild Roos

Refugees, Security and the European Union
Sarah Léonard and Christian Kaunert

The Political Economy of Adjustment Throughout and Beyond the Eurozone Crisis
What Have We Learned?
Edited by Michele Chang, Federico Steinberg and Francisco Torres

Differentiated Integration and Disintegration in a Post-Brexit Era
Edited by Stefan Gänzle, Benjamin Leruth and Jarle Trondal

The Political Economy of Adjustment Throughout and Beyond the Eurozone Crisis

What Have We Learned?

Edited by
Michele Chang,
Federico Steinberg and
Francisco Torres

Routledge
Taylor & Francis Group
LONDON AND NEW YORK

UACES

First published 2020
by Routledge
2 Park Square, Milton Park, Abingdon, Oxon OX14 4RN

and by Routledge
605 Third Avenue, New York, NY 10017

First issued in paperback 2021

Routledge is an imprint of the Taylor & Francis Group, an informa business

British Library Cataloguing-in-Publication Data
A catalogue record for this book is available from the British Library

Library of Congress Cataloging-in-Publication Data
A catalog record has been requested for this book

ISBN 13: 978-0-367-78446-1 (pbk)
ISBN 13: 978-1-138-38615-0 (hbk)

Typeset in Times New Roman
by Wearset Ltd, Boldon, Tyne and Wear

Contents

Figures

Tables

Boxes

Contributors

Editors

Michele Chang has been Professor of European Political and Governance Studies at the College of Europe since 2006 after spending a year as a Fulbright Scholar at the Centre for European Policy Studies. She has taught courses on European integration and political economy across Europe and the US, including Colgate University, Boston University, University of Agder, the Moscow School of International Relations (MGIMO) and American University in Brussels. She has served as Vice Chair of the European Union Studies Association and currently sits on the Board of the Trans European Policy Studies Association. Her research interests include euro area governance, EU fiscal policy and the European Central Bank. She holds a Ph.D. from the University of California at San Diego. Recent publications include: Chang, M. (2017). Brexit and EU Economic & Monetary Union: From EMU Outsider to Instigator. *Law and Politics of Brexit*. F. Fabbrini. Oxford, Oxford University Press. Chang, M. (2016). *Economic and Monetary Union*. London, Palgrave Macmillan.

Federico Steinberg is a Senior Analyst at the Elcano Royal Institute and Lecturer of Political Economy at Madrid's Universidad Autónoma. He holds a Ph.D. in Economics from the Universidad Autónoma, an MSc in Politics of the World Economy from the London School of Economics and a Master in International Affairs from Columbia University. Between 2002 and 2004 he was involved in a variety of development projects for the World Bank as a consultant in Washington DC, Ghana and Bolivia, as well as at the Executive Office of the Secretary General at the United Nations headquarters in New York. He also teaches regularly on a number of Master's degrees, including IE Business School and ICADE. He is a frequent contributor to the Spanish and international media, and has been invited to deliver speeches in more than ten countries. Recent publications include: Otero-Iglesias, M. and F. Steinberg (2017). Following the Franco-German Harbinger? The Footprint of the Euro in Regional Monetary Integration. *Comparative European Politics* 15(2): 220–239. Steinberg, F. and M. Vermeiren (2016). Germany's Institutional

Power and the EMU Regime after the Crisis: Towards a Germanized Euro Area? *Journal of Common Market Studies* 54(2): 388–407.

Francisco Torres is Visiting Professor of European Political Economy at Católica Lisbon School of Business and Economics and has also been since 2014 a Visiting Senior Fellow in European Political Economy at the LSE and a PEFM Research Associate of the European Studies Centre at St Antony's College, Oxford University. He holds a Ph.D. in European Political Economy (UCP, Lisbon), an MSc in Economics (UNL, Lisbon) and a 'licenciatura', also in Economics (UCP, Lisbon). He also studied Economics at the EUI, in Florence (PhD progr.), and holds an MA in International Affairs from the Johns Hopkins University, SAIS. He is EU Steering Committee Member of ECPR. Previously, he was, among other positions, a Visiting Fellow in Oxford, at the EUI, Florence, and the first Robert Schuman Fellow of the European Commission at CEPS, Brussels. He has taught European Political Economy at the Universities of Rome II and Victoria, BC, Canada. Recent publications include: Jones, E. and F. Torres, Eds. (2016). *Governance of the European Monetary Union: Recasting Political, Fiscal and Financial Integration*, London, Routledge. Bongardt, A. and F. Torres (2016). EMU as a Sustainable Currency Area. *The Euro and the Crisis: Perspectives for the Eurozone as a Monetary and Budgetary Union.* N. d. C. Cabral, J. R. Gonçalves and N. C. Rodrigues. New York, Springer: 17–32.

Authors

Kevin Cardiff is a non-executive board member of KBC Bank Ireland and of the think-tank TASC. He is also a member and chairperson of the Board of Auditors of the European Stability Mechanism. He was a member of the European Court of Auditors between 2012 and 2018, where he was responsible for a range of audit products. Previously, Cardiff was a senior official in the Department of Finance of Ireland during the worst periods of the global financial crisis that started in 2007, and was appointed by the Government as Secretary General of the Department in February 2010. In these positions, he was centrally involved in some of the events and policy issues discussed in his chapter. The opinions in this chapter are his own, rather than those of any organization. Recent publications include: Cardiff, K. (2016). *Recap: Inside Ireland's Financial Crisis*. Dublin, Liffey Press.

Miguel Lebre de Freitas is Assistant Professor at Universidade de Aveiro, Adjunct Professor at Nova SBE and Research Fellow at Núcleo de Investigação em Políticas Económicas at Universidade do Minho (NIPE). Miguel has also accumulated significant experience in applied research, having participated in projects involving a variety of countries and regions, for institutions such as the Bank of Portugal, the European Commission, the African, Caribbean and Pacific (ACP) group states and the European Court of

Auditors, among others, and, between 2005 and 2010, he served as Director General at the Ministry of Economy in Portugal. He has published on issues related to macroeconomics, international trade and economic growth. He holds a Ph.D. in Economics from the University of London, Birkbeck College, and an MSc in Economics from Nova SBE. Recent publications include: De Freitas, Miguel Lebre, Luis Catela Nunes and Madalena Sampaio Rodrigues (2018). Euro Area Membership and the Probability of a Sudden Stop: An Empirical Assessment. *JCMS: Journal of Common Market Studies* 56: 818–836. Lebre de Freitas, M., et al. (2015). Productive Experience and Specialization Opportunities for Portugal: An Empirical Assessment. *Portuguese Economic Journal* 15(1): 5–30.

Sven Hilgers is Research Fellow at the Fern Universität in Hagen. He was previously research fellow at the Otto-Suhr-Institute for Political Science of the Freie Universität Berlin (FU Berlin). As part of the research project 'Credit Lending as Two-Level Game: Troika–Debtor Negotiations in the Eurozone', he analyzes the process of negotiation and implementation of financial assistance programs in the Eurozone. His dissertation project investigates the changing nature of the European Central Bank. He studied political science and global studies in Berlin and Roskilde (Denmark) and holds an MA and BA in political science from FU Berlin. Recent publications and works include: Lütz, S. and Hilgers, S. (2018). When Overlapping Organizations Play Two-Level Games: IMF–EU Interaction in Credit Lending to Latvia and Greece. *New Political Economy* 24(3): 299–312. Hilgers, S. (2017). 'Reinterpreting Financial Stability: Seeing Like the European Central Bank on Debt Restructuring'. Paper presented at the Conference of the Society for the Advancement of Socio-Economics (SASE), University of Lyon, France, June 29 to July 1, 2017.

G. Russell Kincaid is Senior Associate Member of the Program on Political Economy of Financial Markets at St Antony's College, University of Oxford. He was Director at the International Monetary Fund until April 2013, serving as the secretariat for the IMF's Advisory Committee on Risk Management. Mr. Kincaid joined the IMF in 1976, working for the Middle East Department, the Asian Department, the European Department and the Strategy, Policy and Review Department. Mr. Kincaid has worked on many advanced and emerging market economies in the context of surveillance and IMF-supported programs and contributed to the development of IMF policies on surveillance and lending as well as on IMF governance matters. He has published on issues related to macroeconomic and financial policies, exchange rate assessments, sovereign debt management and restructuring, and policy implications of trends in international capital markets. Mr. Kincaid holds a Ph.D. in Economics from Columbia University and a BA from the University of California at Los Angeles. Recent publications include: Kincaid, G. R. (2016). Different Lessons for Europe from American Financial History: A Counterpoint to Mr. Gaspar. *Journal of European Integration* 38(7): 823–836.

Kincaid, G. R. and M. Watson (2015). Avoiding Another Crisis in the Euro Area: Public and Private Imbalances and National Policy Responses. *Journal of European Integration* 37(7): 787–801.

Susanne Lütz has been Professor for International Politics at the Fern Universität in Hagen since October 2017. She was previously Professor for International Political Economy at the Freie Universität Berlin. In her work, she focuses on international economic organizations, Eurozone politics, financial markets and financial market regulation, in particular. She received her Diploma in Social Sciences from the University Duisburg-Essen and completed her Ph.D. project in the interdisciplinary Post-Graduate Program on 'Social networks', funded by the Volkswagen Foundation, at the University of Cologne. She habilitated at the FernUniversität in Hagen. In addition, she has been a research fellow at the Max Planck Institute for the Study of Societies in Cologne, the Minda De Gunzburg Center for European Studies at Harvard University and the National Centre for Research in Europe (NCRE) at the University of Canterbury, Christchurch, New Zealand. Professor Lütz has held the Robert Bosch Fellowship for Comparative Public Policy and Institutions awarded by the American Institute for Contemporary German Studies (AICGS). Recent publications include: Lütz, S. and S. Hilgers (2018). When Overlapping Organizations Play Two-Level Games: IMF–EU Interaction in Credit Lending to Latvia and Greece. *New Political Economy* 24(3): 299–312. Lütz, S. and M. Kranke (2014). The European Rescue of the Washington Consensus? EU and IMF Lending to Central and Eastern European Countries. *Review of International Political Economy* 21(2): 310–338.

Benedicta Marzinotto is Lecturer in Economic Policy at the University of Udine and Visiting Professor at the College of Europe. Previous positions include Visiting Fellow at the European University Institute; Economist at the European Commission's DGECFIN; Fellow at Bruegel, the Brussel-based economic policy think tank; Research Fellow at the International Economics Program at Chatham House; and Visiting Researcher at the Free University of Berlin and at the University of Auckland. She has a Ph.D. and MSc from the London School of Economics and Political Science. Her main areas of expertise include international macroeconomics, European economic governance and labor economics. Recent publications include: Hallerberg, M. et al. (2018). Explaining the Evolving Role of National Parliaments under the European Semester. *Journal of European Public Policy* 25(2): 250–267. Marzinotto, B. (2017). Euro Area Macroeconomic Imbalances and Their Asymmetric Reversal: The Link between Financial Integration and Income Inequality. *Economia Politica* 34(1).

Silvia Merler is currently a Ph.D. candidate in European and Eurasian Studies at Johns Hopkins School of Advanced International Studies (SAIS), focusing on European macro-economics and political economy. She also serves as Head of Research at Algebris Policy & Research Forum. Formerly she was Affiliate

Fellow at Bruegel, Brussels Economic Policy Think Tank and an economic analyst at the European Commission's DG ECFIN. Recent publications include: Merler, S. (2018). Europeans and Globalization: Does the EU Square the Circle? *The Crisis of Globalization: Democracy, Capitalism and Inequality in the Twenty-First Century*. Patrick Diamond. London, I.B. Tauris Politics & International Relations. Merler, S. (2018). Varieties of Banking Union: Resolution Regimes and Backstops in Europe and the US. Paper prepared for the Istituto Affari Internazionali (IAI), IAI Papers 18(21).

George Pagoulatos is Professor of European Politics and Economy at the Athens University of Economics and Business and Visiting Professor at the College of Europe in Bruges. He is Vice President of the Hellenic Foundation for European and Foreign Policy (ELIAMEP) and member of the Governing Board of the European Policy Centre (EPC) in Brussels. Author of several books and many articles, he has been a regular columnist in the Sunday edition of the main Greek centrist newspaper *Kathimerini* since 2007. In 2011–12 he served as Senior Advisor and Director of Strategy at the PM Office under the technocratic Prime Minister Lucas Papademos and the interim government of P. Pikrammenos. Recent publications include: Pagoulatos, G. (2014). State-Driven in Boom and in Bust: Structural Limitations of Financial Power in Greece. *Government and Opposition* 49(Special Issue 03): 452–482. Pagoulatos, G. and L. Quaglia (2013). Turning the Crisis on Its Head: Sovereign Debt Crisis as Banking Crisis in Italy and Greece. *Market-Based Banking and the International Financial Crisis*. I. Hardie and D. Howarth. Oxford, Oxford University Press.

Sebastián Royo is a Professor of Government and Acting Provost at Suffolk University in Boston, USA. Royo's articles and reviews on comparative politics and political economy have appeared in leading journals, and he is the author of several books. Royo is a Senior Research Associate at the Elcano Royal Institute in Madrid, and an affiliate at the Minda de Gunzburg Center for European Studies at Harvard University, where he is the co-chair of the Southern Europe in the EU Study Group. Recent publications include: Otjes, S. et al. (2017). War of Attrition and Power of Inaction: The Spanish Financial Crisis and Its Lessons for the European Banking Union. *Revista de Economía Mundial* 46: 1691–1214. Quaglia, L. and S. Royo (2015). Banks and the Political Economy of the Sovereign Debt Crisis in Italy and Spain. *Review of International Political Economy* 22(3): 485–507.

Sebastian Schneider is a Research Fellow at the Fern Universität in Hagen. He previously worked as a Research Fellow at the Otto-Suhr-Institute for Political Science of the Freie Universität Berlin (FU Berlin). As part of the research project 'Credit Lending as Two-Level Game: Troika–Debtor Negotiations in the Eurozone', he analyzes negotiation and implementation processes of financial assistance programs in the Eurozone. His dissertation project analyzes the implications of national growth models for economic policy making. He studied political science in Berlin, Bergen and Friedrichshafen. Sebastian holds an MA in political science from FU Berlin and a BA in Public Management and Governance from Zeppelin University Friedrichshafen. Recent publications and works include: Schneider, S. (with Susanne Lütz and Sven Hilgers) (2018). Games Borrower Governments Play: The Implementation of Economic Adjustment Programs in Cyprus and Portugal. Paper presented at the workshop 'One Crisis, Many Perspectives: Understanding the Politics of the Eurozone Crisis'. Zürich, January 29–30, 2018. Schneider, S. (2017). Growth Models on the European Periphery: The 1980s as a Critical Juncture for Ireland and Portugal. Paper presented at the 113th APSA Annual Meeting, San Francisco, August 31 to September 3, 2017.

Preface[1]

One of the most surprising facts about the sovereign debt crisis that erupted in the Eurozone at the end of 2009 is the way it was misdiagnosed by European policymakers, helped by a number of influential academic economists. The misdiagnosis was in fact a double one. First, the crisis that hit a number of Eurozone countries, especially those of the periphery, was seen as originating from the supply-side of the economy. We were told that these countries experienced structural rigidities, not only in the output markets but even more so in the labor markets. Wages were too high and too rigid; workers could not be sacked easily enough; unemployment benefits were too high, weakening unemployed workers' incentives to look for a job.

The second misdiagnosis consisted in thinking that the sovereign debt crisis had been caused by government profligacy. Governments had been too lax in their fiscal policies and had allowed their debt to explode and to become unsustainable. Financial markets recognized this and dumped the bonds of these governments that had allowed their debt to become unsustainable.

The therapies that followed from these two diagnoses then followed logically. Countries hit by a sovereign debt crisis had to do two things: structural reforms, especially of the labor markets, and fiscal austerity. And thus the Troika was sent out to countries on the periphery of the Eurozone to apply these two therapies. The latter differed in detail when applied to different countries, as the chapters of this book make clear; the essence was the same and consisted of some mix of structural reforms and austerity programs.

Rarely have policies been so ill-conceived, based as they were on a fundamental misdiagnosis of the crisis hitting the Eurozone. The crisis did not originate from the supply side of the economy but from the demand side, and (with the possible exception of Greece) it was not the result of government profligacy but an excessive private debt accumulation prior to the crisis. If the government debt explosion had been the cause of the sovereign debt crisis, we would expect that Eurozone countries that accumulated a lot of government debt prior to the sovereign debt crisis also would have been hit most by this crisis when it erupted in 2010. In other words, we should find that the public debt accumulation is a good predictor of the subsequent sovereign debt crisis. In fact it was not, as De Grauwe and Ji (2018) showed. Instead they found that private debt accumulation before the financial crisis is a good predictor of the sovereign debt crisis, i.e., those countries that tended to accumulate more *private* debt before the crisis were more likely to experience a *public* debt crisis later.

How can we make sense of this? The financial crisis that erupted in 2008 was a classic case of a boom-bust dynamics that capitalism has produced quite often in history. These classical boom-bust episodes have been analyzed by, among others, Kindleberger (1978) and Minsky (1986). During the boom phase optimism and euphoria dominate, blinding consumers and investors in perceiving risks. As a result, consumption and investment soar, made possible by excessive bank credit granted by equally euphoric bankers. This typically leads to bubbles in asset markets (including housing markets), until the crash hits. Then many consumers and firms (including banks) are saddled with unsustainable debt. A process of deleveraging is set in motion, leading to a deep recession. That's when governments have to step in in order to save the market system. Banks and firms have to be rescued, the unemployed have to be paid, leading governments have to issue debt. The countries that have experienced the most intense booms and bubbles also experience the deepest crashes, forcing the governments of these countries to issue an unsustainable level of public debt. As Schularick and Taylor (2012) have shown, most sovereign debt crises in history were preceded by unsustainable booms and bubbles in private markets that forced governments to pick up the pieces.

In a monetary union such a boom-bust scenario leads to additional problems because governments of member countries lack a backstop, i.e., a central bank willing and capable of providing liquidity to the sovereign in times of crisis (De Grauwe 2011). This feature was at first not recognized by most policymakers, until Mario Draghi accepted the need to step in in 2012.

Thus, a misdiagnosis of the crisis and the inability to understand the nature of a monetary union led policymakers to apply the wrong treatment, i.e., structural reforms (supply-side policies) and austerity programs. It should be no surprise that when this treatment was applied with vigor in the periphery countries it did not work; or worse, it helped to aggravate the crisis. This policy failure was also responsible for the fact that in contrast to other industrial countries, the Eurozone countries experienced a double-dip recession during 2011–12.

Why was such a misdiagnosis possible? Why did policymakers in the Eurozone insist on applying the wrong treatment? Sometimes ideas are powerful in influencing policymakers. Here is my hypothesis on how economists' ideas gripped policymakers' minds.

During the 1970s, new academic theories were developed. They came as a reaction to Keynesianism that was widely seen to have failed and to have led to excessive government interventions. A new paradigm was created with the following ingredients. Free markets when left alone lead to efficient outcomes profiting everybody. In addition, markets are inherently stable. The source of instability is to be found in the indiscipline of governments. From this paradigm, two policy conclusions followed. First, markets have to be left free to work well. In other words, 'rigidities' that lead to departures from market equilibrium have to be eliminated by structural reforms. Second, governments have to be disciplined.

Many policymakers were educated in the 1970s and had absorbed this paradigm. The latter worked as rose-tinted spectacles through which to see and interpret the world. Thus, when the crisis erupted, this was immediately seen as originating from the fact that markets had been too much and governments too little constrained. It was time to redress this.

It did not help that at the same time well-known academic economists came up with a theory that promised 'non-Keynesian effects' of austerity programs. They meant that fiscal contraction (less government spending, especially fewer social transfers) would lead to an increase in confidence by private agents, who would then react by increasing spending. Thus by contracting government spending, the economy would actually be stimulated. European policymakers were enthusiastic and toured around the capitals of the Eurozone countries to spread the good news.

A few years later, the IMF (and only the IMF) brought out a 'mea culpa': Sorry, it was all wrong; austerity programs did not have these hoped-for stimulatory effects (see Blanchard and Leigh 2013).

The previous discussion does not mean that some structural reforms are not meaningful. I am thinking of policies aimed at eliminating the dual nature of the labor markets in many countries on the periphery that makes it very difficult for the young to find a job. Similarly, pension reform programs that give more incentives to work longer are desirable. These reforms are desirable in all countries, whether or not they have experienced a sovereign debt crisis. Put differently, the sovereign debt crisis had nothing to do with these supply-side problems, and resolving these structural problems (although desirable in themselves) does nothing to shield countries from the booms and busts that regularly emerge in capitalism.

Where does that leave us? The Eurozone sovereign debt crisis of 2010–12 has led to substantial reforms in the Eurozone. They were aimed at redressing some of the design failures of the Eurozone. As this book makes clear, there was some success in reconstructing the Eurozone so as to make it more sustainable. The progress made in creating a banking union is one of these. But as is stressed in this book, the progress is insufficient to make sure that the Eurozone can survive in the long run. The benefit of this book is that it makes clear the direction we have to take to guarantee long-term success. This direction involves future steps toward political unification.

What is also necessary is that policymakers free themselves from old ideas that do not correspond with reality. The idea that markets are stable and that governments are the sources of trouble continues to shape policies. The reality is that we live in a system that produces great instability when left alone. Capitalism is a wonderful system to generate material welfare. It is, however, also a system that is unstable and that requires stabilization. The Eurozone has stripped the national governments of most of their capacity to stabilize an 'otherwise unstable system', without creating sufficient capacity at the Eurozone level to stabilize the booms and busts that capitalism creates. If we do not manage to create such a capacity, the Eurozone is doomed.

Paul De Grauwe

Note

1 I am grateful to Francisco Torres for useful comments.

References

Blanchard, O. and Leigh, D. (2013). Growth Forecast Errors and Fiscal Multipliers, IMF Working Paper, January. www.imf.org/external/pubs/ft/wp/2013/wp1301.pdf.

De Grauwe, P. (2011). The Governance of a Fragile Eurozone, CEPS Working Documents, Economic Policy, May 2011. www.ceps.eu/book/governance-fragile-eurozone.

De Grauwe, P. and Ji, Y. (2018). Core–Periphery Relations in the Eurozone. Paper prepared for the conference 'The Future of Central Banking: An ECB Colloquium Held in Honour of Vitor Constancio', Frankfurt, May 16–17, 2018.

Kindleberger, C. P. (1978). *Manias, Panics and Crashes: A History of Financial Crises*. New York, Wiley.

Minsky, H. (1986). *Stabilizing an Unstable Economy*. New Haven, CT, Yale University Press.

Schularick, M. and Taylor, A. (2012). Credit Booms Gone Bust: Monetary Policy, Leverage Cycles, and Financial Crises, 1870–2008. *American Economic Review* 102(2): 1029–1061.

Acknowledgments

This project began as a conference at the College of Europe in February 2017, and we wish to thank the funding provided by the College of Europe as well as the original participants of that conference: Istvan Pal Szekely, Daniel Daco, Gabriel Glöckler and Eric De Souza. We also gratefully acknowledge the support of Rector Jörg Monar and the College of Europe's Research Council for supporting a workshop in Bruges that took place in June 2017.

We thank the following colleagues for providing feedback on the drafts of the volume: Lorenzo Codogno, Paul Dermine, David Howarth, Lucia Quaglia and Mattias Vermeiren. All errors remain our own.

Abbreviations

ADR	assets to deposits ratio
Banif	Banco Internacional do Funchal
BCP	Banco Comercial Português
BE	Bloco de Esquerda
BES	Banco Espírito Santo
BPI	Banco Português de Investimento
BPN	Banco Português de Negócios
BPP	Banco Privado Português
BRRD	Bank Recovery and Resolution Directive
BSSF	Bank Solvency Support Facility
CAC	collective action clause
CDS	Centro Democrático e Social – Partido Popular
CDS	Credit Default Swap
CGD	Caixa Geral de Depósitos
CGTP-IN	Confederação Geral dos Trabalhadores Portugueses – Intersindical Nacional
CME	Coordinated Market Economy
CoCos	Contingent Convertible Bonds
CPE	comparative political economy
EBA	European Banking Authority
EC	European Commission
EC	European Community
ECA	European Court of Auditors
ECB	European Central Bank
ECJ	European Court of Justice
EDP	Excessive Deficit Procedure
EFF	Extended Fund Facility
EFSF	European Financial Stability Facility
EFSM	European Financial Stabilization Mechanism
ELA	emergency liquidity assistance
EMF	European Monetary Fund
EMS	European Monetary System
EMU	Economic and Monetary Union

ESFS	European System of Financial Supervision
ESM	European Stability Mechanism
ESRB	European Systemic Risk Board
EU	European Union
FDI	foreign direct investment
FF	Future and Freedom
FITD	Interbank Deposit Protection Fund
GAO	General Accounting Office
GDP	Gross Domestic Product
GIPSI	Greece, Ireland, Portugal, Spain and Italy
GNI	gross national income
HICP	Harmonised Index of Consumer Prices
IMF	International Monetary Fund
LME	Liberal Market Economy
LTRO	Long-Term Refinancing Operations
M5S	Five Stars Movement
MEFP	Memorandum of Economic and Financial Policies
MIP	Macroeconomic Imbalances Procedure
MME	Mixed Market Economy
MOU	Memorandum of Understanding
MPS	Monte dei Paschi di Siena
MTM	monetary transmission mechanism
NAMA	National Asset Management Agency
NATO	North American Treaty Organization
ND	New Dawn
NIIP	Net International Investment Position
NL	Northern League
NPB	National Productivity Board
NPE	non-performing exposures
NPL	non-performing loans
NPV	net present value
OECD	Organisation for Economic Co-operation and Development
OMT	Outright Monetary Transactions
PCP	Partido Comunista Português
PD	Democratic Party
POF	People of Freedom
PPP	public–private partnership
PPS	post-program surveillance
PS	Partido Socialista
PSAPP	public sector asset purchase program
PSD	Partido Social Democrata
PSI	private sector involvement
ROE	return on equity
SGP	Stability and Growth Pact
SMP	Securities Market Program

SOE	state-owned enterprise
SRF	Single Resolution Fund
SRM	Single Resolution Mechanism
SSM	Single Supervisory Mechanism
UGT	União Geral de Trabalhadores
ULC	Unit Labor Cost
VAT	value-added tax
VOC	Varieties of Capitalism

1 After the bailout

10 years of the euro area crisis

Michele Chang, Federico Steinberg and Francisco Torres

Introduction

2019 marks the 10th anniversary of the revelation of the Greek debt crisis that snowballed into the euro crisis and threatened the single currency's very existence. In the course of the euro crisis, a number of euro area countries lost access to market financing and required official assistance: Greece (2010, 2012 and 2015), Ireland (2010), Portugal (2011), Spain (2012) and Cyprus (2013). And while Italy did not receive a bailout, it did face considerable market speculation alongside the other economies in the euro area periphery. Together, those countries were dubbed the GIPSI countries (the crisis in Cyprus came later and no moniker emerged to include it). The speculation against these countries and the existential threat that further spillover posed to the euro area prompted a host of reforms that were enacted over the last decade to improve economic convergence and the resilience of the euro area. Moreover, countries that received bailouts underwent conditionality programs that included major structural reforms.

This volume focuses on the aftermath of the euro crisis and asks whether the reforms have brought about lasting changes to the economic and political structures of the crisis countries or if the changes were short-term and easily abandoned post-bailout and post-recovery. Starting with an analysis of how the crisis led to further constraints on euro area member states, the volume then focuses on how this changed environment, particularly the conditionality programs, disrupted the economic growth models of the GIPSI countries. The case studies analyze in which cases and in which sectors the euro area reforms and the bailout programs were able to promote convergence and alter the domestic political economies of the economies in the euro area periphery. This volume presents an up-to-date analysis of the aftermath of the crisis, how it contributed to lasting change and how various elements of national growth models have either persisted or been altered.

The central argument of the book is that while the crisis had imposed policy constraints on the euro area countries and on the program countries in particular, the national growth models nevertheless persist. Despite the efforts to strengthen euro area governance and impose unprecedented levels of reform on the program countries, it took years for a consensus to emerge on the causes of the crisis

(Baldwin and Giavazzi 2015). Even the institutions of the troika found themselves in conflict on how to address the underlying weaknesses of the euro area and the domestic political economy of the crisis countries (see chapter by Lütz et al. in this volume). Nevertheless, substantial convergence has occurred thanks to the euro area reforms made during the crisis and the program that the adjustment countries underwent as a condition of their bailout(s) from the European Financial Stability Facility (EFSF) and the European Stability Mechanism (ESM).

This introduction provides a brief overview of the volume. It presents the main research questions that all of the case studies deal with and the analytical framework that will be utilized to varying degrees by all of the case studies: the varieties of capitalism. The last section summarizes the volume's case studies, both at the level of the euro area and the country studies.

Analytical framework

The issues confronted in this volume contrast with existing work on the sovereign debt crisis that have considered a wider variety of theories explaining the causes of the crisis itself and the troika programs (Caporaso and Rhodes 2016); or have taken a more sector-specific approach (Johnston 2016; Dølvik and Martin 2017); or works looking at the crisis from a more macro perspective rather than country-level (Caselli, Centeno and Tavares 2016). The theoretically informed chapters draw on the insights from the varieties of capitalism (VOC) literature, specifically in regards to the impact of countries' respective growth models in leading up to the crisis and its response. They explore the politics in Europe and EU member states to look comprehensively at the European and domestic political consequences of the crisis since countries have exited their respective bailout programs, updating previous work on the causes of the immediate repercussions of the crisis to consider their longer-term impact. Enough time has passed to consider how the reforms imposed by the euro area and the troika have fared during more "normal" times and affected the domestic political economy of the program countries.

The VOC literature is a well-established comparative political economy theory that considers institutional variations across states. In contrast to expectations that globalization would lead to similar policies across countries striving to gain a competitive advantage, VOC points out enduring differences in relationships between government and economic actors. When institutional change does occur, such changes are conditioned by a country's VOC and "new practices are developed to cope with the problems generated by past practice and integrated into a network of interacting institutions, some of which remain stable as others change" (Hall 2001, p. 76). In other words, "actors seek institutional and functional equivalents to pre-existing forms of coordination" (Hancké, Rhodes and Thatcher 2007, p. 11).

The three primary models in VOC are the liberal market economy (LME), the coordinated market economy (CME) and the mixed market economy (MME); their characteristics are briefly described in Table 1.1. Within LMEs, an

Table 1.1 Varieties of capitalism traits

	Liberal market economy	*Coordinated market economy*	*Mixed market economy*
Examples	UK, Ireland	Germany, Belgium, Austria, Netherlands	France, Italy, Spain, Portugal, Greece
Growth model	Demand-led	Export-led	Demand-led
Asset specificity	Low	High	Low
Wage coordination	Low	High	Limited
Role of state	Limited	Coordinator	Compensator

arm's-length relationship exists between the state and economic actors operating within a competitive environment. The UK and the US are often presented as the typical LME countries, and Ireland also fits this description. Within CMEs exist more extensive relationships between governments and economic actors, contributing to a more collaborative economic environment. Some of the main differences concern wage-bargaining systems that are coordinated in CMEs but not in LMEs, and the types of skills developed by workers that are more general in LMEs and asset-specific in CMEs (Hall and Soskice 2001). Germany, Belgium, Austria and the Netherlands are typical CMEs. The third model of the MME was introduced later to explain more completely economies like France, Spain, Portugal, Italy and Greece that share characteristics of both LMEs and CMEs. Their hybrid nature lacks the functional coherence and institutional complementarities that characterize LMEs and CMEs, leaving the state to compensate for the country's economic deficiencies through the use of subsidies and protectionism (Molina and Rhodes 2007).

VOC research explained not only different institutional and policy preferences but also how they interacted with the top-down pressure from the Europeanization process. In some instances, member states effectively would re-regulate in bottom-up initiatives rooted in VOC models (Menz 2005). The robustness of the respective VOC models not only relate to the aggregate welfare benefits that they provide, they also reinforce underlying political and social relationships (Hall and Thelen 2009).

These insights had important ramifications for EMU. The euro area consisted of very diverse economies at different levels of development and had different growth models. At the onset of EMU, Greece, Ireland, Portugal and Spain still benefited from EU cohesion funds in order for their economies to catch up to those in the euro area core in the north, which might have dampened reform pressures. Nevertheless, it was assumed that the single currency would encourage economic convergence. The fixed exchange rate system that had been in place since 1979 had contributed to converging interest rates and inflation rates as well as exchange rate stability. Capital controls had already been liberalized through the Single Market program, which presumably would intensify market discipline. The Maastricht Treaty's convergence criteria demanded nominal convergence in long-term interest rates, inflation, debt and deficit levels, and exchange rate stability. Post-euro, adherence to the Stability and Growth Pact (SGP) would ensure continued fiscal probity. The Broad Economic Policy Guidelines and Lisbon Strategy would encourage structural reforms that would include more labor market flexibility and deregulation.

Nevertheless, monetary union did not lead to more convergence. Portugal, for example, was deemed a "big disappointment" after the first decade of EMU because of the "marked deterioration in … the Portuguese economy … with its potential growth rates now pointing to divergence rather than convergence" (Commission 2008, p. 115). EMU did not alter the VOC of the member states, and EMU may have pushed the different VOC to the point of incompatibility by removing their traditional forms of adjustment through exchange rate changes and national central banks targeting convergence in inflation and real exchange rates (Johnston and Regan 2016).

VOC indicated that MMEs would be more likely to engage in behavior that contributed to their vulnerability prior to the crisis despite the EU rules that were in place to promote convergence. Figure 1.1 shows that the deficit to GDP ratios of the MME countries under study exceeded the euro area average once the euro was adopted, though Spanish deficit figures quickly improved. This was on top of the already high debt levels carried by countries like Italy and Greece prior to the crisis, as seen in Figure 1.2. Indeed, Italy was well above the Maastricht Treaty convergence criterion's debt limit of 60 percent of GDP but was able to enter in the first round of EMU thanks to the flexible application of these criteria.

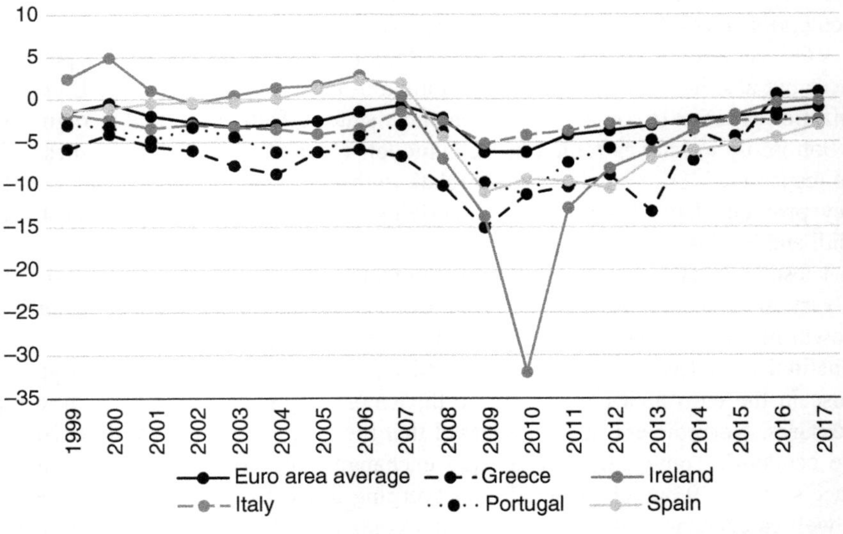

Figure 1.1 Deficit to GDP levels of Greece, Ireland, Italy, Portugal and Spain and the euro area (17) average.

Source: Eurostat.

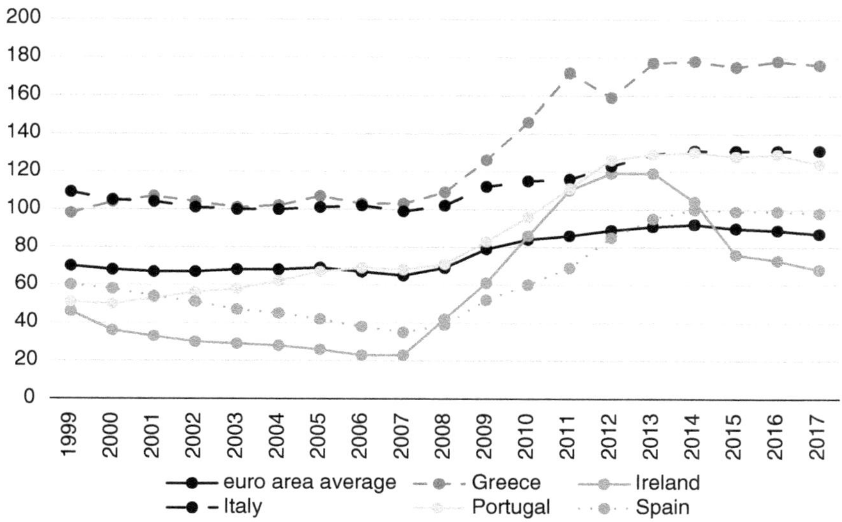

Figure 1.2 Debt to GDP ratio of Greece, Ireland, Italy, Portugal and Spain and the euro area average, 1999–2017.

Source: Eurostat.

While CMEs were more likely to follow an export-led growth model that generated current account surpluses, LMEs and MMEs tended to generate current account deficits, as seen in Figure 1.3. While Portugal and Spain began EMU with current account deficits, Ireland's small surplus turned into a deficit midway through the first decade of EMU and remained in deficit until well into the crisis.

While the run-up to monetary union and its first decade did lead to the liberalization of all euro area economies, MME governments concurrently had ramped up their social spending to compensate domestic actors who otherwise would have suffered as a result of EMU (Hassel 2014). MMEs lost competitiveness as labor costs surged without corresponding gains in productivity, and they could no longer restore competitiveness via devaluation. Figure 1.4 shows the wage discipline in Germany that even had negative changes prior to the crisis, whereas the LME and MME countries under study were significantly higher during this period.

Prior to the crisis, ECB interest rates were too high for the northern economies experiencing a slump and too low for some of the southern economies in a real estate boom. Figure 1.5 shows the inflation rates for the countries under study versus that of the euro area; while the latter mainly followed the 2 percent goal of the euro area, this masked the stronger inflation in the MME and especially LME countries under study compared to the euro area average, some significantly so.

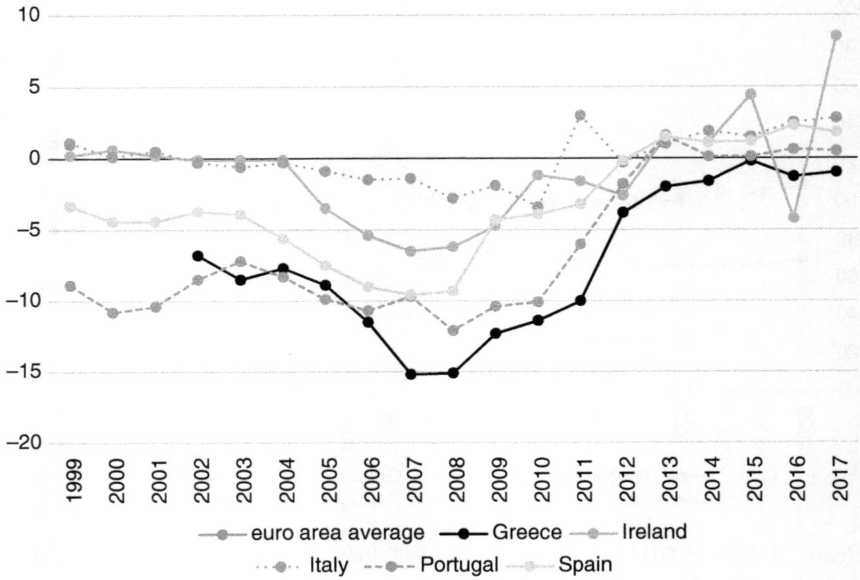

Figure 1.3 Current account balance as a percentage of GDP.

Source: Eurostat.

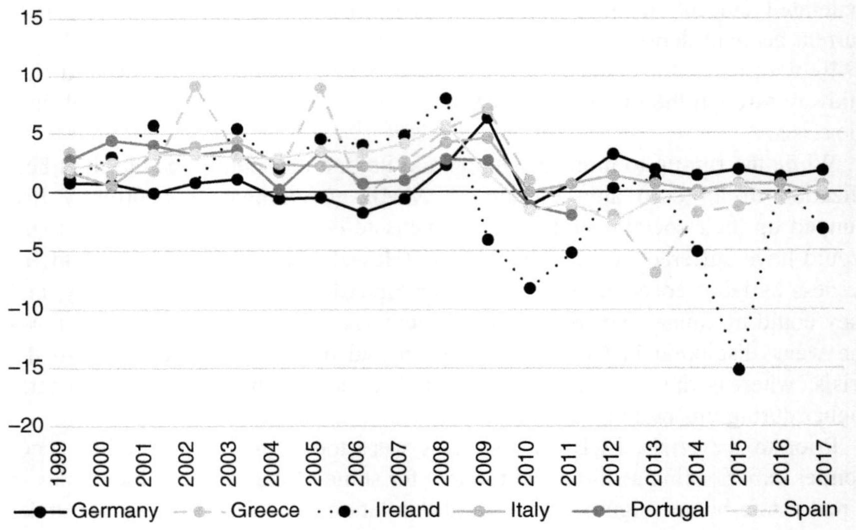

Figure 1.4 Annual percentage change in nominal unit labor costs, 1999–2017.

Source: Eurostat.

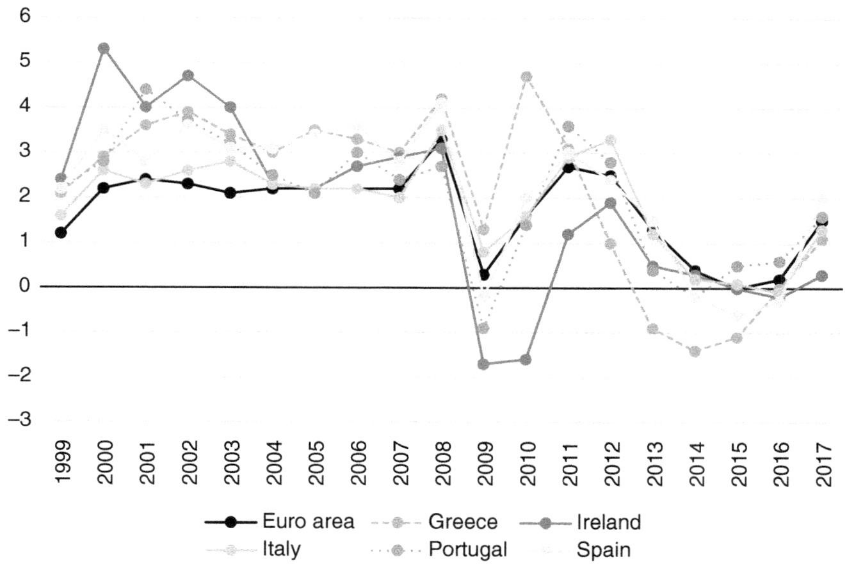

Figure 1.5 Annual inflation rate (measured by rate of change of HICP) for euro area 18, Greece, Ireland, Italy, Portugal and Spain, 1999–2017.

Source: Eurostat.

The historically low interest rates for the MMES combined with the explosion of the finance industry made credit abundant. It thereby created a "fragile and perverse complementarity in financial markets" (Fuller 2018, p. 175), as capital from the north drove demand-led growth in the periphery and promoted the export of goods and capital in the north. Large imbalances arose in the euro area as competitiveness diverged, though the access to this cheap credit during the first decade of EMU allowed MMEs to easily finance their debt (Scharpf 2011): "The euro allowed Germany to pursue real exchange rate depreciation through the exertion wage restraint and facilitated the recycling of its export surpluses, thereby creating incentives for unbalanced consumption-led growth in the MMEs and LME" (Vermeiren 2013, p. 731). Although Ireland and Spain have different VOC models, both grew rapidly as a result of real estate booms enabled by the low interest rates of the period, and neither had coordination systems that could control wage growth (unlike in CMEs), leading to higher wages and diminished competitiveness. In contrast, the euro area's CMEs benefited greatly from EMU and accrued additional monetary power as a result. Monetary union kept down the exchange rate, and combined with their limited wage growth, enhanced the competitiveness of the CMEs.

The global financial crisis revealed the fragility of the economic growth in the euro area periphery and exacerbated its differences with the core countries. The credit crunch made it impossible for the economies on the periphery to finance their deficits, as capital gravitated to the safer economies of the euro area core. The rise of the Asian economies, particularly China, complicated the efforts of southern European economies to restore growth, as their traditional export products went head to head against the products offered by Asian economies. Southern European economies could not compete with the low wages and hence prices offered by these competitors. This contrasts with the CMEs in the core that exported higher value-added goods and sold their goods to Asian economies rather than competing with them.

A myriad of factors contributed to the subsequent euro crisis, including loose fiscal policy, debt overhang (public and private), macroeconomic imbalances and concern over the integrity of the euro area. The incompatibility of the CME and MME growth models in EMU also has been hypothesized as the cause: "the attempt to join together these two distinct capitalist growth regimes into a single currency is the real source of the Eurozone crisis" (Regan 2017, p. 972).

While some of these countries may share a general growth model, lumping them together as the GIPSI countries misses important nuances. While the Greek government had engaged in high deficit spending and public sector debt, Ireland and Spain were among the countries in the best fiscal condition in the euro area prior to the crisis. Ireland and Spain's economic woes stemmed from their financialization (especially in Ireland) and the bursting of the real estate bubble that had fueled both economies. Portugal and Italy had been suffering from weak competitiveness since the start of the euro and had not experienced a similar economic boom, making it difficult to escape the large debt levels. While these countries share some similarities, their differences are significant and critical to understanding the causes for the crisis in these countries and the solutions to improve their economies. All of the countries successfully exited from economic adjustment programs (Ireland and Spain exited in 2013, Portugal in 2014, Cyprus in 2016 and Greece in 2018). Figures 1.1–1.5 indicate convergence along numerous measures, no doubt the result of the euro area reforms and the conditionality programs undertaken by those countries that received bailouts. Did the euro crisis, euro area reforms and conditionality programs finally succeed in creating economic convergence?

This volume sheds light on the convergence that occurred and did not occur as a result of the crisis by posing the following questions:

- How can we understand the differences that emerged regarding how to handle the crisis? Initially analysts viewed the main cleavage to be between creditor and debtor countries, but differences arose within the troika itself. Given the lack of consensus on how to best manage the euro crisis, how can we explain the choices that were ultimately selected?
- How did the euro crisis change the economic and political landscape of the euro area? Much work has been done to indicate the imbalances (fiscal, financial, competitiveness, etc.) leading up to the euro crisis – did the euro area reforms alleviate these imbalances? Why or why not?

- How did the euro crisis change the political fortunes and alliances within the euro area and within program countries? Did the crisis lead to structural changes in these economies, or did existing patterns persist, despite the changes demanded by the conditionality programs? If change occurred in some sectors and not others, why?

Summary of chapters

The first chapter by G. Russell Kincaid gives a macro view of the origins of the euro crisis and the changes that were made to euro area governance. The euro crisis stemmed from deficiencies in the economic architecture of the euro area and policy errors by individual euro members. In response to the euro crisis, significant, albeit incomplete, reforms were made to its economic architecture. But with these reforms came a further transfer of sovereignty to euro area institutions, heightening questions concerning their legitimacy and accountability. Meanwhile the immigration crisis and Brexit placed new strains upon European political solidarity. Against this background, lessons are offered as well as thoughts on how to strengthen the euro project.

The chapter by Susanne Lütz et al. looks at the troika (now sometimes referred to as the "quadriga" to include the ESM) institutions that were charged with overseeing the conditionality programs of countries that sought official assistance. It notes how the three institutions very often conflicted on the policy conditionalities related to financial stability, fiscal and structural adjustment. By drawing on the programs for Greece, Ireland, Portugal and Cyprus, the authors demonstrate different roles and approaches of the troika institutions toward credit lending. The IMF played the role of an "Accountant", seeking to ensure timely repayment of the loans. The EC acted as a "Europeanist" by interpreting the compatibility of conditionalities with European rules and treaties as a way to regain competitiveness, whereas the ECB, as "Monetary Guardian", focused on securing the financial and monetary stability of the Eurozone in general. The chapter tries to explain these differences through an analysis of the different bureaucratic cultures of the three organizations and discusses the implications of these "organizational pathologies" for the implementation of the lending programs.

The country studies in Part II look at the impact of the conditionality programs undertaken. Four of the bailout countries (Greece, Ireland, Portugal and Spain) as well as one non-bailout country (Italy) are covered. They first consider the constraints posed by EMU membership and the initial conditions causing the crisis. This is followed by an assessment of how the government and troika tried to fix the problems, considering both the content and sequencing of the reforms demanded, and whether the bailout program fundamentally altered economic and political conditions in the countries. Specifically, the country studies seek answers to the following questions:

- What was the national growth model before the crisis?
- What were the primary causes of the crisis?

- What problems did the EU/troika identify?
- What were the major reforms undertaken by the government?
- What remains to be done?

George Pagoulatos tackles the country that sparked the financial crisis and the only one to undergo several economic adjustment programs. Lax fiscal oversight, loose credit following euro-accession and credibility conferred by Eurozone membership led Greece to debt-driven growth funded by external capital inflows. These private flows came to a "sudden stop" in 2010, forcing a bailout. The first adjustment program viewed the problem as one of liquidity, imposing front-loaded austerity that accentuated recession and led to target slippage. The second program included debt restructuring and focused on decreasing labor costs to improve competitiveness. The third program contained much of what had been left undone and was the only one completed. Eventually, hard conditionality overcame much of the resistance of status quo coalitions to reforms. Despite the successive reform programs, the Greek economy continues to suffer from a weak public administration, slow-functioning justice system, low savings, high consumption, small average business size and a still weak export sector. Prolonged austerity has left a heavy legacy of poverty, social vulnerability and weakened productive capacity, as steep disinvestment and the decline of employment dragged down the economy's growth potential. On the other hand, the twin deficit (fiscal and current account) has been eradicated, significant structural reforms have been implemented, exports have increased and state administrative capacity has relatively improved. Greece represented a Mediterranean market economy, driven by domestic demand and deficit-financing; the crisis brought about an evolving rebalancing of the economy toward a fiscally disciplined, reform-driven and more export-oriented growth model.

Kevin Cardiff's chapter on the Irish case presents a challenge to the VOC framework given it had a different growth model than the other cases yet still faced similar market pressures during the crisis. He notes the strong public finances of the government prior to the crisis as well as the high levels of private savings, thanks to various government initiatives. Nevertheless, imbalances grew as consumption and wages outstripped productivity, and the economy (including government finances) in a short space of time came to depend hugely on the construction sector, creating a very significant vulnerability. Irish banks' dependence on wholesale funding to support their lending for property and construction exacerbated their vulnerabilities, and the bailout of the financial system and collapse of construction devastated government finances. The subsequent troika program demanded "substantial fiscal adjustments" and structural reforms to address efficiency as well as better banking supervision. The Irish government implemented its troika program in a way that reflected ownership on the part of the government, though the government continued negotiations with the troika throughout the implementation phase to improve the terms, e.g., improving interest rate conditions. Post-exit from the program, the Irish economy has resumed growth and employment. Household and public debt remains high albeit there has been significant deleveraging, banks are much less reliant on wholesale funding and the economy depends less on construction. Moreover, the Irish banking system shrank and deleveraged featuring fewer banks and less competition, making it more concentrated. Finally, the crisis altered the political landscape substantially as it created a backlash against traditional parties and contributed to rising support for independents and the Sinn Fein party.

Francisco Torres and Miguel Lebre de Freitas look at Portugal's difficulties as a member of the euro area. During EMU's first years, Portugal's unsustainable path of debt accumulation on the part of households and non-financial enterprises was disguised by a combination of economic (domestic demand-led) growth, falling interest rates and real exchange rate appreciation. However, unlike the Greek, Irish and Spanish economies, which had been booming up to the financial crisis, the Portuguese economy had, at least since 2002, been suffering from very poor growth and rising unemployment. The chapter reviews the design and implementation of Portugal's adjustment program and the return to the markets and program exit. It also analyzes the bailout program's main achievements, failures and social costs. The program emphasized fiscal consolidation, structural reforms in the labor and product markets, and deleveraging of the banking sector, with fiscal adjustment being frontloaded. It qualifies as a success in terms of addressing Portugal's main macroeconomic imbalances and financial risks within EMU, although expenditure repression dominated expenditure reduction and progress on structural reforms was mixed. The recessive impact of the program was, however, aggravated by the European recession and by limited access to external finance. The authors furthermore explain how the loss of political ownership and reform fatigue came about in the implementation phase (2011–2014) and how after exiting the program in 2014, the remaining reform impetus was lost. The chapter finally assesses the post-program period (2014–2018), characterized by a low reform effort while Portugal abided (by and large) by its fiscal commitments, although at the expense of lower public investment and growth-enhancing reforms.

Sebastián Royo and Federico Steinberg analyze the financial sector bailout of Spain and its consequences. After a prolonged period of economic growth, Spain suffered its worst financial crisis in the years between 2008 and 2014. Although successive governments implemented a number of gradual reforms in the first stages of the crisis, the financial sector-related bailout of 2012 was instrumental in triggering the transformation of the banking sector, as well as other structural policies in areas as diverse as taxation, pensions and the labor market. The Spanish program, which ended in 2014, can therefore be defined as a relative success. Despite a persistently high unemployment rate (particularly as regards youth and long-term) and rapid increases in inequality (and to a certain extent in poverty), credit was restored, strong economic growth resumed and the political system did not implode. This chapter argues that the Spanish government made a strategic use of the bailout program to implement a number of structural reforms that it wanted to pursue but that had been hindered by domestic political constraints. It traces back the use of European (external) influence to advance structural reforms in Spain and modernize the economy, explores who have been the winners and losers of these economic transformations and discusses the nature of the new economic model that has emerged from the crisis.

Silvia Merler's chapter looks at Italy, a country that has long been viewed as the most likely candidate for the next crisis. Nevertheless, the Italian government has yet to request a bailout despite its weak growth, high debt levels and financial instability characterized by a large number of non-performing loans. The lack of market pressure and adjustment program did not provide sufficient incentive for reform. This chapter differs from the others in its focus on Italy's difficulties in its banking sector; given its lack of a bailout program and that its major economic difficulties are linked to its inability to comply with new euro area rules related to banking union, this makes for an interesting test case for the VOC ideas focused on financial systems. In recent years some of the longstanding problems of the Italian financial sector have finally come into the light but have also come at a high political cost.

Benedicta Marzinotto's chapter applies a VOC approach to the study of euro area macroeconomic imbalances. Compared with the available comparative-capitalism literature, it makes three original points. First, EMU does not provide for a common macroeconomic regime. Domestic macro-financial systems contribute significantly to the sign of the monetary regime. Stressed countries could preserve their demand-driven growth model, despite the apparent rigidity of the EMU regime, thanks to the size of financial reform and the aggressive lending behavior of formerly highly regulated domestic credit institutions. Second, current account positions are driven also by the distribution of income, which is per se institutionally entrenched. Stressed countries accumulated significant and persistent current account deficits because financial reform meant that liquidity constraints were relaxed, especially for low-/middle-income groups who represent a high share of the population in relatively unequal societies. Third, growth models are not static. Wage-setting institutions evolved under EMU in a way that reinforced the divide between the demand-driven model in the stressed periphery and the export-led model of non-stressed Continental member states. From a policy perspective, the analysis implies that measures to prevent the future build-up of macroeconomic imbalances and to resolve frictions across persistently divergent growth models should go through tighter top-down macro-prudential regulation and some reduction in inequality across all member countries.

This volume therefore makes numerous contributions to the literature on the euro crisis and its aftermath. Empirically, it provides a comprehensive update of the causes and consequences of the crisis. Second, the case studies provide a nuanced portrait of how these diverse economies found themselves so vulnerable to market pressure and how their economies and institutions adjusted as a result. Third, the volume questions the level of convergence implied by the indicators often used to evaluate growth models in the VOC literature. While the figures in this introduction indicate significant convergence with the euro area average after the crisis, Marzinotto's chapter in particular questions these parameters and suggests the tighter incorporation of domestic financial models in our understanding of the VOC.

References

Baldwin, Richard, and Francesco Giavazzi (eds.). 2015. *The Eurozone Crisis: A Consensus View of the Causes and a Few Possible Solutions* (CEPR Press: London).

Caporaso, James A., and Martin Rhodes (eds.). 2016. *Political and Economic Dynamics of the Eurozone Crisis* (Oxford University Press: Oxford).

Caselli, F., M. Centeno, and J. Tavares (eds.). 2016. *After the Crisis: Reform, Recovery and Growth in Europe* (Oxford University Press: Oxford).

Commission. 2008. 'EMU@10: Successes and Challenges after 10 Years of Economic and Monetary Union', *European Economy*, 2.

Dølvik, Jon Erik, and Andrew Martin (eds.). 2017. *European Social Models from Crisis to Crisis: Employment and Inequality in the Era of Monetary Integration* (Oxford University Press: Oxford).

Fuller, Gregory W. 2018. 'Exporting Assets: EMU and the Financial Drivers of European Macroeconomic Imbalances', *New Political Economy*, 23: 174–191.

Hall, Peter. 2001. 'The Evolution of Economic Policy-Making in the European Union', in A. Menon and V. Wright (eds.), *From the Nation State to Europe?* (Oxford University Press: Oxford).

Hall, Peter A., and Kathleen Thelen. 2009. 'Institutional Change in Varieties of Capitalism', *Socio-Economic Review*, 7: 7–34.

Hall, Peter, and David Soskice (eds.). 2001. *Varieties of Capitalism: The Institutional Foundations of Comparative Advantage* (Oxford University Press: New York).

Hancké, Bob, Martin Rhodes, and Mark Thatcher. 2007. 'Introduction: Beyond Varieties of Capitalism', in Bob Hancké, Martin Rhodes and Mark Thatcher (eds.), *Beyond Varieties of Capitalism: Conflict, Contradictions, and Complementarities in the European Economy* (Oxford University Press: Oxford).

Hassel, Anke. 2014. 'Adjustments in the Eurozone: Varieties of Capitalism and the Crisis in Southern Europe', *LSE 'Europe in Question' Discussion Paper Series*, 76.

Johnston, Alison. 2016. *From Convergence to Crisis: Labor Markets and the Instability of the Euro* (Cornell University Press: Ithaca, NY).

Johnston, Alison, and Aidan Regan. 2016. 'European Monetary Integration and the Incompatibility of National Varieties of Capitalism', *JCMS: Journal of Common Market Studies*, 54: 318–336.

Menz, Georg. 2005. *Varieties of Capitalism and Europeanization: National Response Strategies to the Single European Market* (Oxford University Press: Oxford).

Molina, Oscar, and Martin Rhodes. 2007. 'The Political Economy of Adjustment in Mixed Market Economies: A Study of Spain and Italy', in Bob Hancke, Martin Rhodes and Mark Thatcher (eds.), *Beyond Varieties of Capitalism: Conflict, Contradictions, and Complementarities in the European Economy* (Oxford University Press: Oxford).

Regan, Aidan. 2017. 'The Imbalance of Capitalisms in the Eurozone: Can the North and South of Europe Converge?', *Comparative European Politics*, 15: 969–990.

Scharpf, Fritz W. 2011. 'Monetary Union, Fiscal Crisis and the Preemption of Democracy', *MPIfG Discussion Paper 11/11*.

Vermeiren, Mattias. 2013. 'Monetary Power and EMU: Macroeconomic Adjustment and Autonomy in the Eurozone', *Review of International Studies*, 39: 729–761.

Part I

The European dimension of the crisis

2 The euro crisis

Its unresolved roots and their reform implications

G. Russell Kincaid

Introduction

The euro project was designed as a single currency without a central government to back its financial institutions and without sufficient market and supranational discipline over economic policies. The unwillingness to yield more sovereignty to the center resulted in national governments retaining fiscal authority and financial supervision powers. Thus, the project was situated unsustainably on Rodrick's impossible political tri-lemma (2012), which states that national sovereignty, democracy, and economic integration are mutually incompatible; any two elements can be combined but never all three simultaneously and in full. Efforts to preserve the euro ceded national sovereignty to unelected supra-national institutions, diminishing democratic accountability. Using Crum's corresponding tripartite governance framework (2013), the euro area moved toward "executive federalism" in order to save the euro – avoiding the dissolution that restores "democratic autonomy" for the exiting country – but in the process, euro area governance moved away from "democratic federalism." Thus, democracy has been considered to be the main lasting victim of the euro crisis. As the crisis has abated, the time is now propitious to reflect on lessons learned before considering how to move toward a more sustainable and desirable balance.

The story of the euro crisis is now well known (Bastasin, 2015; Brunnermeier et al., 2016; Henning, 2017). These narratives (and others) provide many explanations for the euro crisis, resulting in an over-determined crisis (Jones, 2015). These explanations should be seen as complementary, and not competing, narratives. Most certainly, poor national policies played a major role as emphasized by other authors in this volume, and are also costly for the individual country and its neighbors. An effective, real-time feedback loop – proper incentives – was also lacking. Private markets and official surveillance (by the European Commission (EC) and International Monetary Fund (IMF)) failed to provide necessary discipline to avert poor national economic policies. Once the euro crisis broke, its institutional structure had to be reinforced to prevent a breakup of the euro.

The economic reforms adopted during the euro crisis succeeded in saving the euro and made its economic architecture more robust than previously, albeit seriously incomplete. This chapter takes stock of the main economic reforms undertaken since the outbreak of the euro crisis, identifies remaining gaps and vulnerabilities, and examines possible actions that attempt to find a more sustainable balance point on Rodrick's tri-lemma. In this effort, priority is given to considerations of efficiency and effectiveness, rather than considerations of proper democratic governance within the euro area. The latter considerations would require a separate chapter to be addressed fully.

Cracks in the euro foundation

The euro area was not envisaged as a political federation like Germany; it was structured like a confederation of still largely sovereign states. This setup represented the political realities in Europe at the time – differences in economic philosophy among national elites and the unwillingness of voters to yield more national sovereignty. These differences were papered over in the expectation – the Monnet process – that Europe would be forged through crises, being the sum of the solutions adopted.

The unwillingness to transfer more sovereignty resulted in national governments retaining fiscal authority and financial supervision powers. At the same time, the Maastricht Treaty contained provisions to prevent monetary financing by the central bank of government deficits and "bailouts" of one government by another. Fiscal discipline after euro adoption (as defined by the Stability and Growth Pact (SGP)) was to be assured by the Excessive Deficit Procedure (EDP). But as the euro's architects did not imagine a sudden loss of market access, no lender-of-last-resort for its sovereigns was envisaged.

The 12 countries that signed the Maastricht Treaty in 1992 did not constitute an optimal currency area (Mongelli, 2008); there existed a core (Belgium, Denmark, France, Germany, Luxembourg, and the Netherlands), and a periphery (Greece, Italy, Spain, Portugal, Ireland, and the United Kingdom). Among the periphery countries only the UK sought, and received, an opt-out for euro membership. EU enlargement was seen to place more strain on the euro project (Bayoumi and Eichengreen, 1992). With the end of the Cold War, the EU expanded rapidly, increasing to 28 members by 2013 with the euro members rising from 11 to 19, making euro economies even more heterogeneous.

While the euro architects were concerned about the implications of an expanded financial market for fiscal discipline, they did not show the same concerns about the implications for private sector behavior (Kincaid and Watson, 2015). The risks associated with private sector imbalances were simply ignored. According to the prevailing "Lawson doctrine," named for UK Chancellor Nigel Lawson who articulated it in the 1980s (Blanchard, 2007), current account imbalances – or investment-savings gaps – were problematic only if they stemmed from government actions because in the absence of distortions private sector imbalances would be rationally determined and welfare improving. In addition, asset prices – bonds and currency in this context – incorporate all available information, and thus were rationally determined per the "efficient markets hypothesis," justifying a strong presumption toward financial deregulation (Turner, 2009).

With efficient markets also came the philosophy of "lite" prudential supervision of financial institutions. With national financial stability assured by their authorities, no provision was made in the euro's governance structure for a euro-level institution to safeguard system-wide financial stability. But national financial supervisors had multiple objectives. In particular, "national champions" were maintained so that banking systems could support domestic industrial policies and ensure governments had favorable access to domestic bank credit. As a consequence, home-country bias in national banks' lending was preserved, while national banks' funding sources became euro-area wide, permitting access to a larger savings pool and heightening exposure to funding risks, or sudden stops. Financial market participants did not find the no-bailout provision to be credible, resulting in the underpricing of sovereign credit risk.

Banking systems typically have a government backstop because they are too important to fail. This status is not unique to the euro area, but it is more potent there, owing to its greater network and contagion effects and larger size (relative to GDP). Also, a banking system can become too big to be saved by its national government without outside help, or without endangering the sovereign's debt sustainability, as was the case for Ireland, Cyprus, and Spain. Greece was a case where fiscal unsustainability contributed to the insolvency of its own banking system as well as that in Cyprus.

In a currency union, common shocks can be addressed by a common – one-size-fits-all – monetary policy, while asymmetric shocks can be handled by national fiscal policies. This principle was well recognized. What was not appreciated was that the internal adjustment dynamics of the euro could be unstable (EC, 2006; Allsopp and Vines, 2008). Specifically, the banking system would suck in foreign savings to feed both public and private imbalances. But when this bank debt-financed boom turned to bust, the resulting bank losses imperiled the sovereign's fiscal sustainability, producing a sudden stop that affected the entire economy.

Efforts to cement the cracks

Official responses to the euro crisis have reshaped its economic architecture in five key areas: a euro bailout mechanism including the Troika; the roles of the ECB; debt restructuring both for sovereigns and banks; financial stability; and fiscal policy and governance reforms. As a result, the euro's foundations became more robust, but this repair work remains incomplete.

Bailout mechanism

To avoid a disorderly default by Greece, euro area governments decided in March 2010 to provide bilateral loans based upon "strong conditionality" negotiated by the EC and IMF and in liaison with the ECB. The EC worked on behalf of the Eurogroup and more pointedly key euro area national capitals, beginning a pattern of decision-making conducted outside of the EU institutional triangle of the EC, European Council, and European Parliament. Intergovernmental agreements amongst euro authorities (rather than Treaty amendments) were utilized to build a European firewall to protect other euro members from contagion. In particular, the temporary European Financial Stability Facility (EFSF), which would later be replaced by the permanent ESM, was erected. Strategically, the ECB waited until the European Council had acted to put in place in 2010 its Securities Market Program (SMP), which formally was intended to repair the monetary transmission mechanism, addressing dysfunctional government debt markets, specifically in Greece, Ireland, Italy, Portugal, and Spain.

However, the EFSF/SMP firewall did not prevent other euro members (Ireland, Portugal, and Cyprus) from having to ask for conditional financial assistance negotiated by the Troika (EC, IMF, and ECB). The "institutions," as the Troika plus ESM became known, generally operated effectively and efficiently in negotiating and monitoring adjustment programs, although policy disagreements arose at times related to fiscal austerity, debt restructuring, and financial reforms (Kincaid, 2016).

Two large euro countries – Italy and Spain – were able to resist ECB pressure in mid-2011 that had in 2010 led Irish authorities to seek a Troika-negotiated macroeconomic program. In August 2011, the ECB President (Trichet) and the Governor of the Bank of Italy (Draghi) and the Governor of the Bank of Spain (Ordoñéz) wrote to the Italian and Spanish Prime Ministers, respectively, outlining the need for measures to restore market confidence. In October 2011, the Italian government committed at the Euro Summit to implement structural reforms and a fiscal consolidation plan. Then in November after a meeting between Berlusconi, Merkel, and Sarkozy at the G20 Leaders summit, they welcomed "Italy's decision to invite the IMF to carry a public verification of its policy implementation on a quarterly basis" (G20 Leaders Communiqué). On November 8, Berlusconi resigned and the proposed IMF monitoring of Italy's policy implementation never took place as market pressures eased.

In Spain the process was more drawn out. But in July 2012, the Eurogroup approved Spain's access to conditional ESM financing for its banks, but without having to ask for concurrent IMF financing or IMF conditionality, albeit IMF technical assistance was requested. This new arrangement came about because the Spanish authorities had insisted to their euro partners that the IMF play only an advisory role and that it not impose any conditionality. On the favorable side, these two cases show a willingness by the Eurogroup to adapt its modalities. Less positively, these cases exhibit a similar uneven treatment of countries based upon their economic size that occurred in 2003 when the Council decided not to proceed with the EDP regarding Germany and France.

By 2015, the EC and ESM had acquired the skills and crisis management experience that they were perceived to lack earlier. At the same time, the systemic implications of the euro crisis had diminished. In August 2015, the EC and ESM agreed on a third program with Greece without a concurrent IMF arrangement. IMF support could not be secured because of differences of opinion between the Eurogroup and the IMF over the achievability of medium-term fiscal targets and the need for a credible strategy to secure sovereign debt sustainability. As a compromise, the IMF Executive Board approved, in principle, in July 2017 a new IMF-supported program with Greece, but this program would only become effective – allowing Fund resources to be committed and then disbursed – once European creditors provided commitments for debt relief sufficient to secure debt sustainability. This approval-in-principle procedure allowed the IMF to endorse formally the Greek authorities' economic policy program, which helped secure approvals by key European parliaments for proceeding with ESM disbursements.

In June 2018, the Eurogroup announced additional debt relief measures plus ESM disbursements to help prepare Greece to exit from its third ESM program. The IMF program expired in July 2018 without ever being activated; therefore, no IMF resources were committed to Greece and no IMF conditionality applied under this IMF program. At the same time, the IMF cautioned that long-term fiscal sustainability remained uncertain and further official debt relief could be needed. The conclusion of the euro crisis was marked by Greece's exit from the third program in August 2018 – more than eight years after it began. Greece is now under post-program monitoring by both the IMF and ESM, but its effectiveness is still very much an open question.

Roles of the ECB

As private markets reassessed euro area sovereign credit risks, national commercial banks purchased their sovereign's debts, using them as repo collateral. Significant ECB exposures to Ireland, Portugal, and Cyprus were acquired prior to their bailouts. In the case of Ireland, exposure concerns prompted a letter in October 2010 from ECB President Trichet warning that "future decisions by the Governing Council of the ECB regarding the terms of liquidity provision to Irish banks will thus need to take into account appropriate progress in the areas of fiscal consolidation, structural reforms, and financial sector restructuring" (Trichet). The following month, Ireland had a bailout program. The ECB also successfully pushed smaller euro members into Troika programs, which became a means for the ECB to manage exposure reductions – a process termed (not wholly appropriately) "deleveraging" by the Troika.

With monetary conditions tighter in periphery countries than in the rest of the euro area, the monetary transmission channel was deemed to be impaired. As already mentioned, the SMP was the first remedy introduced, allowing the ECB to determine yields on periphery sovereign debt, although its practice fell well short of that outcome. In the end, total SMP purchases were modest at €210 billion for five countries (i.e., Greece (€31 billion), Ireland (€14 billion), Italy (€99 billion), Portugal (€22 billion), and Spain (€44 billion)). Empirical analysis indicates that the ECB's repeated interventions had a statistically significant, but small, impact on interest rates (Eser and Schwaab, 2016).

Subsequently, the ECB instituted Long-Term Refinance Operations (LTRO), permitting the ECB to fine-tune its interventions in individual national markets, including euro area countries without adjustment programs, which is discussed more in the next section. More generally, President Draghi announced in a July 2012 speech (Draghi, 2012) that the ECB "is ready to do whatever it takes to preserve the euro. And believe me, it will be enough." Outright monetary transactions (OMT), which replaced SMP but have never been used, are potentially unlimited in scope and were intended to be used only in conjunction with macroeconomic adjustment programs. With these powers, the ECB became a de facto, albeit not de jure, lender-of-last-resort for sovereigns.

This expansion in ECB powers did not go unchallenged. In Germany, complaints were lodged before its federal constitutional court. That court requested in January 2014 an opinion from the European Court of Justice (ECJ) as to whether OMT were consistent with EU treaties. In 2015, the ECJ ruled that the ECB's OMT program was consistent and that the ECB could use OMT to "reduce or eliminate excessive risk premiums in sovereign yields but it should not go further than necessary." The Court added that the ECB had the authority to purchase government bonds in the secondary market, so long as such purchases would not have an effect equivalent to direct purchase of government bonds, undermining the effectiveness of the Treaty provision against monetary financing. This ruling clearly placed limits, albeit vague ones, on ECB powers because "excessive risk premiums" and "equivalent effect" were left undefined.

When designing bailout programs, two major issues emerged related to the financial sector. One issue pertained to appropriate monetary conditions. Specifically, the pace of "deleveraging" by commercial banks – or more precisely, the lowering of their assets to deposits ratio (ADR) – reduced their dependency on wholesale/ECB funding but thereby increased the financing requirements of these programs for the ESM and IMF. ADR reduction also resulted in overly tight credit conditions that undermined real activity. Therefore, the initial ADR targets had to be scaled back in Greece, Ireland, and Portugal.

The second issue related to financial stability. In particular, their banking systems were typically undercapitalized, requiring an effort to identify those banks that needed to be merged or closed. But consolidation of domestic banks could decrease competition among the remaining domestic banks. Maintaining the number of domestic banks to ensure greater competition, however, would increase state aid required for bank recapitalization, widening the program's financing requirement and potentially creating a conflict between EU competition policy and financial soundness efforts of bank supervisors. In the end, uneasy compromises were struck with less consolidation and less recapitalization taking place and leaving these periphery countries at the conclusion of their programs with unfinished agendas in their financial sectors.

The ECB's role in bailout programs has been criticized, owing to conflicts of interest. These conflicts were three fold: (i) a bias toward fiscal consolidation because it facilitates the ECB's price stability objective; (ii) a preference to bail out in public and private sectors to support banks to protect its exposure to those banks; and (iii) a tough line on sovereign debt restructuring and fiscal consolidation to protect its holdings of sovereign debt. As a result, a "silent observer" role has been proposed wherein the ECB would not be a full negotiation partner and would discontinue co-signing mission statements (European Parliament, 2014). A possible ECB OMT program coupled with its supervisory role (discussed later) makes ECB participation in future bailout programs even more crucial and a "silent partner" role less appropriate, while raising fundamental issues pertaining to its independence and accountability.

Debt restructuring by sovereigns and banks

The Eurogroup's approach to debt restructurings evolved considerably during the euro crisis. In early 2010, debt restructuring by Greece was kept "off the table" in program negotiation by a combination of systemic contagion fears and philosophical opposition. Nonetheless, behind closed doors in mid-2010, the IMF made a case for debt restructuring to senior officials of the German and French governments. In a shocking U-turn, Merkel and Sarkozy at Deauville in October 2010 proposed the principle of private sector involvement – bail-in of the private sector or "haircuts." In November 2010, the Eurogroup announced that standardized Collective Action Clauses (CACs) would be introduced in all new euro area government bonds, which would make such debt restructuring less difficult in the future.

Euro area governments, as a whole, only acknowledged in July 2011 that Greece's sovereign debt needed to be restructured "voluntarily." Insistence on a voluntary restructuring – avoiding any payment default – resulted in substantial "sweeteners" from the official sector, reducing the net debt reduction (Zettelmeyer et al., 2013). It was a case of too little, too late, leaving Greece with a need for future official debt relief.

Later in the context of signing the ESM Treaty (February 2012), the euro area governments recognized, "in accordance with IMF practice, in exceptional cases an adequate and proportionate form of private sector involvement shall be considered." ESM loans were also deemed senior to sovereign debt held by private creditors, but not to IMF lending. While the ESM Treaty is silent on ESM-loan forgiveness, it does have loss-sharing provisions. But any loss-sharing would have political ramifications, particularly for some ESM shareholders, who had assured their parliaments and voters that taxpayer funds would not be used to bailout euro members.

Turning to bank debt restructurings, the bailing-in of unsecured bondholders was proposed by the Irish authorities in 2010 and 2011. Strong opposition emerged from euro area officials on grounds of contagion and euro area support for Irish bank recapitalization was conditioned on the absence of private sector involvement. In the end, no private sector involvement by, or bail-in of, holders of Irish bank debt occurred.

Economic conditions in Cyprus deteriorated sharply in late 2010 with the euro crisis. In particular, Cypriot banks, which had assets equivalent to about

750 percent of GDP, were highly vulnerable owing to their large exposure to Greece and extraordinary dependency on foreign funding. Cyprus was not considered to be a systemic case by the IMF, and several euro governments found it politically difficult to authorize a bailout that would benefit rich Russian oligarchs (Brunnermeier et al., 2016), while also burdening Cyprus and their own taxpayers. Consequently, a bail-in of banks' private creditors was necessary. The Troika suggested therefore a double-digit tax on uninsured (large) deposits and unsecured bonds, but the Cypriot government rejected this proposal. Instead, the government proposed (and the Troika accepted) a package that included a 6.7 percent tax on all deposits, including small (insured) ones. This package created a firestorm in Cyprus and adversely affected bank stocks and deposits in other periphery countries. It was quickly rejected by the Cypriot parliament and replaced by a package that protected insured depositors; the Troika also backpedaled from its faux pas.

In April 2014, the EU's Bank Recovery and Resolution Directive (BRRD) was adopted, establishing a bail-in principle for bank equity holders and specified bank creditors, which could impose losses or write-downs. A bail-in of 8 percent of the bank's liabilities is required before public – national or euro-level – support can be provided to a failing bank. Importantly, the BRRD clarifies that deposits covered (insured) by a guarantee deposit scheme are excluded from the banks' liabilities when applying this bail-in mechanism. Presumably, this directive would forestall a repeat of Cyprus. Its application has not been straightforward, however. In Portugal and Italy, owing to the political ramifications of imposed losses on uncovered deposits and bank bonds held by individuals, application has been sidestepped.

Financial stability

Euro area financial stability was predicated upon financial stability at the national level. But the euro crisis has shown this foundational assumption to be flawed, owing to externalities stemming from network effects and cross-border spillovers. The euro architecture was also founded upon national sovereign backstops for their financial systems. But some national banking systems were too large to save by their respective sovereign (e.g., Ireland, Portugal, and Spain), while in some other cases, a weak sovereign took down the banking system (i.e., Greece, Cyprus (by Greece)); this relationship has been termed the "doom loop."

To redress these shortcomings, several institutional changes were implemented with effect in 2011. First, the European Systemic Risk Board (ESRB) came into existence (mid-December 2010) with the objective of providing macro-prudential oversight of the entire EU financial system. Second, microprudential supervision at the union level was reorganized under the European System of Financial Supervision (ESFS). While these reforms were welcome, they were also considered insufficient or to constitute only a halfway house to banking union (Posen and Veron, 2014). In addition, the European Banking Authority (EBA) was made responsible for safeguarding the functioning of the banking sector, contributing to the creation of a single rulebook – harmonized prudential regulations, and promoting convergence in supervisory practices. Unfortunately, EBA got off to a bad start with its first stress test (2011); Dexia bank met the capital benchmarks in July (12th highest capital score out of 91 banks), only to be reorganized three months later with financial support from the Belgium and French governments. The credibility of the stress test and EBA were consequently undermined, casting doubts on the soundness of other banks, particularly in Cyprus, Greece, Italy, and Spain.

Against this background, euro area leaders affirmed in a June 2012 statement that "it is imperative to break the vicious circle between banks and sovereigns" (Euro Area Leaders), launching the process that culminated in the creation of the Single Supervisory Mechanism (SSM) and the Single Resolution Mechanism (SRM) with a corresponding Single Resolution Fund (SRF) to be built up over a period of eight years (2016–2023). The single supervisory task was assigned to the ECB in part so the SSM would benefit from ECB credibility. The BRRD established "bail-in" principles for shareholders and bondholders in order to safeguard taxpayers. Once the SRF was fully in place, direct bank recapitalization by the ESM would be virtually redundant in the view of some key euro area authorities. To make Europe less dependent on bank finance, a plan to form a capital markets union was announced in 2014. These steps will certainly strengthen the euro financial system, but vulnerabilities remain, as will be discussed in the next section.

In 2011, the macroeconomic imbalance procedure (MIP) was introduced for all EU members to identify imbalances, such as excessive current account imbalances or asset bubbles, in one country that could adversely affect another euro country, or the euro area, or EU, as a whole. The MIP is intended therefore as a crisis prevention tool and represents an implicit rejection of the earlier "Lawson Doctrine." Once imbalances are identified (using scoreboard indicators followed up by in-depth reviews as warranted), then country-specific policy recommendations are formulated by the EC. These recommendations are buttressed by, as well as support, the operations of the SGP/EDP.

The ECB is barred from being a lender of last resort for governments, but it is tasked with providing liquidity to banks. Nonetheless, banks can finance their governments and then go to the ECB, conducting repo operations using their government debt as collateral. Collateral eligibility and valuation ("haircut") rules have become important ECB policy instruments. In addition, the pace of ECB exposure reduction was an issue in Greece, Ireland, and Portugal. When collateral is insufficient, national banks can approach their national central banks for emergency liquidity assistance (ELA). The ECB can, and has, capped a national central bank's ELA provision. A national central bank can run payment deficits with other national central banks in the euro area, accumulating in the process TARGET2 liabilities – a form of automatic official balance of payment support.

To ease bank liquidity conditions, the ECB launched Long-Term Refinancing Operations (LTROs) in December 2011. An amount of €489 billion was announced, of which €325 billion, or two-thirds, was tapped by banks in Greece,

Ireland, Italy, and Spain. These banks then purchased their governments' debts, earning a sizable spread with no capital backing required; this activity was termed a "Sarko trade" after Nicolas Sarkozy, who stated that LTRO funds allowed Italian and Spanish banks to buy their government bonds. The second LTRO auction (€530 billion) took place in February 2012 and had similar take-up and impact.

With euro inflation well below its target (2 percent), the ECB in mid-2014 lowered its deposit facility interest rate into negative territory and then in March 2016 launched an expanded asset purchase plan. Under this plan, the ECB purchased by December 2018 about €2.6 trillion in eligible bonds (Table 2.1), of which 82 percent were government debt providing financial relief to these markets. The ECB decided to allocate its purchases of government debt based on the ECB's capital key coupled with security-specific and issuer-specific limits/rules.[1]

Under the ECB's public sector asset purchase program, periphery countries gained an assured new source of unconditional demand for their government debt. Cumulative ECB purchases of euro government bonds by December 2018 amounted to 22 percent of total debt of euro governments excluding Greek debt, which was ineligible. In flow terms, the ECB's purchases were more than six times the increase in gross debt of euro governments over this nearly 36-month period! Focusing on the eligible periphery countries (Cyprus, Ireland, Italy, Portugal, and Spain), the ECB acquired under its public sector asset purchase program (PSAPP) nearly four times the amount acquired under the SMP and more than double the amount provided by various bailout mechanisms to the five program countries. These ratios would have been even greater had Greece been PSAPP eligible! The ECB's PSAPP eased funding pressures on these periphery governments, allowed their bondholders to exit, contributed to the decline in yields on sovereign debt, and facilitated exiting from these programs. Moreover, OMT for these periphery countries were not needed.

Table 2.1 ECB asset purchase program, December 2018

Program	*Amount (in billions of euro)*	*Share (in percent)*
Total	2,569.8	100.0
Covered bonds	262.2	10.2
Asset-backed securities	27.5	1.1
Corporate sector	178.1	6.9
Public sector	2,102.0	81.8
Of which:		
Cyprus	*0.7*	*0.1*
Ireland	*30.1*	*1.4*
Italy	*365.4*	*16.8*
Portugal	*36.8*	*1.7*
Spain	*260.8*	*12.0*

Source: ECB.

Fiscal policy and governance reforms

Fiscal policy is the only instrument available to national governments to address national macroeconomic imbalances in the short run. Monetary policy seeks to achieve an area-wide inflation target; therefore, monetary conditions will tend to be appropriately set for the largest economies and potentially least suitable for the smallest economies. Consequently, the economic stabilization burden of fiscal policy is heaviest in the smallest economies in a currency union, particularly if that economy is not well integrated with the others in the union.

The fiscal governance structure of the euro area was not set up to address asymmetrical shocks because fiscal policy was deemed ill-suited for demand stabilization, owing to political reasons (e.g., deficit bias, procyclicality) and economic reasons (i.e., small fiscal multipliers). The SGP and EDP focused on preventing adverse spillovers to other members from excessive fiscal deficits and public debt sustainability. By construction, the SGP/EDP introduced asymmetric adjustment, as it applied only to economies with "excessive deficits." This construction is not dissimilar to the operation of the Bretton Woods system at the international level. But not all deficit countries were treated the same in practice; despite several years with deficits above 3 percent of GDP, Germany and France were not placed under the EDP by ECOFIN in 2003. As a consequence, the EDP was reformed in 2005, but the fundamental deficiencies remained (Eyraud et al., 2017).

The EC approached fiscal adjustment efforts for bailout cases through the lens of the EDP. Countries were typically expected to exit the EDP after one year or exceptionally after three years. However, these deficit targets were typically considered too ambitious by IMF staff (Kopits, 2016), but slower fiscal adjustment would entail larger official financing for the program, or necessitate diverging resources from the "deleveraging" efforts or bank recapitalization. Slower fiscal adjustment would also mean additional accumulation of government debt, leaving the country further above the 60 percent limit.

Because fiscal multipliers were viewed as relatively small, fiscal consolidation was not seen as counterproductive – deepening recessions – but as a means to increase fiscal credibility, lowering credit risk spreads and stimulating real activity. In October 2012, the IMF published an empirical analysis, showing that fiscal multipliers used for euro area programs had been systematically underestimated, implying that fiscal consolidation produced a drag on real activity. Both the EC and ECB published rebuttals. With real growth underperforming, additional fiscal measures were required to attain program fiscal targets, which were eased too slowly and too little (Kopits, 2016). Fiscal sustainability was also adversely affected as a consequence of slower growth and larger-than-programmed fiscal deficits.

The euro crisis underscored the need to redress weaknesses in its fiscal surveillance. A fiscal compact was introduced in 2012; its "six pack" rules were reinforced for euro area members by the "two pack" provisions. These changes increased dramatically the complexity of SGP/EDP rules, making them less transparent and expanding the scope for discretionary judgments. The importance of the public debt criterion was reinforced by a separate provision calling for a 5 percent decline per year in the excess over the 60 percent of GDP limit. For euro members, draft national budgets were reviewed by the Commission, which could seek revisions under certain circumstances; Brussels has thus become a more intrusive force at the national level – as the non-elected EC has challenged decisions made by elected national Parliaments (e.g., Italy). Finally, EDP policy settings are set independently of macro-imbalances identified by the MIP, potentially leaving vulnerabilities unaddressed.

Further steps to shore up the euro foundation

The euro crisis prompted profound changes to its economic architecture. However, these changes have not been accompanied by a political transformation to create a United States of Europe. The evolutionary – Monnet – process can be expected to continue. And indeed, some further deepening was endorsed at the euro summit in December 2018 (EC, 2018). Thus, it is timely to consider what remains incomplete or should be reshaped. Of course, the political will to act boldly has also weakened, owing to diminished crisis risks, while new challenges (e.g., immigration, nativism, terrorism, and trade wars) have emerged to dominate the political agenda. Against this background, the present euro governance structures will be assessed from an area-wide perspective, focusing upon crisis resolution and crisis prevention aspects.

Crisis resolution

The euro area now has crisis resolution – bailout – arrangements for sovereigns. The EC and the ESM are now responsible – "in liaison" with the ECB – for negotiating conditional financial assistance, while financing is provided by the ESM and possibly the ECB via OMT. Is this structure sufficiently robust? What about IMF involvement? Such bailout arrangements also raise worries about moral hazard; such worries will be addressed under crisis prevention.

The IMF was invited to assist Europe in their bailout programs to provide technical expertise, crisis management experience, negotiation toughness, and credibility. European institutions have acquired all four elements to varying degrees. As Spain and the third Greek program have shown, IMF money is not needed, if it ever was, and IMF advice can be obtained without IMF conditionality. Moreover, in 2018 the IMF adopted its first formal policy on IMF conditionality for members of currency unions (IMF, 2018). This policy specifies that the IMF should seek *ex ante* policy assurances from union-level institutions; in the case of the euro area, the IMF could seek assurances, for example, from the EC, ECB, ESRB, and SSM, when their actions are critical to achieve program objectives. Such policy assurances need to be clear, specific, monitorable, and – where necessary – time bound. However, EU institutions may be reluctant to provide such *ex ante* assurances, seeing them as impeding their policy independence. More importantly, euro area governments may not want to listen to what the IMF has to say.

With the ebbing of the euro crisis, the IMF has presented policy proposals that the EC, ESM, and ECB were not prepared put forward (e.g., private sector involvement, bank debt restructuring). Most recently, the IMF and the Eurogroup agreed to disagree on the prospects for Greek debt sustainability as Greece exited its third program. Would Euro – creditor and debtor – countries be better off if the IMF was not engaged and thus was not in a position to press this issue, and similarly difficult issues? Given possible spillovers to the rest of the world, should non-euro capitals seek IMF involvement in future euro area bailout efforts? The answers to these questions pose difficult political conundrums for all.

Against this background, the Troika has outlived its usefulness from a euro area perspective. Indeed, the EC has proposed (2017) to transform the ESM into a European Monetary Fund (EMF). Aside from the name change, which is resisted by the ECB, this proposal would mainly bring the existing ESM into the EU legal framework and provide a new backstopping role to the SRB/SRF, with a procedure for rapid – 12-hour – drawdown decisions by the EMF. One reason given by the EC for this change in the legal framework is to increase democratic accountability of the ESM. But curiously, the legal process taken by the EC is an EU regulation rather than an EU treaty amendment, which would entail more democratic accountability because, unlike a regulation, an amendment requires ratification by national parliaments. As the sovereign bailout role of the EMF implies a fundamental change to the philosophy underlying the Maastricht Treaty, the amendment process seems more appropriate, albeit more risky, because it could provoke uncomfortable debates. At the December 2018 euro summit, leaders endorsed the ESM backstopping the SRF; however, they didn't agree to incorporate the ESM into the EU legal framework.

Some ESM reforms were approved at this euro summit but several substantive issues remain outstanding. First, although the proposed EMF regulation mandates periodic reporting to the European Parliament, it does not make the Managing Director elected by, or more substantively accountable to, the Parliament, loosening the ESM's present close ties to the Eurogroup, which is not accountable to European Parliament. Second, an upgraded ESM would need considerably more lending firepower than at present. In particular, it should have enough to avoid having euro borrowers also rely on resources from the IMF and ECB, while having the capacity to backstop liquidity, as well as solvency, support by the SRB/SRF. With sufficient EMF resources, the ECB would no longer need to engage in quasi-fiscal operations such as OMT. Three, the EMF should, like the IMF, have readily available resources to avoid entering private financial markets, which could be time consuming, expensive, and in competition with sovereigns.

The EMF should have more independence from the Eurogroup in negotiating policy reforms. Like the IMF, program negotiations should be undertaken by EMF staff and supervised by EMF management. The EMF Board could establish broad policy rules to guide EMF management and staff, but the EMF would no longer be acting on behalf of the Eurogroup. This change would reduce political involvement in program negotiations, but not eliminate it because EMF lending would still need to be approved by the EMF Board – the Eurogroup effectively. EMF management, like IMF management, would inform its Board members as necessary during negotiations to ensure loan approval once program negotiations are completed.

Creation of the EMF with sufficient technical and financial resources would also raise issues pertaining to EMF's responsibilities relative to the EC and the IMF. As regards the ESM and EC, the note signed by the borrowing country that details policy conditionality would now be signed by the ESM as well as the EC. In addition, a cooperation agreement was signed in 2018 that specifies a division of labor – or lead agency model – consistent with existing EU and ESM treaties. Moreover, it was explicitly stated that this agreement would be amended when the ESM becomes part of the Union legal framework – a joint aim of the EC and ESM. As to cooperation with the IMF, overlapping policy mandates and expertise make the lead agency model unsuitable. Instead, a collaboration approach based on a coherent program design with the capability to take mutually independent actions seems more workable.

In any event, program design issues that confronted the Troika will not disappear. For example, the issues associated with the pace of fiscal consolidation and its feedback to real activity and the implications for program financing requirements will remain. Excessive fiscal adjustment could result if the EC keeping to its standard SGP/EDP approach was reinforced by the ESM seeking to minimize its loan exposure. An outside (IMF) perspective would help guard against this risk. Will the ESM and EC take a sufficiently hardheaded look at the debt sustainability of prospective borrowers? Will they be willing to urge an early sovereign debt restructuring when needed, or wait until it is unavoidable? As regards the banking system, the ESM backstop will usefully augment the SRF, although it effectively reduces unencumbered resources available for other ESM lending tools. Even an augmented SRF could prove inadequate to cope with a systemic banking crisis in the euro area. A more robust euro-wide deposit insurance system remains essential.

Structural conditionality in EC-negotiated programs to date has been "extensive and intrusive" (IEO, 2016). The European Court of Auditors (ECA) estimated that the EC's memoranda of understanding (MOUs) for Ireland and Portugal had nearly 400 detailed structural measures. The numerous and detailed structural conditions contained in the EC's MOUs have been criticized as undermining ownership, overwhelming implementation capacity, and contributing to reform fatigue (ECA, 2015). The ECA recommended that structural conditions "should be used sparingly and should clearly relate to reforms that are essential to crisis resolution." In addition, the evaluation report of EFSF/ESM financial assistance (Tumpel-Gugerell, 2017) recommended that priority be given to macro-critical conditionality, rather than structural reforms. The ESM/EMF would do well to make serious changes to their conditionality practices in response to these recommendations.

Policy conditionality associated with bailouts diminishes national sovereignty vis-à-vis its citizens and other countries within the union. While some loss of sovereignty may be acceptable temporarily to resolve a crisis, experience indicates that the effectiveness of policy conditionality declines over time as "reform fatigue" sets in. After exiting from program conditionality, policy tutelage is extended by EC post-program surveillance (plus the ESM's early warning system) and post-program monitoring by the IMF. The absence of policy conditionality incentivized by disbursements leaves the traction of such policy tutelage very much an open question. Keeping countries on a short leash may not, however, ultimately be successful, even if it appears as an attractive tool to unblock political gridlock and achieve further institutional reforms. Lengthy periods of policy conditionality increasingly come into conflict with euro-architecture principles of mutual responsibilities, solidarity, and democratic accountability.

While the financial support can provide an incentive to take actions with unpopular domestic political consequences, this "carrot" may need to be supplemented by a "stick" to ensure implementation of difficult policy actions. Finance Minister Schauble proposed informally a "severed limb" approach under which a country could temporarily "exit," or receive a "timeout," from the euro, but have the right to rejoin later. This approach, if established and credible, would provide an effective stick, particularly for smaller euro economics, to accompany the carrot of financial assistance. But if a large euro member was in trouble, this stick approach might not be credible or effective because of the adverse feedback to the remaining euro area members. The experiences with the dissolutions of Czechoslovakia and Yugoslavia provide recent dueling examples.

Crisis prevention/surveillance

Transforming the euro area surveillance into an effective crisis prevention system requires balancing issues related to moral hazard and official traction, while incentivizing early and more frequent use of crisis resolution tools to meet the challenges posed by stigma, which causes a country to wait too long to seek conditional assistance. In addition, intra-regional transfer mechanisms, which provide automatic fiscal stabilizers, can provide risk-sharing buffers to, or insurance against, asymmetric shocks. But like any insurance, moral hazard risks must be addressed. The need for such balancing is not unique to the euro area. It is also faced by the IMF at the global level and by countries with federal fiscal systems, such as the United States and Germany.

German experience with bailouts of its Länder underlies German worries about moral hazard associated with the ESM/EMF. From this perspective, bailout prospects can heighten fiscal deficit bias and weaken policy discipline, more generally. On the other hand, an inadequately resourced ESM can deter country authorities (particularly for larger economies) from seeking early assistance because the adjustment burden is not lightened sufficiently to overcome stigma. Delay can exacerbate imbalances. Meanwhile, larger economies are more difficult politically for the union to steer into a conditional bailout, as indicated by the cases of Spain and Italy.

Moral hazard can also adversely affect the operation of private financial markets, particularly their assessment of sovereign credit risk, making market discipline less effective. The skepticism of participants in private financial markets over the no-bailout provisions, coupled with regulatory and collateral rules, has been cited as contributing to the unjustified convergence of sovereign credit risk spreads for euro members in the 1990s and 2000s (Buti and Carnot, 2012). Indeed, credit risk spreads operated only weakly on the bonds of German Länder, in part owing to the 1992 bailouts by the German federal government of two Länder.

Moral hazard can be combated by a bail-in of private creditors so that they have more skin in the game, strengthening market discipline. The Greek sovereign debt restructuring, the introduction of CACs for euro area sovereign bonds, and the BRRD's bail-in principle provide much-needed offsets to the moral hazard induced by permanent bailout mechanisms. But will this offset be enough?

While access to private market finance can allow country authorities to delay making difficult economic choices, unconditional access to official financing can also contribute to this problem. Automatic financing of one national central bank by the others via the TARGET2 system helps ensure a single financial market, but it also effectively provides unconditional financing to cover a country's external imbalances and/or fiscal deficits. Under TARGET2, liabilities to these national central banks are treated as equivalent to each other, which contrasts with the credit rating and market pricing of the liabilities of their respective sovereigns. To limit TARGET2 access, proposals have been made to establish liability caps relative to GDP, to settle accounts at year end (modeled after the US Federal Reserve Interdistrict Settlement Accounts), and to charge interest rates on liabilities that reflect credit risk. These actions could provide clearer signals to country authorities of impending trouble, encouraging early policy reaction.

But TARGET2 is not the only official mechanism providing governments with preferred access to financing. Under the ECB's public sector asset purchase program, each country was assured its share based upon the ECB's capital key. But such official purchases substituted for market discipline, while not providing any official discipline (or conditionality) on national policies. The single supervisor for euro banks oversees their treatment of sovereign debt for regulatory purposes (e.g., risk weights (zero), exemption from exposure limits for single borrowers, use in liquidity ratios, and collateral rules for repurchase (repo) operations). These regulations affect the pricing of government debt and availability of finance, and may also reinforce the doom loop.

Moral hazard can also be reduced if the private sector has more "skin in the game" or more to lose. CACs make those losses more credible, although the willingness of governments to trigger CACs is still uncertain. Moreover, European CACs even after the proposed single limb reform need further modification to be made fully effective. Alternatively, the euro area could create a sovereign debt restructuring mechanism (Gianviti et al., 2010).

Banking and capital market unions are still very much works-in-progress. European banks are undercapitalized, making them less competitive, and less able to lend. The high level of nonperforming loans compared with associated provisioning is recognized as a source of financial fragility. Undercapitalized banks are also more vulnerable to shocks and therefore may need to draw upon the national resolution fund, placing additional burdens on national public finances, particularly deposit guarantee schemes. With attention shifted elsewhere, progress toward redressing euro vulnerabilities could well be slow. Moreover, euro area financial services now performed in London are likely to be transferred to the euro area, shifting employment and tax bases in the process. But this move will also expose the euro financial system to new risks, requiring even more bank capital. In addition, euro banks will need to upgrade their risk management practices and European supervisors will need to acquire new skills to monitor new risks.

To focus on financial stability and macroeconomic imbalances generated by the private sector, the ESRB and MIP were established. Both are welcome moves. The ESRB monitors and assesses systemic risks over the entire EU financial system – banks, insurers, asset managers, and market infrastructure – and can issue warnings and recommendations, particularly related to macroprudential tools. The operation of the ESRB was recently reviewed by the EC, identifying several areas for incremental improvements, while more fundamental issues pertaining to overlaps with the SSM and ECB remain untouched.

The MIP attempts to identify macroeconomic imbalances at the national level and then makes country-specific policy recommendations to redress excessive imbalances. The MIP has an elaborate and detailed annual process for identifying macroeconomic imbalances (involving a 14-indicator scoreboard, which has considerable overlap with financial stability measures, followed by in-depth reviews when warranted). This MIP process, however, is insufficiently forward-looking, asymmetrically designed, and missing a key imbalance indicator – national inflation. Thus, the MIP may not identify imbalances promptly enough, is focused more on correcting deficits than surpluses, and may not accurately gauge their magnitudes. So far, the annual country-specific policy recommendations have centered on structural measures, leaving the fiscal stance to the SGP/EDP process, macroprudential tools for the ECB/ESRB, and inflation management to individual EU central banks. This hands-off approach on fiscal, monetary, and macroprudential policies is problematic as a coordinated policy response is still missing at the euro level.

Both the MIP and SGP/EDP suffer from well-known compliance and enforcement problems. In particular, the EC has been criticized by the ECA for exhibiting too much discretion (ECA, 2016, 2018). Moreover, in November 2018, the Italian government rejected the EC's request to bring its draft 2019 budget deficit (2.4 percent of GDP) in line with the EC's deficit recommendation (1.6 percent of GDP). A compromise (2.04 percent of GDP) was reached at the end 2018, avoiding the imposition of disciplinary actions but not resolving the fundamental policy differences. Clearly, these EU surveillance processes have not been sufficiently reformed and require more traction. This latter shortcoming is made more significant because market discipline is still inadequate. Perhaps if a government repeatedly flouts EC recommendations, it may also warrant a time-out from the euro area, or from the process toward euro adoption. Indeed, looking specifically at Italy – the largest periphery country – Bagani et al. (2017) examined the macroeconomic consequences of euro exit, banking crisis, and sovereign debt revaluation using an empirical structural model. They concluded that "the short-term costs of the breakup, while non-negligible, would be manageable" (p. 533). This conclusion implies that a time-out could be credible.

A "third rail" political issue pertains to a fiscal union – which some creditor euro countries refer to despairingly as a transfer union – for the euro area. Such a union could provide, inter alia, automatic stabilizing for intra-regional transfers and significant federal taxes. Such redistributive functions would constitute a fundamental change in the EU – no doubt requiring a Treaty amendment. Skirting this sensitive issue, the EC (2017) proposed to establish a macroeconomic stabilization fund to address only short-term idiosyncratic shocks. In the end, the euro leaders endorsed in late 2018 a convergence and competitiveness instrument that would be folded into overall EU budget and remains very small relative to union GDP. But this tool is likely to prove inadequate. As observed by Feryer and Sacerdote (2017), US federal (net) fiscal stabilizers for regional shocks (20 percent of the per capita shock) operate totally via the federal income tax system; indeed, federal spending funneled to states moves pro-cyclically, rather than counter-cyclically, largely offsetting the impact of federal fiscal stabilization. Experience in other federal systems (Rodden, 2010) indicates that rules-based transfer, or redistributive, systems operate best in political unions. But a pre-condition for political union is a collective identity that includes trust and solidarity – the *demos thesis*. This pre-condition is lacking at this time at the euro area level but is present at the national level. Thus, the euro area may find itself in a suboptimal position that may not be sustainable, while the way out of this fiscal and legitimacy conundrum has no easy solution (Nicoli, 2017).

Conclusions

The euro project has survived its first crisis, growing stronger as a result. New crisis resolution and crisis prevention institutions and procedures have been put in place. But these changes were implemented in a piecemeal fashion and in a rush so as to save the euro. They have also profoundly altered the euro's economic governance. The no-bailout principle was circumvented and a permanent bailout institution (ESM) created. Meanwhile, the ECB greatly expanded its monetary powers and was assigned bank supervision. Even the EC has gained greater sway, with the introduction of the MIP and reforms to the SGP/EDP. Overall, economic decision-making has shifted to union-level institutions, particularly for euro area governments. But vulnerabilities remain and economic policy architecture is still incomplete. Rebuilding now appears stalled by new challenges, such as Brexit, immigration, and trade conflicts.

In thinking about building a more resilient euro architecture, two aspects warrant special attention. First, a proper balance needs to be struck between market discipline and official surveillance, whether conducted at the union level or internationally. With a permanent bailout mechanism, the risk of moral hazard has been heightened, undermining the ability of private markets to send proper signals to sovereigns concerning their policies. To mitigate this problem, bailouts should be focused on mitigating contagion or spillovers, while ensuring appropriate private sector involvement or a form of co-pay for this officially provided insurance. Meanwhile, surveillance processes, whether at the EU level or internationally (IMF, OECD), failed to warn of the impending euro crisis. These surveillance processes have been strengthened and reformed in response, but they remain largely untested and without adequate traction because they rely on soft powers or ineffectual financial penalties. Consideration might be given to shifting from a peer review process, which too often becomes peer protection, to communicating more clearly, directly, and loudly with private financial markets. Working in tandem may prove more effective than individually.

Second, economic governance responsibilities with the euro area have been moved to technical institutions (e.g., SSM, ESM, ESRB, EC, and ECB) with limited public accountability – executive federalism. In crisis resolution mode, the Eurogroup effectively makes policy decisions for the borrowing country, which it is unelected to do. Meanwhile, national parliaments of borrowing countries must implement externally mandated "reforms" or face possible draconic economic disruptions. In prevention mode, the EC has been granted intrusive inputs on draft national budgets and can make annually country-specific policy recommendations on social programs and labor-and-product policies. Efforts to further enhance the resiliency and robustness of the euro's economic architecture are likely to strengthen the powers and responsibilities of technocratic economic institutions. Thus, the euro area continues to struggle with the tri-lemmas of Rodrick and Crum, combining uneasily deep economic integration with national sovereignty and democratic principles.

Acknowledgments

This discussion draft builds upon a paper originally presented at a College of Europe workshop on June 29–30, 2017 and this version benefits from workshop participants' comments.

Note

1 Under issuance limitations rules for the public sector purchase program, Greek debt was ineligible.

References

Allsopp, Christopher, and David Vines, 2008, "Fiscal policy, inter-country adjustment, and the real exchange rate," DG-ECFIN Economic Papers No. 344 (Directorate-General for Economics and Monetary Affairs: Brussels).

Bagani, Alberto, Brigitte Granville, and Christian A. Mongeau Ospina, 2017, "Withdrawal of Italy from the euro area: Stochastic simulations of a structural macroeconomic model," *Economic Modeling*, 64: 524–538.

Bastasin, Carlo, 2015, *Saving Europe: Anatomy of a Dream*, 2nd edition (Brookings Institution Press: Washington, DC).

Bayoumi, Tamin, and Barry Eichengreen, 1992, "Is there a conflict between EC Enlargement and European monetary unification?" NBER Working Paper No. 3950, January (National Bureau of Economic Research: Cambridge, MA).

Blanchard, Olivier, 2007, "Current account deficits in rich countries," *IMF Staff Papers*, June, 54 (2): 191–219.

Brunnermeier, Karl, Harold James, and Jean-Pierre Landau, 2016, *The Euro and the Battle of Ideas* (Princeton University Press: Princeton, NJ).

Buti, Marco, and Nicolas Carnot, 2012, "The EMU debt crisis: early lessons and reforms," *Journal of Common Market Studies*, 50 (6): 899–911.

Crum, Ben, 2013, "Saving the Euro at the cost of democracy?" *Journal of Common Market Studies*, 51 (4): 614–630.

Draghi, Mario, 2012, "Verbatim remarks made at the Global Investment Conference in London," July (European Central Bank: Frankfurt).

Eser, Fabian, and Bernd Schwaab, 2016, "Evaluating the impact of unconventional monetary policy measures: empirical evidence from the ECB's Securities Market programme," January, *Journal of Financial Economics*, 119 (1): 147–167.

Euro Area Leaders, 2012, "Euro Area Summit statement, June 29, 2012," accessed at www.consilium.europa.eu/media/21400/20120629-euro-area-summit-statement-en.pdf.

European Commission, 2006, "Adjustment dynamics in the euro area: the European Commission annual economic report," edited by Mary McCarthy and Maxwell Watson (Directorate-General for Economics and Monetary Affairs: Brussels).

European Commission, 2014, "Report from the Commission to the European Council and European Parliament on the mission and organization of the European Systemic Risk Board," COM (2014) 508 final (European Commission: Brussels).

European Commission, 2017, "Proposal for a Counsel Regulation on the establishment of a European Monetary Fund," COM (2017) 827 final (European Commission: Brussels).

European Council, 2018, "Euro Summit statement, 14/12/2018" (European Union: Brussels).

European Court of Auditors, 2015, "Financial assistance provided to countries in difficulties," Special Report No. 18 (European Union: Luxembourg).

European Court of Auditors, 2016, "Further improvements needed to ensure the effective implementation of the excessive deficit procedure," Special Report No. 10 (European Union: Luxembourg).

European Court of Auditors, 2018, "Audit of the macroeconomic imbalance procedure," Special Report No. 03 (European Union: Luxembourg).

European Parliament, Committee on Economic and Monetary Affairs, 2014, "Report on the enquiry on the role and operations of the Troika (ECB, Commission, and IMF) with Regard to the Euro area programme countries," A7- 0149/2014, February (European Union: Brussels).

Eyraud, Luc, Vitor Gaspar, and Tigran Poghosyan, 2017, "Fiscal politics in the euro area," January, IMF Working Paper WP17/18 (International Monetary Fund: Washington, DC).

Feryer, James, and Bruce Sacerdote, 2017, "How much would U.S. style fiscal integration buffer European unemployment and income shocks? A comparative empirical analysis," *American Economic Review*, 103 (3): 125–128.

G20 Leaders Summit Communiqué, 2011, Cannes, November 3–4, accessed from G20 Information Centre, www.g20.utoronto.ca/2011/2011-cannes-communique-111104-en.html.

Gianviti, Francois, Anne O. Krueger, Jean Pisani-Ferry, Andre Sapir, and Jurgen von Hagen, 2010, "A European mechanism for sovereign debt resolution: a proposal," Bruegel Blueprint 10 (Bruegel: Brussels).

Henning, C. Randall, 2017, *Tangled Governance: International Regime Complexity, the Troika, and the Euro Crisis* (Oxford University Press: Oxford).

Independent Evaluation Office (IEO) of the International Monetary Fund, 2016, *The IMF and the Crises in Greece, Ireland, and Portugal* (International Monetary Fund: Washington, DC).

International Monetary Fund, 2018, "IMF Executive Board discusses program design in currency unions," IMF Press Release 18/90 (International Monetary Fund: Washington, DC).

Jones, Erik, 2015, "Getting the story right: how you should choose between different interpretations of the European crisis (and why you should care)," *Journal of European Integration*, September, 37 (7): 817–832.

Kincaid, G. Russell, 2016, "The IMF's role in the euro area crisis: what are the lessons from the IMF's participation in the Troika?" June, IEO Background Paper BP/16-02/7 (International Monetary Fund: Washington, DC).

Kincaid, Russell, and Maxwell Watson, 2015, "Avoiding another crisis in the euro area: public and private imbalances and national policy responses," September, *Journal of European Integration*, 37 (7), Taylor and Francis: London, UK.

Kopits, George, 2016, "The IMF and the euro crisis: the fiscal dimension," Independent Evaluation Office, IEO Background Paper BP/16-02/07 (International Monetary Fund: Washington, DC).

Mongelli, Francesco Paolo, 2008, "European economic and monetary integration and the optimum currency theory," Economic Papers 302, February (European Union: Brussels).

Nicoli, Francesco, 2017, "Democratic legitimacy in the era of fiscal integration," *Journal of European Integration*, 39 (4): 389–404.

Posen, Adam, and Nicolas Veron, 2014, "Europe's half a banking union," September, Opinion Blog (Bruegel: Brussels).

Rodden, Jonathan, 2010, *Hamilton's Paradox: The Promise and Peril of Fiscal Federalism* (Cambridge University Press: Cambridge, UK).

Rodrick, Dani, 2012, *The Globalization Paradox: Why Global Markets, States, and Democracy Can't Coexist* (Oxford University Press: Oxford).

Trichet, Jean-Claude, 2011, "Letter to Brian Lenihan, November 18, 2010," accessed from www.ecb.europa.eu/press/html/irish-letters.en.html.

Tumpel-Gugerell, Gertude, 2017, *EFSF/ESM Financial Assistance – Evaluation Report*, June, (European Stability Mechanism: Luxembourg).

Turner, Adair, 2009, "The Turner Review: a regulatory response to the global banking crisis," April (The UK Financial Services Authority: London).

Zettelmeyer, Jeromin, Christoph Trebesch, and G. Mitu Gulati, 2013, "The Greek debt restructuring: an autopsy," *Economic Policy*, 28 (75): 513–563.

3 When numbers don't add up

Bureaucratic culture and conflicts in EU–IMF programs

Susanne Lütz, Sven Hilgers and Sebastian Schneider

Introduction

In early 2010, the International Monetary Fund (IMF), the European Commission (EC) and the European Central Bank (ECB) formed the so-called troika. Since then, the troika has monitored financial assistance to five Eurozone members. Despite earlier collaboration between the EC and the IMF on Central and Eastern Europe, the steep crisis in the currency union institutionalized cooperation and increased its complexity (Henning 2017). The three institutions may not have gotten together by choice, but they had a common understanding of the causes of the Eurozone crisis, the objective of the assistance programs and the imperative of austerity (Blyth 2013). Yet, this is where similarities end. Evaluating its role in the troika, the IMF states that the 'difference of views that arise from fundamentally differing institutional mandates and priorities will continue to pose challenges' (IMF 2013a: 22). In a similar vein, a report prepared on behalf of the European Parliament points to 'priority differences between the IMF and the Commission' and an 'inconsistency of goals between the two institutions' (Karas and Hoan Ngoc 2014: 15). These differences were discussed with regard to credit lending to Central and Eastern Europe (Lütz and Kranke 2014; Piroska 2017), institutional change (Moschella 2016) and inter-organizational negotiations (Lütz and Hilgers 2018). However, these studies do not show how these different approaches played out across program countries. Our contribution addresses this gap and analyzes how the troika institutions approached credit lending and policy implementation in Cyprus, Greece, Ireland and Portugal, all of which received a full troika program.

Research drawing on the seminal work by Barnett and Finnemore (2004) has established that international organizations are more than 'mere instruments for the interests of powerful member states' (Nelson and Weaver 2016: 920). Rather, they have the autonomy to develop and pursue their own preferences independently of individual member states (Bauer and Ege 2016). When international organizations cooperate, we can expect that they conflict with each other when their preferences interfere and that there is potential for dysfunctional or even pathological behavior (Barnett and Finnemore 1999; Biermann and Koops 2017; Weaver 2008).

Our argument draws on the literature on bureaucratic culture. Informal and external rules and routines define an organization's purpose, specify its functions and direct its activities while being ambiguous enough to leave room for interpretation. We argue that these internal bureaucratic features and processes shaped how the troika institutions approached financial assistance. Our explanation focuses on the causes of conflict, not who eventually prevailed (Lütz and Hilgers 2018); the individual case studies in this volume provide information on the latter. Empirically, we scrutinize the conflicts and different positions of the three troika institutions on loan conditionalities which became apparent in all of the four Eurozone programs. Since the focus of this chapter is on the troika institutions, we do not trace the interaction of the troika with debtors and creditors in detail. Although they were provoked by the international organizations themselves, some conflicts were resolved through member state intervention.

In several cases, internal divisions and debates occurred. However, all three organizations ultimately pursued distinct and coherent individual approaches. The EC acted as the group's *Europeanist* and foregrounded the programs' potential implications for the European project and the need to align them with the European legal framework. The ECB served as the Eurozone's *Monetary Guardian* and prioritized avoiding negative effects on financial and monetary stability. Finally, the IMF, the troika's *Accountant*, focused on safeguarding that the numbers 'add up' (Interview IMF 13) and on timely implementation. Conflicts emerged in all programs and often produced delayed and inconsistent policy measures. Over the course of the Greek programs, for instance, the European institutions engaged in lengthy debates with the IMF about debt restructuring. Equally controversial was the role and design of fiscal policies, and eventually they failed to deliver the expected results. Finally, conflicts were not always resolved but often gave rise to overburdened program governments, especially in the area of structural adjustment.

In order to empirically substantiate our claim, we draw on official documents and more than 110 expert interviews. We conducted these interviews between 2009 and 2018 and talked to representatives from the troika, creditor and debtor governments and interest groups. We mostly use the interviews as background information. In some cases, they are quoted with reference to anonymized codes, because we have guaranteed our interview partners confidentiality.

In the following section, we present our analytical framework. We then provide a systematic account of the approaches of the three troika institutions and their origins. The following section compares how these approaches played out in the cases of Cyprus, Greece, Ireland and Portugal and shows their implications for program design and implementation. A final section concludes.

Bureaucratic cultures

Sociological institutionalism and constructivism state that international organizations are more than just the tools of powerful member states. Member states are not irrelevant, but most international organizations rely on an influential executive. These executives, or bureaucracies, have a certain degree of autonomy. They are staffed by professional public servants who follow and apply the internal and external rules of the organization (Bauer et al. 2017). They do not solely execute member state interests but develop their own strategies of problem solving. In this contribution, we show the distinct and consistent approaches toward financial assistance taken by the troika institutions.

In order to systematically reconstruct these approaches, we draw on the literature on bureaucratic cultures. By bringing in cultural factors and not only focusing on political power or material factors, this literature recognizes that international organizations do not always do what their principals intend them to do or what is 'optimal'. Member states decide on the fundamental mandate of an international organization. However, these mandates are ambiguous enough to leave room for interpretation (Best 2012). This allows the executive to develop and legitimize their own tasks and solutions (Barnett and Finnemore 2005; Nelson and Weaver 2016). Furthermore, bureaucracies 'are organized around rules, routines, and standard operating procedures designed to trigger a predictable response to environmental stimuli' (Barnett and Finnemore 2004: 38).

In the narrowest sense, (legal) rules directly prescribe the actions of member states and bureaucrats, but partly also those of actors outside the organization. In a broader sense, they define and redefine which classifications and categorizations an organization makes, its primary tasks and how it interacts with its environment (Barnett and Finnemore 1999). When carrying out their day-to-day operations, international organizations do not always begin anew but rely on already established and institutionalized routines. These routines may be adapted to provide solutions for novel problems and structure 'the kinds of responses the organization will entertain and, eventually, implement' (Barnett and Finnemore 2004: 9). Taken together, established rules and routines shape the identity of an organization and provide it with legitimacy.

Bureaucratic organization can cause dysfunctional 'behavior that undermines the IO's stated objective' (Barnett and Finnemore 1999: 716). The main purpose of bureaucratic rules and routines is to rationalize the work of an organization and make it more predictable. By design, they are supposed to be universal and to provide generalizable answers to a wide range of problems. Following the rules, however, can become an end in itself. At times, organizations adjust their tasks to their rules and routines instead of developing solutions suitable for their respective missions. Another cause of dysfunctional behavior is the assumed universality of a bureaucracy's technical knowledge that is applicable to a range of different contexts. Even if standardized procedures allow an organization to respond to a variety of challenges, their application under the wrong circumstances can have negative consequences (Barnett and Finnemore 2004: 38–39).

Rules and routines are the building blocks of what we identify as approaches. They give an organization a main purpose it tries to fulfill with its activities. They also prioritize their objectives and provide them with specific solutions to the problems they face. On the other hand, institutionalized rules and routines can have negative effects and may induce dysfunctional behavior, especially when an organization faces tasks without precedent. Furthermore, when organizations cooperate, established approaches might lead to conflictual behavior that can impede how the organizations fulfill their tasks.

Troika approaches to credit lending

The European Commission as Europeanist

The Treaty of the European Union (TEU) and the Treaty of the Functioning of the European Union provide the legal basis for the European Commission. Article 17 of the TEU specifies that the main purpose of the Commission is to 'promote the general interest of the Union', to 'ensure the application of the treaties' and to 'oversee the application of Union law'. The Commission therefore primarily considers the implications of its own activities as well as those of the EU's member states for the Union overall. Consequently, member states are called on to treat their economic policies 'as a matter of common concern'. More specific regulations – such as the Stability and Growth Pact (SGP) – are also part of the Treaties. The fundamental objective of these rules is that member states give priority to the common European good, as opposed to short-term political goals (Buti and Pench 2004). Consequently, the Commission assesses the adjustment programs with regard to their legality as well as their potential impact on integration and the interests of the Union.

Owing to its legalistic and transnational approach, the Commission tends to focus on compliance with the treaties as well as Union-wide harmonization and convergence as the building blocks of the Common Market. It pursues an integrationist agenda to promote the political and economic significance of Europe's emerging Common Market (Becker et al. 2016). Two things follow from that. First, 'to preserve [...] the credibility of the rules-based framework' (EC 2002: 2) of the EU is a major priority of the Commission. Non-compliance with the treaties threatens this credibility. Second, the Commission's agenda is mainly liberal and aims at liberalizing and deregulating domestic markets in order to increase their competitiveness (Crespy and Menz 2015). Ultimately, a consummate Common Market would render 'the importance of national desiderata' (EC 2008: 18) irrelevant. Consequently, the programs are not only supposed to solve economic problems in the Eurozone but also 'to further the European integration project' (Interview EC 03).

At least since the Maastricht Treaty, the European Commission has been executing important monitoring functions over the economies of member states. In doing so, it has been developing a range of specific policies such as Broad Economic Policy Guidelines, Stability and Convergence Programs and especially the Excessive Deficit Procedure. The Commission also gained experience with regard to conditionality as part of the balance of payment programs for Hungary, Latvia and Romania. Conditionality also played a role in the accession process during several rounds of EU enlargement. The latter was especially also in line with the Commission's well-established liberal agenda (Bruszt and Vukov

2017). Part of this agenda is the Lisbon Strategy (later to be renamed Europe 2020) and its focus on competitiveness. For the Commission, the sovereign debt crisis created a window of opportunity to reframe the Lisbon Strategy 'as the EU's exit strategy from the crisis' (Copeland and James 2014: 1).

The Commission is the EU's 'guardian of the treaties'. It acts as a 'Europeanist' that intends to promote European integration against a strictly legalistic backdrop. In doing so, it monitors the activity of both public and private agents in key political areas (Ellinas and Suleiman 2012: 94). In this context, conditionality refers not only to specific policies, but also to 'the acceptance of the rules governing the monetary union as a whole' (Bini Smaghi 2015: 757).

The ECB as Monetary Guardian

The European Central Bank has a high degree of independence and a very narrow mandate. Both are established in the European treaties. Safeguarding monetary stability is the primary mandate of the ECB, which it defines as maintaining an average annual rate of inflation 'below but close to 2 percent' (Chang 2016: 70; McNamara 2006: 179–180). Given further treaty provisions such as the 'prohibition of monetary financing', the ECB has to justify every decision with regard to its primary mandate. Over time, the ECB has become known for its 'anti-inflationist rigor' (Lebaron 2013: 89). It also has some responsibilities with regard to supporting the general economic policies of the EU and the stability of financial markets (Chang 2016: 69). Because of the formation of the European Systemic Risk Board (ESRB) and the Single Supervision Mechanism (SSM) during the Eurozone crisis, the ECB now plays a central role in banking supervision and financial stability. At an early stage of the Eurozone crisis, ECB representatives began to assess the potentially catastrophic risks associated with disorderly sovereign default. They concluded that 'there would have been unpredictable contagion effects to other euro area Member States and to their banking sectors, threatening the stability of the euro area as a whole' (ECB 2014). From the ECB's point of view, the purpose of the financial assistance programs is to avoid financial contagion in order to preserve monetary stability and, thus, the common currency.

By design, the ECB features the 'stability culture' of the Bundesbank that informs not only its stability-oriented monetary policy but also its view on other matters such as financial markets and fiscal policy (Dyson 2008: 26; Umbach and Wessels 2008: 62). In the financial crisis, the ECB quickly acted to preserve financial stability by providing exceptional liquidity of €95 billion to Eurozone banks followed by further measures to support the banking system (Brunnermeier et al. 2016: 324; Irwin 2014). The ECB supports a rigorous interpretation of the EMU's fiscal rules and frequently engaged in conflicts over excessive fiscal policy, which the central bankers identified as a potential cause of inflation (Hodson 2011: 29; Howarth 2004: 848; Kaltenthaler 2006: 98). Apart from giving priority to preserving financial stability, the ECB intends to prevent moral hazard resulting from member states' exceptional access to funding (Yiangou et al. 2013). The ECB's 'very narrow interpretation' of the provision on monetary financing reduced its flexibility in the financial assistance programs (Interviews IMF 08; IE 06).

To cope with the challenge of conducting a single monetary policy for a group of states, ECB bureaucrats have developed a specific understanding about the link between monetary policy decisions and price developments, i.e., monetary transmission mechanism (MTM) (Marcussen 2009). In so doing, they have made the Eurozone amenable to monetary policy intervention based on models and analyses to support a monetary policy for countries with different inflation dynamics (Padoa-Schioppa 2004: 86; Issing 2008: 78). Focusing on financial aspects such as bank rates and risk premia as well as economic conditions in the real economy, the MTM constrains the central bankers' view by emphasizing factors and events according to their perceived impact for monetary transmission. Therefore, the ECB favors policies in the program countries that are expected to further the transmission of monetary policies in the Eurozone and conversely opposes policies that risk impairing monetary transmission. During the Eurozone crisis, ECB staff was mostly concerned about financial instability in sovereign-debt markets and the transmission of monetary policies through private banks. Focusing 'on the banks, the liquidity of the banks, (and) collateral' (Interview ECB 01), its mission teams promoted a creditor-friendly consolidation and initially ruled out losses for the banking sector (Interview EC 01).

Based on its centrality for monetary union and the Euro, the ECB acts as a 'Monetary Guardian'. Its key priority is to protect the common currency against threats resulting from financial instability and defaulting member states. Therefore, the ECB prioritizes measures and policies that support its monetary policy, promote a sound fiscal stance and ensure financial stability.

The IMF as Accountant

The IMF's Articles of Agreement establish its main purposes. Among them are to promote financial stability and to lessen the degree of balance of payment disequilibria. In order to maintain financial stability and to prevent economic crises, the IMF regularly reviews country policies and financial developments through its surveillance activities (based on Article IV). It identifies itself as a 'ruthless truth-teller and trusted policy advisor' (Strauss-Kahn 2010). The IMF's financial assistance programs are meant to support member countries in correcting balance of payment problems. The use of the resources is temporary, and loans have to be repaid. To this end, conditionalities are to provide adequate safeguards (IMF 2001: 3). Although it is not part of the Fund's legal basis, its so-called preferred creditor status means that the IMF must be repaid before all other creditors (Blustein 2016: 24; Interview IMF 17). Another important norm for the IMF is the 'uniformity of treatment', which applies to all IMF activities including lending programs (Cottarelli 2005: 19; IMF 2007: 9). As in other IMF programs, the purpose of financial assistance in the Eurozone is to restore the borrower's access to private capital markets.

As a technocratic organization, the IMF has developed various macroeconomic models, using econometric formulas and mostly quantitative data to evaluate financial stability, the economic situation of member states and the progress of program countries. Over time, debt sustainability has become the crucial norm for the IMF. In 2001, Argentina defaulted on its debt. The lesson learned was that 'in a situation in which debt dynamics are clearly unsustainable the IMF should not provide financing' (IMF 2003: 70–72). Consequently, the IMF's key priority is to ensure debt sustainability (Interviews EC 01; EC 02; EC 03). This criterion is formulated in the exceptional access policy. It takes effect when the Fund lends above its regular access limits, which was the case in all Eurozone programs. Based on a systematic analysis, the IMF staff has to establish that there is a 'high probability' that the member's public debt is sustainable in the medium term. If this standard cannot be met, the Fund provides aid usually only under the condition that the country's debt is restructured (IMF 2015a: 6–11).

The IMF draws on a rich experience with financial assistance programs. Fund staff drafted the Stand-By Arrangement as the principal lending facility as early as 1952 (Barnett and Finnemore 2004: 58). Thus, it has developed specific solutions for different economic problems in a program context. Over time, the Fund changed its policies on conditionality. During the 1980s and 1990s, both the number and scope of the conditions linked to lending programs expanded far beyond its initial focus on macroeconomic key figures (Killick 1995). Following the Asian financial crisis, program countries and economists criticized the IMF for this 'one-size-fits-all' approach (Stone 2008: 598; Park 2017). As a result, the IMF has returned to the practice of imposing fewer 'micro-critical' conditions and has replaced structural performance criteria with softer 'benchmarks' (IMF 2012; Lütz 2015). In terms of lending policies, IMF staff tend to favor a narrow approach with realistic fiscal objectives and targeted measures, and evaluates structural reforms mainly in terms of what it considers as 'macro-critical'. Unlike the Commission and the ECB, the IMF focuses on the impact on the respective program country and pays less attention to the effects of program policies on the Eurozone as a whole. It plays the role of an 'Accountant', who ensures that the 'numbers of the program add up' (Interview IMF 13). The overall purpose of an IMF program is to restore the borrower's access to private capital markets in order to repay their loans.

Country studies

Greece

The aftermath of the financial crisis and an unexpectedly large national deficit in 2009 compromised Greece's ability to repay its government debt. European leaders were confronted with the possibility of sovereign default in the Eurozone. By May 2010, EU member states reluctantly agreed to provide financial assistance to Greece. However, the first adjustment program was not sufficient to allow Greece to return to capital markets and neither was a second program.

After leftwing party SYRIZA was elected and a negative referendum on the program measures had been conducted, a third program was designed in August 2015 and completed three years later. In addition to a lack of ownership on the Greek side that impaired implementation, the Troika institutions clashed over several issues over the course of the three programs in Greece.

The prevalent conflict between IMF, EC and ECB concerned Greece's debt profile and the *restructuring of public debt*. In all three programs, IMF staff argued in favor of a restructuring of public debt and were met with the Commission's and the ECB's opposition. At the outset of the first program, IMF staff elaborated on a 'Plan B' – that is, a debt restructuring strategy – in case the far-reaching austerity measures ('Plan A') failed to significantly reduce public debt (Blustein 2016: 108; Papaconstantinou 2016: 126). The ECB in particular was worried about the implications for the banking sector and financial stability (Bastasin 2015: 135). Former ECB president Jean-Claude Trichet forewarned that 'once faith in the creditworthiness of one euro-zone country was shattered, bonds issued by other European governments would be destroyed' (Blustein 2015: 11). When the second program was being discussed in 2011, the IMF's stance on debt restructuring hardened, and it made the measure a precondition for participation (Moschella 2016: 11; Interview IMF 13). Still worried about potential contagion effects and less concerned with debt sustainability, the Commission and the ECB continued to oppose the measure. They agreed to a voluntary private sector involvement (PSI) by July 2011 (Interview EC 03). Bonds held by the ECB and other central banks were explicitly excluded from the PSI, but it was agreed that profits from their holding of Greek debt would be passed back to Greece (Papaconstantinou 2016: 233; Zettelmeyer et al. 2013: 524). After the PSI had been conducted, IMF staff continued to cast doubt on the sustainability of Greece's debt. As a third program became imminent in 2015, the IMF again made a credible and far-reaching commitment to debt restructuring a precondition for its participation. Given that the measure would mostly affect bonds held by public entities and not by banks, the ECB was more flexible. The Commission continued to oppose public debt restructuring. Eventually, IMF staff did de facto participate in review missions, but it neither wrote reports to the Executive Board nor contributed funding (Interview IMF 18). By July 2017, IMF staff initiated an 'approval in principle' by the Executive Board that linked a €1.6 billion IMF program for Greece to debt restructuring (IMF 2017). In so doing, the IMF signaled further willingness to participate in a third program but also its insistence on means to achieve debt sustainability. In the end, the Eurozone's member states agreed on several measures to improve the debt profile and on the prospect of further measures following a debt sustainability analysis in 2023 (Eurogroup 2018). For the IMF, however, these measures were not sufficient to mitigate concerns about long-term debt sustainability (IMF 2018). The program was concluded in August 2018 without a financial involvement by the Fund.

The IMF and its European counterparts also took different approaches toward *fiscal adjustment*. The conflicts over fiscal adjustment mostly reflected the IMF's concerns about debt sustainability. At the outset of the Greek program, all three institutions agreed on ambitious fiscal targets in order to improve the debt-to-GDP ratio. However, the IMF repeatedly advised the Commission and the ECB against 'too-fast fiscal adjustment' and 'too much austerity' (Interviews IMF 13; IMF 14). In the fifth review of the first program, IMF staff signaled that the underlying projections had been too optimistic and the fiscal targets too ambitious (IEO 2016). Failing to deliver the required results, the extensive fiscal adjustment was criticized internally and externally as 'self-defeating austerity' (IMF 2013b: 26; Kopits 2016: 25). While the Commission and the ECB emphasized the importance of complying with the (nominal) Maastricht criteria, from the fifth program review onwards, the IMF provided rather conservative projections. The conflict over growth projections, fiscal targets and the means to achieve it continued during the second and third program (Interviews GR 01; GR 20). As a result, the parliament frequently had to approve additional measures. This further decreased the government's ownership and undermined investors' confidence in the country's finances.

The IMF and the EC repeatedly clashed over *structural adjustment measures*, whereas the ECB took a backseat. The IMF primarily focused on the measures it considered necessary to meet short-term fiscal targets so that the numbers 'add up' (Interview IMF 13). The Commission took a more comprehensive view on structural reforms. It was criticized as being preoccupied with 'compliance with EU norms' (IMF 2013b: 31). These differences about the general purpose of structural adjustment induced disagreements on issues such as pension or tax administration reform. However, more often the IMF did not oppose the EC's requests but concentrated on its macro-critical issues. Rather than resulting in a division of labor, this increased the number of conditions. In all three programs, the EC and the IMF followed their respective rules and routines and in so doing often overwhelmed a fragile Greek administration (IMF 2013b; IEO 2016; Park 2017: 451).

According to a Greek official, 'everything that could go wrong went wrong' (Interview GR 01). Because of the inconsistent fiscal approach, the recession was steeper than anticipated, which caused high numbers of non-performing loans in the banking sector. Moreover, the discussions about private sector involvement, defaults and Grexit resulted in a banking crisis and further financial instability. Partly because of a lack of prioritization of the vast amount of structural reforms, its implementation stalled and failed to produce the expected effects. Thus, the first and second program not only failed to deliver the short-term numbers, but also many reforms needed for economic progress in the long and medium term were not implemented.

Ireland

In December 2010, Ireland was the second Eurozone country to request financial assistance. In the run-up to the global financial crisis, Irish banks had been investing heavily in domestic real estate. This housing bubble burst and the Irish government found itself constrained to issue a blanket guarantee for the ailing banking sector in September 2008. The guarantee weighed heavily on government debt and how it was assessed by private investors. Additionally, tax revenues, which were skewed toward the property sector, collapsed and government spending surged (Donovan and Murphy 2013). Consequently, the adjustment program for Ireland prioritized fiscal consolidation and deleveraging the banking sector. Structural reforms were of lesser importance, 'particularly for the ECB and the IMF' (EC 2015: 79). The troika institutions evaluated implementation very positively (EC 2015; IMF 2015b). They disagreed on a number of policies, however, mainly with regard to the substantial *financial sector* part of the program.

The proposal to bail-in senior bank bondholders was put forward by the IMF when the program outline was discussed in November 2010 (Véron 2016: 18–19). At that time, IMF staff called into question the sustainability of Irish government debt because of its exposure to the banking sector (IMF 2010: 29). It argued that a bail-in would improve debt sustainability and at the same time decrease overall IMF lending (Cardiff 2016: 187–188; Interview IMF 08). The ECB was vehemently opposed, as it intended to prevent contagion effects on the rest of the Eurozone at any rate (Interviews ECB 02; IMF 08; EC 04). Arguing that the European Union did not have an appropriate legal basis, the European Commission sided with the ECB (Interview EC 02). On financial issues, the ECB was much more involved than the European Commission, which 'was not in the driving seat' (Interview IE 05). Eventually, the member states stepped in, most prominently the U.S., rejecting the proposal in late November (Interview IE 03; Cardiff 2016: 189–190; Véron 2016: 19). In its report to the Executive Board, IMF staff nevertheless adhered to its opinion (Banking Inquiry 2015a: 10; IMF 2010: 22). The issue came up again when in February and March 2011 snap elections had resulted in a new coalition government. Both coalition parties had campaigned for a bail-in of senior bondholders (Interview IE 06; Véron 2016: 19). The ECB again confronted the IMF and the Irish government, as it still feared spillover effects (Asmussen 2012). Finally, the ECB threatened to cut its liquidity support for the Irish banking sector, and a bail-in was finally taken off the agenda (Banking Inquiry 2015b: 921–923; Banking Inquiry 2015c: 799–802). The EU institutions prioritized their concerns for the Eurozone as a whole over what may have been appropriate for the Irish case when viewed in isolation. The estimated loss for the Irish government ranged from €2–3 billion to €16–17 billion (Véron 2016: 18–19). This resulted in a strong sense of unfairness in the wider Irish public, which was in parts shared by IMF staff (Banking Inquiry 2015a: 8; Véron 2016: 19).

The IMF and its European counterparts also disagreed over the appropriate path of *fiscal adjustment*. For both the ECB and the EC, the targets of the Stability and Growth Pact were decisive (IMF 2015b: 22). The ECB in particular asked for comprehensive measures at the outset of the program (Interviews EC 02; IE 07). By contrast, IMF staff cautioned against 'excessive front loading' (Banking Inquiry 2015a: 16). Including also cyclical factors, it was 'mindful of debt sustainability' (IMF 2015b: 38) and considered the compromise struck with the European Commission and the ECB 'more aggressive than warranted' (Banking Inquiry 2015a: 16). However, the agreement on the ambitious adjustment path was much in line with the preferences by the Irish government that it independently had laid out in its National Recovery Plan (Interview IE 15; EC 2015: 63).

Portugal

Over the past two decades, Portuguese governments were running high deficits. Economic growth was sluggish, unemployment rising was constantly and current account deficits were persistently large because of massive capital inflows. Government deficits skyrocketed in 2009 and 2010. Economic turmoil in Europe and especially in Ireland and Greece resulted in soaring borrowing costs and a sudden stop of capital inflows (Reis 2013). The program identified government spending and the rigidity of labor and product markets as the main problems of Portugal's economy. Consequently, it focused on structural adjustment as well as reforming fiscal and budgetary institutions.

Since Portugal was not perceived as having a banking crisis, the ECB remained 'very silent' over the course of the program (Interviews PT 11; PT 12). This was an immediate result of the discussions about the *financing envelope* of the program. In order to reduce its exposure to the Portuguese banking sector, the ECB did prefer a larger amount of direct financing. Furthermore, it argued in favor of including expenditures for state-owned enterprises. By contrast, the IMF made the case for a smaller program and a larger contribution by the ECB in the form of liquidity provision. The IMF's position was also due to its overly optimistic projections and an internal bias to perceive the Portuguese crisis as 'mostly fiscal' (Véron 2016: 24; Interview PT 01). The EC steered a middle course. It rejected the inclusion of state-owned enterprises, as this would impede necessary reforms (Interview EC 01). Both European institutions sided with the Bank of Portugal, which refused an independent assessment of the banking sector. Finally, the IMF gave in, as it did not want to impair domestic ownership but to maintain consensus with its European partners (Véron 2016: 24). In general, however, all three institutions were reluctant to give too much weight to banking recapitalization, as this would have massively increased Portugal's financing needs (Interviews PT 08; EC 08). What is more, they saw the need to swiftly complete program negotiations (Véron 2016: 24–25). When the condition of the Portuguese banks eventually worsened, the financing envelope of the program was too small to allow for a comprehensive financial sector strategy (Interview PT 02). As a result, non-performing loans rose sharply and access to bank credit and investment deteriorated significantly (Interviews PT 02; EC 08; IMF 2016a: 37–40; IMF 2016b: 23).

Fiscal targets were also a source of conflict. Both European institutions, and especially the ECB, were in favor of bringing the deficit in line with the SGP as soon as possible. The IMF preferred a slower adjustment path, and its main concern was to restore debt sustainability (IMF 2016a: 46; Kopits 2016: 25). It argued for the application of more flexible targets, whereas the European Commission insisted on more ambitious targets as percentages of GDP (Eichenbaum et al. 2016: 53). However, in combination with the IMF's overly optimist projections, the targets compelled the Portuguese government to find additional measures when GDP contracted more than expected, which negatively affected program ownership (Interviews PT 12; PT 01).

Finally, IMF and European Commission took different views on *structural adjustment*. The Commission pressed for a broad and detailed reform agenda that included a range of microstructural measures in accordance with EU law (Interview IMF 06; Eichenbaum et al. 2016: 29). The IMF, on the other hand, 'focused on relatively few big things' (Interview IMF 06), in order to comply with its guidelines on conditionality (Eichenbaum et al. 2016: 28–29). In place of the possibility of a currency devaluation, one of the measures suggested by the IMF was 'fiscal devaluation', a concept already developed for Portugal in 2007. The idea was to reduce labor costs offset by an increase in the VAT, which was met with skepticism by the EC (Interview EC 01). After two failed attempts to implement it, the Portuguese government dismissed the measure. In the aftermath of the program, the IMF also quoted constraints by EU rules as another reason why the measure failed (IMF 2015c: 20). With regard to the general reform agenda, the IMF did focus on macro-critical measures but did not prevent the Commission's detailed in-depth approach (Interview IMF 06). As a result, the reform agenda for Portugal was overloaded and overexerted the capacities of the Portuguese government (Interview PT 01; Eichenbaum et al. 2016: 28).

Cyprus

Over the last decades, Cyprus had emerged as a major banking hub for the eastern Mediterranean. It initially weathered the global financial crisis without significant bankruptcies and was able to join the Euro in 2008. However, repercussions from the Greek haircut and an indecisive response by the Cypriot government to problems in the banking sector caused a severe financial crisis in 2011 (Michaelides 2014). Despite early calls by its European partners, it took the Cypriot government until June 2012 to formally request an EU-IMF program. After another nine months and a new government in office, a program was agreed. It focused on banking and fiscal consolidation as well as on privatizations (Charalambous 2014).

During the negotiations of the program, there had already been intense disagreements between the troika institutions. They mostly concerned the *handling of the oversized banking sector* and particularly of the two largest banks – Laiki Bank and the Bank of Cyprus. While the Commission opted for a standard program without a bail-in, the IMF proposed a direct recapitalization of Cypriot banks by the European Stability Mechanism (ESM) as an alternative to a full program (Henning 2017: 195; Blustein 2016: 364). Given the size of the banking sector and the magnitude of financial assistance requested (100 percent of GDP), the IMF cast doubt on debt sustainability and was reluctant to even discuss a program with the national authorities (Michaelides 2014: 641, Interview CY 14). When the IMF realized that a direct recapitalization was politically not feasible, its mission team demanded a bail-in of depositors and other private creditors of the two banks to reduce the size of financial assistance (Henning 2017: 195). Just like the Commission, the ECB initially opposed a bail-in (Demetriades 2017: 96). Yet, by January 2013, the ECB had prepared different scenarios for a bail-in that would avoid contagion to Greece and the wider European banking sector (ThePressProject, March 5, 2015). Given the amount of emergency liquidity assistance (ELA) provided by national central banks, the ECB pressed for a program to protect the balance sheets of the Eurosystem (Interview CY 14). The Commission remained concerned about the risks of a bail-in and its staff were 'doing everything in their power to block it' (Blustein 2016: 364).

During the crucial negotiations between March 15 and 25, 2013, the IMF, with crucial support from the German government, insisted on a bail-in of depositors. The ECB was open to it, and the Commission sided with the Cypriot government in trying to limit the impact on the domestic banking sector (Interview CY 02). The Eurogroup and Cyprus agreed to impose a levy on insured and uninsured deposits of Cypriot banks (Blustein 2016: 367). However, the proposal was rejected by the Cypriot parliament. Intense negotiations followed, after which a bank holiday was imposed and the ECB threatened to cut ELA (Interview CY 02, 11). Eventually, it was agreed that one of the biggest Cypriot banks (Laiki) would be dissolved. The arrangement entailed even harsher losses for the bank's depositors than the bail-in that was planned initially. This was to ensure that the IMF's contribution did not exceed 500 percent of Cyprus' quota (Henning 2017: 195; Blustein 2016: 367). By this time, the ECB also demanded a certain bail-in to consider the 'reinstatement of Bank of Cyprus as a counterpart for monetary policy operations' (Demetriades 2017: 159). Moreover, the agreement involved the implementation of capital controls and a carve-out of Cypriot bank branches in Greece to prevent contagion effects (Interview CY 05). In the end, consequences for the Cypriot economy have not been as negative as expected. However, an earlier agreement would have arguably allowed for a program with minor losses for depositors, and without bank closures, capital controls and damage to the Cypriot business model as well as the trust in domestic political institutions (Charalambous 2014: 94).

Conclusion

The three troika institutions pursued distinctive and partly conflicting approaches to *financial*, *fiscal* and *structural adjustment measures* in European lending programs. These approaches reflect different bureaucratic cultures – that is, formal and informal rules – as well as routines of problem solving. The European Commission as 'Europeanist' focused on structural adjustment measures in order to harmonize the debtor's economies in line with European rules and the overall priority to increase domestic competitiveness. As 'Monetary Guardian', the ECB was most vocal on financial issues and on compliance with the fiscal rules of the Monetary Union. The IMF's overall concern as 'Accountant' was that loans would be repaid on schedule, which in turn required sustainability of public debt. Unlike the European institutions, the Fund evaluated program measures in terms of their 'macro-criticality' and refrained from micro-managing structural adjustment conditions.

The majority of conflicts can be traced back to disagreements between the IMF on the one side and the European institutions on the other. They were most pronounced with regard to financial sector stability, where the EC figured less prominently. Here, the IMF sometimes felt that the ECB was sitting on 'the wrong side of the table' (Interviews IMF 17; ECB 01). Usually, in IMF-supported programs, the central bank co-signs the Memorandum of Understanding and is required to implement conditional measures. On more than one occasion, the IMF urged the ECB to use its monetary policy to mitigate the risk of contagion evolving from potential debt restructuring (Blustein 2016: 119, 173). Given its crucial role in liquidity provision, the independent ECB got its way in the conflicts over debt restructuring in the first Greek and the Irish programs. Disputes over the path of fiscal adjustment mostly resulted in rather hawkish compromises in accordance with the SGP criteria. In the area of structural reforms, the EC's role was more substantive, in that it was able to add its own agenda to the IMF's macro-critical strategy. In general, the IMF's single country focus collided with the considerations for the Eurozone as a whole as prioritized by the EC and the ECB. European rules were in many cases at odds with the more pragmatic solutions brought forward by the IMF. It is not the focus of this chapter, but the reason for the European institutions frequently winning through may be related to three factors. First, they provided a significantly larger amount of financing, directly and indirectly, than the IMF. Second, the IMF and most of its non-European principals were less affected by the Eurozone crisis than the EC and ECB. This held especially true at later stages of the crisis, when its potential repercussions on the global economy had largely diminished. Finally, the EU's rules served as a major limitation in many cases. Our findings convey that the European institutions operate within a much more restrictive legal framework than the IMF. Moreover, the borrower governments were not able or not willing to exploit the divisions between IMF and Europeans. In the negotiations with debtor governments, the troika tried to appear united. In general, the balance of power was tilted toward the troika institutions (Table 3.1).

The 'troika regime complex' may have been created by powerful member states in order to reduce agency slack and, thus, to control the outcome of crisis resolution (Henning 2017). However, our study shows that this complex produced dysfunctional behavior resulting from strong IO preferences. First, the ECB and the Commission faced a novel task in designing and overseeing financial assistance programs. Both often made recourse to established routines and

Table 3.1 Approaches of troika bureaucracies on loan conditionalities

	IMF	*EU Commission*	*ECB*
Financing/ Financial stability	Debt sustainability as crucial norm and debt restructuring	Lack of legal framework for sovereign debt restructuring	Focus on financial stability of Eurozone and skeptical toward debt restructuring
Fiscal	Structural and flexible fiscal targets depending on economic conditions	Ambitious, nominal fiscal targets in line with Stability and Growth Pact	Ambitious, nominal fiscal targets in line with Stability and Growth Pact
Structural adjustment	Focus on 'macro-critical' measures	Detailed reform agenda, harmonization and competitiveness of Eurozone economies	No explicit position
Role in troika	'Accountant'	'Europeanist'	'Monetary Guardian'

policies in line with their primary mandate. Second, the process of cooperation often protracted conflicts stemming from the IO's approaches and a lack of division of labor. These unintended consequences of the troika complex led to various difficulties in the programs such as *inconsistencies*, *delays*, *overburdening* and a *shift of the burden of adjustment*. In the Greek program, the inconsistent approach toward debt restructuring thwarted reform efforts and discouraged potential investors. Delayed debt restructuring in the second program then undermined the effect of the PSI so that Greek debt remained unsustainable. Thus, another debt restructuring exercise became inevitable. It caused another conflict leading to a reserved commitment by the IMF to the third Greek program. In the end, the Greek taxpayers had to endure a lengthy and painful reform process. What is more, disagreements on fiscal projections and targets gave rise to inconsistencies, which again irritated investors and resulted in even more measures and an erosion of program ownership. In Portugal and Greece, conflicts over structural reforms overburdened program implementation by increasing the number of measures without a clear prioritization and overwhelmed national authorities. In the end, crucial reforms were delayed or not implemented at all. Finally, the absence of a bail-in in Ireland and the design of the bail-in in Cyprus shifted the burden of adjustment toward taxpayers and depositors, causing public outrage in both program countries.

We have illustrated the difficulties of cooperation between IOs with different core tasks. Cooperation between the three troika institutions was created ad hoc and in a context of high uncertainty. It lacked clear criteria of responsibilities and mechanisms to achieve a division of labor. In such an environment, IOs tend to refer to long-established 'standard operating procedures' that are likely to reproduce bureaucratic pathologies and even generate new ones.

A long-term solution for the EU could be replacing the Fund with an eventual 'European Monetary Fund' (EMF) on the basis of the ESM (see also the chapter by G. Russell Kincaid in this volume). Given our findings, the EMF should be the single authority to provide financial assistance and be in charge of program design and supervision. This would avoid conflicts of interest between organizations with potentially contradictory mandates and which have to answer to different principals. The EMF could make use of the expertise of other institutions but without unnecessarily protracting decision-making processes. This would accommodate notably the ECB, which does not intend to fully participate in future programs but to concentrate on financing and financial sector aspects (ECB 2018: 3). Such an arrangement would improve program consistency, even though it would not eliminate potential conflicts between the interests of the Eurozone in general and those of individual member states. Further political and economic integration may therefore be necessary (Matthijs and Blyth 2015). It would increase both the political legitimacy of financial assistance and its technical feasibility. As a result, policies that one-sidedly favor (or disadvantage) particular member states would be less probable and some of the bureaucratic pathologies that we identified could eventually be prevented.

Acknowledgments

A former version of this chapter was presented at the College of Europe workshop on June 29–30, 2017 in Bruges. We are indebted for helpful comments to Michele Chang, G. Russell Kincaid, the workshop participants and an anonymous reviewer. The chapter presents findings of a larger empirical research project on Troika–debtor negotiations in the Eurozone. The project was financed by the German Research Association (Deutsche Forschungsgemeinschaft, DFG, No. LU 867/2–1).

References

Asmussen, Jörg (2012), The Irish case from an ECB perspective, Speech by Jörg Asmussen, Member of the Executive Board of the ECB at the Institute of International and European Affairs, Dublin, April 12.

Banking Inquiry (2015a), Witness Statement of Ajai Chopra, Joint Committee of Inquiry into the Banking Crisis, Session 63(a), September 10, Dublin: Houses of the Oireachtas.

Banking Inquiry (2015b), Hearing Transcript of Kevin Cardiff, Joint Committee of Inquiry into the Banking Crisis, June 24, Dublin: Houses of the Oireachtas.

Banking Inquiry (2015c), Hearing Transcript of Michael Noonan, Joint Committee of Inquiry into the Banking Crisis, June 10, Dublin: Houses of the Oireachtas.

Barnett, Michael N. and Martha Finnemore (1999), The politics, power, and pathologies of international organizations, *International Organization*, 53(4), 699–732.

Barnett, Michael N. and Martha Finnemore (2004), *Rules for the World: International Organizations in Global Politics*, Ithaca, NY: Cornell University Press.

Barnett, Michael N. and Martha Finnemore (2005), The power of liberal international organizations, in: Michael Barnett and Raymond Duvall (eds.), *Power in Global Governance*, Cambridge: Cambridge University Press, 161–184.
Bastasin, Carlo (2015), *Saving Europe: Anatomy of a Dream*. Washington D.C.: Brookings Institution Press.
Bauer, Michael W. and Jörn Ege (2016), Bureaucratic autonomy of international organizations' secretariats, *Journal of European Public Policy*, 23(7), 1019–1037.
Bauer, Michael W., Steffen Eckhard, Jörn Ege and Christoph Knill (2017), A public administration perspective on international organizations, in: Michael W. Bauer, Christoph Knill and Steffen Eckhard (eds.), *International Bureaucracy: Challenges and Lessons for Public Administration Research*, London: Palgrave Macmillan, 1–12.
Becker, Stefan, Michael W. Bauer, Sara Connolly and Hussein Kassim (2016), The Commission: boxed in and constrained, but still an engine of integration, *West European Politics*, 39(5), 1011–1031.
Best, Jacqueline (2012), Ambiguity and uncertainty in international organizations: a history of debating IMF conditionality, *International Studies Quarterly*, 56(4), 674–688.
Biermann, Rafael and Joachim A. Koops (2017), Studying relations among international organizations in world politics: core concepts and challenges, in: Rafael Biermann and Joachim A. Koops (eds.), *The Palgrave Handbook of Inter-Organizational Relations in World Politics*, London: Palgrave Macmillan, 1–46.
Bini Smaghi, Lorenzo (2015), Governance and conditionality: toward a sustainable framework?, *Journal of European Integration*, 37(7), 755–768.
Blustein, Paul (2015), Laid low: the IMF, the Euro Zone and the first rescue of Greece. *CIGI Papers No. 61*, April, Waterloo: Centre for International Governance Innovation.
Blustein, Paul (2016), *Laid Low: Inside the Crisis That Overwhelmed Europe and the IMF*, Waterloo: CIGI Press.
Blyth, Mark (2013), *Austerity: The History of a Dangerous Idea*, Oxford: Oxford University Press.
Brunnermeier, Markus K., Harold James and Jean-Pierre Landau (2016), *The Euro and the Battle of Ideas*, Princeton, NJ: Princeton University Press.
Bruszt, Laszlo and Visnja Vukov (2017), Making states for the single market: European integration and the reshaping of economic states in the Southern and Eastern peripheries of Europe, *West European Politics*, 40(4), 663–687.
Buti, Marco and Lucio R. Pench (2004), Why do large countries flout the Stability Pact? And what can be done about it?, *Journal of Common Market Studies*, 42(5), 1025–1032.
Cardiff, Kevin (2016), *Recap: Inside Ireland's Financial Crisis*, Dublin: The Liffey Press.
Chang, Michele (2016), *Economic and Monetary Union*, Basingstoke: Palgrave Macmillan.
Charalambous, Giorgos (2014), *Political Culture and Behaviour in the Republic of Cyprus during the Crisis*, PCC Report No. 2, Oslo: Peace Research Institute Oslo.
Copeland, Paul and Scott James (2014), Policy windows, ambiguity and Commission entrepreneurship: explaining the relaunch of the European Union's economic reform agenda, *Journal of European Public Policy*, 21(1), 1–19.
Cottarelli, Carlo (2005), *Efficiency and Legitimacy: Trade-Offs in IMF Governance*. IMF Working Paper WP/05/107. Washington D.C.: International Monetary Fund.
Crespy, Amandine and Georg Menz (2015), Commission entrepreneurship and the debasing of social Europe before and after the Eurocrisis, *Journal of Common Market Studies*, 53(4), 753–768.
Demetriades, Panicos (2017), *A Diary of the Euro Crisis in Cyprus Lessons for Bank Recovery and Resolution*, Basingstoke: Palgrave Macmillan.

Donovan, Donal and Antoin E. Murphy (2013), *The Fall of the Celtic Tiger: Ireland and the Euro Debt Crisis*, Oxford: Oxford University Press.

Dyson, Kenneth (2008), The first decade: credibility, identity, and institutional 'fuzziness', in: Kenneth Dyson (ed.), *The Euro at 10*, Oxford: Oxford University Press, 1–34.

EC (2002), Public finances in EMU, *European Economy No. 3*, Brussels: European Commission, Directorate-General for Economic and Financial Affairs.

EC (2008), EMU@10: successes and challenges after ten years of Economic and Monetary Union, *European Economy 2*, Luxembourg: Office for Official Publications of the European Communities.

EC (2015), Ex post evaluation of the economic adjustment programme: Ireland, 2010–2013, *Institutional Papers 004*, Luxembourg: Publications Office of the European Union.

ECB (2014), *ECB's replies to the questionnaire of the European Parliament supporting the own initiative report evaluating the structure, the role and operations of the 'troika' (Commission, ECB and the IMF) actions in euro area programme countries*. www.ecb.europa.eu/pub/pdf/other/140110_ecb_response_troika_questionnaireen.pdf (accessed April 6, 2017).

ECB (2018), Opinion of the European Central Bank of 11 April 2018 on a proposal for a regulation on the establishment of the European Monetary Fund, CON/2018/20.

Eichenbaum, Martin, Sergio Rebelo and Carlos de Resende (2016), The Portuguese crisis and the IMF, *IEO Background Paper BP/16-02/05*, Washington, D.C.: Independent Evaluation Office of the International Monetary Fund.

Ellinas, Antonis A. and Ezra Suleiman (2012), *The European Commission and Bureaucratic Autonomy*, Cambridge: Cambridge University Press.

Eurogroup (2018), *Eurogroup statement on Greece of 22 June 2018*, Press Release 390/18, Brussels: Council of the EU.

Henning, C. Randall (2017), *Tangled Governance: International Regime Complexity, the Troika, and the Euro Crisis*, Oxford: Oxford University Press.

Hodson, Dermont (2011), *Governing the Euro Area in Good Times and Bad*, Oxford: Oxford University Press.

Howarth, David (2004), The ECB and the Stability Pact: policeman and judge?, *Journal of European Public Policy*, 11(5), 832–853.

IEO (2016), *The IMF and the Crises in Greece, Ireland, And Portugal*, July 8, Washington, D.C.: Independent Evaluation Office of the International Monetary Fund.

IMF (2001), *Conditionality in Fund-Supported Programs – Policy Issues*, February 16, Washington, D.C.: International Monetary Fund.

IMF (2003), Lessons from the crisis in Argentina. Prepared by the Policy Development and Review Department. October 8, 2003. www.imf.org/external/np/pdr/lessons/100803.pdf (accessed April 6, 2017).

IMF (2007), *International Monetary Fund Handbook: Its Functions, Policies and Operations*. Washington D.C.: International Monetary Fund.

IMF (2010), Ireland: Request for an Extended Arrangement – Staff Report, IMF Country Report No. 10/366, Washington, D.C.: International Monetary Fund.

IMF (2012), 2011 Review of Conditionality. Overview Paper. Prepared by the Strategy, Policy and Review Department. June 19, 2012. www.imf.org/external/np/pp/eng/2012/061912a.pdf (accessed April 6, 2017).

IMF (2013a), *Stocktaking the Fund's Engagement with Regional Financing Arrangements*, April 11, Washington, D.C.: International Monetary Fund.

IMF (2013b), Greece: ex post evaluation of exceptional access under the 2010 stand-by arrangement. *IMF Country Report No. 13.156.* Washington, D.C.: International Monetary Fund.

IMF (2015a), The fund's lending framework and sovereign debt: further considerations. April 9, 2015. www.imf.org/external/np/pp/eng/2015/040915.pdf (accessed April 6, 2017).

IMF (2015b), Ireland: ex post evaluation of exceptional access under the 2010 extended arrangement, *IMF Country Report No. 15/20*, Washington, D.C.: International Monetary Fund.

IMF (2015c), Portugal: selected issues, *IMF Country Report No. 15/127*, May, Washington, D.C.: International Monetary Fund.

IMF (2016a), Portugal: ex post evaluation of exceptional access under the 2011 extended arrangement, *IMF Country Report No. 16/302*, September, Washington, D.C.: International Monetary Fund.

IMF (2016b), Portugal: 2016 Article IV consultation, *IMF Country Report No. 16/300*, September, Washington, D.C.: International Monetary Fund.

IMF (2017), *IMF Executive Board Approves in Principle €1.6 Billion Stand-by Arrangement for Greece*. www.imf.org/en/News/Articles/2017/07/20/pr17294-greece-imf-executive-board-approves-in-principle-stand-by-arrangement (accessed September 15, 2017).

IMF (2018), Greece: 2018 Article IV consultation and proposal for post-program monitoring, *IMF Country Report No. 18/248*. Washington, D.C.: International Monetary Fund.

Irwin, Neil (2014), *The Alchemists: Three Central Bankers and a World on Fire*, London: Penguin Books.

Issing, Otmar (2008), *The Birth of the Euro*, Cambridge: Cambridge University Press.

Kaltenthaler, Karl (2006), *Policy-Making in the European Central Bank: The Masters of Europe's Money*, Lanham, MD/Plymouth: Rowman & Littlefield.

Karas, Othmar and Liem Hoan Ngoc (2014), REPORT on the enquiry on the role and operations of the Troika (ECB, Commission and IMF) with regard to the euro area programme countries, A7-0149/2014, Strasbourg: European Parliament, Committee on Economic and Monetary Affairs.

Killick, Tony (1995), *IMF Programmes in Developing Countries: Design and Impact*, London and New York: Routledge.

Kopits, George (2016), The IMF and the euro area crisis: the fiscal dimension. *IEO Background Paper* BP/16-02/07.

Lebaron, Frédéric (2013), ECB leaders: a new European monetary elite?, in: D. Georgakakis and J. Rowell. (eds.), *The Field of Eurocracy: Mapping EU Actors and Professionals*, New York: Palgrave Macmillan, 87–104.

Lütz, Susanne (2015), From Washington Consensus to flexible Keynesianism? The International Monetary Fund after the financial crisis, *Journal of International Organization Studies*, 6(2), 85–98.

Lütz, Susanne and Sven Hilgers (2018), When overlapping organisations play two-level games: IMF–EU interaction in credit lending to Latvia and Greece, *New Political Economy*, 24(3), 299–312.

Lütz, Susanne and Matthias Kranke (2014), The European rescue of the Washington Consensus? EU and IMF lending to Central and Eastern European countries, *Review of International Political Economy*, 21(2), 310–338.

Marcussen, Martin (2009), Scientization of central banking: the politics of a-politicization, in: Kenneth Dyson and Martin Marcussen (eds.): *Central Banks in the Age of the Euro: Europeanization, Convergence, and Power*, Oxford and New York: Oxford University Press, 373–390.

Matthijs, Matthias and Mark Blyth (2015), Conclusion: the future of the Euro – possible futures, risks, and uncertainties, in: Matthias Matthijs and Mark Blyth (eds.), *The Future of the Euro*, Oxford: Oxford University Press, 248–269.

McNamara, Kathleen R. (2006), Managing the Euro: the European Central Bank, in: John Peterson and Michael Shackleton (eds.), *The Institutions of the European Union*, Oxford: Oxford University Press, 169–188.

Michaelides, Andreas (2014), Cyprus: from boom to bail-in, *Economic Policy*, 29(80), 639–689.

Moschella, Manuela (2016), Negotiating Greece: layering, insulation, and the design of adjustment programs in the Eurozone, *Review of International Political Economy*, 23(5), 799–824.

Nelson, Stephen C. and Catherine Weaver (2016), Organizational culture, in: Jacob Katz Cogan, Ian Hurd and Ian Johnstone (eds.), *The Oxford Handbook of International Relations*, Oxford: Oxford University Press, 920–939.

Padoa-Schioppa, Tommaso (2004), *The Euro and Its Central Bank Getting United after the Union*, Cambridge, MA/London: MIT Press.

Papaconstantinou, George (2016), *Game Over: The Inside Story of the Greek Crisis*, Athens: Papadopoulos Publishing.

Park, Yung Chul (2017), The role of the IMF in managing the euro area sovereign debt and banking crises: perspectives from East Asia, *Global Policy*, 8(4), 443–454.

Piroska, Dóra (2017), Funding Hungary: competing crisis management priorities of troika institutions, *Third World Thematics: A TWQ Journal*, 2(6), 805–824.

Reis, Ricardo (2013), The Portuguese slump and crash and the euro crisis, *Brookings Papers on Economic Activity*, 46(1), 143–210.

Stone, Randall W. (2008), The scope of IMF conditionality, *International Organization*, 62, 589–620.

Strauss-Kahn, Dominique (2010), Crisis and beyond: the next phase of IMF reform, *Speech delivered at the Peterson Institute for International Economics*, Washington, D.C., June 29.

ThePressProject. (2015), Special Report: how the Troika and Piraeus Bank sealed Cyprus's fate, March 5. www.thepressproject.gr/article/73470/How-the-troika-and-Piraeus-Bank-sealed-Cypruss-fate (accessed April 6, 2018).

Umbach, Gaby and Wolfgang Wessels (2008), The changing European context of economic and monetary union: 'deepening', 'widening', and stability, in: Kenneth Dyson (ed.): *The Euro at 10*, Oxford: Oxford University Press, 54–68.

Véron, Nicolas (2016), The IMF's role in the euro area crisis: financial sector aspects, *IEO Background Paper 16-02/10*, Washington, D.C.: Independent Evaluation Office of the International Monetary Fund.

Weaver, Catherine (2008), *Hypocrisy Trap: The World Bank and the Poverty of Reform*, Princeton, NJ: Princeton University Press.

Yiangou, Jonathan, Mícheál O'Keeffe and Gabriel Glöckler (2013), 'Tough love': how the ECB's monetary financing prohibition pushes deeper euro area integration. *Journal of European Integration*, 35(3), 223–237.

Zettelmeyer, Jeromin, Christoph Trebesch and Mitu Gulati (2013), The Greek debt restructuring: an autopsy, *Economic Policy*, 28(75), 513–563.

Part II

Country studies

4 Greece after the bailouts

Assessment of a qualified failure

George Pagoulatos[1]

Introduction

In the comparative analysis of the Eurozone bailout programs, Greece stands out as an uncontroverted failure of historic proportions. The first country to resort to a financial assistance program in May 2010, Greece was the only country to require three consecutive programs, and the last to graduate, in August 2018, having spent over eight years subject to heavy monitoring and conditionality. An endless succession of policy reforms and heavy austerity measures were applied, contributing to a steep recession.

Since its first year of recession in 2008, Greece registered an eight-year-long equivalent of a Great Depression, as steep as that of the US in the 1930s, but twice as long. By the time it completed its third program, Greece had lost a quarter of its 2008 GDP, unemployment was at 20 percent (having reached 27.5 percent at its peak), one out of three Greeks were below the poverty line, and youth unemployment affected four out of ten young Greeks. Over 400,000 people (some 9 percent of the country's labor force) were estimated to have emigrated during the crisis. By the end of the third program, even the lender institutions agreed that the handling and outcomes of the Greek crisis suggested a case of grave failure, though the exact allocation of responsibility varied.

What were the reasons why Greece ended up in such a sadly exceptional state? Why did it fail to graduate following its second bailout? What were the policy errors and failures, and what is the legacy of Greece's bailout programs? We explore these questions, looking at (a) the content of the conditionality programs and what was left behind; (b) the surrounding macroeconomic conditions; (c) the sociopolitics of Greece's "forced adjustment"; and (d) the implications for Greece's variety of capitalism.

The tyranny of antecedent circumstances: from boom to crash

Greece's main incentive for pursuing euro-accession in the 1990s was two-fold. First, all governments, across party lines, had pursued being at the inner core of European integration, with the EU viewed at the time as the main provider of political security and institutional stability, and the driver of domestic economic modernization. Second, for an economy with a legacy of high fiscal deficits, public debt, inflation, and a weak currency, the EU provided the vital external constraint (the *vincolo esterno* – Dyson and Featherstone 1996) that would catalyze macroeconomic adjustment to overcome the lack of domestic fiscal discipline and the low reform capacity (Featherstone and Papadimitriou 2008).

Indeed, Greece entered the 1990s with high fiscal deficits, public debt, and inflation, bequeathed by a period of expansionary economic policies that followed the country's transition to democracy (1974) and the first socialist government of PASOK under A. Papandreou (1981–85). Macroeconomic adjustment was pursued throughout the 1990s, initially under the center-right ND government (1990–93), and subsequently (and more successfully) under PASOK led by A. Papandreou (1993–96) and Kostas Simitis (1996–2004). Stabilization was initiated in 1985–87, interrupted in 1988–89, relaunched after 1990, but began to deliver after 1994.

Macroeconomic stabilization was tightly interwoven with the EU single market program. The objectives of coping with the single market (culminating with the liberalization of short-term capital movements in 1994) and fulfilling the EMU nominal convergence targets implied a rigorous framework within which Greece should achieve macroeconomic stabilization, market liberalization, and institutional modernization. In the constraining Maastricht framework, inflation declined, fiscal discipline was restored, and from the mid-1990s the government began to post primary budget surpluses.

As part of the single market process, the financial system was gradually liberalized over the second half of the 1980s and into the 1990s, in view of the liberalization of the capital account scheduled for 1994. Under financial "repression", the public sector had enjoyed below-market borrowing costs, which rose sharply in the early 1990s, as interest rates adjusted to market levels, pushing the public debt/GDP ratio upwards. Over the 1990s, financial liberalization allowed monetary policy to become assertive as interest rates increased, aligned behind the Bundesbank after 1994. But financial liberalization also brought about an important reallocation of resources from sectors traditionally favored for developmental or redistributive purposes (manufacturing, small- and medium-sized enterprises, agriculture, public investment), to increasingly modernizing non-tradable sectors (banking, real estate, constructions, media, retail trade) that corresponded to the strong demand for consumption created by trade and capital liberalization (Pagoulatos 2003). Following financial liberalization, private sector creditors and financial institutions expanded, fueling consumption-driven growth.

High real interest rates in the mid-1990s, and the Maastricht-induced fiscal discipline, reduced inflation and suppressed budget deficits, allowing Greece to narrowly satisfy the EMU accession criteria and join the single currency with the second wave on 1 January 2001. In 1998 Greece implemented a final devaluation of the drachma before "irrevocably" joining the Exchange Rate Mechanism (ERM) of the European Monetary System (EMS), the official antechamber of the single currency. After that, real interest rates began to decline, which, combined with the prospect of euro accession, led to a financial market boom, typical of an "emerging" and euro-denominated market. Government access to globalized financial markets allowed cheap government borrowing and expansion. Boosted by the cost of the 2004 Olympic Games, primary budget deficits (i.e., net of interest payments on the public debt) re-emerged from 2003 and would last for a decade. The government (whose public debt was increasingly held by foreign investors) became subject to the power of global financial markets, susceptible to a self-fulfilling debt crisis at the first serious sign of financial vulnerability.

At first sight, EMU offered a much-anticipated framework of imported stability and growth. Low financing costs and ample supply of investment capital provided the Greek economy the opportunity to build productive capacity, develop comparative advantages, address structural deficiencies, and expand in a rule-based macroeconomic environment. However, these advantages were overridden by the irresponsible economic governance exercised by the Greek authorities up to the end of 2009. The social-democratic PASOK was succeeded in power by the conservative ND, which governed between March 2004 and October 2009. Greece posted a primary budget deficit every single year from 2003 until 2013, despite the economy growing at one of the fastest rates in the Eurozone until 2007 (annual GDP growth averaged 4.1 percent in 2000–07). The governments failed to use the opportunity of rapid growth and low interest rates to generate primary surpluses and reduce the stock of debt. While public spending grew (financing pension and wage increases, investment, and personnel expansion), tax revenues remained stagnant. The externally imposed fiscal discipline lost its teeth, as the "hard" Maastricht constraint (where fiscal divergence carried the maximum cost of EMU exclusion) was succeeded by a Stability and Growth Pact which became "softer", flexible, and politicized after its deficit limits were defied by France and Germany in 2003 (Blavoukos and Pagoulatos 2008). The Commission was incapable of imposing or reluctant to impose fiscal discipline, and the Eurostat lacked the power to independently audit the numbers presented by a Greek Statistical Authority which (until its 2010 reform) remained subservient to the government (see Savage and Verdun 2016).

Up to 2008, annual credit expansion grew at average double-digit rates, pulling GDP growth. Below the surface of a prosperous-looking economy lay deep-rooted structural deficiencies: an unsustainable pension system, a wasteful and corrupt health sector, an excessively rigid labor market, closed products and services markets, an antiquated, inefficient, and corrupt tax administration, a slow and overburdened justice system, and a public sector overwhelmed by patronage appointments and red tape. Instead of using the high-growth period to implement long-needed reforms, the governments by and large refrained from any significant reform in the above sectors from 2001 to 2009. The Lisbon scorecard pre-crisis showed Greece lagging on nearly all Lisbon reform indicators regarding competitiveness and social protection (Tilford and Whyte 2010). The rapid economic growth inside the euro, fueled by low-interest debt financing, generated complacency and an illusion of perpetual prosperity. Cheap finance and exuberant credit growth sustained an inordinate expansion of consumer demand. Fiscal deficit creation was again a major driver, to which growing private sector liabilities were added, both mainly funded by copious capital inflows. The twin deficit, which peaked when the 2007/08 financial crisis shook the global economy, summarized the profound macroeconomic destabilization (Table 4.1).

The stealthy destabilizing factor at work were the growing external imbalances. Cheap capital inflows ended up a factor of macroeconomic divergence rather than convergence, funding a steadily expanding current account deficit. The economy grew through foreign debt-fueled financial and credit expansion, visible in the rapid growth of real estate, consumption (government and private), and other non-tradeable sectors of the economy. Between 1998 and 2008, private sector debt (which had been low, with consumer and mortgage debt at dormant levels) almost tripled as GDP share, funded by annual credit expansion rates higher than the European average, though the stock of private debt always remained lower than the EU average. Contrary to the debt creation of the 1980s (funded mainly by domestic banks and general government entities), debt-driven growth after the late 1990s was financed predominantly by external capital inflows, via capital, debt, or interbank channels. Inside the euro, reflecting the deficient EMU structure, external deficits reached levels hitherto unseen, as they would have otherwise necessitated an adjustment via exchange rate depreciation or devaluation. Indicating the economy's overall net exposure to foreign creditors, the net foreign debt grew as GDP ratio from single digit in the mid-1990s to well over 90 percent on the eve of the debt crisis (Meghir et al. 2017: 17).

As an economy in the Eurozone periphery, Greece experienced a far-reaching distortion (though less extreme for Greece compared to Spain or Ireland): an inflation of the non-traded sectors (banks, public enterprises, imports, constructions, telecoms, services, retail trade, media, etc.) at the expense of exports and tradables. Higher returns on capital and labor (given the ample possibilities for private sector deficit financing) directed resources to these sectors, away from manufacturing, where global competition compressed profits. Traditional local industrialists turned into financiers or investors in real estate, where prices and returns rallied every year (Pagoulatos 2014). The significant increase of wages in the sheltered, non-tradable sectors (led by the public sector, utilities, and banks, all heavily unionized and over-represented in the national confederation of labor unions) passed on their higher prices to the rest of the economy, undercutting competitiveness. Since euro accession, the Greek economy had suffered a severe erosion of competitiveness, the result of lax fiscal and incomes policies, large capital inflows, rapid credit expansion, and higher inflation compared to its Eurozone partners. Between 2000 and 2010, the unit-labor cost-based real effective exchange rate rose by 26 percent, while the nominal unit labor cost increased by 47 percent, among the highest increases in the Eurozone. The Greek and Southern European erosion of competitiveness and divergence up to the crisis was magnified by the opposite policy of aggressive wage deflation pursued by the German economy through most of the 2000s.

Table 4.1 Economic indicators for Greece 2001–07

	2001	*2002*	*2003*	*2004*	*2005*	*2006*	*2007*
GDP growth at constant prices (AMECO) *National currency: aggregates: average of national growth rates weighted with current values in EUR (billion)*	197.7	205.5	217.4	228.4	229.8	242.8	250.7
GDP growth at constant prices (AMECO) – relative to EU 15 *GDP at 2010 reference levels: performance relative to the rest of the former EU-15: double export weights (national currency)*	96.4	99.1	104.1	107	105.8	108.4	108.8
TFP growth (AMECO) (Unit: 2010=100)	100.3	101.8	105.5	108	107.3	110.8	111.9
CPI inflation (AMECO) ***(harmonized)*** (2015=100)	73.6	76.5	79.1	81.5	84.3	87.1	89.7
Unemployment rate (AMECO) ***(% of active population)***	10.7	10.3	9.7	10.6	10	9	8.4
Real exchange rate (ULC) (AMECO) *Real effective exchange rates, based on unit labor costs (total economy) – performance relative to the rest of the former EU-15: double export weights Unit: 2010=100*	78.4	83.9	85.7	86.2	93	91.4	92.4
Household savings (% of disposable income) (AMECO) *Saving rate, gross: households and NPISH (gross saving as percentage of gross disposable income)*	6.2	5.9	8.4	8.5	4.9	7.5	6.5
Gross fixed capital formation (% of GDP) (EUROSTAT)						23.7	26.0
General government balance (% of GDP) (AMECO)	–5.5	–6	–7.8	–8.8	–6.2	–5.9	–6.7
General government primary balance (cyclically adjusted, % of trend GDP at current prices) *Net lending (+) or net borrowing (–) excluding interest of general government adjusted for the cyclical component: Adjustment based on trend GDP*	1.6	0.1	–3.6	–6	–2.8	–5.1	–7.4

continued

Table 4.1 Continued

	2001	*2002*	*2003*	*2004*	*2005*	*2006*	*2007*
General government primary balance (cyclically adjusted, % of potential GDP at current prices) *Net lending (+) or net borrowing (−) excluding interest of general government adjusted for the cyclical component: Adjustment based on potential GDP*	0.2	−1	−4	−5.6	−2	−3.5	−4.8
Current account balance (% of GDP) (AMECO)	ND	ND	ND	ND	−8.9	−11.5	−15.2
Exports of goods and services (% of GDP)	22.8	20.1	18.5	20.7	21.3	21.2	22.5
Government bond yields (AMECO) (Nominal long-term interest rates, %)	5.3	5.1	4.3	4.3	3.6	4.1	4.5
Private sector debt (% of GDP) EUROSTAT (*consolidated*)	60.0	63.8	67.9	73.6	85.7	92.5	101.5
Government gross debt (% of GDP) (AMECO)	107.1	104.9	101.5	102.9	107.4	103.6	103.1
Net international investment position (% of GDP) EUROSTAT	–	–	−59.6	−66.9	−75.6	−82.6	−93.7
Banks: loans/deposits **(Bank credit as % of bank deposits[1])**	56.6	61.2	69.7	76.8	84.3	90.7	94.2
% non-performing loans ratio (consumer loans) (BoG)	–	–	8.8	7.9	8.4	8.0	6.5
% non-performing loans ratio (residential loans) (BoG)	–	–	4.8	4.7	4.7	3.8	3.8
% non-performing loans ratio (business loans) (BoG)	–	–	9.8	9.5	9.4	8.0	6.5
Capital-labor substitution: total economy (AMECO) (2010=100)	106.5	106.6	105.7	105.5	105	104.5	103.3

Note
1 www.theglobaleconomy.com/Greece/bank_credit_to_deposits.

The state-driven expansion and debt-driven growth up to the debt crisis not only contravened EMU fiscal rules but could not be justified on economic grounds, either. The fiscal expansion was highly procyclical, at a time when the ECB monetary policy was too loose for the peripheral economies that were growing rapidly and with consistently positive inflation differentials from the Eurozone average. In that, the growth of private debt in Greece up to 2008 was not a substitute or compensation for fiscal consolidation, but grew in parallel with the persistently high levels of public sector indebtedness. The Eurozone was too coy to intervene in the fiscal transgressions, and (perhaps even worse) was agnostic regarding the accumulation of large external imbalances in the Eurozone periphery, which under a single currency were perceived as almost immaterial. As the opportunity to exploit the unique conjuncture of high GDP growth and low-cost government borrowing to reduce the debt stock was squandered, and huge net foreign liabilities were accumulating, the economy was becoming increasingly susceptible to an external shock. The Greek state ended up crashing under its extreme vulnerability, as illustrated in a gaping current account deficit of 15 percent in 2008, and 15 percent fiscal deficit and 127 percent public debt to GDP in 2009. The structure of capital inflows pre-crisis (debt rather than equity – FDI inflows being shallow) amplified crisis vulnerability. The shock, the debt crisis, came as a "sudden stop" of private sector capital inflows, in 2010 (Baldwin and Giavazzi 2015), which had to be compensated for by Eurosystem or official bailout lending.

From crash to bailout: the first and second financial assistance programs

The 2010 debt crisis terminated the illusive pursuit of debt-financed growth. When the global financial crisis erupted in 2008, the ND government rushed to shore up the banks, making available a total of €28 billion by way of government bonds, preferred shares, and state guarantees (Pagoulatos and Triantopoulos 2009). However, very little was done to restore fiscal discipline, especially as elections were approaching and the economy was halting. In February 2009, for the second time since 2004, Greece came under the Excessive Deficit Procedure. In 2008–09 tax revenues declined and the economy was heading unhinged to the October 2009 elections. The socialist PASOK under George Papandreou won the elections on an expansionary platform, but directly sought to acquire an accurate picture of the fiscal situation. What was officially projected to be a fiscal deficit of 6 percent for 2009 was gradually revealed to be double-digit, eventually settling at 15 percent GDP.

By the end of 2008 the 10-year government bond spread over the German bund was over 200 bps; by the end of 2009 it had stabilized just below 300 bps. During the first months of 2010, as the fiscal outlook was revealed to be far worse than expected, markets were panicking, every fiscal package announced was deemed insufficient, and the Eurozone was wavering on how to deal with an imminent sovereign default, which only made things worse. Lehman provided a cautionary tale on what can happen if a systemically important debtor is left to collapse. Eurozone banks (predominantly French and German) were heavily exposed to Greek debt,[2] and Greece's bailout emerged as the only way to avoid catastrophic financial contagion in a Eurozone that lacked substantial crisis reaction instruments. By April 2010, days before the bailout package would be decided, the 10-year government bond spread over the German bond had exceeded 700 bps, rendering it clear that the government was unable to access the market.

The predominant emphasis of the first financial assistance program, signed in May 2010, was on rapidly reducing the budget deficit. It contained a wide array of fiscal austerity measures split between the revenue and the spending side, ranging from public sector wage and pension cuts to the increase in VAT and other tax rates and the abolition of tax credits (see Table 4.2). Many of the policies implemented under the first program represented critical structural reforms that would enhance fiscal discipline and the overall efficiency of the economy:

- the full institutional independence to the Greek Statistical Office;
- a new organic budget law requiring multi-year top-down budgeting with expenditure ceilings for the state budget and deficit targets for the general government;
- a Parliamentary Budget Office;
- strengthening of the General Accounting Office (GAO) in budget planning and control and publication by GAO of timely monthly statistics on revenue, expenditure, and financing, including arrears;
- establishment of a single authority for the payment of public sector wages that until then were scattered between different public sector entities;
- comprehensive pension reform consolidating the highly fragmented pension system (many more rounds of pension reform would follow);
- establishment of a central directorate general for debt collection with a large-scale taxpayers unit;
- comprehensive reform to rationalize public health spending (until then, among the most inefficient and corrupt sectors of government), including strengthening central procurement, e-health capacity, and pharmaceuticals savings by expanding generics;
- merging the largest four health insurance schemes into one national organization for the provision of health services;
- and merging municipalities, prefectures, and regions to reduce operating costs.

Thus, the Greek economy was subjected to far-reaching externally forced adjustment (Pagoulatos 2012). The program(s) represented the hardest conditionality, with each review attached to a tranche disbursement merely sufficient to prevent a sovereign default. Greece's eventually three consecutive bailout programs imposed fiscal consolidation, internal devaluation, and market-liberal structural reforms. Welfare state retrenchment became a priority, focusing on pension system and health sector structural spending cuts, primary sources of government deficits. Failure to adjust in good times necessitated harsh, painful, and heavily frontloaded fiscal and external adjustment. The harshness was amplified by a punitive approach of the Eurozone lenders, who preferred to view the Greek crash as an exclusive result of Greek fiscal recklessness, overlooking lenders' responsibilities and Eurozone-level systemic flaws and policy omissions.

From the crisis onset, the Greek sovereign debt problem was officially branded one of illiquidity rather than insolvency. The creditors were unwilling to even discuss a mild reprofiling, let alone restructuring the debt. An admission of state insolvency would have required debt restructuring, which German and French banks (heavily exposed to the Greek debt) and an ECB concerned about Eurozone systemic stability vehemently opposed. Moral hazard and financial contagion considerations (firewalls not yet there) prevented treating the Greek state as insolvent, which raised the overall adjustment cost.[3] A heavily front-loaded schedule of fiscal adjustment was imposed, targeting a primary budget surplus for 2013, thus foreseeing an end of the program in three years, instead of the five to six years proposed by the IMF. The first bailout program, funded by guarantees provided by the Eurozone member states, made it difficult for the euro area governments to obtain agreement by their Parliaments to bailout a country still running a primary budget deficit. Thus, the EU chose to buy time, both for itself and for Greece, until the Eurozone had erected the firewalls, and Greece had adopted front-loaded painful austerity to both address moral hazard and eradicate the primary deficit. Front-loading adjustment went together with backloading the issue of debt sustainability, in a strategy of "extend and pretend".

In summer 2010, the European Commission (2010: 22) acknowledged half of the fiscal adjustment envisaged up to 2014 was implemented within the first semester of 2010. Many rounds of additional fiscal measures would be demanded from the Greek governments. The first program proved excessively optimistic on the deficit and debt reduction targets, GDP growth assumptions, and anticipated speed of recovery. The overambitious fiscal targets were a function of the unwillingness of the Eurozone to consider additional concessional financing or to frontload debt relief, as was also observed by the IMF's ex post independent evaluation (IMF IEO 2016: viii). The European Commission's October 2011 (5th) Review of the program began acknowledging a contraction in economic activity "substantially deeper than previously projected" (European Commission 2010: 1). The main driver of the recession was the magnitude of austerity measures, implemented in a sociopolitical environment that soon became extremely confrontational and would remain so throughout most of the crisis. Grexit speculation, the Eurozone's reluctance to provide a definitive backstop to the Greek crisis, and the slowdown of the European economy only made things worse. The subsequent upward revisions of the 2009 budget deficit by Eurostat in 2010 exacerbated conditions further, necessitating additional fiscal measures that created a vicious cycle that worsened the recession and resulted in target slippage, while destroying the political capital of the Papandreou government.

Table 4.2 Greece bailout programs

1st economic adjustment program
Agreed: 2 May 2010

PM: George Papandreou, PASOK

Tenure: May 2010 to June 2013

Size: *110 billion

Contributors: GLF (Bilateral Loans pooled from the EA) (€80 billion), IMF (€30 billion)

Objectives:

- Implementation of sustainability-enhancing fiscal consolidation;
- Implementation of financial sector policies to stabilize the system;
- Reforms in the economy's structure toward a more investment- and export-led growth model;
- Restore Greece's credibility for private investors.

Status: *€72.8 billion were disbursed by March 2012, when the program was superseded by the 2nd economic adjustment program.*

**This amount was eventually reduced by €2.7 billion, as Slovakia decided not to participate in the GLF while Ireland and Portugal stepped down from the facility as they requested financial assistance themselves.*

2nd economic adjustment program
Agreed: 1 March 2012 (PM: Lucas Papademos, ND, PASOK)

Tenure: March 2012 to end 2014

Size: €130 billion + €34.5 billion (undisbursed amounts of the GLF)

Contributors: EFSF (€144.7 billion), IMF (€19.8 billion until 2016)

Objectives:

- Restructuring debt held by private creditors to bring the total debt level back to a sustainable path;
- Underpin fiscal consolidation efforts with structural reforms, to boost growth and improve competitiveness.

Status: *The program was extended to 30 June 2015 and expired. The Greek government failed to repay about €1.5 billion to the IMF. A three-week bank holiday took place.*

Total amount disbursed: €153.7 billion *(on 27 February 2015, the €10.9 billion that were earmarked but not needed for bank recapitalization were returned by the Hellenic Financial Stability Fund (HFSF) to the EFSF)*

3rd economic adjustment program
Agreed: 19 August 2015 (PM: Alexis Tsipras, SYRIZA/ANEL)

Tenure: August 2015 to August 2018

Amount: up to €86 billion*

Contributors: ESM

Objectives:

- Restoring fiscal sustainability;
- Safeguarding financial stability; boosting growth, competitiveness, and investment;
- Reforming the public administration.

Status: *Greece successfully concluded the program*

**€61.9 billion were disbursed*

Given the steep fall of nominal GDP, public debt soon became glaringly unsustainable. Even following the adoption of the first program, government bond and CDS markets continued to price in a very high probability of sovereign default, as the Commission recognized from summer 2010 (European Commission 2010: 16). Though the markets had briefly stabilized during the first good months of program implementation, peripheral spreads shot up after October 2010, when, in Deauville, Merkel and Sarkozy agreed that private sector debtholders would take a hit next time a Eurozone government was to be bailed out. The massive sellout of Greek bonds by international investors (including French and German banks) had dire consequences for Greek banks, major investors, and holders of their sovereign's paper.

The second bailout was thus necessitated by the looming funding gap of the first program and Greece's indubitable inability to access the markets upon its conclusion. Thus, the second program *ipso facto* represented an admission of failure of the first program, with two new elements.

First, the second program, which contained what had been left incomplete from the first, was now more focused and detailed interventions not only on fiscal reforms but on a range of competitiveness-enhancing reforms, featuring among others an expansion of labor market liberalization initiated by the first program, including a sharp reduction of the minimum wage by 22 percent (32 percent for the subminimum wage of young employees) that affected labor costs in the private sector. The reforms of the first program (tax governance, pension system and health system reform, labor market flexibility, liberalization of market entry, etc.) were strengthened and expanded to include reforms in public administration and the justice system, regulatory reform, and extensive market liberalization. Importantly, the second program contained a controversial obligation to sharply reduce public employment, including the transfer of 25,000 employees to the mandatory mobility ("availability") scheme, an antechamber for layoffs. During the program, further reforms improving the business environment were added, such as establishing a "one-stop shop", reducing administrative burdens for business, setting up a general commercial registry, reducing the minimum required capital for establishing a limited liability company, and introducing a new legal type of low-capital and flexible private company. In 2013–14, the government adopted much of the so-called OECD toolkit, containing hundreds of specific measures aimed at reducing restrictions to competition in retail, tourism, construction materials, and food processing.

Second, the second program introduced public debt restructuring. A mild 20 percent reprofiling agreed in July 2011 was revised upward to 50 percent in October 2011, while it was also agreed that Greece would need a new second bailout, possibly exceeding the first. Finally, private sector holders of Greek public debt were forced to "voluntarily" accept a haircut of 53.5 percent on the nominal value of their Greek government bonds. This unprecedented and highly complex exercise (euphemistically named "private sector involvement" – PSI) wiped out €106 billion (54 percent GDP)[4] from the total €198 billion of privately held Greek government bonds. Some €50 billion from the second financial assistance program were earmarked for the recapitalization and resolution of Greek banks, whose initial losses were multiplied by the effects of PSI on their portfolios. In November and December 2012, additional reprofiling interventions were implemented (this time affecting the debt held by the official creditors – official sector involvement, OSI), including the repatriation of profits made on GGBs by Eurosystem central banks, and a bond buy-back scheme amounting to a net debt reduction of €21 billion (10.8 percent GDP). From 2011 to 2015, the creditor institutions defined debt sustainability in (stock) terms of debt/GDP, setting an arbitrary target of a medium-term reduction of the ratio at 120 percent GDP or below. Only in 2015, the official stance shifted into realizing that debt sustainability was a matter of ability to service the debt, thereby shifting to the (flows) concept of gross financing needs (GFN), not to exceed 15 percent GDP annually. By that time, and following the 2012 PSI, several additional reprofiling interventions had taken place, significantly reducing the net present value of the debt.

The first and second programs were pursued under conditions of grave political instability, fierce political opposition, and social tensions, but the period was marked by considerable policy and government continuity, instilled by the tight conditionality of the program(s). Program implementation and the economy were seriously derailed on the way to national elections (in May and June 2012, and in January 2015) or by domestic political crises. Such was the announced and subsequently revoked referendum under George Papandreou, which led to his resignation from prime minister and succession, in November 2011, by a grand coalition government under former ECB vice-president Lucas Papademos, backed by a three-party majority (PASOK, ND, and the ultraright-wing LAOS). Typically, different governments and ministers displayed a diverse record on program implementation, either moving fast and efficiently in completing milestones and reviews (as in the first months of the first program in 2010, or in 2013) or, more frequently, dragging their feet. Overall, program "ownership" by the governments remained low, if compared to Ireland, Portugal, Spain, and later Cyprus. Both ND under Antonis Samaras and SYRIZA under Alexis Tsipras, when in opposition, vigorously campaigned against the program, promising to "renegotiate" it (Samaras) or to entirely repeal it (Tsipras), only to change tack after coming to government. In the case of Samaras, this happened within days after his election as prime minister in June 2012. In the case of Tsipras in 2015, it would take six months, culminating in the July 2015 referendum and capital controls, which brought Greece to the verge of Eurozone exit, before implementing a momentous U-turn and signing a third financial assistance program.

The second program was negotiated and voted by the coalition government of L. Papademos, but mostly implemented (after being updated) by the Samaras coalition government. Samaras came to power in June 2012, initially as a three-party coalition between ND, PASOK, and the Democratic Left. The insistence of the IMF on redundancies of public sector employees contributed to the Democratic Left eventually leaving the coalition. Nonetheless, the government registered considerable progress in implementing a large number of reforms and in achieving the fiscal targets after the fiscal adjustment path was extended by two years in November 2012, to make up for the steep deterioration of the economy under two consecutive elections in May and June 2012. The more realistic fiscal path now involved a reduction of the primary surplus target for 2014 from an extreme 4.5 percent to 1.5 percent GDP, and an even annual adjustment of 1.5 percent GDP targeting a primary surplus of 4.5 percent GDP for 2016.

Four reviews of the second program were successfully completed by April 2014, which lasted much longer than intended, a demonstration of implementation delays. Through summer 2014, the economy was recovering on all counts: investment, consumption, exports, consumer confidence, employment – all were showing signs of improvement. The fourth review registered that the 2013 fiscal target had been exceeded with a 0.8 percent GDP primary surplus. In spring 2014 the government tapped the bond market successfully for the first time since 2009, and two of the four systemic banks raised more than the capital required fully from private investors. By 2014 the banks had substantially reduced reliance on Eurosystem funding.

Following the May 2014 European elections, and alarmed by the rise of SYRIZA, the Samaras government implemented a cabinet reshuffle that signaled a populist shift. From summer 2014 progress stalled under the spectrum of an early election in early 2015, if the government failed to gather the necessary Parliament supermajority to elect a President. The risk became imminent in autumn 2014, and the government geared toward an election which SYRIZA was projected to win. The fifth review, which was to complete the second program and open a way to a softer conditionality under an ESM precautionary credit line, was never completed.

The 3rd financial assistance program and the political economy of bailouts

The norm of overall policy continuity between 2010 and end 2014 was interrupted in January 2015, when the coalition of SYRIZA and Independent Greeks (ANEL) rose to power, representing the most populist government coalition in Europe at that time. They were a radical left-wing party and an ultraright-wing nationalist party, united by their virulent opposition and demonization of the adjustment programs (the "Memoranda") applied since 2010, elected with the extravagant promise to unilaterally terminate the programs, end austerity, restructure the public debt, and remain in the euro.

Alexis Tsipras came to power with his own "impossible trinity": he could not implement his program of repealing the Memoranda, keeping Greece inside the Eurozone, and remaining in government all at the same time. One of the three would have to give. In order not to be accused of betraying the anti-austerity cause and committing the "somersault" pundits expected, the Tsipras government, with Varoufakis as finance minister, applied extreme brinkmanship. The newly elected government announced the termination of the second MOU program and the troika. Then an erratic back and forth with the creditors took the negotiation to the wire for five months, in what many viewed as a chicken game, finally calling a referendum advocating for the rejection of the troika proposals. This prompted a run on the banks (whose deposits were flowing out from the end of 2014 and through the first half of 2015) which could only be halted through the imposition of capital controls.[5]

In the aftermath of a resounding "No" in the July 2015 referendum, the Tsipras government, under the imminent threat of disorderly default and Grexit, was forced to capitulate into accepting a new €86 billion ESM program. Its large size corresponded to the funding gap which had grown rapidly, and the higher recapitalization needs of the banks whose capital had severely deteriorated. The conditionality program featured bold reforms and a gradual path to a primary surplus of 3.5 percent in 2018. Notably, by extending ESM loans at very low interest rates and long maturities (amortization not before 2034, some maturities extending over 40 years), the third bailout brought about a significant reduction in the refinancing needs and net present value of the (officially held) sovereign debt.

The third program was a continuation of the second, containing what had been left incomplete. However, by that time the anti-austerity arguments had been gaining momentum in Europe, the Eurozone economy was more confident under the ECB's public sector purchase program (PSPP) and was finally growing, and the European Commission had become more politically thoughtful in its approach. The third program allowed a smoother fiscal adjustment path than any previous program, taking into account the severe economic derailment. Indeed, the economy had returned to recession (after 0.8 percent GDP growth in 2014), and the public debt (which in 2014 was viewed by the IMF as "sustainable but highly vulnerable" (IMF 2015a)) by July 2015 had become "highly unsustainable" (IMF 2015b). The primary surplus targets agreed (-0.25 percent for 2015, 0.50 percent for 2016, 1.75 percent for 2017, and 3.5 percent GDP for 2018) ensured continuation of austerity, but less aggressively this time.

The reforms were bold and more focused than before. Some of the most controversial items such as public sector layoffs not only were absent, but the Tsipras government had been allowed to rehire those laid off directly upon coming to power. Apart from fiscal austerity, reforms prioritized financial stability, pensions, and the business environment, including, among others: the introduction of a framework to enable the reduction of non-performing exposures (NPEs) of banks; adoption of an out-of-court workout mechanism and the relevant electronic platform for debt restructurings and NPL resolution; reform of household and corporate insolvency legislation; full autonomy to the Independent Authority for Public Revenue; further pension reform and consolidation; completion of the merge of all insured persons and related data into the single pension fund (EFKA); centralized collection of the social security contributions and debt into EFKA; completion of public procurement and health system expenditure reform; corporate governance reform in the four systemic banks and the HFSF; further liberalization of regulated professions and product markets; the establishment of a new independent privatization and investment fund to manage and maximize the value of important Greek assets; more privatizations; liberalization of gas and electricity markets; public administration reforms including the annual performance assessments for all public officials; and the acceleration of the judicial process.

The three consecutive economic adjustment programs represented an integral policy framework, despite differences. Each program was more realistic in its assumptions and forecasts compared to its predecessor. The second program incorporated more flexibility than the first (in 2012 the 4.5 percent primary budget surplus target was deferred from 2014 to 2016), and the third program had the mildest fiscal adjustment path compared to both previous ones. The second and third programs were combined with debt relief. The second program was able to incorporate better terms on the back of the sizeable adjustment implemented until then, but also the serious macroeconomic deterioration that resulted from two consecutive national elections (in May and June 2012) that led the program implementation off-track. The third program drew on the magnitude of adjustment implemented between 2010 and 2014, combined with the severe destabilization caused by the plebiscite of July 2015 and imposition of capital controls. Each program drew its existence from the failure of the previous.

The second program was more successful than the first in achieving its revised fiscal targets, even though the economy deteriorated worse than projected, and the third was the most successful. In all three programs, structural reforms were harder to implement compared to legislated austerity measures. In a social economy of traditionally weak supply and even weaker demand for productivity-enhancing reforms, only hard externally imposed conditionality could bring about any substantive progress. Many politically costly reforms (opening up professions or liberalizing product markets) were legislated but not fully implemented, as some link in the policy chain was typically missing. Vocal interest groups such as lawyers, doctors, engineers, and pharmacists mobilized to obstruct implementation of reforms affecting their status quo, with eventually limited success. The implementation deficit, exacerbated by the weak administrative capacity, systematically undermined the credibility of the Greek governments. It was repeatedly castigated by the troika, leading them to introduce a steadily growing number of reforms as specific prior actions, ministerial decisions, or cabinet acts which had to be completed before any program money was disbursed. During the various program reviews, a number of additional "structural benchmarks" were transformed into "prior actions" to ensure completion of implementation. Under the first program, 32 of the prescribed reforms were implemented (80 percent success rate), while in the second program 58 reforms were implemented (66 percent success rate given the much larger number of reforms contained in the second program) (Katsikas et al. 2018: 34). The case with the third program was similar. Reforms requiring simple legislation or government act were easier to implement compared to reforms requiring multiple actions by various branches of the executive. Obstacles were also posed by the courts: austerity measures such as public sector wage cuts were repeatedly challenged in the Council of the State, the country's supreme administrative court, whose rulings created financial liabilities such as wage refunds, financed by further cuts, usually on the public investment program.

The third program enjoyed unprecedentedly favorable circumstances. First, EU leaders were relieved to see a leftwing firebrand Tsipras sign on to Eurozone orthodoxy, thus also reducing the threat represented by Podemos in Spain. Second, the Eurozone was finally growing, including all bailout countries, the shrinking Greek economy of 2015 and 2016 being the only exception. Third, Greece enjoyed sociopolitical stability, as none of the main opposition parties (ND, PASOK, and some smaller centrist parties) was willing to wage the kind of extreme opposition they themselves had faced by SYRIZA-ANEL during 2010–14. The third program was voted in Parliament by an unprecedented majority of five parties and 222 out of 300 MPs, which following the September 2015 elections (also won by SYRIZA) represented over 250 out of 300 parliament seats. The second Tsipras government of September 2015 was practically the first crisis government elected with the commitment to implement an adjustment program it had negotiated and signed. Such political consensus was unprecedented, and so was the social peace following the tumultuous summer of 2015. While massive and often violent demonstrations and strikes had escalated between 2010 and 2014, reaching record numbers, mass protests and industrial action declined rapidly after the July 2015 referendum, and remained subdued throughout the second Tsipras government.

Program compliance by the Tsipras government led to a significant reduction of political risk, especially since the major opposition party of ND carried a moderate market-liberal agenda representing policy continuity to a large extent. From the beginning of Greece's debt crisis, the Grexit speculation had severely undermined the economy's effort to adjust. The "currency redenomination" threat was accentuated by the intense sociopolitical instability and uncertainty about the future continuation of economic adjustment. Extravagant major opposition parties until 2015 promising to abolish the Memorandum policies if elected to power raised political risk as Grexit risk, driving away deposits, investment, raising the country's risk premium and financing costs, and deterring business commitments. The Grexit speculation hovered between 2010 and end 2012, subsided in 2013–14, reemerged and peaked in 2015, and left the picture from 2016.

The second Tsipras government oversaw the return to positive growth from 2017 (albeit the weakest in the Eurozone), tapped the market for a small bond issue in 2017, and completed the program in August 2018. It graduated the program with the Eurogroup agreeing to extend the grace period on the EFSF loans from 2022 to 2032 (theoretically – but overoptimistically – ensuring debt sustainability until 2032), but subject to a post-program framework of "enhanced surveillance" tighter than the other post-bailout countries, given the size of the public debt held by the EU official sector. A primary budget surplus of 4.2 percent was registered in 2017, way above the program target of 1.75 percent. Program fiscal targets were overachieved in 2015 and 2016 as well. Fiscal overperformance (drawn from over-taxation) became a political strategy of overcompensating for the accumulated credibility deficits of the past.

Under the inexorable pressure of the official creditors, since 2010, inconceivably unpopular measures were taken, reducing the life span of any government and severely weakening the two main pillars of the post-1974 two-party system, ND and, especially, PASOK. The socialist PASOK was reduced from 44 percent of the national vote in the 2009 national election to 12 percent in June 2012 to a humiliating 5 percent in January 2015. Following the reverse course, the radical left SYRIZA went from 5 percent in 2009 to become the major opposition party in 2012 to winning the January 2015 elections with 36 percent and September 2015 with 35.5 percent. Tsipras turned out to be the most resilient prime minister of the bailout era, and his coalition the only one to have both voted on and completed a bailout program.

The crisis had a far-reaching impact on Greek society. The main victims left behind were the long-term unemployed, low-wage earners, and the new poor, suffering from the massive job losses, wage cuts, and rise of indirect taxes. Income and wealth losses went across the board, affecting former protected groups (such as civil servants, higher-income pensioners, employees of public enterprises) who were specifically targeted by the wage and pension cuts. At the same time, other formerly privileged groups (liberal professions, lawyers, notaries public, engineers, pharmacists, etc.) lost much of their protected status and favorable social security benefits, and from 2016 saw their contributions increase. Even the long-cherished institution of private property was not spared, as owners were forced to pay unprecedentedly high and quite progressive property taxes. So the burden of austerity was spread relatively proportionately in the population, but the weakest suffered the most. Tax evaders (or large tax avoiders) continued to evade but doing so became relatively harder.

The radical left SYRIZA graduated from the extreme populism of its opposition years to a more pragmatic discourse of necessity. Public opinion has acquired a new "folk memory" against (private or public) over-indebtedness, a new consensus for fundamental fiscal discipline. However, though a solid public opinion majority continues to support euro membership, trust in the EU institutions, as shown in Eurobarometer surveys, reached historic all-time lows.

A forced adjustment under the bailouts: the vicious cycle of contraction

Greece implemented one of the toughest fiscal consolidation programs ever pursued in the OECD, heavily frontloaded and recessionary. A primary fiscal deficit of 10.1 percent in 2009 was turned into a 0.4 percent surplus in 2013, and a 2009 fiscal deficit of 15.1 percent became a surplus of 0.8 percent in 2017. In addition to fiscal consolidation, income policies became very restrictive, culminating in a 22 percent reduction of the statutory minimum wage in 2012 (pushing downwards private sector wages across the board), aiming to sharply reverse the unit labor cost increases of the previous period and restore cost competitiveness.

The magnitude of procyclical fiscal adjustment was directly correlated with the loss of output, as can be seen in Figure 4.1. In the year of the deepest

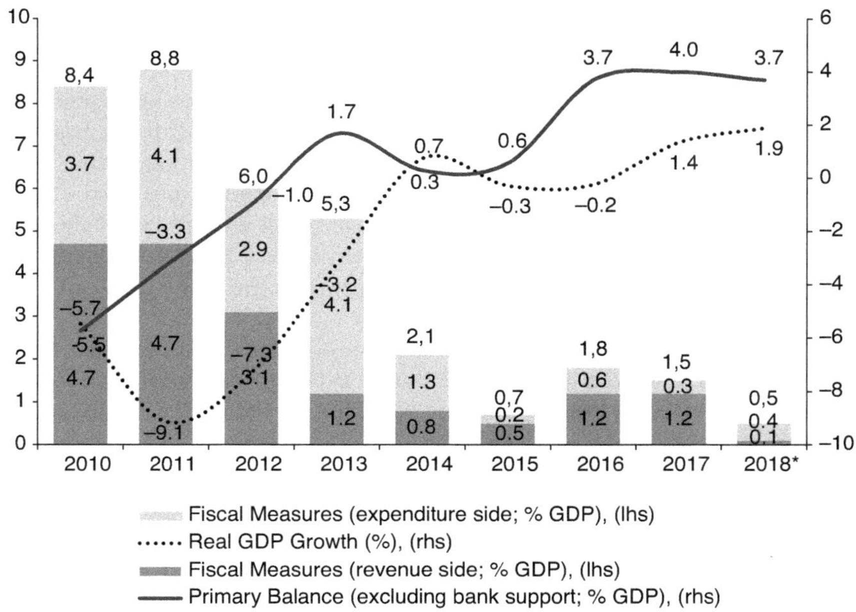

Figure 4.1 Fiscal measures and outcomes.

recession (2011), when the economy shrank by 9.1 percent GDP, the Greek government took the largest amount of fiscal measures, equal to 8.8 percent GDP. The total scale of fiscal retrenchment was huge and explains the magnitude of GDP loss from 2010 on.

The doctrine of expansionary fiscal contraction (Giavazzi and Pagano 1990), also known as expansionary austerity, was invoked in the Eurogroup to justify the severe public expenditure cuts. Under certain conditions, reducing public spending would make room for the private sector to expand. Such conditions (the economy near full employment, declining interest rates, lack of credit constraint, rapid international economic growth) were observed by Giavazzi and Pagano in Ireland and Denmark in the 1980s, but none of them held for Greece. In an institutional *mea culpa* for the IMF, Blanchard and Leigh (2013) concluded that the fiscal multiplier for government spending was not 0.5 (as the IMF initially assumed) but substantially above 1.[6] In addition, the impact of fiscal austerity on the Greek economy was accentuated by the relatively closed economy (depending excessively on domestic demand), the lowest savings rate in the EU during the crisis, the combination with steep income decline, the credit crunch, and the severe confidence effect, associated with the threat of Grexit. Gros and Alcidi (2010) had an estimated 2.5 multiplier, predicting 15 percent GDP loss.

The simultaneous application of contractionary policies was left without significant offsetting instruments: the accommodative monetary policy applied by the ECB failed to pass on to the periphery. Financial fragmentation and the infamous bank-sovereign doom loop had broken the monetary transmission mechanism. The crisis broke up as a sovereign debt crisis in the case of Greece, then via channels of portfolio exposure to sovereign debt and the real economy spread to the banking sector. "Double drowning" took over, when banks had to be recapitalized with public money, raising the bailout bill, adding to the debt burden, and so on. Credit contraction made it hard even for the most efficient Greek firms to access credit at reasonable rates, while the looming Grexit risk drove away prospective investors, froze economic activity, and pushed the economy deeper into the vortex of recession.

By 2018 real gross disposable incomes had lost over one third of their pre-crisis levels. The unit labor cost-based real effective exchange rate was down to the levels of 1999, meaning that the economy had more than offset the real exchange rate appreciation under the euro. These significant improvements in cost competitiveness were translated into a limited improvement in the export of goods, as discussed below. The current account deficit was eradicated mostly as a result of the sharp contraction of imports due to the recession, and to a secondary extent an increase in exports. During 2013–15, the economy recorded negative inflation. This improved cost-competitiveness, but also demonstrated the pain of adjustment achieved through internal devaluation, especially with an average Eurozone inflation below 1 percent, suggesting that adjustment in the euro-periphery could only be achieved through suppression of prices and wages. Price inflation should have been much more negative than wage inflation to preserve purchasing power, and thus product market reforms deeper than what we have seen.

Negative inflation and the steep reduction of nominal GDP during the crisis years led to debt deflation, with both sovereign and private sector debt burden growing in real terms as a result. As private debt turned into public debt (non-performing bank loans necessitating bank recapitalizations that raised public debt), the reverse process also took place. Excessive public debt necessitated such a steep fiscal consolidation that the tax burden for a wide array of taxpayers became impossible to meet. Thus, public debt was converted into private debt, owed by failing enterprises and distressed households. In 2018, a total of €102 billion of tax arrears (to which another €6 billion of customs debt are added) and €35 billion of unpaid social security obligations were estimated, alongside the €92 billion NPLs (some 45 percent of total loans). Altogether, these added up to a staggering private sector debt of €235 billion, far exceeding the country's GDP. An estimated four million tax citizens (almost one out of two) owed some debt to the state.

The mostly negative legacies of massive austerity and positive reforms

The scope of adjustment and reforms were unprecedented for any advanced democracy, especially undergoing a modern-era Great Depression. There is no doubt that the magnitude and harshness of adjustment (in terms of both reforms and eliminating macroeconomic imbalances) were a direct result of the low starting point of the Greek economy as it entered the crisis. Poor performance on Lisbon indicators such as market openness, innovation, enterprise, and social protection also helps explain why the crisis lasted so long, and why large groups fell through the social safety net.

Even excluding reforms not fully completed, the scope of the overall adjustment remained exceptional by standards of advanced democracies. In terms of cyclically adjusted fiscal balance improvement, Greece posted the largest and fastest fiscal consolidation among OECD countries (Table 4.3). For consecutive years after 2012, Greece was listed first in reform responsiveness on the OECD *Going for Growth* reports. Significantly, the programs forced the Greek government to operate upon measurable targets and milestones, bringing about an improved executive capacity.

The legacies of heavy and prolonged austerity weighed heavily on the Greek economy, not only regarding high unemployment and poverty levels, but also in terms of the economy's productive capacity. Unemployment in 2018 was down to 19.6 percent, a marked improvement from the 27.5 percent peak but in stark contrast to a Eurozone average of 8.6 percent. In GDP per hour worked, Greece was the only OECD economy with a negative performance during the period 2010–16.[7] During the crisis years, the rate of GDP decline exceeded that of unemployment growth, which accounts for the negative growth of labor productivity. Total factor productivity growth was weak as well, and historically among the lowest before the crisis, because of the relatively low openness of the economy and a high share of labor in non-tradeable sectors (IMF 2018: 56). Restoring productivity growth will be among the country's greatest challenges in the years to come, so that incomes can grow and the economy can expand healthily. Productivity growth has been the target of many implemented structural reforms, and those that remain on the agenda.

As a result of the crisis, national savings declined to a mere 9 percent GDP in 2017, the lowest in the EU (against a Eurozone average 23.9 percent; Spain 22.5 percent; Portugal 16 percent). Household savings collapsed from 4.2 percent pre-crisis to a negative balance of –7.2 percent in 2017. Consumption this time exceeded earnings because Greeks, suffering income and wage reductions, were using their savings to cover daily expenses and meet growing tax obligations.

Fixed capital formation at the end of the bailouts was 13 percent GDP (from 24 percent pre-crisis), and the employment rate (defined as aged 15–64, as a percentage of the total population) at 53.5 percent in 2017, against a Eurozone average of 66.5 percent (European Commission 2018). Both the large investment gap and the low employment rate undermine the growth potential of the economy. Demonstrating the combined recessionary impact of these factors, potential GDP (the output the economy could be producing if all its resources – workforce, capital equipment, technology, natural resources – were fully utilized) was negative through most of the crisis. Indicative of the austerity path ahead, the European Commission estimated a negative output gap of –7.7

Table 4.3 Economic indicators for Greece 2008–17

	2008	*2009*	*2010*	*2011*	*2012*	*2013*	*2014*	*2015*	*2016*	*2017*	*2018*
GDP at constant prices (AMECO) ***national currency: aggregates: average of national growth rates weighted with current values in EUR (billion)***	249.9	239.1	226	205.4	190.4	184.2	185.6	184.8	184.4	187.2	191
GDP growth at constant prices (AMECO) – relative to EU 15 ***GDP at 2010 reference levels: performance relative to the rest of the former EU-15: double export weights (national currency)***	108.1	108.5	100	89	82.9	80.2	79.5	77.5	75.9	75.4	75.5
TFP growth (Unit: 2010=100)	109.5	104.4	100	94.7	91.6	90.6	91.4	91.2	91.2	92.2	93.6
CPI inflation (AMECO) ***(harmonized)*** (2015=100)	93.5	94.8	99.3	102.4	103.4	102.5	101.1	100	100	101.2	102
Unemployment rate (AMECO) (% of active population)	7.8	9.6	12.7	17.9	24.5	27.5	26.5	24.9	23.6	21.5	19.6
Real exchange rate (ULC) (AMECO) *Real effective exchange rates, based on unit labor costs (total economy) – performance relative to the rest of the former EU-15: double export weights Unit: 2010=100*	95.7	99.1	100	97.9	93	85.9	83.4	81	81.2	81.6	80.8

Household savings (% of disposable income) (AMECO) *Saving rate, gross: households and NPISH (gross saving as percentage of gross disposable income)*	4.2	6.6	1.8	0.9	–0.2	–4.8	–3.6	–5.4	–6.9	–7.2	–6.7
Gross fixed capital formation (% of GDP) (EUROSTAT)	23.8	20.8	17.6	15.3p	12.6p	12.2p	11.5p	11.6p	12.1p	12.9p	–
General government balance (% of GDP) (AMECO)	–10.2	–15.1	–11.2	–10.3	–8.9	–13.2	–3.6	–5.6	0.5	0.8	0.6
General government primary balance (cyclically adjusted, % of trend GDP at current prices) *Net lending (+) or net borrowing (–) excluding interest of general government adjusted for the cyclical component: adjustment based on **trend GDP***	–10.7	–14	–7.4	–1.6	–0.1	–5.1	3.2	0.4	5.9	5.3	4.5
General government primary balance (cyclically adjusted, % of potential GDP at current prices) *Net lending (+) or net borrowing (–) excluding interest of general government adjusted for the cyclical component: adjustment based on **potential GDP***	–7.3	–10	–3.1	2.5	3.7	–1.5	6.8	3.7	8.9	8.1	6.8
Current account balance (% of GDP) **(AMECO)**	–15.1	–12.3	–11.4	–10	–3.8	–2	–1.6	–0.2	–1.2	–1	–0.2

continued

Table 4.3 Continued

	2008	*2009*	*2010*	*2011*	*2012*	*2013*	*2014*	*2015*	*2016*	*2017*	*2018*
Exports of goods and services (% of GDP)	23.4	19.0	22.1	25.5p	28.7p	30.4p	32.4p	31.6p	30.1p	33.0p	–
Government bond yields (nominal long-term interest rates, AMECO)	4.8	5.2	9.1	15.8	22.5	10.1	6.9	9.7	8.4	6.0	ND
Private sector debt (% of GDP) (consolidated) EUROSTAT	113.0	116.5	128.1	130.2p	131.5p	130.3p	129.2p	126.7p	124.0p	116.4p	–
Government gross debt (% of GDP) **(consolidated)**	109.4	126.7	146.2	172.1	159.6	177.4	178.9	175.9	178.5	176.1	182.5
Net international investment position (% of GDP) (EUROSTAT)	–75.8	–87.5	–99.0	–88.8	–115.9	–130.4	–131.9	–136.1	–139.7	–142.5	–
Banks: loans/deposits (bank credit as % of bank deposits[1])	94.4	90.2	101.8	127.6	136.5	131.0	126.2	138.7	153.2	–	–
% Non-performing loans ratio (consumer loans) (BoG)	7.3	13.2	22.3	33.8	46.7	54.1	58.0	61.3	63.3	61.2	55.8*
% Non-performing loans ratio (residential loans) (BoG)	4.7	7.9	12.3	18.5	26.1	31.4	36.8	39.0	41.7	43.0	44.3*
% Non-performing loans ratio (business loans) (BoG)	5.4	7.3	10.2	15.9	25.7	36.4	42.9	47.9	50.0	49.2	48.3*
Capital-labor substitution: total economy (AMECO) (2010=100)	102.6	101.5	100	96.5	94	93.4	94.6	95.7	96.5	97.8	99.2

Notes
1 www.theglobaleconomy.com/Greece/bank_credit_to_deposits.
* data available until September 2018

percent of potential GDP for 2017, and –5.2 percent for 2018, an output gap projected negative for every year until 2022.

Austerity left a lasting legacy in the form of low employment rates, brain drain, and capital destruction, which, combined with worse than EU average ageing of the population, are negatively affecting the country's growth potential. The IMF has invoked these exact factors (combined with the political system's reform fatigue) to estimate Greece's long-term real GDP growth rate at a paltry 1 percent (instead of over 1.3 percent supported by the EU institutions). Moreover, affecting its future path, Greece graduated from the programs subject to a fiscal framework of prolonged austerity, foreseeing primary surpluses of 3.5 percent until 2022, and an average 2.2 percent GDP for 2023–60. The IMF (among many others) has forcefully challenged the assumption that any economy (let alone one exiting a prolonged and deep recession) can realistically sustain these fiscal targets for such an extended period (IMF 2018: 60), suggesting that to pursue them in the longer run would suffocate growth of the Greek economy.

On the positive side, Greece graduated from its three adjustment programs with a legacy of productivity- and growth-enhancing structural reforms, whose favorable impact will unfold with a time lag after the economy has entered recovery. Significant improvements in overall competitiveness, as a result of structural reforms undertaken by the three adjustment programs, can be substantiated if one looks at relevant indicators pre- and post-crisis (see Table 4.4). In the World Bank *Doing Business Report 2009* (World Bank 2008) Greece was ranked 96th in 181 countries on the ease of doing business, and had one of the worst scores in regulating business startups and property registration, ranking at 133 in starting a business, 109 in getting credit, 133 in employing workers, 150 in protecting investors, 62 in paying taxes, and 85 in enforcing contracts. In the World Bank *Doing Business Report 2015* (World Bank 2014) in a total of 189 countries, Greece had climbed to 61 in ease of doing business, and was listed as having made the largest improvement in the area of registering property in 2013/14; it also made transferring property easier, and enforcing contracts easier, by introducing an electronic filing system for court users (World Bank 2014: 42). Greece was now ranked at 52 in starting a business, 88 in dealing with construction permits, 116 in registering property, 71 in getting credit, 59 in paying taxes, 62 in protecting minority investors, 48 in trading across borders, and 52 in resolving insolvency, though it retained a low score in enforcing contracts (155). Other reports by the OECD noted the progress made in reducing rigidities in the labor, product, and service markets. OECD indicators show the sharpest reduction in the rigidity of product market regulation among OECD countries in 2008–14, but Greece remained one of the highest regulated in the OECD. In 2015, an ambitious agenda of streamlining and simplifying investment licensing was launched, with the technical assistance of the World Bank, resulting in the simplification of 328 sectors between 2016 and 2018 (European Commission 2018: 23).

In terms of political economy, the burden of price adjustment fell heavily on labor and wages (starting from the general government and extending to the

Table 4.4 Competitiveness and inequality measurements 2008–17

	2008	*2009*	*2010*	*2011*	*2012*	*2013*	*2014*	*2015*	*2016*	*2017*
Competitiveness										
Product market regulation (OECD):	**2.21**	NA	NA	NA	NA	**1.74**	NA	NA	NA	NA
i. *State control*	**3.33**	NA	NA	NA	NA	**2.82**	NA	NA	NA	NA
ii. *Barriers to entrepreneurship*	**2.53**	NA	NA	NA	NA	**1.91**	NA	NA	NA	NA
iii. *Barriers to trade and investment*	**0.79**	NA	NA	NA	NA	**0.49**	NA	NA	NA	NA
Strictness of employment protection (OECD) (EPRC – V3)	2.85	2.85	2.85	2.44	2.44	2.41	NA	NA	NA	NA
Ease of doing business (rank)	96	109	109	100	78	72	61	60	61	67
• Starting a business score	133	140	149	135	146	36	52	54	56	37
• Getting credit	109	87	89	78	83	86	71	79	82	90
• Paying taxes	62	76	74	83	56	53	59	66	64	65
• Trading across borders	70	80	84	84	62	52	48	27	29	29
• Enforcing contracts	85	89	88	90	87	98	155	132	133	131
• Resolving insolvency	41*	43*	49*	57	50	87	52	54	52	57
Political stability**	0.27	–0.21	–0.13	–0.10	–0.22	–0.17	–0.14	–0.23	–0.12	–0.13
Inequality										
Income inequality (GINI)	0.328	0.330	0.336	0.333	0.338	0.342	0.339	0.340	0.333	NA
Poverty rate (OECD)	0.129	0.129	0.141	0.151	0.149	0.151	0.148	0.149	0.144	NA
Long-term unemployment (EUROSTAT)	3.7	3.9b	5.7	8.8	14.5	18.5	19.5	18.2	17.0	15.6
Youth unemployment (EUROSTAT)	21.9	25.7	33.0	44.7	55.3	58.3	52.4	49.8	47.3	43.6

Notes
* = closing a business.
** Governance Score (–2.5 to +2.5).
Estimate of governance measured on a scale from approximately –2.5 to 2.5. Higher values correspond to better governance.
http://info.worldbank.org/governance/WGI/#reports.
b = break in time series.
NA = Not available.

private sector), and less so on the product and service markets, where powerful interest coalitions (including sector oligopolies) resisted liberalization. The labor market was profoundly transformed, acquiring features of a liberalized market economy. Among others, reforms introduced especially by the two first programs contained: the liberalization of wage bargaining, transition from sector-level to firm-level collective agreements; easing dismissals, aligning labor conditions in former state-owned enterprises with those in the rest of the private sector; extending the use of fixed-term contracts; reducing overtime premia; and extending part-time shift work (or partial lay-off) (European Commission 2014).

Though the official objective (and proclaimed European strategy) was that of flexicurity, the reforms brought about flexibility without the security element. Given the fiscal constraint on welfare spending, and the sheer magnitude of unemployment, only a tiny percentage of long-term unemployed were receiving any state income support. During much of the crisis, after unemployment had peaked and had begun to de-escalate, long-term unemployed represented about 70 percent of all unemployed, and less than 20 percent of all unemployed were receiving an unemployment allowance, the system excluding long-term unemployed, self-employed, and the young.

Active labor market policies and the expansion of vocational education and training, funded copiously by the EU budget, were relied upon as a strategy for tackling the high levels of unemployment and youth unemployment. Takeover rates and effectiveness have been questionable, but the systematic activation of such policies represents the strengthening of a structural shift from passive to active labor market policies more fit for the era of capital and labor mobility and rapid changes in the business environment.

Labor market flexibility facilitated the reduction of unemployment by 6 percentage points between 2013 and 2017, even though GDP growth remained nearly stagnant. It also accounted for the large majority of new jobs created during the last years of the crisis being flexible, low-paying, part-time jobs. Greece pre-crisis had one of the most rigid labor markets in the OECD, which justified much of the labor market liberalization agenda, promising to allow easier hiring of employees when the economy recovered. However, the situation of an economy in recession, with investment rapidly declining, meant that during the first years of recession labor market flexibility facilitated the cyclical rise of unemployment.

Internal devaluation (the downward adjustment of nominal prices and wages) became a key external adjustment strategy, substituting for the lack of currency redenomination. Internal or fiscal devaluation aims to mimic the effects of a currency devaluation through fiscal measures. An example of proper fiscal devaluation would be a revenue-neutral increase in the value-added tax (VAT) and social security contributions paid by employees combined with a reduction in the payroll taxes paid by employers. There was an obvious sociopolitical limitation to how far regressive tax measures could advance, at a time when VAT rates had already been increased, and private sector nominal wages (especially after 2012) were falling. Even employer associations were not receptive. Moreover, the already high VAT rates, combined with depressed demand, would only exacerbate tax evasion. Thus, fiscal devaluation measures were applied inconsistently, as the need to reduce short-term fiscal deficits overruled the longer-term reorientation of the Greek economy.

Overall, despite lip service to strengthening tradable sectors and improving export performance, the adjustment policy mix was only partly and belatedly successful on these objectives. The performance of manufacturing was undermined by the increasing tax burden, the delayed product market reforms, and the high cost of capital. While the reduction of social security contributions (the tax wedge) was emphasized in the second program, targeting a 5pp. reduction, the fiscal constraint led to more modest adjustment. The employer social contribution marginal rate went from 28.6 percent in 2011 gradually to 27.5 percent in 2013, 26 percent in 2014, and 24.6 percent in 2015, to rise again to 25.1 percent in 2017 (OECD data).

The large improvement in price competitiveness and unit labor costs achieved during the crisis was not mirrored in a proportionate improvement of Greek exports, which was delayed, and did not reach the annual growth rates achieved by Ireland, Spain, and even Portugal. Greek exports significantly recovered only after 2017. Percentage-wise, total exports of goods and services went from 19 percent GDP in 2009 to 33 percent in 2017, an improvement reflecting the recovery of goods exports as well as the fall of GDP.

Explanations for the delayed recovery of Greek exports include: the currency redenomination risk and paralyzing economic and political uncertainty during much of the crisis; the prohibitive cost of capital, including trade credit, affecting Greek exporters importing raw materials and intermediate goods for their exports; low institutional quality (lack of regulatory predictability, red tape, regulatory barriers); and the small size of Greek companies, prohibiting them from better accessing export markets (Bŏwer et al. 2014).

A crippling legacy involved the banks, heavily affected by a crisis which (contrary to Spain or Ireland) originated from the sovereign sector. Non-performing loans from 7 percent in 2009 had reached 14.4 percent of total gross loans in 2011, 23.3 percent in 2012, 31.9 percent in 2013, 33.8 percent in 2014, and 37 percent in 2016, and continued to rise to the 45 percent area in 2018, against a Eurozone average 6.2 percent for 2009–16. Three waves of bank recapitalization unfolded between 2010 and 2018. The first, in 2011–13, was financed with €41.2 billion from the bailout; the second in 2014 was entirely privately funded, raising €8.3 billion mainly from foreign investors optimistic about the recovery prospects of the banking system. The third recapitalization became inevitable after the collapse of share prices following the July 2015 capital controls. Between November 2014 and June 2015, the banks lost €40 billion worth of deposits (26 percent of the total) and were subsisting on Emergency Liquidity Assistance. The state injected another €5.4 billion in the December 2015 recapitalization, while a total of €9 billion was raised from existing private sector investors.

The authorities were late in devising and implementing a strategy to deal with NPLs, which became a priority only under the third program. Until then, all borrowers were legally protected from auctions of primary residence regardless of income, wealth, or size of mortgage loan, which created a category of strategic defaulters. Banks, borrowers, and politicians for different reasons converged in delaying dealing with NPLs until creditors pressure became inescapable. From 2016 a process began of selling NPLs in the secondary market, establishing an out-of-court workout scheme, reforming the household insolvency law, and setting up an e-auction framework, all of which were producing results by the time the program was completed (European Commission 2018). However, the banks were left in a fragile position, incapable of providing credit to the economy, facing very ambitious NPL reduction targets for the following years and the menacing specter of a new recapitalization.

Given the dearth of national savings, the weakness of banks, and the framework of fiscal austerity affecting public investment, the Greek economy is and will be forced to rely extensively on foreign investment. Far-reaching privatizations were implemented toward the end of the programs, for debt reduction and attracting foreign investment, including plots of land, airports, ports, and utility companies. Foreign direct investment (FDI), however, remained low during the crisis as much as pre-crisis, despite depreciated asset prices, mainly because of poor institutional quality and legal and administrative impediments discouraging foreign firms from investing and producing in Greece (Meghir et al. 2017: 12).

The socioeconomic effects of the crisis weighed heavily as the programs failed to effectively target protection to the weakest groups, especially the long-term unemployed. In 2013, Greece posted the highest percentage in the EU (60 percent) of individuals aged 18–59 living in jobless households at risk of poverty, whose total benefits received were less than 10 percent of total net disposable household income (EU average 25 percent) (Maquet et al. 2016: 43). Poverty rates severely deteriorated: the percentage of people at risk of poverty or social exclusion climbed from 28 percent in 2009 to 36 percent in 2016 (against a Eurozone average 23 percent). The World Bank estimated an annualized income decline of 8.4 percent among the bottom 40 percent in 2010–15, the worst performance among 91 economies (World Bank 2018: 51). The OECD found that Greece recorded the largest drop in equivalized disposable income for children in low-income two-parent families between 2007 and 2014, 50 percent for the poorest 25 percent, and over 60 percent for the poorest 10 percent (OECD 2018: 4). The inequality impact was tempered by the steep decline of profits during the initial crisis years. Moreover, wage and pension cuts were mainly focused on higher incomes, and progressive tax policies (income and real estate tax) spread the burden of adjustment. This still left intact tax-evading groups, mainly the self-employed, but significant reforms on tax administration and bank secrecy have rendered tax evasion much more difficult. The elderly improved their relative position in the income distribution, while there was substantial deterioration in the relative position of the enlarged group of the unemployed (Andriopoulou et al. 2018). In conclusion: income losses were large across the board, and greater than average at the bottom of the distribution; the population in poverty changed significantly during the crisis, to comprise fewer pensioners and more low work-intensity families with children (see Table 4.4).

Social spending cuts aside, the programs rationalized social expenditure and welfare state organization in several respects. Consecutive pension reforms improved the sustainability of a system that was heading to bankruptcy before the crisis hit. According to the IMF, pension expenditure increased from 14.8 percent GDP in 2010 to 17.7 percent in 2015, as pensions lagged behind the fall in GDP. After a 2016 reform, pension expenditure remained above 16 percent of GDP, the highest in the Eurozone. Unemployment, early retirement, and steep recession severely affected pension sustainability. Health and pharmaceuticals spending, an area of extreme corruption and waste of public resources, was overhauled and rationalized. These savings allowed for a more efficient establishment of safety nets targeting vulnerable social groups toward the end of the programs. A minimum guaranteed income scheme was adopted during the second program, beginning on a pilot basis and subsequently generalized. The troika supported the introduction of a Social Solidarity Income in 2017, providing income support to the poorest households, covering some 600,000 individuals, as well as means-tested housing benefits from 2019 (European Commission 2018: 13–14). The other safety net was the extension of universal health care coverage to uninsured Greeks and other vulnerable categories such as immigrants, entitled to receive public health care and medicines under the same conditions as insured citizens.

Toward a new growth model?

The crisis terminated or certainly disrupted the unsustainable growth "model" of a demand-driven, Mediterranean economy, which can no longer rely on deficits, fiscal or external. Post-crisis, deficit-financed growth is not an option for a peripheral economy that will need to maintain a balanced current account and to generate large and sustained primary budget surpluses.

The less efficient mixed version of a capitalist economy identified as a mixed market economy or (more descriptively) as a Mediterranean market economy (Hall 2018) has included liberal features following the adoption of market-oriented reforms, cohabiting with patterns of coordination secured by the actions and policies of the interventionist state. There arises the need to shift to a greater reliance on exports, higher value-added tradable activities, and private investment, including FDI, areas in which Mediterranean economies are less well equipped compared to export-led CMEs (Hall 2014; Regan 2016).

The pursuit of external competitiveness drives the post-crisis growth model, emphasizing the supply side and export-orientation, seeking to strictly align wage increases to productivity gains (or otherwise rely on wage deflation), and pursuing the latter through extensive structural reforms of the general government sector and the markets. A fiscally sustainable, liberal-type welfare state, focusing on active labor market policies and the provision of an adequate minimum safety net, complements the post-crisis growth model, which also transforms a statist economy into one containing stronger liberalized features.

The direct legacies of depression, however (extensive disinvestment, erosion of capital, employment decline), and the resulting decrease of potential growth cast doubt on the prospects of the said growth strategy. It indeed points to a direction of parallel reform, at national and Eurozone level, the Eurozone supporting (or necessitating) national reforms, establishing a capacity for short-term countercyclical stabilization and institutionalizing greater risk-sharing for risk reduction.

Various growth studies have outlined comparative advantages of the Greek economy, apart from tourism and shipping, in sectors such as agro-industry, logistics, renewable energy and energy transport, pharmaceuticals, and others, while some dynamic clusters are developing in high technology and software. Some of these sectors (tourism, logistics, agro-industry, energy, renewables, software and technology startups) have seen significant growth around the end of the crisis, while manufacturing companies have increased their export orientation to compensate for the loss of domestic consumer demand. So the rebalancing of the economy is happening, albeit at slower than desirable speed.

The Greek case points to a broader research question: what becomes of a Mediterranean state and the surrounding political economy inside an imperfect single currency regime, with a strict institutionally prescribed and market-imposed fiscal framework, an only limited ability to rely on foreign borrowing, and the need to maintain competitiveness by means other than resorting to the exchange rate fix? This remains an open question for future research.

Notes

1 A version of this chapter was published as GreeSE Discussion Paper 130/2018 in the Hellenic Observatory Series of the European Institute, LSE. The paper has benefited from useful comments by Michele Chang, Federico Steinberg, Francisco Torres, Spyros Economides, Vassilis Monastiriotis, Lorenzo Codogno, Manos Matsaganis, Panos Tsakloglou, and Christos Triantopoulos, and the excellent research assistance of Dimitra Tsingou.

2 According to the Bank for International Settlements (BIS), in 2010 total exposure of French and German banks to the Greek sovereign and banks amounted to $120 billion, which by mid-2011 had been reduced by $35 billion.

3 Between May 2010 (when the first bailout program was launched) and February 2012 (when the second was adopted), an approximate €58 billion of Greek public debt matured and was repaid at face value. If debt restructuring had taken place at the 53.5 percent haircut rate, this would have reduced the public debt by €31 billion, equivalent to 16 percent of the 2012 GDP (to which lower interest payments should be added). A non-negligible difference, which would have allowed milder austerity.

4 The net reduction of public debt actually amounted to €68 billion (34 percent GDP), as the PSI had a cost of €38 billion (20 percent GDP) for the Greek banks whose GGB portfolio was written down, and which were subsequently recapitalized with public funds from the second bailout program earmarked for bank recapitalization.

5 The Bank of Greece has estimated the overall cost of the 2015 brinkmanship and capital controls at over €86 billion, equal to the size of the third bailout program; Klaus Regling of the ESM put the number at over €100 billion. This included, among others, profits of Eurosystem central banks that were lost to the Greek budget, an approximate €25 billion of market value of the country's systemic banks that evaporated when the stock market

crashed following capital controls, at a loss for the banks' principal public shareholder, the Hellenic Financial Stability Fund (HFSF). One could also add the opportunity cost resulting from two additional years of recession or zero growth (2015 and 2016) instead of the strong growth that was widely forecast by institutions and market analysts.

6 A fiscal multiplier of 1 implies that 1 percent GDP expenditure-based fiscal consolidation reduces the GDP by an equal amount.

7 https://read.oecd-ilibrary.org/economics/oecd-compendium-of-productivity-indicators-2018_pdtvy-2018-en#page1.

References

Andriopoulou, E., A. Karakitsios, P. Tsakloglou (2018) "Inequality and Poverty in Greece: Changes in Times of Crisis", in Katsikas D., D. Sotiropoulos, M. Zafiropoulou (eds) *Socioeconomic Fragmentation and Exclusion in Greece under the Crisis*, Basingstoke: Palgrave Macmillan.

Baldwin, R. and F. Giavazzi (eds) (2015) *The Eurozone Crisis: A Consensus View of the Causes and a Few Possible Remedies*, A VoxEU.org eBook, CEPR Press.

Blanchard, O.J. and D. Leigh (2013) "Growth Forecast Errors and Fiscal Multipliers", *IMF Working Paper* No. 13/1.

Blavoukos, S. and G. Pagoulatos (2008) "The Limits of EMU Conditionality: Fiscal Adjustment in Southern Europe", *Journal of Public Policy*, 28/2, 229–253.

Böwer, U., V. Michou and C. Ungerer (2014) "The Puzzle of the Missing Greek Exports", *European Economy*, Economic Papers, 518, June.

Dyson, K. and K. Featherstone (1996) "Italy and EMU as a 'Vincolo Esterno': Empowering the Technocrats, Transforming the State", *South European Society and Politics*, 1(2).

European Commission (2010) "The Economic Adjustment Programme for Greece – First review – summer 2010", *European Economy*, Occasional Papers, 68, August.

European Commission (2014) "The Second Economic Adjustment Programme for Greece – Fourth Review", *European Economy*, Occasional Papers, 192, April.

European Commission (2018) "Compliance Report – ESM Stability Support Programme for Greece – Fourth Review", July.

Featherstone, K. (2008) "Varieties of Capitalism' and the Greek Case: Explaining the Constraints on Domestic Reform?", GreeSE Paper No 11, Hellenic Observatory Papers on Greece and Southeast Europe, February 2008.

Featherstone, K. and D. Papadimitriou (2008) *The Limits of Europeanisation: Reform Capacity and Policy Conflict in Greece*, Basingstoke: Palgrave Macmillan.

Giavazzi, Fransesco and Marco Pagano (1990) "Can Severe Fiscal Contractions Be Expansionary? Tales of Two Small European Countries", *NBER Macroeconomics Annual*, 5, 75–111.

Gros, D. and C. Alcidi (2010) "Is Greece Different? Adjustment Difficulties in Southern Europe," *VoxEU*, 22 April.

Hall, P. (2014) "Varieties of Capitalism and the Euro Crisis", *West European Politics*, 37/6, 1223–1243.

Hall, P. (2018) "Varieties of Capitalism in Light of the Euro Crisis", *Journal of European Public Policy*, 25/1, 7–30.

IMF (2015a) "Preliminary Draft Debt Sustainability Analysis", IMF Country Report 15/165, 26 June. www.imf.org/external/pubs/ft/scr/2015/cr15165.pdf.

IMF (2015b) "An Update of IMF Staff's Preliminary Public Debt Sustainability Analysis", IMF Country Report 15/186, 14 July. www.imf.org/external/pubs/ft/scr/2015/cr15186.pdf.

IMF (2018) "Greece", Country Report No. 18/248, July.
IMF IEO (2016) "The IMF and the Crises in Greece, Ireland and Portugal: An Evaluation by the Independent Evaluation Office", 6 July.
Katsikas, D., M. Anastasatou, E. Nitsi, A. Petralias, K. Filinis (2018) *Structural Reforms in Greece During the Crisis (2010–2014)*, ELIAMEP/Crisis Observatory and Bank of Greece (in Greek).
Maquet, I., V. Maestri, and C. Thévenot (2016) "The Coverage Rate of Income Support Measures in the EU: Measurement and Challenges", European Commission, Working Paper 2/2016.
Meghir, C., C.A. Pissarides, D. Vayanos, and N. Vettas (2017) "The Greek Economy Before and During the Crisis", in Meghir, Pissarides, Vayanos, Vettas (eds) *Beyond Austerity: Reforming the Greek Economy*, Cambridge, MA: MIT Press.
OECD (2018) "Poor Children in Rich Countries: Why We Need Policy Action", *Policy Brief on Child Well-Being*, October. www.oecd.org/social/family/Poor-children-in-rich-countries-Policy-brief-2018.pdf.
Pagoulatos, G. (2003) *Greece's New Political Economy: State, Finance and Growth from Postwar to EMU*, Houndmills: Palgrave Macmillan.
Pagoulatos, G. (2012) "The Political Economy of Forced Reform: Reflections on the 2010 Greek Economic Adjustment Program", in S. Kalyvas, G. Pagoulatos and H. Tsoukas (eds) *From Stagnation to Forced Adjustment: Reforms in Greece, 1974–2010*, London and New York: Hurst/Oxford University Press.
Pagoulatos, G. (2014) "State-Driven in Boom and in Bust: Structural Limitations of Financial Power in Greece", *Government and Opposition*, 49/3, 452–482.
Pagoulatos, G. and C. Triantopoulos (2009) "The Return of the Greek Patient: Greece and the 2008 Global Financial Crisis", *South European Society and Politics*, 14/1, 35–54.
Regan, A. (2016) "The Imbalance of Capitalisms in the Eurozone: Can the North and South of Europe Converge?" *Comparative European Politics*, 15/6, 969–990.
Savage, J. and A. Verdun (2016) "Strengthening the European Commission's Budgetary and Economic Surveillance Capacity Since Greece and the Euro Area Crisis: A Study of Five Directorates-General", *Journal of European Public Policy*, 23/1, 101–118.
Tilford, S. and P. Whyte (2010) *The Lisbon Scorecard X*, London: Centre for European Reform.
World Bank (2008) *Doing Business 2009*, Washington, DC: World Bank.
World Bank (2014) *Doing Business 2015*, Washington, DC: World Bank.
World Bank (2018) *Piecing Together the Poverty Puzzle*, Washington, DC: World Bank.

5 Ireland

Back to a different normal

Kevin Cardiff

Introduction

A long period of truly extraordinary economic performance in Ireland continued, despite building vulnerabilities, into the mid-2000s. However, the economy, the fiscal position and the banking system became highly dependent on activity levels in the construction sector, and when these fell off sharply at a time of fragility in financial systems and weaker economic performance in the US and Europe, Irish economic activity collapsed, and the domestic banking system experienced huge losses which were much greater than could be met by shareholder funds and were instead offset principally by very large Government interventions. Determined and early fiscal adjustments in 2008, 2009 and 2010, including wide-scale adjustments in wages, benefits and other spending levels, were insufficient, given the absence of growth and the building cost of the banking interventions, to convince increasingly risk-averse markets to continue to finance the country, leading to the need for an EU/IMF lending program agreed at the end of 2010. Of course, the economic crash created considerable hardship, with reducing earnings, increasing unemployment and emigration and with many bank customers falling into arrears. Both the electoral performance of political parties and some long-established consultative and decision-making systems were, naturally, heavily affected also.

By mid-2012, though, there were signs that a sufficient stabilization of the fiscal position had taken place to allow a gradual return to markets, and over the subsequent years the scale of the rebound in economic terms has been remarkable. Ireland has put the crisis behind it, in many ways, but there remain issues arising directly from the crisis period to be addressed, as well as new challenges to be met. These developments are described in this chapter.

The pre-crisis position

The Irish economy started its "crash" in 2007 and especially 2008, after a long period of extraordinary performance that had earned it the sobriquet "Celtic Tiger". By then, Ireland had moved in a liberal direction over the previous decades, and many of the characteristics of a liberal economic model were clearly visible in the Irish picture. There was a business-positive orientation to government policies, a liberalization of key utility markets, a relative openness to new entrants and a lighter approach to regulation in some areas. As Hardiman says, "growth was based on a progressive opening up of trade and investment opportunities, and full engagement with the European integration project. Ireland came to be among the most open economies in the world" (Hardiman, 2015). Successive Irish governments and state agencies had set out to make Ireland a welcoming environment for business, especially international business, with very considerable success.

Financial market liberalization was also a feature of the decades leading up to the crisis. Ireland was taking advantage of both globalization and Europeanization (Donovan & Murphy, 2013), and this was impacting directly on the financial sector. In monetary matters, Ireland's official policy was very pro-European and liberalizing. The Maastricht Treaty was adopted in 1992 after a referendum. In line with European rules, the last capital controls were abolished in late 1992, ironically in the middle of the 1992/93 currency crisis, and remaining agreed controls on retail interest rates were also removed later (Bredin, Fitzpatrick & O'Reilly, 2001). There was little serious opposition to joining the single currency, and there was a belief that it would both better position Ireland within the European system and also address some of the problems of the old Exchange Rate Mechanism. Initial rejections of the Nice and Lisbon Treaties in referenda in Ireland in 2001 and 2008 were reversed in subsequent votes after reassurances about military neutrality, abortion and institutional issues, and the overall trend of liberalization and Europeanization was continued.

But liberalization is not the whole story. Marzinotto (this volume) explains some of the implications of institutional features of the economies of Spain, Greece, Portugal and Ireland, in terms of the variety of capitalism literature of Hall and Soskice (Hall & Soskice, 2001), but is careful to note that these features are not static. A simple labeling of Ireland as a Liberal Market Economy in the definition of the varieties of capitalism literature, as compared to a Co-ordinated Market Economy, such as Germany, must take into account certain specificities of the Irish situation. In some important ways, the liberal model is not followed. A key example is the adoption of a social partnership model for economic decision making. Emanating from a tradition of centralized wage bargaining, at least for the public sector and often also for the private sector, that extended back for some decades, the Social Partnership model of the period 1987–2009 was characterized at the core by discussions around wage setting between labor and employer representatives, but with significant discussion also of related economic policy orientations, including in relation to tax and social welfare policies. Over time the model extended to include representatives of farmer interests and the "Community and Voluntary Pillar" as a proxy for the community and disadvantaged interests. At its height, this process was a substantive input into much of the economic and social policy-making of the State. The model was of planned state action, almost German in inspiration (O'Donnell, 1998). However, policymakers resolutely avoided any interference with the successful formula of reliance on deliberately invited foreign direct investment. A simplistic example is the very consistent application of a single low tax rate to trading activities of businesses operating in Ireland, unvarying over decades. This is simplistic because the actual tax paid by a company depends on a myriad of factors and may, of course, vary from the headline tax rate, but the point is valid – a consistent long-term approach to FDI.

Moreover, at the same time as the Irish economic and fiscal model has been very welcoming to investing firms, there has also been a highly progressive tax and social welfare system, designed to protect the vulnerable from the worst of the inequalities of the liberal model (indeed without these elements, Ireland would have one of the most unequal income ratios in the developed world). Elements of the Irish institutional structure remain determinedly statist in character (Hardiman, 2015). So, to a large extent, Ireland has not just evolved, but has actively chosen a hybrid economic model, coordinated and corporatist in some areas and deliberately very liberal in orientation in others.

Supported by this hybrid approach, in the late 90s and early 2000s (notwithstanding short-term fluctuations) the basic pattern for Ireland was of strong growth, exceeding 5 percent in most of the years from 2001 to 2007 (see Table 5.1), and increasing employment. There was a significant increase both in labor force participation rates and in inward migration, in turn fueling a demographic pattern that in subsequent years supported a growing level of housing construction and significant increases in house prices.

By the 2000s, this construction trend was turning into a boom and was supported by easy credit and low eurozone interest rates, at least by comparison with Irish historical patterns. However, the boom in bank credit could not be supported by the more stable domestic deposit base, so loan to deposit ratios went up (see Table 5.1) and, as a corollary, Irish banks became increasingly dependent on external wholesale funding sources to finance its domestic Irish business.

The Government finances, too, were doing very well – strong revenues, coming especially from the construction sector, and boosted in other sectors by strong domestic consumption and higher incomes, allowed the Government to run budget surpluses in most years from 1997, and even to develop some mechanisms for setting money aside for the future, such as a state-incentivized medium-term savings scheme and the establishment of a sovereign wealth fund, the "National Pension Reserve Fund", into which the Government would make annual payments. As a proportion of GDP, the national debt had been greatly reduced and was by the early 2000s among the lowest in the Eurozone, and falling (Table 5.1).

Private wealth was also reflecting several years of economic growth. The Central Bank reported that the net wealth of Irish households had increased by over 130 percent between 1999 and the end of 2005, most of this arising from the net equity in the principal residence (Kelly, 2006), but businesses and private individuals were also often involved in other investments, often leveraged property investments.

Table 5.1 Economic indicators for Ireland 2001–2007

	2001	*2002*	*2003*	*2004*	*2005*	*2006*	*2007*
GDP growth at constant prices (AMECO)	5.3	5.9	3.0	6.6	5.7	5.0	5.3
TFP growth % (AMECO)	1.2	2.6	–0.5	2.0	–0.1	–0.4	0.2
CPI inflation % (HICP) (Central Statistics Office)	4.3	4.5	3.0	2.4	1.9	3.0	3.2
Unemployment rate (AMECO)	4.2	4.7	4.8	4.7	4.6	4.8	5
Real exchange rate (ULC) (AMECO)	85.3	86.66	96.14	99.14	102.27	104.99	110.34
Household net savings as % of net disposable income (AMECO)	1.0	–0.8	–0.1	0.7	1.4	–1.0	–1.5
Gross fixed capital formation as % of GDP (AMECO)	24.0	23.6	24.9	27.0	29.8	31.0	28.7
General government debt (% of GDP) (AMECO)	33.2	30.6	29.9	28.2	26.1	23.6	23.9
General government surplus/deficit (–) (% of GDP) (AMECO)	1.0	–0.5	0.4	1.3	1.6	2.8	0.3
Exports of goods and services (% of GDP) (AMECO)	95.3	90.5	80.9	80.5	79.6	79.0	80.8
Government bond yields % (AMECO)	4.3	4.5	3.0	2.4	1.9	3.0	3.2
Private sector debt (% of GDP) (Eurostat)	139.3	137.4	141.3	149.5	170.1	190.6	198.1
Net international investment position (% of GDP) (Eurostat)		–21.0	–23.5	–22.3	–46.2	–25.8	–31.4
Banks: loans/deposits % (ECB risk assessment indicators)	135.5	135.3	138.1	157.4	162.0	161.7	176.0
Banks: NPL % (IMF GFSR)					0.5	0.5	0.6

Given the solid performance of the economy in general, there were huge political demands on the Governments of the day to reduce taxes further and to increase spending, in areas such as health, social welfare, justice and so forth. By the mid-2000s, government spending was increasing much more quickly than the economy was growing. At the same time, the Government had been able to reduce personal taxes. Lowering the tax wedge was a target, and by the 2008 budget announcements (Department of Finance, 2007), it was projected that workers on the average wage in Ireland would not pay income tax that year.

A key feature of the increase in Government spending was the growth in public sector wages. Driven by private sector comparisons organized by way of a benchmarking process, and moderated through regular public sector pay agreements, as well as a growth in numbers to meet service demands, the Irish public sector was still not large by international comparisons but had indeed become more expensive. The increased income of the nation was being shared with the public sector, and policymaking was increasingly shared through the "social partnership" process with unions (mostly representing the public sector), employer bodies, community and voluntary bodies and the agricultural sector. The availability of growing resources and the varied demands of different sectors allowed (but also demanded) the establishment of some level of consensus about how the cake might be distributed.

Growing vulnerabilities

By the mid-2000s, however, there were increasing imbalances that might, in the wrong circumstances, prove to be very significant vulnerabilities. At the macroeconomic level, Ireland had moved from a current account surplus position through most of the 1990s into a deficit which persisted at around or over 5 percent of GDP (sometimes well over) from 2005 to 2008. Irish wages were growing much faster than in other parts of the Eurozone, and whereas Ireland had performed well in terms of productivity over the previous decades, outperforming the EU, there was a new danger that the growth in wages would outpace productivity increases. In effect, the Irish growth model was changing towards a demand-led one. In prior years, this might have given rise to currency and interest rate pressures that could not easily be ignored, but in the single-currency era, these imbalances could more easily build.

Moreover, after years in which demand had exceeded supply, the construction sector was by 2006 now delivering over 90,000 new homes per year (Department of Housing, Planning, Community and Local Government, 2017a), a pace that would very quickly outstrip demand. Construction was now such a large part of the economy, and such a contributor to employment, that the economy and fiscal position had become very vulnerable to changes in construction output.

Not just the economy in general, but also the Government's fiscal position was very vulnerable to sharp turnarounds in construction. Constant increases in spending in the years leading up to the crisis, and a growing dependence on the construction sector for tax revenues, meant that the Government's fiscal plans were heavily based on a continuation of the revenue stream from this activity. At the peak, nearly one-fifth of tax revenue was coming from the construction sector (Donovan & Murphy, 2013).

The strong supply of houses was, of course, a response to the high prices which consumers and were willing to pay for them, but houses were being constructed and bought not just as a good in themselves, but also for speculative reasons. Small- and medium-sized business had also often engaged in some property speculation, using equity in property to finance expansion or diverting business revenues from other potential investments into property (McAnn & McIndoe-Calder, 2015).

However, a sense that the top of the market had been reached was reflected in a reduction in housing starts in 2007, and in the Government's budget for 2008, authorities allowed for a significant fall-off in house completions. The Minister for Finance of the day explained that the dynamics of the housing market had changed fundamentally (Cowen, 2007), but he was underestimating the change that was coming. Ireland was on the cusp of, and very vulnerable to, a great downturn in construction and housing activity.

The banking system also was a store of imbalances and potential vulnerabilities. Even more than the Government, it had become increasingly dependent on the construction sector, via loans for development and for house purchases, for its revenues and growth, and shareholders had been hugely rewarded for the willingness to expand lending in this sector. This very significant domestic vulnerability of the financial sector was exacerbated by developments internationally.

The US sub-prime crisis of 2007 initially seemed to have only limited impacts for Ireland – after all, the Irish banks were so busy expanding their activities in direct property lending, they had little scope for engaging in speculation in the slightly more exotic financial instruments at the center of the sub-prime collapse. Irish banks, therefore, declared themselves unlikely to be much affected by the sub-prime problem. However, they were rather missing the point, which was that large home-grown imbalances would not be ignored by a market which was already becoming considerably more risk-sensitive in reaction to the sub-prime crisis. Moreover, although there was formally no significant "sub-prime" sector in the Irish mortgage market, the mainstream lenders were, in keeping with the liberalization trend, more willing to lend to borrowers on higher loan to value and loan to income ratios. In fact, there was a very significant shift in the customer profile towards lower-income groups: "between 1994 and 2007, the share of the top income quintile in annual mortgage originations decreased from 57 per cent to 27 per cent" while the proportion of new mortgages to the middle 20 percent and the bottom 40 percent rose from 13 percent and only 2 percent respectively of the market, to 29 and 11 percent respectively (Lydon & McCann, 2017). And at the same time as providing increased finance to house buyers, they were busily lending large amounts to property developers also.

By this time, banks in Ireland had, relatively, very high dependence on that international wholesale funding. The Northern Rock collapse of September 2007 showed the penalty that a bank could pay for an overdependence on short-term wholesale funding to finance longer-term lending, if the wholesale market, with all its new-found wariness, came to doubt the quality of its credit. Now, the global funding pool that had come with increasing international integration of the market was gradually becoming shallower and more national, as the months passed. For the Irish banks, this combination of risk-aversion and de-internationalization would have created real dangers, even if their underlying asset base had been strong, but the value of these assets was highly sensitive to the now shaky construction and housing market.

The onset of the crisis

The economic edifice started to crumble in earnest in 2008. Instead of the growth rate of around 3 percent predicted by the authorities (Department of Finance, 2007), GDP fell precipitously. There was a contraction of over 4 percent in the single year of 2008, and a further substantial contraction of 5 percent again in 2009 (see Table 5.2). Figures for modified GNI, a measure developed to try to separate out some of the impacts of the non-domestic activities of multi-national firms in Ireland, and therefore to present a better picture of the domestic economy (Department of Finance, 2018), show even greater adjustments in nominal terms (see Table 5.3).

Housing activity in 2008 did not just reduce, it collapsed. From nearly 80,000 in 2007, completions fell to around 50,000 in 2008 and 26,000 in the following year (Department of Housing, Planning, Community and Local Government, 2017a). Housing starts followed a similar pattern, though naturally leading the completions somewhat. From a peak of around 78,000 in each of the years 2004 to 2006, the rate of housing starts adjusted sharply. The fall to just under 50,000 in 2007 was a first response to changing market circumstances and expectations, and there was, in any event, a strong pipeline of projects already started to keep construction workers busy and exchequer revenues flowing. However, in 2008, starts fell to 23,000 and by 2009 they were below 9,000. They continued to fall so that at the trough of activity, housing starts were only 1/20th of the peak levels (Department of Housing, Planning, Community and Local Government, 2017b). Moreover, just as prices had been driven upwards by a self-sustaining speculative demand that led to a substantial price overshoot, demand also quickly dried up as soon as the market topped out and prices started to fall, exacerbating the price and activity declines.

Soon, it was not only challenging to sell a house at reduced prices, but also very difficult to say at what price any house might sell. There were few transactions and very little price formation in the market. Official house price statistics suggest that Dublin house prices fell nearly 20 percent from end 2006 levels by the end of 2008, and by 40 percent by the end of 2009, and they continued to fall after that (Central Statistics Office).

Table 5.2 Economic indicators for Ireland 2008–2018

	2008	*2009*	*2010*	*2011*	*2012*	*2013*	*2014*	*2015*	*2016*	*2017*	*2018*
GDP growth at constant prices (AMECO)	–4.4	–5.0	1.9	3.7	0.2	1.3	8.8	25.1	5.0	7.2	7.8
TFP growth % (AMECO)	–5.9	–1.8	4.0	4.3	–0.4	–0.9	6.2	22.1	0.2	5.8	6.6
CPI inflation % (HICP) (Central Statistics Office)	1.3	–2.6	–0.2	1.5	1.7	0.3	–0.3	0.2	–0.2	0.5	0.8
Unemployment rate % (AMECO)	6.8	12.6	14.6	15.4	15.5	13.8	11.9	10	8.4	6.7	5.6
Real exchange rate (ULC) (AMECO)	120.24	112.63	100	94.45	89.65	92.40	86.90	86.16	68.29	69.26	67.60
Household net savings as % of net disposable income (AMECO)	3.9	8.3	6.2	3.7	6.6	4.9	2.7	2.2	1.9	4.0	
Gross fixed capital formation as % of GDP (AMECO)	24.8	21.1	17.5	16.8	19.7	18.7	20.7	24.2	35.7	23.5	20.7
General government debt (% of GDP) (AMECO)	42.4	61.5	86.0	110.9	119.9	119.7	104.1	76.8	73.4	68.4	63.9
General government surplus/deficit (–) (% of GDP) (AMECO)	–7.0	–13.8	–32.0	–12.8	–8.1	–6.1	–3.6	–1.9	–0.5	–0.2	–0.1
Exports of goods and services (% of GDP) (AMECO)	84.1	93.2	103.0	103.6	104.4	103.5	109.8	122.1	120.1	119.9	116.5
Government bond yields % (AMECO)	4.53	5.23	5.74	9.60	6.17	3.79	2.37	1.18	0.74	0.80	N/A
Private sector debt (% of GDP) (Eurostat)	236.4	256.1	257.0	274.0	279.6	267.7	278.3	306.0	283.3	243.6	
Net international investment position (% of GDP) (Eurostat)	–95.3	–115.7	–113.5	–139.1	–137.7	–133.3	–164.3	–198.7	–170.7	–149.3	
Banks: loans/deposits % (ECB risk assessment indicators)	190.1	173.4	170.7	161.9	151.6	142.2	124.5	115.9	111.0	111.6	117.5
Banks: NPL % (IMF GFSR)	1.9	9.8	13.0	16.1	25.0	25.7	20.6	14.9	13.6	11.5	

Table 5.3 Some competitiveness indicators for Ireland

a OECD product market regulation

	2003	*2008*	*2013*
PMR overall	1.58	1.35	1.45
State control	2.50	1.84	2.12
Barriers to entrepreneurship	2.02	1.99	1.98
Barriers to trade and investment	0.23	0.23	0.26

b OECD: strictness of employment protection (dismissals)

2008	*2013*
1.98	2.07

Of course, less activity meant less work. Construction-related employment numbers fell a relatively small amount – about 35,000, from a peak around 270,000, in the four quarters to September 2008, but then they fell much more quickly in the following four quarters to about 150,000 and continued to plummet (Central Statistics Office).

Even before the worst of the construction employment falls occurred, unemployment went up by over 3.5 percent points in 2008, to 8.6 percent, before climbing much higher (Table 5.2). Moreover, with a significant and unexpected fall in economic activity, and increased demands for services, the Government had to react to the resultant changing fiscal position. As revenues fell and expenditures increased, the Government announced some immediate, if relatively small, fiscal adjustments in mid-2008, and brought forward the announcement date for the 2009 budget by two months, to prepare for worse to come. Even with this initial corrective action, the deficit outturn for 2008, at about seven percent of GDP, was much weaker than the 1 percent deficit that had been expected at the start of the year (Department of Finance, 2007). The over-reliance on taxes from property was already starting to take its toll, as taxes from property transactions relative to GDP halved (Donovan & Murphy, 2013).

A collapsing construction industry at a time of a general and severe recession was bound to have implications for a banking system which was heavily invested in that industry. As 2008 developed, Irish banks' access to funding became increasingly restricted until, in the immediate aftermath of the Lehman collapse in mid-September 2008, the third-biggest Irish headquartered bank ran out of cash. Another smaller bank was likely to follow very soon afterwards, and the market signals were that all Irish banks would have a more difficult time funding in the following weeks, especially, of course, if any one of them failed (Cardiff, 2015).

It was the policy of all EU governments that banks would not be allowed to fail, and several rescues had already taken place, so it was no surprise that the Irish Government intervened. However, the scale of the intervention did surprise the market.

The Government guaranteed most of the liabilities of seven domestic banks, ranging from the largest to quite small institutions, regarded as having an important enough domestic footprint to justify the intervention. From then on, the fate of the State's finances and those of the banks were tied closely together for years to come.

Multiple crises

The story of the following two years was of continued economic collapse. Despite significant efforts by the Government sector, businesses and individuals to react and adapt to these crises, 2009 and 2010 saw further deteriorations in the economic and fiscal position, as the economy contracted even more deeply in 2009 and managed only feeble growth in 2010. Unemployment continued to rise, reaching over 15 percent in 2010, despite significant outward migration of both Irish nationals and of foreign nationals who had come to Ireland in very large numbers in response to labor demand during the boom years.

The fiscal position was terrible. In 2009, the Government sector revenues covered only about 70 percent of expenditures, and in 2010 the ratios were even worse – amazingly, only about half of the expenses of the Government sector were covered by its income – the deficit/GDP ratio peaked at over 30 percent (Table 5.2). These headline figures, however, are complicated by large one-off charges for bank recapitalization measures, but even when these are excluded the deficit peaked at around 11.6 percent of GDP in 2009 (Smyth, 2017), and fell only slowly in the following two years.

This fiscal outturn arose in those two years despite discretionary fiscal measures – adjustments in Government spending and taxing policies – amounting to nearly 15 percent of GDP (Smyth, 2017). These consisted of various tax-raising measures, as well as pay and numbers reductions in the public service, adjustments in social welfare provisions for certain groups, reduced services and so forth. These measures could not be taken without having a real impact on the people of the country, many of whom were suffering their own severe adjustments at household level, arising from the crisis. Of course, the benefit of such fiscal measures in terms of budget savings is always offset to some extent by the negative effect on economic growth of the measures themselves.

Also in these years, ongoing instability in the banking system led to one initiative after another:

- Nationalization of the Anglo-Irish bank;
- The announcement of recapitalization after recapitalization as the valuations of bank assets kept sinking;
- The establishment of the National Asset Management Agency (NAMA) as a piece of financial engineering which aimed to reduce the risks held within the banks' balance sheet, by stripping away the worst classes of property loans, while keeping the cost off the balance sheet of the State, and bringing tens of billions of ECB funding into the system, with the kind cooperation of the ECB;

- Multiple attempts to more fully understand the real balance sheet position of the banks, culminating in a major capital assessment in April 2010, for most of the Irish banks, and a further exercise in September 2010 in relation to the Anglo-Irish bank (Cardiff, 2016).

All these efforts did not save the financial system – it remained in grave danger – but they did manage to put some brakes on the deterioration. The main banks were still more or less intact, the deposits of Irish citizens and others were protected, and the guarantee held together.

The credibility of the banks rested on the credibility of the state, but the state had its own fiscal problems, just described. So, when the fiscal problems of the State were added to by the costs of the banking crisis, the two together started to seem to market participants, already reeling from developments in Greece, as potentially overwhelming.

The program period

In the autumn of 2010, a further acceleration of bank outflows and a withdrawal of investors from the Government bond market was prompting a negative cycle in which investor flight led to a weaker banking system and undermined the State's apparent creditworthiness, leading to further flight. Bond yields were rising in response, increasing the reward for investors in assets that were becoming riskier, but also themselves adding to the State's cost-base, in a vicious cycle.

While the Government had deliberately ensured that it had considerable cash holdings in reserve, the banks did not have any cash reserves, and they could only continue to operate with the continuing support of the ECB and the Irish Central Bank. This liquidity support for the banking system was in turn dependent on the central banks' willingness to accept Government assets pledged by the banks as security, and thus on the creditworthiness of the State itself. The situation was becoming untenable, in the absence of outside assistance. Moreover, various elements of the external economic and policy environment were making the situation worse. Something had to give.

In the end, despite massive efforts by Ireland, often applauded by market participants and EU officials, the "Credibility Equation" just did not add up. So, after a short period of informal and then more formal negotiations during November 2010, the Government decided to accept an EU/IMF loan of €67.5 billion. About one-third of that was from the IMF; the rest was from the EU, the European Financial Stability Facility (a company formed for the purpose by the Eurozone Governments) and the UK, Danish and Swedish Governments. Ireland's own reserves would bring the total amount of the program to some €85 billion.

The program laid out in indicative terms how Ireland would finance itself, with the help of fiscal adjustments and the program loans, but receipt of the ongoing loans was contingent on satisfactory adherence to fiscal conditions.

Irish authorities were themselves already committed to a very substantial set of fiscal adjustments and had been engaged in these since mid-2008. Moreover, the authorities had already set out their broad fiscal targets some weeks earlier, after considerable discussion with EU partners. These plans allowed for a total program of adjustment amounting to some €15 billion or around 9 percent of GDP. Shortly before the program for Ireland was agreed, the Irish authorities published their own "National Recovery Plan" (Government of Ireland, 2010) and this plan set out in considerable detail the areas of fiscal adjustment intended. A broader tax base and various tax increases were to provide about one-third of the adjustment, while expenditure measures including additional wage cuts, public sector numbers reductions and more, as well as specific efficiency measures, social welfare adjustments and so forth, were to provide the balance of adjustments. The fiscal measures set out in the Program for National Recovery then formed the basis for the agreement with the program lenders.

Beyond fiscal conditionality, there were to be legislative and other structural measures, too, to improve the efficiency of the economy, addressing issues such as the level of the minimum wage and wage-setting systems in specific sectors, the level of competition in sheltered sectors, such as legal and healthcare, the efficiency of the insolvency and bankruptcy systems, and the impact of activation policies in the social welfare system as it affected working-age individuals. Again, these measures were quite closely aligned with the policies already announced in the Irish Government's National Recovery Plan (Independent Evaluation Office of the IMF, 2016) (Box 5.1).

Box 5.1 Economic adjustment program for Ireland – summary of elements

Initially agreed: 28 November 2010.
PM: Brian Cowen until March 2011, followed by Enda Kenny until 2017.
Tenure: December 2010 to end 2013.
Size: €85 billion, of which 17.5 billion to be provided by Ireland from its own resources.
Contributors: IMF (€22.5 billion), EFSM (€22.5 billion), EFSF, together with bilateral loans from UK, Sweden, Denmark (€22.5 billion).
Objectives: Restore Irish economy and fiscal and financial systems to health, allowing the Irish state to regain market access for financing.

Main areas of intervention

- Extensive and frontloaded actions to restructure the banking system, including stress tests, recapitalizations, deleveraging, reorganization of the banks and burden sharing with subordinated bond holders. Legislation to provide for a resolution regime
- Ensure fiscal adjustments on lines already announced by Irish authorities, in National Recovery Plan

- Take longer-term fiscal-structural measures, for example in relation to reducing the long-term pension burden, base-broadening, etc.; establish a Fiscal Advisory Council
- Make structural and legislative changes to address labor market rigidities (including in the original plan, later set aside, to reduce the minimum wage), adjustments to the social welfare system to enhance labor activation
- Promote efficiency and competition in the service sector by removing remaining restrictions on trade and competition; at the same time look for ways to enhance the efficiency of the energy sector
- Reforms of the aspects of the legal services system, reform of insolvency/bankruptcy systems.

Status: *The program ended without any extensions, and the government opted to make early repayments elements of the program loans, specifically from the IMF, to avail of lower interest rates.*

The program announced in November 2010 also included a detailed set of actions to be taken in relation to banking, building on initiatives already taken or announced, but going beyond those in several ways, including new more aggressive stress testing with the potential for further recapitalizations arising from that exercise. (For example, paras 9–20 of the Memorandum of Economic and Financial Policies, IMF, December 2010.)

Concerns about the asset quality of the banking system were to be addressed by continuing with the planned recapitalization and instituting very quickly new aggressive stress testing against tough benchmarks to underpin depositor confidence and provide a base for private investment. Constant funding concerns and unsustainable demand for non-deposit funding from central bank funding, including Emergency Liquidity Assistance, would be addressed by significantly reducing the size of the banking system, divesting of non-core assets and making other appropriate assets ready for sale where possible, amounting to a significant program of targeted deleveraging. The structure and resilience of the banking system would be enhanced by providing enhanced supervisory structures, raised capital requirements, and by targeting core banks to be protected while failed entities, the Anglo-Irish bank in particular, would be prepared for resolution. The program would also require the development of legislation for a special resolution regime for the banking sector. Meanwhile, additional recourse to asset purchases from banks by the already established National Asset Management Agency would assist with both the deleveraging of banks and the reduction of asset quality concerns.

All of this banking support could cost a great deal of money, eventually to be paid by Irish taxpayers, and up to €35 billion of the program was notionally earmarked for these purposes. While sharing the objectives of the banking measures, Irish authorities, however, were concerned that the already very difficult position in relation to the sustainability of the State's debt would be made even more precarious by these banking measures. Discussions between the various parties to the program often revolved around how to do enough to solve the banking problems, but not to spend more than required, to avoid even greater strain on the State's capacity to service and repay debt. There had been considerable disappointment when plans of the Irish Government (initially supported by the IMF) to insist that bond investors in Irish banks would accept some of the losses inherent in their investment had to be pared back at the insistence of the lenders. They were concerned about contagion implications in the broader financial system if senior bond holders were forced to take losses in any part of the European banking system. In the end, only subordinated bondholders took losses, but it was not necessary to use the full €35 billion, and the eventual call on the State was closer to €17 billion under the Program. This was in addition to many more billions previously committed, however.

Implementation

Irish authorities set about managing the EU/IMF program with a view to full implementation. Once agreed, the program became a clear guideline for policy actions in the years to come. Deadlines and so-called "structural benchmarks" of the program were made to act as real targets for Irish action. Various evaluations reflect closely on the domestic "ownership" of the program and its careful and smooth implementation as a factor in Ireland's relative success (Independent Evaluation Office of the IMF, 2016).

However, policy in Ireland was never to simply accept and implement the program. Instead, it was to implement but renegotiate. Even before the signature of the program, Irish authorities were considering how to persuade the program partners to improve the terms to make the program more supportive and sustainable. The first tentative discussions on ameliorating the high interest rates on program loans were taking place early in 2011, even before the first quarterly review (Cardiff, 2016). Moreover, as soon as a new Government was in place in the first quarter of 2011, efforts commenced to have the program adjusted to better match their priorities. There was still no progress on letting bondholders take losses, but new terms were agreed on some labor market measures and on asset sale plans and how receipts from such sales would be applied, for example.

Throughout subsequent years, Ireland took advantage of a number of important opportunities to benefit from improvements in program terms, while at the same time meeting, or even outperforming, its commitments to the program partners. This combination of determined and credible implementation, together with improvements in interest rate conditions of the loans, extensions of maturities of loans etc., and even an apparent (if ultimately undelivered) European promise in July 2012 to use the new European Stability Mechanism to help alleviate Ireland's bank recapitalization burden, all helped to improve the conditions which eventually allowed for a return to market access for the Irish sovereign.

One key example was the "promissory note deal" agreed in early February 2013. After years of tentative discussions, a very complex mechanism was designed (Department of Finance, 2017; White & Casey, 2013) to alleviate the debt service and refinancing burden arising from the capital support given to Ireland's most problematic defunct bank, the Anglo-Irish bank, while at the same time liquidating the bank itself, now operating under the name of IBRC. Overall, it was expected at the time that the package of measures in the promissory note deal would reduce the Government deficit by around one billion euro per year, for a number of years after the first year, that Government funding requirement would be reduced by around 20 billion euro over a decade (White & Casey, 2013) and that the NPV of the outstanding debt would reduce by nearly seven billion euro, using discount rates and assumptions appropriate to that point in time (Whelan, 2013). Whelan noted that the "dramatic reduction" in the ongoing financing requirements of the State would alleviate investor concerns.

Analysis (Smyth, 2017) of Ireland's fiscal performance relative to initial expectations for the five years from 2011 to 2015 inclusive shows that spending was kept close to target – there was an annual "overspend" of around half a billion euro. However, this modest figure may be deceptive. Debt service costs were somewhat lower than expected, especially in the later years of this period. A self-reinforcing combination of growing market confidence in Ireland, and associated substantial reductions in bond yields (from nearly 10 percent for 10 year bonds at end 2011, as shown in Table 5.2, to below 1 percent), lower program interest rates and lower service costs arising from the promissory note deal, allowed the Irish authorities to keep close to overall spending plans but with much lesser adjustments in primary (pre-debt service) expenditures. Austerity impacts were, therefore, less than they might otherwise have been, helping to reinforce the resumption of growth, and growth allowed the Government to take a more relaxed fiscal stance, in turn.

Political developments

By the time the program negotiations had commenced in late 2010, the ruling Government coalition between the Fianna Fáil Party and the Green Party had become deeply unpopular, arising from the unpopularity of both the austerity measures and the banking support measures that had taken place. Trust in government institutions had declined considerably (Boda, Medgyesi, Fondeville & Özdemir, 2018), reflected in a number of high-profile public demonstrations against Government policy. The two Government parties were themselves no longer happy that they retained a mandate, but believed they had some duty to manage any transition in a way which would not further destabilize the situation. The Green Party decided to leave the Government, but with effect from after the expected passing of the 2011 Finance Bill in early 2011. This Bill would put into law the measures that would be required to meet the fiscal targets already agreed for 2011 and make for an easier transition period for a new Government. Meanwhile, Fianna Fáil selected a new party leader, with the current leader, Brian Cowen, remaining as Taoiseach until after the coming election.

In the election that followed, both Fianna Fáil and the Greens were heavily penalized by the electorate. Fianna Fáil lost 51 of its 71 seats in the more important lower house of Parliament, the Dáil, while the Green Party lost all six of its seats. This left a new coalition of Fine Gael and Labour in charge, with for them an unprecedented gain in electoral support, with Sinn Féin (a more radical republican party) and smaller parties and independents also picking up seats from Fianna Fáil losses. The scale of the Fianna Fáil loss was unprecedented, allowing the new Government to speak of "democratic revolution" and "political whirlwind" (Government of Ireland, 2011). But it was the size of the swing in voter sympathies that was revolutionary. In fact, the "new" Government coalition of center-right Fine Gael and moderate left Labour represented a traditional alternative to Fianna Fáil, these two parties having been in Government together a number of times in the past, rather than a demand by the electorate, at this stage, for an electoral revolution, and their aim was not to overturn the adjustment program agreed by the prior Government, but to renegotiate various elements of it, to make it more sustainable and acceptable to citizens.

Trust in EU institutions was also declining in the crisis period (Boda, Medgyesi, Fondeville & Özdemir, 2018), though Ireland remained a relatively strong supporter of the European project and EMU. Despite strong views in media discussions on the role of the ECB, especially in relation to banking interventions, Irish people generally continued to believe that the Euro was a positive factor for both Ireland and the EU. At 68 percent of a surveyed population, this belief was significantly stronger in Ireland than in the Eurozone as a whole (55 percent) (European Commission, 2012), though it had fallen from a very high level of 81 percent in 2007 (then the highest of the Euro countries) (European Commission, 2007). Even despite this significant loss of confidence in Government and the EU, Irish people were not all questioning every aspect of EU and national policy. While far from popular, there was more support for fiscal reforms, for example, in Ireland than in most other Euro countries (European Commission, 2010).

Emerging from the crisis and the post-crisis period

The successful outcome of the program and the emergence from crisis seems in hindsight almost predestined, but in fact, it was not. Conditions got worse before they got better. The EU/IMF program insulated Ireland from an even stormier period in 2011, when bond yields for Irish debt of two-year maturity went over 20 percent, signaling that many in the bond market believed that the Irish state would default on its obligations. The Irish problems were part of a wider systemic situation, and other countries were in great difficulty, too. Portugal and Spain required their own EU/IMF packages. The Greek picture was sometimes hopeful, sometimes bad, but always worse than Ireland's.

However, credibility was, indeed, slowly rebuilt. By early 2012 the tide seemed to be turning, at least regarding investor interest in Irish credit. By mid-2012 Ireland could again tentatively find buyers for its sovereign bonds. As already noted, successive improvements in the terms of the deal with the EU/IMF made it more affordable, more sustainable. Consistent meeting of program targets and implementation of announced policy measures added to the credibility of the program. At the same time, the measures in relation to the banking system were also commanding a good deal of market respect. Interest rates on Irish bonds fell to the point where instead of being a destabilizing sustainability problem, they started to represent a good return for more modest risk. Moreover, in the reverse of the negative cycle of 2010, as the involvement of early investors pushed these interest rates down, other investors were incentivized to participate. EU and ECB measures and announcements, including Mr. Draghi's "whatever it takes" announcement (Draghi, 2012), underpinned market sentiment and created a real downward momentum in bond yields in Europe. Finally, things seemed set to get better.

A sudden start

If Ireland entered the crisis with a classic "sudden stop" in its economic performance, the post-program recovery of the Irish economy looks like a "sudden start". On many measures, the economy is performing so much better now that one is tempted to wonder if things are back to normal for Ireland. This is not the case, or at most one might say there is a new normal, with significant reverberations of the crisis and the boom-bust cycle still in play.

Nonetheless, the performance is impressive. As measured by GDP, after two disastrous years of contraction in 2008 and 2009, the economy first flattened out, then recovered very strongly. Even discounting a huge GDP increase in 2015, arising from multi-national activities and not reflecting domestic economic reality, there has been a clear recovery trend since 2013, and the economy is now performing strongly. Although certain transactions of a small number of international firms have distorted the usefulness of GDP as a measure of underlying economic activity within the Irish economy (Department of Finance, 2018), the alternative growth measure of modified GNI, or GNI*, unfortunately not yet available in constant price terms, nonetheless confirms that the trend is highly positive (Table 5.3).

This performance is reflected most clearly in employment and unemployment statistics. Unemployment, which peaked at over 16 percent at the start of 2012, has been on a strong, consistent downward trend since then and has now fallen below 6 percent (Table 5.2). Similarly, employment started to pick up strongly from 2013 onwards, in line with the recovery in economy, and by the second quarter of 2018, employment growth had offset most of the jobs lost from 2007 to 2011 and 2012. Migration flows which had been strongly negative in the crisis period, mitigating the headline unemployment figure, are now significantly positive, providing a source of labor as the available domestic pool reduces.

These new jobs, however, are not principally in the construction sector. Although more than 40 percent of the net jobs losses during the period from Q4 2007 to Q4 2011 were attributable to the construction sector, only about 16 percent of the employment rebound up to Q4 2017 was in this area, and the percentage of construction employment in the total has only recently exceeded six percent compared to a pre-crisis peak of 11 percent, and 8 percent in 2000.

So far as housing construction is concerned, activity remained very low for a number of years, reflecting a combination of factors, including weakened financial infrastructure and heavy damage to the construction industry during the crisis period, but also a fall in house prices below the level at which developers were prepared to build. Lower supply relative to the release of several years of pent-up demand has meant a steady increase in prices, and at the same time a fall in the proportion of households living in their own house, so putting severe upward pressure also on rents.

The Central Bank has shown itself much more activist in its approach to macroprudential stability than in the pre-crisis period and has put in place macroprudential rules on residential mortgage lending, restricting borrowing above certain loan-to-value and loan-to-income levels. The aim of these measures is to increase the resilience of both borrowers and the banking sector to house price adjustments, and they act to offset some part of the upward pressure on house prices by damping demand somewhat (Central Bank of Ireland, 2018).

Moreover, it looks like there had been a conscious effort by Irish households to deleverage their household balance sheets in response to the crisis conditions. Some research (Lydon & McIndoe-Calder, 2017) managed to provide a more sophisticated understanding of this household balance sheet picture. They show, as might be expected, that certain sectors were more affected by the crisis than others, and unfortunately that the rising tide post-crisis has been kinder to some boats than others. Their analysis shows that older age groups who tend to have lower incomes on average, and a greater concentration of their wealth in property, suffered the most significant decline in the wealth-to-income ratio since 2006 (based on data to 2014). However, they crucially also identify a group of "Younger households … born in the 1970s and 1980s, [which] see almost all their wealth wiped out by the property crash" (ibid., pp. 19 and 20) compared to large, but much lesser property wealth losses in other age groups. Notwithstanding that some of these younger borrowers enjoyed the considerable benefit of interest rate reductions directly related to ECB policy rate changes as a term of their mortgage contract, this cohort suffered harder than most.

Some sectors of society were less well equipped to cope with the crisis than others. Although the boom period had provided very broad employment opportunities and allowed for better social provision by the Government, it did not benefit all equally, or even proportionately. The OECD examined income inequality before and after the crisis, noting that Ireland's tax and social welfare systems are relatively very effective in redistributing income to reduce income inequality. However, the huge increase in unemployment during the crisis period, including in particular in sectors where lower-skilled employees could find employment, such as construction, meant that lower-income lower-skilled households had more than their share of the burden. Alternatively, as the OECD put it, "market income inequality increased markedly during the recession, owing to the dramatic rise in employment losses" (OECD, 2015). Table 5.4 provides some of the key income inequality and poverty measures for the period.

Table 5.4 Inequality measures for Ireland

a Gini coefficient (source: Central Statistics Office)

2004	*2005*	*2006*	*2007*	*2008*	*2009*	*2010*	*2011*	*2012*	*2013*	*2014*	*2015*	*2016*	*2017*
31.7	32.3	32.4	31.7	30.6	29.3	31.4	31.1	31.7	31.8	32.1	30.8	30.7	31.5

b Consistent poverty rate (source: Central Statistics Office)

2004	*2005*	*2006*	*2007*	*2008*	*2009*	*2010*	*2011*	*2012*	*2013*	*2014*	*2015*	*2016*	*2017*
6.6	7.0	6.6	5.1	4.2	5.5	6.3	6.9	8.2	9.0	8.3	8.5	8.2	6.7

c Poverty rate before taxes and transfers, poverty line 50% (source: OECD)

2004	*2005*	*2006*	*2007*	*2008*	*2009*	*2010*	*2011*	*2012*	*2013*	*2014*	*2015*
0.34	0.33	0.35	0.36	0.39	0.43	0.44	0.42	0.43	0.41	0.39	0.38

d Poverty rate after taxes and transfers, poverty line 50% (source: OECD)

2004	*2005*	*2006*	*2007*	*2008*	*2009*	*2010*	*2011*	*2012*	*2013*	*2014*	*2015*
0.13	0.11	0.11	0.10	0.09	0.09	0.09	0.10	0.09	0.09	0.09	0.10

e Youth unemployment rate % (age 15–24) (source: OECD)

2004	*2005*	*2006*	*2007*	*2008*	*2009*	*2010*	*2011*	*2012*	*2013*	*2014*	*2015*	*2016*	*2017*
9.5	9.8	10	10.3	12.6	26	28.8	30.4	33.4	29.6	26.5	21.5	18.4	16.1

f Incidence of long-term unemployment (over 1 year) (source: Central Statistics Office)

2004	*2005*	*2006*	*2007*	*2008*	*2009*	*2010*	*2011*	*2012*	*2013*	*2014*	*2015*	*2016*	*2017*
34.9	33.4	31.6	30.0	26.5	29.1	49.1	59.3	61.7	60.6	59.2	57.6	55.3	47.0

Policymaking processes, including the negotiations between Irish authorities and the Troika parties, did try, with some effect, to mitigate the social and economic damage for the more vulnerable (Chopra, Witness Statement of Ajai Chopra, 2015; Kennedy, Jin, Haugh & Lenain, 2015). Resources at that point were limited, of course, and even if basic social welfare payment rates could be protected to some extent, they could only mitigate the income reductions and the huge social stresses arising from a shift from employment into unemployment. Job and income losses were broadly spread, and the highly progressive tax and welfare systems "were critical in helping Ireland to avoid the rise in income inequality seen in many other countries" (Callan, Regan, Savage & Walsh, 2017), even as overall incomes and employment fell.

Ireland, post-crisis, is left with a high level of pre-tax/benefit income inequality – the most unequal in the EU according to the think-tank TASC (Wickham, 2017), offset by a quite highly redistributive tax and benefit system (Kennedy, Jin, Haugh & Lenain, 2015; Wickham, 2017). However, data for the 2013–2016 period contain some hopeful signs that the level of deprivation and inequality is indeed responding to growth and employment increases in the Irish economy (Central Statistics Office, 2018), with significant income increases across all income deciles, especially the lowest.

Banking sector developments have also helped considerably to underpin improved confidence and the ability to invest in Ireland. Around 64 billion euro was transferred to the banks to offset losses and maintain their capital positions. By end 2016, the Department of Finance estimated that returns on this investment and the current valuation of the remaining ownership positions in the banks amounted to over 28 billion (Department of Finance, 2016). As the remaining stakes are sold, this will reduce the exposure to the banking sector and at the same time allow for a reduction in debt to international creditors, adding to sustainability. Moreover, the exposure to contingent liabilities represented by the balance sheet of the National Asset Management Agency, which had issued over €30 billion in bonds to take bad assets off the balance sheets of banks, has now been eliminated. Indeed, NAMA is now forecasting a modest surplus on its operations; it may even make a small eventual contribution to debt reduction (Daly, 2018).

At the same time, the remaining banks have themselves become smaller, substantially deleveraged entities, reliant principally on customer deposits for their funding, with much more sustainable business plans. However, despite considerable progress in reducing non-performing loans over time, the levels remain significant, attracting the continuous attention of supervisors, and act as something of a brake on a return to fuller performance of the system. Credit conditions remain relatively tight in Ireland, and interest rates for customers reflect relatively higher funding costs for Irish banks. Moreover, after closures and consolidations, the system has fewer banks and less competition than in the pre-crisis period. Banking business in Ireland, therefore, remains highly concentrated.

In considering the recovery of the Irish economy, however, it would be a mistake to forget that amidst all that went wrong in the bubble and bust period, there were some underlying strengths. Proposed structural reforms in the EU/IMF programs were relatively modest because economic structures were, overall, not performing very badly. Therefore, "structural reforms were never front and centre … as a part of addressing this crisis", according to Ajai Chopra (Chopra, 2015).

One of the underlying strengths of the Irish economy – its ability to attract foreign direct investment – is sometimes characterized as being a sort of accounting and taxation trick without much reality. The position is somewhat different. According to the relevant State agency, IDA Ireland, FDI-related employment reached just over 210,000 persons in 2017, with net job creation in the sector of some 10,000 (IDA Ireland, 2018). These are all essentially exporting companies and are central to any strategy of export-led growth. Even through the crisis period, efforts were made to ensure that Ireland protected its business-friendliness (see Table 5.5 for some measures), including in relation to the tax system.

Regan and Brazys (2017) argue that Ireland's post-crisis growth was driven by this FDI sector, notwithstanding some real political risks to the growth model in the longer term. Moreover, the IMF also notes that "the flexibility and openness of the Irish economy where multinationals – including international financial institutions – are major employers and investors, were key for the recovery" (IMF, 2016).

The post-crisis period has also seen important shifts in key institutional and political structures. There were considerable changes in the structures of financial sector regulation, in many aspects of the public sector's productivity and governance, and the fiscal and economic decision-making system is now subject to considerably more oversight. An Irish Fiscal Advisory Council has now been in place for some years and regularly challenges Government thinking on planning and fiscal matters. Domestic fiscal responsibility legislation and, of course, the full range of EU surveillance in its post-crisis enhanced form are now in place (Kopits, 2014) to act as a moderating influence on any future irrational exuberance in Ireland.

The tax base has also been broadened, with residential property taxes and a Universal Social Charge now a more or less accepted feature of the tax system (though there are divergences of view as to how universal the USC should be). By contrast, residential water charges did not seem to catch on in Ireland, meeting very considerable popular opposition – all well described recently (O'Leary, 2018). State asset sales (other than those related to bank rescues) were much less a feature of the program and post-program period than had been anticipated, though there were some, and the reforms to address competitiveness of the legal systems also made limited progress.

There has also been considerable shift in the political landscape of Ireland, though perhaps less pronounced than in some other countries. The principal party of Government for much of the 20th century, Fianna Fáil, had been in power for the pre-crisis period and was responsible for the initial responses to the crisis. As noted above, it suffered huge losses in the 2011 election as a result. It had then been replaced by a coalition of Fine Gael and the Labour Party, which were committed to maintaining the broad outlines of the EU/IMF program while working to improve the terms and to achieve the successful emergence of Ireland from the program. Their electoral successes in 2011 were of course founded in part on the backlash against Fianna Fáil, but they also suffered their own electoral reversal at the election in 2015, when the Labour Party was reduced to just seven seats out of 158 in the Dáil, the principal house of the parliament, compared to 37 out of 166 after the 2011 election. Fine Gael remains in power after 2016, but only with the acquiescence of the Fianna Fáil party (which has recovered some of its 2011 losses), through a so-called "confidence and supply arrangement" and in coalition with a loose grouping of independent

Table 5.5 Modified gross national income (GNI*) for Ireland

€millions	*GDP at current market prices*	*GNI* at current market prices*	*GNI* as % of GDP*	*Change in GDP (current prices, %)*	*Change in GNI* (current prices, %)*
2000	108,380	94,108	86.8	17.0	16.8
2001	121,959	103,496	84.9	12.5	10.0
2002	135,960	112,787	83.0	11.5	9.0
2003	145,556	123,714	85.0	7.1	9.7
2004	156,143	132,446	84.8	7.3	7.1
2005	170,187	144,016	84.6	9.0	8.7
2006	184,994	157,896	85.4	8.7	9.6
2007	197,202	165,560	84.0	6.6	4.9
2008	187,769	156,906	83.6	–4.8	–5.2
2009	170,101	134,841	79.3	–9.4	–14.1
2010	167,721	128,949	76.9	–1.4	–4.4
2011	171,140	126,621	74.0	2.0	–1.8
2012	175,216	126,444	72.2	2.4	–0.1
2013	179,922	136,906	76.1	2.7	8.3
2014	195,293	148,628	76.1	8.5	8.6
2015	262,466	161,382	61.5	34.4	8.6
2016	273,238	175,827	64.3	4.1	9.0
2017†	294,110	181,182	61.6	7.6	3.0

Source: Central Statistics Office.

Notes

* While GDP in Ireland is calculated according to international standards and norms, the large and complex involvement of multi-national firms in the Irish economy gives rise to particular problems of interpretation. For this reason, an Irish-specific measure, called modified GNI, or GNI, has been instituted to give policymakers and analysts a better picture of the economy, controlling for some of the impact of globalization on Irish economic statistics. For the moment at least, a constant price series is not available. The Department of Finance has produced an explanatory note (Department of Finance, 2018).

† Preliminary.

members of the Dáil, some of whom have ministerial portfolios. Indeed, the rise of the independents, and the growth in electoral support of the Sinn Fein party (now the principal left-wing party), has undermined old political patterns and left the two traditionally most dominant parties relying on each other.

How has the Irish economic model changed post-crisis, in comparative terms? The institutional changes of the crisis period suggest that there is now a much greater emphasis on regulation, particularly in the financial sphere, and there has not been a broad return to procyclical construction tax breaks of the sort that were hugely overused in the 90s and 2000s. Recent strong growth has not been based on credit-led consumer consumption. However, the generally highly welcoming approach to FDI and a generally liberal approach to business activity, supported by low corporation tax rates, has continued to provide strong employment growth at a time of constrained public sector expansion and near morbidity in the construction sector. In this key area, Irish policy has retained an extraordinary consistency before, during and since the crisis.

Notwithstanding that the social partnership model of economic management, described earlier, had been promoted and accepted as having been a positive element of the development of the country from its origins to the late 90s or early 2000s, grand formal social partnership arrangements and discussions were set aside during the fiscal crisis period and the regular cycle of formal discussions leading to social partnership-based "programs" has fallen into disuse during the crisis period and since. As a result, social partnership has been "declared dead" (Teague & Donaghey, 2015), so this key anomaly in the picture of Ireland as a liberal market economy may seem to have receded.

It is certainly true that the crisis provided its own, often unpleasant, organizing principle for the distribution of public resources. However, the relationships that existed between Government, unions and other partners did not dissolve overnight. The core trade union–government relationship was strong enough that both parties were able to institutionalize in formal industrial bargaining the crisis measures that had been taken by the Government in relation to public sector pay, and even to extend the bargaining into areas of productivity. As the crisis unwinds, the need for an organizing mechanism for managing conflict around disruptive wage and income distribution demands may yet give rise to a renaissance of social agreements in some form.

Notwithstanding the ups and downs of the Irish–EU relationship over the past decade, Irish people remain heavily committed to the EU and to the EMU. Eurobarometer data show 85 percent of the respondents indicating that they regard the Euro as good for Ireland, well over the Eurozone average. But this support should not be misunderstood as trust in the EU institutions. Data show that trust in EU institutions, like trust in the national Government, has nonetheless rebounded from crisis lows (as is the case in Portugal and Spain), and trust in EU institutions remains consistently above trust in National Government, according to Eurofound data (Boda, Medgyesi, Fondeville & Özdemir, 2018). In this area, Ireland can be said to be back to the pre-crisis normal: supportive of the EU, but as is the case in much of Europe, somewhat skeptical of its institutions.

Conclusions

The Irish economy is steaming ahead, but it is not back to "normal". It is in many respects performing better than the word "normal" might imply, suggesting at least the possibility of an overshoot in growth rates and in employment growth, which, if it continues, must soon start to test the capacity constraints of the economy.

In other ways, damaging impacts of the crisis have been somewhat remediated, but the repair work is far from complete and necessary corrections are still working themselves through the system. For example, the fiscal position of the State and the capital position of the banking system are on a much more stable footing, but the new stability is less comfortable than might be preferred. High indebtedness of the State and individuals might leave the economy more vulnerable to any new shocks, and in the banking system, one could say the same of the high, albeit reducing, level of outstanding non-performing loans.

Moreover, there are some areas in which the crisis adjustment significantly overshot any likely equilibrium point and remains to re-adjust. Construction is an example, because activity fell so close to zero for years that natural demand cannot now be met, with serious consequences for rental markets and house prices. Here, a failure of the market to adjust to create more supply would risk a deepening housing crisis, and damage competitiveness, but if the market does adjust, the demand for workers to meet this pent-up demand at a time of near full employment could put considerable upward pressure on wages, again with the potential for damaged competitiveness.

There is pent-up demand, too, in the area of public spending, where demands for service improvements after the austerity period will need to be carefully and well managed to avoid an overshoot in the other direction. There is a natural resistance to the adoption of a strongly counter-cyclical fiscal stance, while the economy and many of its people feel they are still trying to "catch up" after the crisis.

Ireland remains an anomaly in a European context. The scale of its "bust", the resilience of critical elements of the economy and its institutions, and the scale of the recovery since the crisis all stand out. Its liberal-oriented but hybrid political-economic model has sustained an enormous impact and emerged in a slightly different but still fluid constellation. Whether the institutions of political and economic decision making see a return toward some former equilibrium or find a new one is still to be determined, because the reverberations of the crisis, albeit more than half a decade since the worst period, are still far from complete.

The demand for responses to all of these forces – many of them now problems of success – as well as the major disruption threatened by Brexit will have to be organized by a more disparate parliamentary system in which the crisis has accelerated the pace of change, leaving political parties which shared power for most of the last 50 years with less influence and with a greater role for "newer" parties (at least in terms of participation in parliamentary politics) and independents. The current Government now operates from a minority position in the parliament, and majorities may be more difficult to form in the future, albeit the more "centrist" parties still dominate the parliament.

Focused on the aftermath of the crisis, this chapter has not dealt with Brexit or certain other longer-term threats, which are beyond its scope and, at the time of writing, exceptionally difficult to predict with certainty. The Central Bank of Ireland, while trying to give some indication of the scale of impact of a disorderly Brexit, indicates that "compared to a scenario where the UK remained an EU member, a disorderly Brexit would result in a substantial and permanent loss of output in the Irish economy" (Central Bank of Ireland, 2019), but it also threatens a real shift in the geo-political situation of Ireland, the UK and the EU, perhaps of greater long-term significance than many of the issues dealt with above. These issues are for another article, perhaps.

References

Boda, Z., Medgyesi, M., Fondeville, N., & Özdemir, E. (2018). *Societal Change and Trust in Institutions: Eurofound Report.* Luxembourg: Publications Office of the European Union. Retrieved 19 02 2019, from www.eurofound.europa.eu/publications/report/2018/societal-change-and-trust-in-institutions.

Bredin, D., Fitzpatrick, T., & O'Reilly, G. (2001, December). Retail Interest Rate Pass-Through: The Irish Experience. *The Economic and Social Review, 22*(2).

Callan, T., Keane, C., & Walsh, J. (2010, Spring). What Role for Property Taxes in Ireland. *The Economic and Social Review, 41*(1), 87–107.

Callan, T., Regan, M., Savage, M., & Walsh, J. R. (2017, June). Income Distribution in Ireland: Through Recession Towards Recovery. *Economic and Social Research Institute, Budget Perspectives 2018*(2).

Cardiff, K. (2015, 18 06). *Witness Statement to the Oireachtas Banking Inquiry.* Dublin: Houses of the Oireachtas. Retrieved 18 06 2017, from Houses of the Oireachtas (Irish parliament): https://inquiries.oireachtas.ie/banking/wp-content/uploads/2015/06/Opening-Statement-Kevin-Cardiff.pdf.

Cardiff, K. (2016). *Recap: Inside Ireland's Financial Crisis.* Dublin: Liffey Press.

Central Bank of Ireland. (2018). *Review of Residential Mortgage Lending Requirements.* Dublin: Central Bank of Ireland. Retrieved 21 January 2019, from https://centralbank.ie/docs/default-source/financial-system/financial-stability/macroprudential-policy/policy-documents/2018-review-of-mortgage-market-measures.pdf?sfvrsn=4.

Central Bank of Ireland. (2019, January). Irish Economy: Overview. *Central Bank of Ireland Quarterly Bulletin*(1).

Central Statistics Office. (2018, 18 September). *SILC.* Retrieved from Central Statistics Office: www.cso.ie/en/silc.

Chopra, A. (2015, 10 09). *Oral Evidence of Ajai Chopra.* Retrieved 18 06 2017, from Houses of the Oireachtas (Irish parliament): https://inquiries.oireachtas.ie/banking/hearings/ajai-chopra-former-deputy-director-imf.

Chopra, A. (2015, 10 09). *Witness Statement of Ajai Chopra.* Retrieved 18 06 2017, from Houses of the Oireachtas (Irish parliament): https://inquiries.oireachtas.ie/banking/wp-content/uploads/2015/09/Ajay-Chopra-Opening-Statement.pdf.

Cowen, B. (2007, 7 December). *Financial Statement of the Minister for Finance (Budget Speech for Budget 2008).* Retrieved 18 06 2017, from Budget Website: www.budget.gov.ie.

Daly, F. (2018, 13 June). *Chairman Frank Daly's speaking notes for NAMA Annual Report press briefing.* Retrieved from NAMA website: www.nama.ie/about-us/publications/annual-reports.

Department of Finance. (2005). *Summary of Budget Measures, 2006.* Dublin: Department of Finance.

Department of Finance. (2007, 07 12). *Stability Programme (part of the Budget 2008 documentation).* Retrieved 18 06 2017, from www.budget.gov.ie: http://budget.gov.ie/Budgets/2006/Documents/StabilityProgramme.pdf.

Department of Finance. (2007). *Summary of Budget Measures 2008.* Dublin: Department of Finance.

Department of Finance. (2016, December). *Ireland's Economy and Finances.* Retrieved 18 06 2017, from Department of Finance: http://finance.gov.ie/sites/default/files/Ireland_Report_Card_Economy_and_Finances_Dec2016.pdf.

Department of Finance. (2017). *Irish Bank Resolution Corporation.* Retrieved 18 06 2017, from Department of Finance: http://finance.gov.ie/what-we-do/banking-financial-services/shareholding-management-unit/irish-bank-resolution-corporation.

Department of Finance. (2017, 04). *Stability Programme Update, April 2017.* Retrieved 18 06 2017, from Department of Finance: http://finance.gov.ie/sites/default/files/170502%20Final%20SPU%202017.pdf.

Department of Finance. (2018). *GDP and 'Modified GNI' – Explanatory Note.* Dublin: Department of Finance.

Department of Housing, Planning, Community and Local Government. (2017a). *Construction Activity – Completions.* Retrieved 19 06 2017, from Department of Housing, Planning, Community and Local Government: www.housing.gov.ie/housing/statistics/house-building-and-private-rented/construction-activity-completions.

Department of Housing, Planning, Community and Local Government. (2017b). *Construction Activity – Starts.* Retrieved 6 19, 2017, from Department of Housing, Planning, Community and Local Government: www.housing.gov.ie/housing/statistics/house-building-and-private-rented/construction-activity-starts.

Donovan, D., & Murphy, A. (2013). *The Fall of the Celtic Tiger* (First Edition). Oxford: Oxford University Press.

Draghi, M. (2012). *Verbatim of the remarks made by Mario Draghi: Speech by Mario Draghi, President of the European Central Bank at the Global Investment Conference in London, 26 July 2012.* Frankfurt: European Central Bank. Retrieved 15 02 2019, from European Central Bank website: www.ecb.europa.eu/press/key/date/2012/html/sp120726.en.html.

European Anti Poverty Network Ireland. (n.d.). *Tax in Ireland and Europe.* Retrieved 15 06 2017, from EAPN Ireland: www.eapn.ie/eapn/policy/resources-on-taxation/tax-in-ireland-and-europe.

European Commission. (2007). *Flash Eurobarometer 216: Public attitudes and perceptions in the euro area: Analytical report.* European Commission. Retrieved 19 02 2019, from http://ec.europa.eu/commfrontoffice/publicopinion/flash/fl_216_en.pdf.

European Commission. (2010). *Flash Eurobarometer 306: The euro area, 2010 – Public attitudes and perceptions: Analytical report.* European Commission. Retrieved 19 02 2019, from http://ec.europa.eu/commfrontoffice/publicopinion/flash/fl_306_en.pdf.

European Commission. (2012). *Flash Eurobarometer 362.* European Commission. Retrieved 19 02 2019, from http://ec.europa.eu/commfrontoffice/publicopinion/flash/fl_362_en.pdf.

Farrell, C. (2017). *Deprivation*. Retrieved 19 06 2017, from Publicpolicy.ie: www.publicpolicy.ie/wp-content/uploads/deprivation.pdf.

Government of Ireland. (2010). *National Recovery Plan, 2011–2014*. Dublin: Government of Ireland. Retrieved from www.budget.gov.ie/The%20National%20Recovery%20Plan%202011-2014.pdf.

Government of Ireland. (2011). *Programme for Government: Statement of Common Purpose*. Government of Ireland. Retrieved 19 02 2019, from www.taoiseach.gov.ie/eng/Work_Of_The_Department/Programme_for_Government/Programme_for_Government_2011-2016.pdf.

Hall, P. A., & Soskice, D. (2001). *Varieties of Capitalism: The Institutional Foundations of Comparative Advantage*. Oxford: Oxford University Press.

Hardiman, N. (2015, October). *Tracking the State in a Liberal Economy*. Retrieved from University College Dublin: www.ucd.ie/t4cms/Hardiman,%20Tracking%20the%20State%20in%20a%20Liberal%20Economy.%20GFG,%20Oct%202015.pdf.

IDA Ireland. (2018, 03 01). *Annual Report and Accounts for 2017*. Dublin: IDA Ireland. Retrieved 18 06 2017, from IDA Ireland: www.idaireland.com/newsroom/fdi-employment-hits-new-l/index.xml.

IMF. (2016, July). Ireland – Financial Stability Assessment. *IMF Country Reports, 16*(258).

IMF. (2016, September). Ireland, Financial Sector Assessment Programme, Technical Note – Financial Safety Net, Bank Resolution and Crisis Management. *IMF Country Reports, 16*(313).

Independent Evaluation Office of the IMF. (2016). *The IMF and the Crises in Greece, Ireland and Portugal*. Government of Ireland. Washington, DC: IMF.

Kelly, J. (2006). The Net Worth of Irish Households. *Central Bank Quarterly Journal, 2006*(3).

Kennedy, S., Jin, J., Haugh, D., & Lenain, P. (2015). Taxes, Income and Economic Mobility in Ireland. *OECD Economics Department Working Papers*(1269).

Kopits, G. (2014, Spring). Ireland's Fiscal Framework: Options for the Future. *The Economic and Social Review*, *45*(1), 135–158.

Lydon, R., & McCann, F. (2017). The Income Distribution and the Irish Mortgage Market. *Central Bank of Ireland Economic Letter Series*(5). Retrieved 19 02 2019, from www.centralbank.ie/docs/default-source/publications/economic-letters/vol-2017-no-5-the-income-distribution-and-the-irish-mortgage-market.pdf?sfvrsn=6.

Lydon, R., & McIndoe-Calder, T. (2017, May). The great Irish (de)leveraging 2005–14. *ECB Working Paper Series*(2062).

McAnn, F., & McIndoe-Calder, T. (2015, Spring). Irish SME Property Exposure: What Do We Know. *The Economic and Social Review*, *46*(1), 119–132.

O'Donnell, R. (1998, December). Ireland's Economic Transformation: Industrial Policy, European Integration and Social Partnership. *University of Pittsburgh, Centre for West European Studies, Working Paper series*.

OECD. (2015). *OECD Economic Surveys: Ireland 2015*. Paris: OECD. Retrieved 14 03 2019, from https://doi.org/10.1787/eco_surveys-irl-2015-en.

OECD. (2019, 19 02). *Household Spending*. Retrieved from OECD: https://data.oecd.org/hha/household-spending.htm#indicator-chart.

O'Leary, J. (2018). *How (not) to do public policy*. Galway: Whitaker Institute, NUI Galway.

Quinn, R. (1996, 21 09). Remarks to RTE (Irish Television). *RTE News Report*. (G. Lee, Interviewer) Retrieved 19 02 2019, from www.rte.ie/archives/category/business/2016/0920/817906-single-currency.

Regan, A., & Brazys, S. (2017, 01 12). Celtic Phoenix or Leprechaun Economics? The Politics of an FDI Led Growth Model in Europe. *UCD Geary Institute for Public Policy Discussion Paper Series, 2017*(01).

Rob Wright, H. B. (2010). *Strengthening the Capacity of the Department of Finance ('the Wright Report')*. Dublin: Department of Finance.

Smyth, D. (2017, 25 05). *The Recovery in the Public Finances of Ireland following the Financial Crisis, Paper presented to the Statistical and Social Inquiry Society of Ireland.* Retrieved 06 18, 2017, from Statistical and Social Inquiry Society of Ireland: www.ssisi.ie/Public_Finances_and_the_Crisis_in_Ireland_v1_8.pdf.

Teague, P., & Donaghey, J. (2015). The Life and Death of Irish Social Partnership: Lessons for Social Pacts. *Business History*, *57*(3), 418–437.

Whelan, K. (2013, 11 02). *Ireland's Promissory Note Deal*. Retrieved 18 06 2017, from Forbes: www.forbes.com/sites/karlwhelan/3013/02/11/irelands-promissory-note-deal.

White, R., & Casey, E. (2013, 07 02). *Promissory Note Transaction*. Retrieved 18 06 2017, from National Treasury Management Agency: www.ntma.ie/download/investor_presentation/PromissoryNoteTransaction070213.pdf.

Wickham, J. (2017). *Cherishing All Equally 2017.* Dublin: TASC.

6 Portugal's adjustment program

The run-up to the sovereign debt crisis, program design, implementation and legacy

Francisco Torres and
Miguel Lebre de Freitas

Introduction

In Portugal, the 2008 financial crisis was less of a bursting bubble type of shock than in other Eurozone countries like Ireland or Spain. The Portuguese economy had been suffering from very poor growth and increasing unemployment at least from 2002. Since EMU's inception, Portugal did not breach the 3 percent threshold of the Stability and Growth Pact (SGP) only in 1999 and 2007. The crisis hit the country after a long period of (slow and partial) fiscal adjustment. Following in the footsteps of Greece and Ireland, Portugal was shut out from external financing in the sovereign debt crisis and in April 2011 the Government was forced to ask for financial assistance.

The European institutions saw the bailout as an opportunity for Portugal to implement long-overdue structural reforms. The program encompassed three pillars: structural reforms to boost potential growth and improve competitiveness; a fiscal consolidation strategy, supported by structural measures; and a banking sector strategy based on recapitalization and deleveraging.

The issue of Portugal's adjustment program raises a number of pertinent questions, which this chapter aims to address. To start with, what were the factors that forced Portugal to ask for financial assistance? And how did the initially (relatively high) political consensus and low levels of contestation, an indication that there was a general understanding that the country had to go through some adjustment, give way to a more widespread opposition to the reforms and to reform fatigue well before the end of the program? What were the program's main achievements and failures and its social costs? If and how did the program alter the economic structure and the political landscape in Portugal? What is the impact of the different policy stance adopted in the post-bailout period, with some reforms having not been pursued or even reversed?

The chapter is structured as follows. The second section sets the stage by briefly examining Portugal's initial phase of adjustment within the Euro between 1999 and 2007 and by providing a description of the country's attempt to respond to the twin (global financial and sovereign debt) crises in 2008–2011. The third section reviews the design and implementation of Portugal's adjustment program and the return to the markets and program exit. The fourth section analyzes the bailout program's main achievements, failures and social costs. The fifth section explains how the loss of political ownership and reform fatigue came about in the implementation phase. The sixth section assesses the post-program period (2014–2018), characterized by a low reform effort while Portugal abided (by and large) by its fiscal commitments. The seventh section discusses the pre-conditions for sustained structural change versus short-term adjustment. The final section concludes.

The pre-bailout period: the boom, the slump and the crisis (1999–2011)

The boom followed by the slump (1999–2007)

At the time when Portugal joined the European Community (EC) in 1986, the Portuguese economy was characterized by extensive financial repression (Beleza and Macedo, 1991; Torres, 1990). In 1992, just before the launch of the Single Market, however, a significant (regime) change occurred: from discretion to rules and from capital controls to free capital mobility (Torres, 1998: 176). On 6 April of that year, during (and probably also thanks to) the Portuguese presidency of the European Council, the escudo joined the exchange rate mechanism of the European Monetary System (EMS). That decision also marked an important change of attitude toward a more open and constructive political stance vis-à-vis the process of European integration (Torres, 1998: 176). Complete liberalization of international capital flows (the return to full currency convertibility) was also achieved in 1992 ahead of schedule (Portugal had been granted a derogation until 1996). Thereafter, the inflation rate declined and the government increased its reliance on market financing, which opened a window for banks to lend to the private sector.

In 1999, Portugal became a founding member of the European Economic and Monetary Union (EMU). However, in a way it fell victim to its success (Torres, 2009). Apart from an initial impetus to comply with EMU entry criteria, the anticipation of EMU benefits took away pressure for further reforms (Torres, 2007), in particular with regard to the need for improving fiscal governance (EC, 2008a). Being part of (protected by) EMU, therefore, further anesthetized Portugal's capacity to implement reforms.

Already during the convergence phase, in the late 1990s, the expected positive wealth effects of EMU, associated with the decline in interest rates, gave a significant boost to domestic demand (Blanchard and Giavazzi, 2002). On the other hand, the elimination of the exchange rate risk and the easing of constraints in regard to the external financing of domestic credit operations by the banking sector allowed for a substantially higher indebtedness of households and non-financial enterprises.[1] The Portuguese financial sector, which had been progressively liberalized since the mid-1980s and held to be well capitalized (EC, 2004), was able to sustain the expansion in domestic credit. However, the growth in bank loan portfolios outpaced the growth in domestic deposits, so that the credit boom was financed substantially by the external sector. The current account deficit rose steadily to 10.8 percent of GDP in 2000, implying a significant deterioration of the net international investment position (NIIP), from –13 percent of GDP in 1996 to –42 percent in 2000.

Given the continuation of this trend (massive capital inflows and easy access to external credit, intermediated by domestic banks), a substantial "expenditure effect" materialized, whereby the increase in aggregate demand translated into an increase in the relative price of non-tradable goods and a reallocation of production away from tradables. Between 1995 and 2003 the real exchange rate based on unit labor costs (ULC-based RER) relative to the rest of the EU15 appreciated by almost 15 percent. Throughout this period, resources were not necessarily put to the most productive use but invested in non-tradable "less productive and more protected industries" (Reis, 2013: 146, 2015: 443) and also in non-priority (and non-sustainability enhancing) infrastructures ("wrong investment projects", in the words of Blanchard and Portugal, 2017).

During this period budgetary policy was mostly pro-cyclical and failed to attain the SGP's medium-term objective of a balanced budget. As argued in Torres (2007), EMU had not been presented as a desirable political reform, being instead perceived as an external constraint – the need to remain in the first tier of EU integration. That circumstance might also explain a budgetary reactive policy stance, translating into the need to comply with EMU entry criteria, and eventually with the SGP's public deficit threshold when the Excessive Deficit Procedure (EDP) applies, while there is no pressure to take action when there is an easing of borrowing constraints.

Arguably, accountancy issues, rather than fundamental concerns, drove much of the policy decisions at that time. The increasing reliance on public-private partnerships (PPPs) and other contingent liabilities through state-owned enterprises (SOEs), together with weak control over local governments' and autonomous bodies' debt, are revealing in this respect. Still, thanks to the favorable borrowing conditions and real GDP growth above 3 percent, the "snowball effect" remained basically negative and the government debt-to-GDP ratio declined from 58.3 percent in 1995 to 50.3 percent in 2000 (Table 6.1).[2]

In contrast to Greece, Ireland or Spain, all of which grew significantly until 2007, the boom was much shorter and was followed by a slump after 2001, leading to what became known as the "difficult adjustment within the euro" (Blanchard, 2007). Ever since, the Portuguese economy has been one of the poorest performers among EU member states in terms of economic growth, only comparable to Italy's. Real convergence toward the EU-15/EU-27 averages was interrupted (Tables 6.1 and 6.2).[3] This interruption was to be protracted by the financial and sovereign debt crises and the bailout program.

The poor growth performance after 2001 led to a steady increase in unemployment. Nevertheless, inflation stayed significantly above the euro area average, reflecting the continuous inflow of capital. The current account deficit remained high (and did not fall much below 10 percent of GDP) despite the long economic downturn.[4]

In 2001, the general government deficit had risen to 4.8 percent of GDP. The government was forced to take some pro-cyclical one-off measures in an attempt to bring it below the 3 percent threshold. As the European Commission (2008a) stressed, the medium-term budgetary plans remained a moving target. There were successive updates of the stability programs and frequent one-off measures to reduce the deficit, even though the latter never went below the 3 percent limit. Both the general government deficit and the structural adjusted deficit deteriorated significantly in 2004 and 2005, leading to a steady increase in public debt (EC, 2008a). Fiscal governance had not improved.[5]

In 2006, the budgetary consolidation process was slowly taken up again (although with a significant amount of expenditures left out of the state perimeter through SOEs and PPPs) by the new Socialist majority government (led by Prime Minister José Sócrates), which had been elected in 2005.[6] By 2007 the government deficit had eventually converged to the SGP threshold of 3 percent, which in turn led to the closure of the EDP in 2008.

On the financial front, Portuguese banks seemed to have adapted successfully to the new competitive and macroeconomic environment (EC, 2004). Having consolidated and improved efficiency during the second half of the 1990s, they managed to remain profitable and with sound solvency ratios during the 2001–2006 downturn (credit continued to grow faster than income and deposits). The main causes for concern resided in the exposure to the real-estate sector, the large external debt and the very high level of indebtedness of the private sector that reached 185 percent of GDP in 2007. The main (systemic) Portuguese banks seemed not to be particularly exposed to the so-called financial toxic assets, unlike in Ireland or Spain. In Portugal, there was no speculative bubble in the housing market, nor was there a subprime segment in the credit to the housing sector (Banco de Portugal, 2008). The banking system had, however, become highly leveraged, with the loan-to-deposits ratio reaching 160 percent in 2007 (Table 6.2). As pointed out in various program evaluations, all those developments signaled a deterioration in credit underwriting standards before the crisis and, according to Véron (2016: 22 and 24), complex governance structures and supervisory weakness.

In 2007, just before the eruption of the financial crisis, Portugal was not only in external imbalance but also in internal imbalance, with the unemployment rate peaking at 9.1 percent (Table 6.1).

Furthermore, public debt as a percentage of GDP had increased from 53.4 percent in 2001 to 68.4 percent in 2007. Over this period, household savings continued to decline, driving up the consolidated private sector debt to 185 percent of GDP in 2007 despite a fall in investment. In this phase, both the private sector and the government sector contributed to the deterioration of the country's NIIP (Table 6.1).[7]

Table 6.1 Portuguese macroeconomic indicators, 1995–2007 (boom and slump)

		1995	*1996*	*1997*	*1998*	*1999*	*2000*	*2001*	*2002*	*2003*	*2004*	*2005*	*2006*	*2007*
Real GDP growth	% ch	2.3	3.5	4.4	4.8	3.9	3.8	1.9	0.8	–0.9	1.8	0.8	1.6	2.5
Relative to rest of EU 15	% ch	–0.2	1.6	1.4	1.6	0.6	–0.1	–0.4	–0.6	–2.1	–0.6	–1.4	–1.7	–0.6
GNI at current PPS per head of population	PPS, EU = 100	69.0	68.6	69.2	70.0	71.7	70.6	69.9	70.3	70.9	69.7	71.5	70.7	70.3
TFP growth	% ch	1.7	1.2	1.2	1.2	1.0	0.6	–0.8	–0.8	–1.3	1.3	0.2	0.5	1.6
Output gap	%	–1.1	–0.4	0.8	1.9	2.4	2.9	2.0	0.7	–1.6	–1.0	–1.1	–0.4	1.3
Employment	% ch	NA	1.8	2.7	2.8	1.6	2.3	1.7	0.3	–1.0	–0.6	–0.3	0.6	0.3
Unemployment rate (total)	%	7.9	8.0	7.5	6.1	5.5	5.1	5.1	6.2	7.4	7.8	8.8	8.9	9.1
Of which: share of long-term	%	NA	NA	NA	38.9	38.9	43.0	34.7	32.3	38.5	45.4	49.2	50.1	47.3
GDP deflator	% change	5.6	2.4	3.9	3.8	3.4	3.5	3.7	4.2	3.4	2.4	3.3	3.2	3.0
CPI inflation	% change	4.0	2.9	1.9	2.2	2.2	2.8	4.4	3.7	3.2	2.5	2.1	3.0	2.4
Nominal compensation per employee	% ch	10.3	6.1	5.7	5.9	5.1	6.0	4.2	3.6	3.6	2.8	4.7	1.8	3.5
Nominal ULC (total economy)	% ch	7.0	4.3	3.9	3.9	2.8	4.4	4.0	3.2	3.6	0.2	3.4	0.7	1.0
RER ULC (relative to EU 15)	1995 = 100	100	103	104	106	107	108	111	112	114.7	113	115	114	113
Exports of goods and services	% ch	13.6	5.9	7.4	8.0	3.6	8.4	2.3	3.1	3.3	4.5	0.5	12.4	7.3
Imports of goods and services	% ch	9.4	5.9	10.4	14.7	9.1	5.5	1.1	–0.2	–0.4	7.6	2.2	7.5	5.4

Current account	% of GDP	NA	–4.5	–6.2	–7.5	–8.9	–10.8	–10.4	–8.5	–7.2	–8.3	–9.9	–10.7	–9.7
Household savings rate	% disp. Inc.	12.5	11.4	10.9	12.0	11.4	10.5	11.0	10.9	10.0	10.0	9.2	8.0	7.0
Gross fixed capital formation	% of GDP	23.3	23.8	26.0	27.3	27.6	28.0	27.4	25.8	23.7	23.4	23.1	22.5	22.5
Of which: private sector	% of GDP	19.8	19.5	20.9	23.2	24.1	24.2	23.1	21.4	19.3	19.7	19.6	19.9	19.9
Government: net lending	% of GDP	–5.2	–4.7	–3.7	–4.4	–3.0	–3.2	–4.8	–3.3	–4.4	–6.2	–6.2	–4.3	–3.0
General government primary balance (cycl.adj.)	% pot. GDP	0.7	0.2	–0.1	–1.9	–1.0	–1.3	–2.8	–0.9	–1.0	–3.1	–3.1	–1.3	–0.7
(diff. relative to previous year)	% pot. GDP	–	–0.5	–0.4	(1.8)	1.0	(0.3)	(1.5)	1.9	(0.1)	(2.2)	0.1	1.7	0.6
Private sector debt, consolidated (MIP)	% of GDP	81.5	87.9	94.4	108.9	124.5	137.1	149.8	155.9	162	165.8	171.4	176.5	185
Gen. government consolidated gross debt	% of GDP	58.3	59.5	55.2	51.8	51.0	50.3	53.4	56.2	58.7	62.0	67.4	69.2	68.4
Government bond yields	%	11.5	8.6	6.4	4.9	4.8	5.6	5.2	5.0	4.2	4.1	3.4	3.9	4.4
Implicit Int. rate on gov. debt	%	n.d.	8.8	7.0	6.2	6.1	6.3	6.3	5.6	4.8	4.5	4.3	4.3	4.5
Net International Investment Position	% of GDP	n.d.	–12.9	–14.8	–24.4	–34	–41.5	–49	–58.4	–62.4	–66.7	–69.9	–79.3	–88.8
Overdue credit (households)	%, e.o.p.	n.d.	n.d.	3.2	2.5	2.1	1.8	2.0	2.1	2.4	2.2	2.0	1.7	1.7
Overdue credit (NF corporations)	%, e.o.p.	n.d.	n.d.	6.4	4.7	3.2	2.5	2.4	2.4	2.1	1.7	1.7	1.5	1.5

Sources: AMECO, Bank of Portugal, Eurostat.

Crises and policy responses (2008–2011)

The global financial crisis

Before the eruption of the financial crisis, the Portuguese economy had been suffering from very poor growth at least from 2002, unlike the Greek, Irish and Spanish economies (Pagoulatos; Cardiff; Royo and Steinberg; this volume), which had been booming until then.

Portugal had breached the 3 percent threshold of the SGP almost every year since EMU's inception. EU pressure had led to some pro-cyclical fiscal adjustment within a phase of low growth and, as referred to above, the EDP was closed in 2008. It was hence after a phase of (albeit slow and partial) fiscal adjustment that Portugal was caught in the financial crisis.

The crisis brought back the long-forgotten external (borrowing) constraints. Although not directly impacted by the global financial crisis, Portugal was badly hit by the collapse of world trade that followed: in 2009 exports of goods and services fell by over 10 percent and GDP fell by 3 percent.[8]

In 2008, the Government had to step in to support two small national banks, with market shares of around 2 percent each, Banco Português de Negócios (BPN), and Banco Privado Português (BPP); the nationalization of BPN and the state guarantee to BPP were justified on the grounds of safeguarding the deposits held by those institutions and avoiding a bank run. These interventions generated a significant political debate on the role of the government and the responsibilities of the banking supervisory authorities and also on the redistribution effects of rescuing banks. This debate would continue during the bailout program and its aftermath, with the recapitalization of major banks and the failure of Banco Espírito Santo (BES) in 2014, one of the country's four major banks. These episodes marked the beginning of a new phase of public distrust in national (and European) institutions (Eurobarometer), the political establishment and the financial sector in particular.[9]

Since 2008, against the background of the freeze in interbank money markets, the Portuguese banks had come to rely on European Central Bank (ECB) loans (Table 6.2). In January 2009, following the financial downgrades of Greece and Spain, Portugal became the third Eurozone economy that suffered from a reduction of its long-term credit rating (by Standard & Poor's) on the grounds of "its failure to tackle deteriorating public finances". These downgrades followed the increase of sovereign debt yields within the Eurozone, reflecting higher risk perceptions regarding solvency. With the rise in yields, a vicious circle emerged, as the costs of servicing the debt augmented. Moreover, as banks held sovereign bonds, the value of their portfolios fell (feedback loop effects from sovereign risk into bank risk), augmenting the risk that governments would need more money to help them out, thereby impacting on sovereign yields.

The Council of the EU approved Portugal's 2009 update of the stability program on 10 March 2009. Still, it was noted (EC, 2009 and Council of the EU, 2009) that fiscal consolidation measures were insufficient, that the competitiveness gap remained a major weakness and that weak economic growth could not underpin fiscal consolidation as envisaged.

In 2009, there was wide EU and international support for a coordinated fiscal expansion, albeit only for the countries with the necessary fiscal space to do so.[10] In Portugal, the fact that the EDP had been closed in 2008 may have given the government the illusion of some margin of maneuver for a fiscal expansion in 2009, which would be particularly convenient in a year of general elections.

The government re-focused its economic policy onto mitigation of the crisis effects, with support for investment and other measures such as protecting employment and strengthening social protection (MFAP, 2008, 2009). Also, in 2009 real wages grew as opposed to the three previous years. In the event, the incumbent government of Partido Socialista (PS) still won the 2009 elections but lost its absolute majority of seats in parliament.

In 2009–2010 there was a significant fiscal expansion: the fiscal deficit rose from 3.8 percent of GDP in 2008 to 9.8 percent in 2009 and 11.2 percent in 2010 and the public debt to GDP ratio increased sharply from 71.7 percent in 2008 to 96.2 percent in 2010, also reflecting the output contraction.[11] In 2010, the country's NIIP was already –104.3 percent of GDP, which meant a heavy reliance on external funding and increased vulnerability to sudden stops in capital inflows.[12]

In a context of uncertainty regarding the sustainability of government finances, as was the case of the sovereign debt crisis, fiscal expansion may be counterproductive. Given the country's fragile financial position, and the risks involved with regard to the costs of servicing the debt, it would have been essential for the government to credibly pre-commit to medium-term budgetary objectives with accelerated corrective measures to ensure that the temporary fiscal expansion would not mark a departure from fiscal sustainability (Torres, 2009).

The sovereign debt crisis

With the eruption of the sovereign debt crisis, spreads on government bonds widened and the country's ratings were downgraded several times. There was also a rise in credit default swaps (CDS) for main banks, which, as a result, became dependent on the Eurosystem for financing. It became clear at the outset of the crisis that the banking sector was vulnerable.

In March 2011 the main credit rating agencies (Moody's, S&P and Fitch) downgraded Portugal's sovereign rating. An updated Stability Program with further adjustment in 2012–2013 was rejected by parliament, and the government resigned.[13] Spreads rose to more than 500 basis points in early April, further credit downgrades took place and Portugal was shut out from external financing. During this period, the government became increasingly reliant on borrowing from domestic banks, but the latter were facing their own liquidity problems, and put pressure on the government to request financial assistance. On 7 April 2011, the Government asked for financial assistance from the European Financial Stabilization Mechanism (EFSM) and the European Financial Stability Facility (EFSF), totaling €52 billion, and from the IMF, amounting to €26 billion.

The bailout period (2011–2014)

The design of the conditionality program

The European institutions saw the bailout as an opportunity for Portugal to implement long-overdue structural reforms that typically lack social support. For that reason, the program was not designed as a mere two-year stand-by arrangement but rather as an Extended Fund Facility (EFF)-supported program, with a scope that went far beyond the typical areas of macroeconomic stabilization (Eichenbaum et al., 2016: 29; see also Lütz et al., this volume).

The program's strategy envisaged a return to the markets within two years. It was based on the following three pillars:

1. Structural reforms to boost potential growth and improve competitiveness, viewed as an opportunity to address reforms (notably in the labor and product markets) that had not been implemented before the crises;
2. A fiscal consolidation strategy, to be achieved mainly (by about two thirds) through expenditure cuts and to a lesser extent (by about one third) through tax increases, and supported by structural fiscal measures, such as improvements in the tax administration, on spending procedures, and better fiscal control over PPPs and SOEs;
3. A banking sector strategy based on recapitalization and deleveraging, with a capital backstop for banks of 12 billion euro by the Bank Solvency Support Facility (BSSF).

The Troika (the European Commission, the ECB and the IMF) ensured the support for key program parameters from the three major political parties: the PS, in government, and the Partido Social Democrata (PSD) and Centro Democrático e Social – Partido Popular (CDS), which formed the center-right opposition (both parties are members of the European People's Party) (Box 6.1).

Box 6.1 The economic adjustment program

Agreed: 3 May 2011.
PM: José Sócrates. PS until June 2011; Passos Coelho, PSD until end of program.
Tenure: May 2011 to June 2014.
Size: €78 billion, including €12 billion to be used in the financial sector.
Contributors: EFSF (€26 billion), EFSM (€26 billion), IMF/EFF (€26 billion).
Objectives: Restore Portugal's credibility for private investors and promote long-term growth.

Main areas of intervention

- Frontload fiscal adjustment, reducing the fiscal deficit to 3 percent of GDP in 2013

- Fiscal-structural consolidation, improving the efficiency of the public administration and entities, streamlining the budgetary process, strengthening risk management and accountability
- Ensure financial sector stability, improve regulation and supervision
- Promote adaptability in the labor market, eliminating rigidities while strengthening safety nets
- Promote efficiency and competition in the product market, with specific measures for the energy sector, telecommunications and postal services, transport; elimination of entry barriers in other services and regulated professions; promote mobility in the house rental market
- Reforms of the judicial system, facilitate out-of-court settlements

Status: *The government opted not to complete the final review of the bailout and to forgo the last tranche of the program that amounted to €2.6 billion.*

The competitiveness agenda included upgrading the regulatory framework, divesting SOEs, fostering competition, reforming civil and commercial claims enforcement and improving labor market flexibility. Benchmarks included measures to reduce severance pay and amend the insolvency law, eliminate golden shares and revise the competition law. Some important reforms were chiefly spelled out in the Memorandum of Economic and Financial Policies (MEFP) rather than in the Memorandum of Understanding (MOU), notably reforms in product markets to open up professional services and reduce rents in energy, telecommunications and transport.[14]

While the program had relatively few quantitative performance criteria, it featured higher than average structural conditionality. It tried to combine upfront fiscal measures with upfront access to funds in order to address short-term financing needs with growth-supporting gradualism (IMF, 2017). Contrary to the case of Ireland, there were no frontloaded interventions to address the banking system vulnerabilities.[15] Targets for public debt and the current account deficit at the end of the program were 115 and 4 percent of GDP, respectively.

Program implementation

Structural reforms and competitiveness

The implementation of the structural reforms and competitiveness pillar of the program, which was rather large, was relatively frontloaded. It went relatively well, at least formally (IMF, 2017), since of the 60 structural measures specified over the course of the program, all except the fiscal devaluation (discussed below) were fulfilled (Eichenbaum et al., 2016).

As for the labor market, Portugal had managed in the years before the crisis to achieve significant progress as far as the regulation of collective lay-offs is concerned but with respect to individual lay-offs it was still ranking the worst performer in the OECD sample. During the bailout program, some significant reforms were successfully implemented: a lowering of severance pay (which had been one of the highest in Europe); a reduction in the maximum duration of unemployment benefits to 18 months; the introduction of a cap on unemployment benefits; working time flexibilization, through the adoption of a "bank of hours" negotiated at the plant level. However, the initial intention to limit the extensions of collective agreements to non-participating firms was reversed before the program's completion (IMF, 2015: 10). As for individual dismissals, the Constitutional Court ruled against a government initiative to relax employment protection in the cases of unsuitability or redundancy. In 2013, Portugal was still ranking last among OECD countries (Table 6.3), even though there had been some positive changes in the value of the indicator in absolute terms.

In Portugal, many product market reforms were still lagging before the crises. They encountered resistance from vested interests (electricity; transport; public sector). Portugal had been performing quite poorly in terms of product market regulation – according to the OECD's overall indicator, it ranked 24th in a sample of 29 countries in 2008. During the program, the main areas of intervention included increasing competition in non-tradable industries, including the electricity and gas markets, postal services, telecommunications, railways, ports, housing market, regulated professions and privatization. The framework law for the functioning of regulators was enacted, reinforcing the independence of sectoral regulators, and the competition law was strengthened. However, tackling rents in the non-tradable good sectors turned out to be more difficult than planned. In the electricity market, the government succeeded in phasing out regulated tariffs, but it fell short in terms of renegotiating high existing feed-in tariffs. In the ports sector, the failure to renegotiate existing concession contracts prevented the benefits from additional flexibility in work arrangements (achieved in the new Port Works Law) to pass through to final users in the form of lower prices (IMF, 2014). As for regulated professions, a new framework law was approved, but the adoption of new by-laws for the 18 professional bodies was delayed and not implemented before the program's completion (IMF, 2015). During the program period, the government gave up its golden shares and privatized airport infrastructures, ANA, the postal company, CTT, as well as the national electricity network, REN, and sold its remaining position in the electricity company, EDP, but it failed to privatize the state-owned rail cargo operator. The privatization of the national air carrier, TAP, was partly reversed after the PS government took charge in 2015. At least in the case of EDP (and possibly REN) and ANA, immediate revenue considerations came at the cost of excessive rents and monopoly rights. PPP contracts were renegotiated, mainly reducing the scope of investments. Other areas of reform include the introduction of out-of-court systems for corporate debt restructuring.

Fiscal policy

On the fiscal front, the government deficit went down from 11.2 percent in 2010 to 4.8 percent in 2013 of GDP. The size of the fiscal adjustment is, however, better measured by the cyclically adjusted primary balance that turned from a deficit of 8.3 percent in 2010 into a surplus of 2.1 percent in 2013 (Table 6.2). This was an impressive adjustment in the context of the Eurozone.

Fiscal targets had to be softened during the program's implementation. Already in 2011, there had been significant fiscal slippages on expenditure, including one-off support for SOEs (notably the recapitalization of BPN and of the state-owned Caixa Geral de Depósitos, CGD) and PPPs and some other more permanent ones.[16] The government then resorted to one-off measures on the revenue side. A temporary surcharge on 2011 personal income and the transfer of bank pension fund assets to the general government (that the Troika only allowed to occur once) more than compensated for one-off measures on the expenditure side.

Government spending was basically on track in 2012, thanks to a larger than planned fall in the number of public sector workers. The expenditure effort in 2012 also accounted for the suspension of the 13th and 14th month component of wages and pensions, which, however, only remained in place in 2012, given that the Constitutional Court reversed the measure for 2013. As a consequence, the wage bill and social expenditure increased in 2013. Despite measures directed at improving the targeting of social transfers and health sector and SOE reforms, the primary expenditure reached 45.1 percent of GDP. The Constitutional Court also overturned envisaged pension cuts and an extraordinary levy on unemployment and sickness benefits for 2014, which prompted the government to search for alternative measures with the same budgetary impact, albeit of lower quality. Apart from the above-mentioned one-off measures, on the revenue side, there was an increase of the value-added tax (VAT) base. However, the nominal revenue from indirect taxes actually decreased over 2011–2013 (due to the recession, the changing composition of production toward exports and the fall in imports), which obliged the government to resort in 2013 to a temporary surcharge and an increase in personal income taxes. This change of strategy extended the austerity measures beyond the more protected public sector to other groups already more penalized by the economic downturn and thus contributed to eroding public support for the program (Box 6.2).

Box 6.2 Constitutional court reversals of cost-cutting and flexibilization measures (13 out of 494 measures)

- July 2012 Rejected the **cut of the 13th and 14th month wage**
- April 2013 Rejected **cuts in 14th monthly wage to public servants and pensioners**
- April 2013 Rejected **cuts of 90 percent of the 13th and 14th month payment to pensioners**
- April 2013 Rejected the **5 percent cut in sick-leave subsidies**
- April 2013 Rejected the **6 percent cut in unemployment subsidies**
- Aug 2013 Rejected **proposal to re-qualify civil servants**
- Aug 2013 Rejected a **bill allowing the state to fire public sector workers**

- Sept 2013 Rejected **2012 reforms on eliminating jobs and firing unsuitable workers**
- Dec 2013 Rejected **equalization of pension benefits for contributors to CGA/SS**
- Dec 2013 Blocked **proposed cuts of up to 10 percent in civil service pensions**
- May 2014 Rejected **2014 budget cuts of 2–12 percent in civil service pay**
- May 2014 Rejected **amendment to formula for survivor dependants' pensions**
- May 2014 Rejected **extraordinary levy on unemployment and sickness subsidies**

Source: IMF Country Report No. 16/302, drawing on two other sources:
The Portuguese Crisis and the IMF, Eichenbaum et al., IEO, 2016;
The Economic Adjustment Programme for Portugal,
European Commission OP 202, 2014

In a context of increased social and political resistance to the program, the initially planned fiscal devaluation – which was to reduce reliance on social security contributions while offsetting revenue losses through higher VAT and expenditure cuts – was no longer feasible. Given low VAT revenues and slippages in expenditures, in September 2012, the government attempted to shift social security contributions from employers to employees. That move, after previous setbacks, generated widespread protests that led to the abandonment altogether of the fiscal devaluation plans.

After three years of implementation and in spite of an impressive adjustment in the government deficit in 2011 and 2012 (Table 6.2), the objectives of the fiscal consolidation agenda were nevertheless only insufficiently met. In addition, the program ended up relying mainly on tax increases (about two thirds) rather than on expenditure cuts (about one third).[17] Much of the latter was the result of wage repression and temporary savings, rather than reform of the public administration. With further reversals of measures in 2014 and uncertainty about future bank needs, the debt outlook remained fragile.

The banking sector

Financial conditionality was applied to implement the agenda to strengthen bank balance sheets and the legal framework for oversight and intervention. At the outset of the stabilization program, banks were overleveraged and dependent on the ECB for liquidity. After the long-term refinancing operations (LTRO) in December 2011, they had enough liquidity but insufficient capital to meet the tighter capital requirements defined by the European Banking Authority (EBA).[18] With low capital relative to the more demanding adequacy ratios, banks had to downsize their assets, which meant less credit for the economy, affecting small- and medium-sized enterprises (SMEs) most. In June 2012, a major bank recapitalization through the emission of contingent convertible bonds (CoCos) was implemented. Millennium Banco Comercial Português (BCP) and Banco Português de Investimento (BPI) used funds provided by the BSSF[19] while CGD relied on the government budget. Only BES, the third largest bank in Portugal, did not request state funding. Recapitalization helped banks to meet capital requirements but, as they were still struggling with high levels of NPL, credit to the economy did not recover immediately.

In 2013, several banks returned to debt markets and dependence on ECB funding started to decline (Table 6.2). Yet, limits to capital increases through shareholders were still binding because bank profitability had stagnated, credit had contracted dramatically and overdue credit (non-financial corporations) had risen sharply (Table 6.2). In a context of significant bank deleveraging (the loan-to-deposits ratio decreased to less than 100 percent in 2015), financial stability was maintained and some reforms were enacted but, as stressed by Véron (2016: 27), the program did not sufficiently address important banking system vulnerabilities. The overdue credit to non-financial corporate firms increased significantly along the adjustment period (from 6.0 percent in 2011 to 14.2 in 2014, reaching its peak in 2015; Table 6.2). Banks also delayed loan restructuring given that their capacity to absorb losses was limited.

Return to the markets, exiting the program and post-program surveillance

Already in January 2013 Portugal successfully floated a five-year (syndicated) bond, followed by a 10-year bond in May 2013, a five-year bond in January 2014 and a 10-year bond in April 2014, just before exiting the program. With financing conditions increasingly favorable, rising opposition to the program and some reform fatigue, the government opted for letting the arrangement expire without trying to find additional measures required to complete the final review. In July 2014 Moody's upgraded Portugal's government bond rating to Ba1 from Ba2.

As the European Commission (EC, 2016) put it, "In June 2014, Portugal exited its three-year economic adjustment program which included the implementation of an ambitious reform agenda and contributed to regaining economic growth and restoring investor confidence". Since then Portugal has been and will be under post-program surveillance (PPS) until it has repaid at least 75 percent of the received financial assistance (to the EFSM and the EFSF). Post-program surveillance consists in a broad monitoring of the economic, fiscal and financial conditions with a view to assessing repayment capacity. There is no policy conditionality but the Council can issue recommendations for corrective actions. Of course, the country is also under the Macroeconomic Imbalances Procedure (MIP) surveillance mechanism and the European Semester.

Portugal was supposed to start repaying its debt to the IMF only in 2019 but the country anticipated a first reimbursement to January 2015, taking advantage of lower market rates. The new PS government pursued this strategy and by December 2018 it had fully reimbursed the IMF loan. The early repayment of

Table 6.2 Portuguese macroeconomic indicators, 2007–2018 (the crises, the program and PPS)

		2007	*2008*	*2009*	*2010*	*2011*	*2012*	*2013*	*2014*	*2015*	*2016*	*2017*	*2018*
Real GDP growth	% ch	2.5	0.2	–3.0	1.9	–1.8	–4.0	–1.1	0.9	1.8	1.9	2.8	2.2
Relative to rest of EU 15	% ch	–0.6	–0.3	1.3	0.0	–3.2	–3.3	–1.0	–0.7	–0.5	–0.2	0.4	0.1
GNI at current PPS per head of population	PPS, EU = 100	70.3	70.1	71.4	71.6	68.6	66.7	68.9	69.0	68.8	70.0	70.0	70.7
TFP growth	% ch	1.6	–0.8	–1.8	2.4	–0.7	–1.2	1.0	0.3	1.2	1.1	0.8	0.8
Output gap	%	1.3	0.9	(1.9)	0.0	(1.2)	(3.9)	(4.1)	(3.1)	(1.7)	(0.7)	0.7	1.2
Employment	% ch	0.3	0.5	–2.9	–1.4	–2.3	–4.0	–2.7	1.5	1.2	1.5	3.4	2.2
Unemployment rate	%	9.1	8.8	10.7	12.0	12.9	15.8	16.4	14.1	12.6	11.2	9.0	7.1
Of which: share of long-term	%	47.3	44.2	47.8	52.4	47.4	51.2	58.0	59.3	56.8	55.2	46.5	40.6
GDP deflator	% change	3.0	1.7	1.1	0.6	–0.3	–0.4	2.3	0.8	2.0	1.8	1.5	1.4
CPI inflation	% change	2.4	2.7	–0.9	1.4	3.6	2.8	0.4	–0.2	0.5	0.6	1.6	1.5
Nominal compensation per employee	% ch	3.5	2.6	2.4	2.1	–1.8	–3.1	3.6	–1.8	0.4	1.7	1.6	1.8
Nominal ULC (total economy)	% ch	1.0	2.8	2.7	–1.2	–2.0	–3.2	1.8	–1.3	0.0	1.4	2.1	1.8
RER ULC (relative to EU 15)	1995=100	113	113	113	112	109	104	105	103	102	104	106	106
Exports of goods and services	% ch	7.3	–0.3	–10.2	9.5	7.0	3.4	7.0	4.3	6.1	4.4	7.8	5.5

Imports of goods and services	% ch	5.4	2.5	–9.9	7.8	–5.8	–6.3	4.7	7.8	8.5	4.7	8.1	6.0
Current account	% of GDP	–9.7	–12.1	–10.4	–10.1	–6.0	–1.8	1.6	0.1	0.1	0.6	0.5	0.2
Household savings rate	% disp. Inc.	7.0	6.8	10.4	9.2	7.5	7.7	7.8	5.2	5.3	5.0	4.7	4.6
Gross fixed capital formation	% of GDP	22.5	22.8	21.1	20.5	18.4	15.8	14.8	15.0	15.5	15.5	16.7	17.1
Of which: private sector	% of GDP	19.9	19.8	16.7	15.8	15.1	13.2	12.4	13.3	13.5	14.2	15.0	15.2
Gen. government: net lending	% of GDP	–3.0	–3.8	–9.8	–11.2	–7.4	–5.7	–4.8	–7.2	–4.4	–2.0	–3.0	–0.7
Gen. government primary balance (cycl.adj.)	% pot. GDP	–0.7	–1.1	–5.9	–8.3	–2.5	1.2	2.1	–0.7	1.0	2.5	0.5	2.1
Gen. government struct. balance (cycl. adj.)	% pot. GDP	NA	NA	NA	–8.5	–6.7	–3.6	–3.0	–1.8	–2.3	–2.1	–1.3	–0.9
(diff. relative to previous year)	% pot. GDP	NA	NA	NA	NA	1.8	3.0	0.6	1.3	(0.5)	0.2	0.8	0.4
Gen. govern. prim. struct. bal. (cycl. adj.)	% pot. GDP	NA	NA	NA	–5.6	–2.3	1.3	1.8	3.1	2.3	2.1	2.5	2.5
(diff. relative to previous year)	% pot. GDP	NA	NA	NA	NA	3.2	3.6	0.6	1.3	(0.9)	(0.2)	0.4	(0.0)
Private sector debt, consolidated (MIP)	% of GDP	185.0	196.2	204.2	201.5	204.1	210.3	202.4	190.5	179.4	170.3	163.5	NA
Gen. government consolidated gross debt	% of GDP	68.4	71.7	83.6	96.2	111.4	126.2	129.0	130.6	128.8	129.2	124.8	121.5

continued

Table 6.2 Continued

		2007	2008	2009	2010	2011	2012	2013	2014	2015	2016	2017	2018
Government bond yields	%	4.4	4.5	4.2	5.4	10.2	10.6	6.3	3.8	2.4	3.2	3.1	NA
Implicit int. rate on gov. debt	%	4.5	4.6	4.1	3.6	4.4	4.2	3.9	3.9	3.6	3.4	3.1	NA
Net International Investment Position	% of GDP	–88.8	–95.1	–107.9	–104.3	–100.7	–116.5	–116.3	–118.6	–113.2	–106.1	–105.7	NA
Loans to deposits	ratio	160.1	160.3	161.5	157.8	140.2	127.9	111.8	102.1	96.1	95.3	94.0	NA
Overdue credit (households)	%, e.o.p.	1.7	2.2	2.7	2.8	3.3	3.8	4	4.3	4.2	3.7	3.8	NA
Overdue credit (NF corporations)	%, e.o.p.	1.5	2.2	3.9	4.1	6.0	9.4	11.8	14.2	15.2	15.0	12.7	NA
ECB loans/liabilities	% of asset	1.3	3.0	3.8	9.3	9.9	11.4	11.2	7.9	7.0	6.4	6.3	NA
Funding from other banks	% of asset.	16.3	15.7	14.8	15.4	14.6	12.4	10.3	10.5	8.9	9.0	8.8	NA

Sources: AMECO, Bank of Portugal, Eurostat.

the IMF loan has allowed for the reduction of financing costs (by €1.6 billion, according to the Government) and has provided a positive signal for markets and creditors alike.[20]

Main achievements, failures and (social) costs

The bailout program for Portugal simultaneously aimed at the recovery of macroeconomic balances and the implementation of long-delayed growth-enhancing structural reforms. In the end, however, it turned out that the more visible achievements were the elimination of macroeconomic (flow) imbalances and the return to markets. In this respect, the program can be qualified as a success: the fiscal deficit was significantly reduced, the current account turned into balance and international market access was rapidly regained.

Debt stocks have gradually decreased albeit at a slow pace, with public debt stabilizing around 130 percent of GDP in 2013–2016 before starting to decline thereafter. Consolidated private sector debt fell below 2007 levels (185 percent of GDP) from its peak in 2012 (210.3 percent of GDP). Private sector deleveraging was mirrored by the above-mentioned fall in bank loan-to-deposits rates. The country's NIIP reached –118.6 percent of GDP in 2013 (its worst level) but, despite the valuation effects related to the decline in bond yields, has since then improved continuously to –105.7 in 2017, reflecting the emergence of small current account surpluses.

Most structural benchmarks (about 80 percent) were achieved on time and compliance was good. However, the fact that there were significant political obstacles to implementation meant that outcomes were mixed. The reform agenda was perhaps too wide to be successfully implemented with national ownership.[21] Adopting a country comparison perspective, the program implementation made it clear that it matters to have a good sequencing of reforms or to have the economy prepared for shocks. The case of Ireland (see Cardiff, this volume), which had performed relatively well under the Lisbon Strategy, is illustrative in that respect.

The economic downturn during the program's implementation phase was substantially larger than expected. It reflected much weaker external demand and a more pronounced and faster than anticipated deleveraging (because of the limited ability to borrow abroad), weighing on private consumption and investment. The restricted access to external finance helps to explain the much faster than expected current account adjustment.[22] In the context of adverse credit conditions, the fiscal multiplier turned out to be much larger than anticipated.

Fiscal structural adjustment

As for fiscal structural reforms, a number of improvements were achieved in the fiscal administration, increasing transparency and accountability, and giving the minister of finance more control over the various budgetary perimeters. The law to strengthen expenditure commitment controls that entered into force in 2012 is a milestone in this respect. Other improvements include a tighter control over SOEs and more rational prescription rules in the national health care system.

Nonetheless, the opportunity to implement a major reform in the public administration was missed. The program failed in its design since the very beginning in that it did not address a fundamental problem in the government sector, which is the inability to dismiss public servants, even in the cases of extinction or restructuring of administration services. Instead it relied on a slow reduction in the number of public employees, with a rule of only having one new hiring for every two retirees, which delivered lower spending but not necessarily an efficient allocation of resources. The plan envisaged the merging of services and the movement of civil servants across departments and ministries to save on the wage bill, often at the expense of entropy and demotivation, yet without solving a fundamental problem in the public administration, which resides in the lack of expertise in key areas and excess supply in other areas. That rigidity has prevented the government, against a background of fast technological change, from empowering the services with the required capabilities, delaying the process of modernization, and ultimately conditioning the effectiveness of the government in providing the economy with the right balance between the tax burden and the quality of public services.

In that context, much of the fiscal adjustment during the bailout period consisted in measures of expenditure repression, such as freezes on new hiring, horizontal wage cuts irrespective of performance, the freeze in career promotions and savings in social spending. Such an expenditure repression combined with an overall increase in tax rates and tax surcharges can hardly be qualified as a structural reform. Not surprisingly, when the economy started to recover and the fiscal position improved, the new government was urged by those with a stake in the budget to alleviate the repressed spending.

The financial sector

Most banks have been recapitalized and emerged from stabilization with much lower loan-to-deposit ratios. They also realized capital gains arising from the decline in government bond yields and the increase of real estate prices after 2014. However, because of the combination of high debt and low growth, there was a steady increase in the share of non-performing loans (NPLs; "overdue credit" in Table 6.2): from 2.2 percent in 2008 for both households and firms, to 4.2 percent for households and 15.2 percent for firms in 2015. Only in 2016 did the NPL ratios start to decline, as a result of the improvement in the general economic situation but also of the banks' efforts to finally clean up their respective balance sheets. By 2017 the European Commission was still concerned about the high level of NPLs and low profitability of Portuguese banks (EC, 2017).

As far as banking supervision is concerned, there was significant progress, with the Bank of Portugal becoming progressively more intrusive with respect to financial institutions' activities and balance sheets, and with the ECB stepping in as the main supervisory authority. Still, prior to and still during the program, supervision had been weak. The failures of two banks, BES and BANIF, just after the completion of the adjustment program revealed a still-lagging quality of surveillance. The government had to rescue BES at a cost of €4.4 billion (it was resolved by the central bank in August 2014) and a new bank, Novo Banco, was created in its place (its initial recapitalization – a one-off fiscal expenditure – amounted to 2.9 percent of GDP in 2014 alone) and BANIF required intervention at the end of 2015. Nevertheless, both throughout the crisis and during the post-crisis period aggregate deposits have remained stable.

Generally speaking, progress made in banking supervision is on the whole aligned with the steps undertaken at the EU level to build a banking union. It follows that it is hard to disentangle what the specific achievements of the bailout are in Portugal.

Competitiveness

The OECD's index of product market regulation is only available for 2008 and 2013, which makes it difficult to disentangle what was achieved along the program. Over this period, the general index improved from 1.69 to 1.29, denoting a climb to the 11th position in the OECD's 29-country ranking (Table 6.3). This move reflected improvements in positions in the "state control" (from 26th to 19th) and "barriers to entrepreneurship" (from 17th to 7th) dimensions, with no improvement, however, in the dimension "barriers to trade and investment". In the ranking on doing business, which is available on a yearly basis, perceptions regarding the Portuguese economy improved between 2011 and 2015 in two dimensions only, namely "dealing with construction permits", thanks to improvements in licensing procedures, and "getting credit". In terms of the "resolving insolvency" dimension, an area covered by the MoU, Portugal fell 10 positions in the ranking (Table 6.3). As for the quality of domestic competition, while more independence was given to the competition authority, which constitutes a positive development, Portugal maintains one of the most restrictive business services regulations in the EU, namely with remaining barriers to access to professions where, as recently pointed out by the European Commission (EC, 2017), reforms have been halted or even reversed.

The labor market saw the implementation of measures to allow for a better alignment of incentives with regard to unemployment benefits and the lowering of severance payments on new hires. However, the program did not deliver on a less segmented labor market than before. Portugal is still ranking last among the 34 OECD countries in terms of the strictness of employment protection on individual dismissals, and dismissals in the government sector remain virtually impossible. The preservation of a segmented labor market is not only socially unfair but it also undermines incentives, reducing the public administration's effectiveness and the economy's attractiveness for private investment as well as its ability to retain young skilled workers.

Table 6.3 Portuguese competitiveness indicators, 2008–2018

	Unit	*2008*	*2009*	*2010*	*2011*	*2012*	*2013*	*2014*	*2015*	*2016*	*2017*	*2018*
Strictness of employment protection												
Strictness of empl. protection – individual	Rank/34	34	34	34	34	34	34	NA	NA	NA	NA	NA
Strictness of empl. protection – collective	Rank/32	7	7	6	6	6	6	NA	NA	NA	NA	NA
Product market regulation												
Product market regulation	Rank/29	24	NA	NA	NA	NA	11	NA	NA	NA	NA	NA
State control	Rank/29	26	NA	NA	NA	NA	19	NA	NA	NA	NA	NA
Barriers to entrepreneurship	Rank/29	17	NA	NA	NA	NA	7	NA	NA	NA	NA	NA
Barriers to trade and investment	Rank/29	8	NA	NA	NA	NA	11	NA	NA	NA	NA	NA
Ease of doing business												
Ranking doing business	Rank/174	NA	NA	32	27	28	27	29	24	25	27	29
Starting a business	Rank/174	29	27	33	36	24	25	18	34	37	42	47
Dealing with construction permits	Rank/174	124	132	120	94	70	36	35	34	35	39	42
Getting electricity	Rank/174	NA	NA	84	84	96	90	94	94	99	96	100
Registering property	Rank/174	73	73	61	23	23	21	23	23	24	24	25
Getting credit	Rank/174	74	81	88	91	94	97	98	85	91	96	101
Protecting minority investors	Rank/174	39	44	44	49	52	49	46	49	51	52	55
Paying taxes	Rank/174	46	51	57	49	50	50	50	57	56	42	53
Trading across borders	Rank/174	23	26	26	26	27	23	28	29	15	15	15
Enforcing contracts	Rank/174	61	54	30	30	31	31	27	28	19	19	18
Resolving insolvency	Rank/174	20	21	21	22	24	22	22	32	31	30	35

Source: OECD.

Social costs

Not only the various achievements of the program, but also and possibly especially its failures carried a social cost. First, the internal imbalance worsened significantly in the first years of the program, with the unemployment rate rising to 16.4 percent in 2013, although it has recovered substantially since then. Moreover, in a context of high unemployment, real wages declined and so did ULC. However, final goods prices did not decline proportionally. This combination caused a fall in the share of labor in national income, which reached the lowest level since at least 1960. The trend suggests that low competition in product markets has prevented the decline in labor costs being passed through to consumers and also to final goods producers of tradable goods, hampering competitiveness.[23]

As for the impact of the crisis on income inequality and poverty rates, the situation is less straightforward than in the cases of the other program countries. There was a substantial impact of the crisis on income inequality among the working-age population, when measured before taxes and subsidies. Fiscal policy was, however, successful in mitigating these impacts, so that in the end one cannot conclude that the program increased inequality relative to the period before. Notably, Gini coefficients averaged less over 2011–2013 than over 2004–2010 (Table 6.4).

The findings are in line with Perez and Matsaganis (2018), who conclude that Portugal achieved lesser inequality than Greece, Italy and Spain despite significant fiscal consolidation and having entered the crisis with the highest level of inequality among the four countries. According to the authors, not only did Portugal manage relatively well as far as the direct and immediate effects of austerity measures on inequality (higher taxes, lower benefits, public sector wage cuts and job losses) are concerned, but also in terms of the second-order short-term effects, whereby lower consumption and investment tend to depress economic activity.

Nevertheless, there is a potential non-negligible long-run cost when higher current expenditures that come at the expense of public investment are not used to partly compensate the losers in welfare-improving reforms but rather in exchange for political stability. In addition, the fact that some interest groups remain powerful implies that the fight for scarce resources is bound to be tight, with the result of a likely further postponement of needed reforms.

On the other hand, the burden of the adjustment could have been more evenly shared across public workers, private sector workers, self-employed and the young, had the segmentation of the labor market been mitigated in time. In the event, the less protected workers hit by unemployment, notably the young (see youth unemployment in Table 6.4) and temporary workers, were induced to migrate or to accept low pay in a new job. Although in relative terms the emigration situation in Portugal in the period 2010–2015 was not as dramatic as in Greece or in Spain, it was considerably higher than in Italy (Table 6.4; and Royo and Steinberg, this volume).

Table 6.4 Inequality, unemployment by category and emigration, Portugal 2008–2017

	Unit	*2008*	*2009*	*2010*	*2011*	*2012*	*2013*	*2014*	*2015*	*2016*	*2017*
Inequality											
Total population											
Poverty rate before taxes and transfers	% (i)	0.30	0.31	0.29	0.32	0.35	0.36	0.35	0.34	NA	NA
Poverty rate after taxes and transfers	% (i)	0.11	0.12	0.11	0.11	0.13	0.14	0.14	0.13	NA	NA
Market income (before taxes and transfers)	GINI (ii)	0.52	0.51	0.52	0.53	0.53	0.55	0.55	0.54	NA	NA
Disposable income (post taxes and transfers)	GINI (ii)	0.36	0.34	0.34	0.34	0.34	0.34	0.34	0.34	NA	NA
Population>65											
Market income (before taxes and transfers)	GINI (ii)	0.80	0.79	0.80	0.80	0.79	0.79	0.80	0.80	NA	NA
Disposable income (post taxes and transfers)	GINI (ii)	0.34	0.34	0.34	0.34	0.33	0.32	0.32	0.34	NA	NA
Working-age population											
Market income (before taxes and transfers)	GINI (ii)	0.46	0.45	0.46	0.47	0.48	0.50	0.48	0.47	NA	NA
Disposable income (post taxes and transfers)	GINI (ii)	0.35	0.33	0.34	0.34	0.34	0.34	0.34	0.33	NA	NA
Unemployment by category											
Youth unemployment	%	16.7	20.3	22.8	30.3	37.9	38.1	34.8	32.0	28.0	23.9
Lower education	%	7.9	10.3	11.8	13.9	16.5	17.4	15.3	13.6	12.1	9.8
Upper secondary education	%	7.8	9.6	11.4	13.4	17.7	17.4	15.3	13.9	12.3	9.9
Tertiary education	%	6.8	6.5	7.0	9.0	11.7	12.7	10.0	9.3	8.4	6.5
Emigration											
Emigration	th	20.4	16.9	23.8	44.0	52.0	53.8	49.6	40.4	38.3	31.8
of which: 16–25 yrs	(%)	37.9	37.9	37.9	26.6	37.3	30.0	29.8	32.5	33.5	32.7

Source: OECD. Notes: (i) Percentage of the population with income that is less than half of the median household income; (ii) GINI index is equal to 1 in cases of extreme inequality, and equal to 0 in cases of extreme equality.

Losing ownership over the implementation phase

Political and social contestation and reform fatigue

As Moury and Standring (2017) argue, governments (initially the PS and after the 2011 elections the coalition between the PSD and the CDS-PP) used the bailout program to push for policies that would advance their agendas. After the 2011 elections, the center-right coalition government acknowledged a strong match between their own views and those of the international lenders. The then Prime Minister, Pedro Passos Coelho, had publicly stated his ownership of the reforms and his desire to go further in certain areas than had been initially agreed. As Reis (2015) and Moury and Standring (2017) observed, the Troika found a very committed and cooperative government in Portugal throughout the bailout program.

There was even a general understanding in the Portuguese society that the country had to go through some macroeconomic adjustment and enact long-due reforms, as can be inferred from the initially very low levels of contestation (demonstrations, strikes) as compared to Greece or even Spain. During an initial, albeit short, phase (basically only in 2011) there was also a national consensus among major political actors and wide social support for the program.

Early in the adjustment the President of the Republic, Aníbal Cavaco Silva, incidentally from the same party as the Prime Minister, had warned against what he termed the risk of a "recessionary spiral". In January 2013, he sent the budget to the Constitutional Court for review and in April the Court ruled against four out of nine contested austerity measures in the 2013 budget. Throughout the implementation phase, the Constitutional Court would become a de facto veto player, obliging the government to retreat from a series of reforms affecting mainly public sector wages, pensions and labor code revisions (see Box 6.2).[24] Overruling of measures by the Constitutional Court, together with the President's criticism,[25] disagreements within the government coalition and, given their different institutional natures, mandates and approaches, even within the Troika,[26] fed resistances and negatively affected ownership of reforms.

The government measures taken to compensate for lower than expected revenues and the Constitutional Court reversals, as well as the failed attempt to shift social security contributions from employers to employees, generated widespread protests in the context of a larger than anticipated downturn. These events marked the beginning of a more vocal and systematic opposition to austerity by opposition parties, trade unions and various parts of society, including vested interests opposing some of the reforms. The government lost much of its remaining ownership of the program.

Those developments reinforced the ongoing political contestation, led by left-wing opposition parties, Partido Comunista Português (PCP) and Bloco de Esquerda (BE) together with the PCP-aligned trade union, CGTP-IN. Also, the initially more moderate opposition of the PS, which had signed the MOU with the Troika while still in government, and of UGT, the more center-left-positioned trade union, intensified.

Vitor Gaspar resigned as minister of finance in July 2013 and the government almost fell when Paulo Portas, the leader of the junior coalition party CDS-PP, also offered his resignation as minister of state and foreign affairs. The prime minister did not accept the latter's resignation and instead reshuffled the government. Portas became vice prime minister, in charge of the program negotiations that he had publicly criticized, and the former treasury secretary Maria Luis Albuquerque replaced Gaspar.

The PS distanced itself from what it called an excess of austerity based on the government's neo-liberal agenda rather than necessary measures to conclude the program. Its change of attitude would become even more pronounced in the run-up to the PS leadership contest and after the change in leadership (already after Portugal's exit from the program in 2014) from António José Seguro to António Costa, the current prime minister, prior to the 2015 general elections. The same holds true for the UGT's stance.

In a context of increased political and social friction, lessened financing pressures as a result of the ECB's Outright Monetary Transactions (OMT) and of successful bond issues from January 2013 to April 2014, the Government accommodated reform fatigue by means of reducing the pace of economic reforms.

The post-program period (2014–2018): banking on the ECB

An anti-austerity discourse with reform reversals but fiscal compliance

In October 2015, the center-right coalition consisting of the PSD and the CDS-PP won the general elections with 38.6 percent of the vote but failed to secure a majority of seats in parliament.[27] The PS, which had come second with 32.4 percent of the vote, reached agreements with the three other left-wing parties, BE, PCP (and its junior coalition party). In November 2015 the government program of the upcoming center-right coalition led by Pedro Passos Coelho was rejected in parliament by a vote of 123 to 107 MPs and a new PS minority government led by António Costa was established.

To be able to govern, the new government had to ensure the support of the left-wing anti-Euro parties. It embarked on an anti-austerity discourse, blaming EU institutions and policies and German-led European fiscal orthodoxy.

In the first years after the bailout, the new government managed to go back on some of the earlier repressed expenditures, taking advantage of the higher tax revenues and low interest payments that came with the economic recovery and ECB policies. The government also reversed several measures, notably by re-establishing four public holidays, going back to a 35-hour working week in the public sector (wages and promotions had been frozen), hiring more people in the public sector (putting an end to the pre-Troika procedure of admitting only one civil servant for each two leaving) and reintroducing automatic rather than evaluation-based career progressions for school teachers. It also made "limited progress" on addressing the 2016 country-specific recommendations (EC, 2017). The Government accommodated those current expenditures at the expense of a delay in recouping public investment, which stood at 2.0 percent of GDP in 2018, thereby corresponding to only half of its average level during the pre-crisis slump phase (2001–2007).

According to the European Commission's assessments (EC, 2017, 2018), the reform momentum has weakened since 2014 and policy gaps have persisted in the areas of product and services markets, skills and innovation, fiscal sustainability, corporate debt restructuring and in the labor market (rigidities). At the same time, the opportunity for public sector reform was not made use of, and pressures on employment and wages in the government sector have remained high.[28]

In the labor market, policy reversals include the return of collective agreement provisions to replace the previously established "bank of hours based on individual agreement" and "collective bank of hours with individual agreement origin" (EC, 2018: 28) with a new bank of hours based on group agreements and a new tightening on dismissals. Measures that have been adopted to reduce labor market segmentation have relied solely on tightening the regulation of temporary contracts, discouraging their use, without easing regulation in the more protected segments.[29] Those moves constituted a retreat in an already incomplete reform agenda and increased the benefits for those who were already privileged in the Portuguese segmented labor market. As for the product market, the new government adopted a more restrictive stance, imposing barriers to entrepreneurship in a number of small business sectors (e.g., individual transport, short-term residential leases).

In the bailout period (2011–2014), the general government structural primary balance, which besides one-off measures also excludes interest payments and therefore provides a measure of the discretionary fiscal stance or the fiscal consolidation effort, improved every year, and quite significantly. In contrast, in the post-bailout period (2015–2018), which includes the electoral year of 2015, the contribution of discretionary fiscal policy to fiscal consolidation was basically negative: the structural primary balance deteriorated 0.7 percent in 2015–2018 (Table 6.2).

Portugal had been subject to an excessive deficit procedure since December 2009. The Council repeatedly extended the deadline for correcting the deficit. In July 2016 it concluded that Portugal's response to its recommendations had been insufficient, although it decided not to impose a fine. However, the general government deficit for 2016 turned out to be on target (2.0 percent of GDP) for the first time in many years and the Council concluded that Portugal's deficit had been corrected.[30] As a consequence, in early 2017, yields on Portuguese debt started to decline again, after an interruption that had started in late 2015. This was an important milestone in rebuilding market credibility, paving the way for rating upgrades.

In the short to medium term, the recovery of macroeconomic imbalances, the return to markets, improved external conditions and the ECB provided sufficient breathing space to the economy and growth started to pick up, though at modest rates in light of the previous downturn. There was also good news related to the recent attractiveness of the country for a new type of tourism and for foreign residents and with regard to innovation (e.g., web summits in Lisbon). Portuguese business was successful in accommodating the increased demand, improving infrastructures and attractiveness.

Those developments contributed to a "feel-good" factor (Macedo, 2017), which can also be partly explained by a good management of expectations. By "decreeing" that austerity was over but just changing the way of complying with fiscal targets (lower public investment and higher indirect taxation and current expenditures), the Government was also able to establish a climate of relative social peace and optimism, thereby avoiding the erosion of support for EU-*cum*-EMU membership and pre-empting the success of any new Euroskeptic parties.

However, excessive (stock) imbalances across all agents, including banks, and product and labor market rigidities weigh on growth, slowing down a sustained recovery. Notably, private investment has remained low at 15 percent of GDP in 2018, well below its 20 percent average during the slump phase of 2001–2007, which is symptomatic of the economy's low attractiveness to new businesses in general.

The minister of finance, Mário Centeno, gained the trust of the markets and of European institutions, notably of his Eurozone colleagues who elected him Eurogroup President in December 2017.[31] His political capital in the government and in the country was reinforced as a consequence and the left-wing parties that support the government in parliament, their political rhetoric notwithstanding, had to put up with the "fiscal orthodoxy" of the Government although they remained opposed to many of the reforms, notably those initiated under the program.

As from 2017 Portugal has been subject to the preventive arm of the SGP only. The country should progress toward its medium-term budgetary objective at an appropriate pace, including respecting the expenditure benchmark and complying with the debt criterion. The structural deficit (excluding one-off measures) improved by 0.8 percent in 2017, thereby meeting the EC's recommendation. However, the recapitalization of CGD triggered another aggravation of the total deficit to 3 percent. In 2018 the government deficit was 0.7 percent of GDP and the gross government debt-to-GDP ratio declined to 121.5. While the Commission's 2018 autumn forecasts project a decrease in Portugal's gross government debt to GDP ratio to 119.2 percent in 2019, external conditions seem to be deteriorating and the pace of growth is slowing down. Throughout the post-bailout period (2015–2018), Portugal continued to experience imbalances (MIP) and has not always been in line with its SGP medium-term objective. The challenge in the near future continues therefore to be compliance with the SGP in a context of adverse macroeconomic conditions and continuing political pressures on the expenditure side.

Legacy: short-term adjustment versus sustained structural change and the (lack of a) growth model

It is in times of crisis that Portugal tends to enact protracted reforms, when there is external pressure to do so. Yet, when the pressure lessens reforms tend to be reversed or impaired by other institutional weaknesses (Torres, 2009).[32] This is what happened upon Portugal's accession to EMU and also with the end of the program's (effective) conditionality.

Perceptions of the desirability or urgency of advances in economic coordination and national economic reform may, of course, vary across EU member states. The issue of economic reform testifies to the difficulties of internalizing spillovers in the EU and the Eurozone. Soskice and Hope (2016) shed light on why external pressure might fail to foster structural reform at the member state level.[33] Their argument is that external pressure works better with respect to austerity than to the reform of institutions. The reason is that austerity is a more immediate concern in contrast to reforming institutions, whose necessity is not so well perceived and which takes longer to produce results. The authors attribute the difficulties underlying reforms to different member state preferences, which are in turn rooted in countries' different growth models. In the Eurozone Soskice and Hope (2016) distinguish an export-led north, which is characterized as traditionally harboring preferences for fiscal discipline, monetary stability, and wage coordination, from a demand-led south, which they qualify as more inflation-prone, with strong public sector unions and low wage coordination.[34] They argue that in the Eurozone the two pre-existing growth models have ceased to function in symbiosis since the crisis, and that the lack of reform has, in turn, put a strain on EMU. Put differently, some Eurozone countries had failed to internalize the constraints associated with being members of a monetary union. As for the issue of convergence of preferences to a compatible and consensual sustainable growth model, one may note that the Europe 2020 Strategy marked an attempt to that end but it still needs to be further fleshed out and implemented.

Still, the acceptance of structural reforms at the member state level can be facilitated if attention is paid to the timing and mix of reforms. The fact that structural policies may often produce results with a time lag, have costs in the shorter run or do not necessarily lead to more demand and output (De Grauwe and Ji, 2016; Campos et al., 2018) makes it politically important to get the timing right, for instance by anticipating those reforms that already produce benefits in the short run (Bongardt and Torres, 2016). They can be implemented even under crisis-induced constraints. In this context, and with regard to the political sustainability of structural reforms, sequencing is a relevant concern: to a certain extent, some reforms that are growth enhancing in the short run should be front-loaded, and private investment encouraged in ways compatible with fiscal constraints. This will help to compensate the more negative social impact of other necessary reforms, thereby avoiding that structural reform and austerity come to mingle in such a way as to push countries into problems they did not have.

In Portugal, the deterioration of international conditions during the adjustment period, notably slower growth, an unclear institutional framework and political uncertainty, has contributed to weakening the government's capacity to steer the program. Those developments paved the way for vested interests, which have managed to retain some of their privileges throughout the adjustment, to erode social support for the program. Moreover, other discriminatory measures have been introduced already in the post-program phase, favoring particular activities or segments in the society.

In this respect, the quality of national political institutions did not improve and the main handicap in Portuguese governance – the low capability to shield the social common interest from pressures by influential groups – remained unaltered.[35] This fragility weighs on the medium-term fiscal sustainability and long-term growth.

In short, the issue of structural reform became too politically charged once it became entangled with austerity in the public debate. At the domestic level, it would have been essential to ensure stable and comprehensive social and political support (ideally around a forward-looking and sustainable model of development, as argued in Bongardt and Torres, 2016), to create ownership of the program and hence to safeguard the continuation of reforms once the program elapsed. As it is, Portugal remains not only extremely vulnerable to changing economic circumstances (tourism is highly sensitive to the global business cycle) and rising financing costs, but its development will remain very much conditioned by external pressure.

Of course, there have been important structural changes, not least an as yet difficult to assess change in mentality in various segments of the population toward a more entrepreneurial attitude, after a difficult weathering of the crisis, and a more sustainable (not only financially or economic but also in terms of the environment and quality of life) growth model. It is, however, still too early to tell to what extent the legacy of the crisis in general and those changes in particular will give rise to a new sustainable growth model.

Conclusion

Portugal's adjustment program can be qualified as a success in terms of addressing its main macroeconomic imbalances and financial risks within EMU. Its more visible outcomes consist in a sharp reduction in fiscal deficits, the regaining of international market access and the current account adjustment. In spite of the vulnerabilities (and failures) of various banks, depositors maintained their confidence in the banking system. Various reforms were implemented, mainly regarding the labor market, the effectiveness of the judicial system and public finances' and bank supervision procedures. However, despite the fact that many structural benchmarks were achieved, even on time, and compliance was good, there were significant (economic and political) obstacles to implementation, which meant that outcomes were mixed.

There were three main types of obstacles to implementation, which, however, are not totally separable from each other.

First, the economic downturn during the program's implementation phase was much larger than expected due to weaker external demand and a more pronounced and faster than anticipated deleveraging, weighing on private consumption and investment. To a large extent, deleveraging resulted from restricted access to external finance, which partly explains the faster than expected current account adjustment. Second, the reform agenda, already difficult to pursue in such a recessionary environment, was perhaps too wide, especially given the lack of prioritization of the various measures, to be successfully implemented with national ownership. Third, after the first revenue slippages and the reversals of measures by the Constitutional Court, it was difficult to find compensatory measures. Alternative measures, more discussed in terms of their distributional impact – as that meant higher and/or more taxes and/or more expenditure cuts affecting certain groups in society more than initially planned – than in terms of their (economic and social) quality, increased political and social contestation. This contestation turned into a more systematic opposition to reforms, which intermingled with austerity in the public debate. At that point the easing of financing pressures accommodated reform fatigue.

Throughout the program, high labor market segmentation contributed to an asymmetric distribution of costs between civil servants (sheltered against unemployment) and private sector workers with temporary contracts and small businesses and the young, by far the most affected by unemployment, emigration and poverty. In spite of very high social costs, the aggregate indicators of income inequality suggest that Portugal was more successful than the other program countries in mitigating the direct and immediate effects of the adjustment on inequality. Fiscal policy was relatively successful in lessening those impacts, to the extent that inequality indicators did not increase when compared to the period before. This specificity may help to explain why the political system did not change at all, nor did vote shares for the main parties change much in the last three elections (since the eruption of the crisis).

After exiting the program in 2014, the reform impetus was basically lost. Since then, reforms in the areas of product markets and in the labor market were halted or even reversed. Still, improved external conditions and the ECB's policies have helped the economy grow, albeit at modest rates given the previous downturn and if compared with the situation in Ireland or Spain.

However, the fact that the focus of policy shifted away from structural reforms to (not necessarily fairer) income distribution in a context of lessened external pressure can be expected to have a negative impact on private investment, which has remained low during the upswing, and on future growth and, by then, on the opportunities of the poorest. One can therefore conclude that the post-program period has been a phase of political and social truce, but that it was only possible thanks to a favorable international economic situation, which is, however, deteriorating. Such a strategy of avoiding political unrest by favoring current expenditures at the expense of lower public investment and growth-enhancing reforms, which eventually would deliver a higher social return, comes at a high long-run cost, and may not prove sustainable in a phase of cyclical downturn.

Acknowledgments

We would like to thank Lorenzo Codogno and Marina Costa Lobo for very useful comments on a previous version of this chapter and João Amador, João Borges Assunção, Paul De Grauwe, Francisco Pereira Coutinho and Ricardo Reis for very fruitful conversations. We are also grateful to the participants in our two Bruges workshops and colleagues in this volume, in particular Michele Chang, George Pagoulatos, Sebastian Royo and Federico Steinberg, for very useful comments and discussions. Of course, the responsibility for any mistakes and opinions is entirely ours.

Notes

1 Between 1995 and 2000, household savings as a percentage of disposable income declined by 2 percentage points, and gross fixed capital formation (GFCF) increased 4.7 percentage points, reaching the impressive level of 28 percent of GDP in 2000.

2 Note that these figures hide contingent government liabilities, namely those generated by entities that were considered outside the government sector perimeter at the time the liability was contracted.

3 The real exchange rate appreciation helped, however, to maintain living standards, masking the stagnation of real output.

4 According to Lebre de Freitas et al. (2017), the various bonanza episodes (of capital inflow) that hit the EU periphery before 2007 were mainly explained by global factors rather than by country idiosyncrasies, while EMU membership might have helped mitigate the risk perceptions regarding fiscal unsustainability.

5 As Macedo (2007) points out, from 1995 to 2006 the delegation to the Minister of Finance remained weak. Reis (2013: 437) stresses instead the generous past promises on old-age pensions as the cause for continuous increases in taxes that discouraged work and aggravated the slump.

6 As pointed out by Eichenbaum et al. (2016), the treatment of SOEs and PPPs was not merely an accounting issue; it also augmented Portugal's exposure to a sudden stop.

7 As pointed out by Eichenbaum et al. (2016), domestic institutions, the European Commission and the International Monetary Fund (IMF) paid little attention to the building up of a large foreign debt and the probability of a sudden capital flow reversal. The dominant wisdom at that time (see for instance IMF, 2003: 9) was that within a monetary union, the current account was a useful, albeit less proximate, indicator of macroeconomic imbalances.

8 Exports of goods and services fell from 31 to 27 percent of GDP.

9 Interestingly, and unlike in the cases of Greece, Italy and Spain, the (initially not so high) levels of support for the Euro in Portugal had remained stable throughout 1998–2007 (Eurobarometer).

10 The European Economic Recovery Plan, launched by the European Commission in November 2008 and approved by the European Council in December 2008, provided the framework for the national counter-cyclical fiscal policies. It has been pointed out, however, that member states facing significant external and internal imbalances should aim at correcting those imbalances.

11 For a discussion on the policies then implemented, see Torres (2009). There were also various statistical reclassifications of SOEs, pension funds, swaps, transport companies and PPPs (brought inside the deficit perimeter), amounting to 0.6 percent in 2009 and 3.5 percent of GDP in 2010.

12 The slight improvement in NIIP in 2010 relative to 2009 despite the current account deficit amounting to 10 percent of GDP reflects a large valuation change, whereby the rising yields on external debt reduced its market value.

13 See Eichenbaum et al. (2016: annex 1) for a timeline of key events from March 2011 until January 2015.

14 See IMF (2017). A list of structural conditionality measures for Portugal can be found in annex 3 of Eichenbaum et al. (2016). The MEFP and the Technical Memorandum of Understanding (TMU) were sent in attachment to a letter of intent addressed to the IMF's Executive Board by the State of Portugal while the MOU between the Portuguese State and the European Commission was signed in Lisbon on 17 May 2011.

15 Despite the heavy dependence on the ECB for liquidity, Portugal was not perceived as having a banking crisis and the three troika institutions did not favor giving too much weight to bank recapitalization, which would have increased the country's financing needs (Lütz et al., this volume). According to Véron (2016: 24 and 27), the IMF approached the Portuguese crisis as "mostly fiscal" and not directly linked to financial sector weakness, which, with hindsight, proved suboptimal.

16 The program had aimed at addressing fiscal risk from public enterprises and PPPs but underestimated the corresponding (difficulties in renegotiating contracts and financing) needs.

17 See Alesina et al. (2019), for the impact of the type of fiscal consolidation adopted on output and on the reduction of the debt ratio.

18 Higher capital requirements were imposed by the EBA in December 2011 as a new buffer against sovereign debt risk. Moreover, the partial transfer of bank pension funds also caused losses in 2011 while the special on-site inspection program, by revealing imparities, contributed to additional capital needs.

19 In December 2012, also Banco Internacional do Funchal (BANIF), a small bank based on the island of Madeira, made use of those funds.

20 In the Eurogroup meeting of 16 June 2017, the German finance minister, Wolfgang Schäuble, supported Portugal's request for an additional early repayment to the IMF, saying that it was a clear sign of the fact that the adjustment program was a success.

21 According to the European Commission (EC, 2016), there was a "lack of prioritization particularly in the product markets field". Kincaid (this volume) discusses how the numerous and detailed structural conditions contained in the MOU may have undermined ownership. Eichenbaum et al. (2016: 29) also suggest that the set of reforms was perhaps too ambitious, broad and detailed.

22 In June 2011, the IMF (2011) forecast the current account deficits to fall from 11.3 billion euro in 2012 to 4.2 billion euro in 2016, totaling 33.9 million euro over 2012–2016. The actual current account adjustment turned out to be much faster, with the cumulative deficit reaching 3.9 billion in the same period only (AMECO). This means that the effective monetary conditions were much tighter than anticipated.

23 As the IMF stated in its 11th review (IMF, 2015), in spite of product market reforms, excessive rents remained in non-tradable network industries, including electricity and ports.

24 According to Pereira Coutinho (2017: 82), the Constitutional Court declared "against all evidence" that the MOU had not foreseen any of those measures, thereby overstepping its mandate since the MOU was EU law, which binds national law. In his opinion, the Court would have been more coherent if it had questioned the validity of the MOU by sending a preliminary reference to the European Court of Justice.

25 In spite of (strong) occasional criticisms, the President maintained his support for the Government throughout the entire bailout period.

26 See Lütz et al. (this volume) for examples. Also, as pointed out in Eichenbaum et al. (2016: 53), "numerous interviewees stressed that the IMF and the EU could have coordinated their public communications better".

27 This was an impressive result for a government that had enacted such a strong adjustment program. To put it into perspective, in the same year the UK conservatives led by David Cameron obtained a lower percentage of the vote, only 36.9 percent, and that was considered an enormous victory that, given the UK's electoral system, gave the conservatives an absolute majority in parliament.

28 Employment in the Public Administration went up – see EC (2018).

29 As recently pointed out by the IMF (2018: 23), reducing the regulatory gap between permanent and temporary contracts is fundamental for the country to be able to absorb adverse shocks and facilitate structural change.

30 Still, in 2016, the structural balance improved by only 0.2 percent of GDP (below 0.5 percent) and the structural primary balance even deteriorated slightly (0.2 percent).

31 The last rating agency to upgrade Portugal's credit profile back to investment grade was Moody's on 12 October 2018, on account of sustained decrease in its debt levels and of real GDP growth.

32 For Barta (2018), fiscal consolidation also tends to be protracted in countries where fiscal policies generate intense conflicts of vested interests while large parts of society remain unaffected by the negative economic side effects of the imbalances.

33 See also Macedo (2003).

34 See also Marzinotto, in this volume, for a review of the literature and different models of varieties of capitalism (VOC) in the context of the crisis: the liberal market economy (LME), including Ireland, the coordinated market economies (CMEs) and the mixed market economy (MME), including Greece, Portugal and Spain.

35 See also Afonso et al. (2015).

References

Afonso, Alexandre, Sotirios Zartaloudis, and Yannis Papadopoulos (2015), "How party linkages shape austerity politics: clientelism and fiscal adjustment in Greece and Portugal during the eurozone crisis", *Journal of European Public Policy*, 22, 3, 315–334.

Alesina, Alberto, Favero, Carlo and Francesco Giavazzi (2019), *Austerity: When It Works and When It Doesn't*, Princeton, NJ: Princeton University Press.

Banco de Portugal (2008), "Sistema Bancário Português no decurso de 2008", Textos de Política e Situação Económica, *Boletim Económico*, 14, 3, 99–167.

Barta, Zsófia (2018), *In the Red: The Politics of Public Debt Accumulation in Developed Countries*, Ann Arbor, MI: University of Michigan Press.

Beleza, L. Miguel and Jorge Braga de Macedo (1991), "Implicit taxes and credit ceilings: the treasury and the banks in Portugal", in J. Silva Lopes and L. M. Beleza (eds), *Portugal and the Internal Market of the EEC*, Lisboa: Banco de Portugal, 57–72.

Blanchard, Olivier (2007), "Adjustment within the euro: the difficult case of Portugal", *Portuguese Economic Journal*, 6, 1, 1–22, May.

Blanchard, Olivier and Francesco Giavazzi (2002), "Current account deficits in the euro area: the end of the Feldstein-Horioka puzzle?", *Brookings Papers on Economic Activity*, 2, 147–209.

Blanchard, Olivier and Pedro Portugal (2017), "How to strengthen the Portuguese recovery", draft paper, May.

Bongardt, Annette and Francisco Torres (2016), "EMU reform and resilience in a re-dimensioned EU", *Journal of Economic Policy*, XXXII, 3, Dec., 575–596.

Campos, Nauro, Paul De Grauwe, and Yuemei Ji (eds) (2018), *The Political Economy of Structural Reforms in Europe*, Oxford: Oxford University Press.

Council of the European Union (2009), "Council Opinion on the updated Stability Programme of Portugal", as adopted by the Council (ECOFIN) on 10 March, General Secretariat of the Council, 7330/09, UEM85.

De Grauwe, Paul and Yuemei Ji (2016), "Crisis management and economic growth in the Eurozone", in F. Caselli, M. Centeno and J. Tavares (eds), *After the Crisis: Reform, Recovery, and Growth in Europe*, Oxford: Oxford University Press.

EC (2004), "The Portuguese economy after the boom", Directorate-General for Economic and Financial Affairs, Occasional paper 8, April.

EC (2008a), "EMU@10: successes and challenges after 10 years of Economic and Monetary Union", *European Economy* 2.

EC (2008b), "European Economic Recovery Plan", Communication from the Commission to the European Council, COM(2008) 800 final, Brussels, 26 November 2008.

EC (2009), "On the updated stability programme of Portugal, 2008–2011", Recommendation for a Council Opinion, Brussels, 25.2.2009, SEC(2009) 234/2.

EC (2016), Ex-post evaluation of the economic adjustment programme – Portugal, 2011–2014, Institutional Paper 040, November.

EC (2017), Country report, including an in-depth review on the prevention and correction of macroeconomic imbalances, 22 February.

EC (2018), Portugal: Post-Programme Surveillance Report, September.

Eichenbaum, Martin, Sérgio Rebelo, and Carlos Resende (2016), "The Portuguese Crisis and the IMF", *IEO Background Paper BP/16-02/05*, Washington, D.C.: Independent Evaluation Office of the International Monetary Fund.

IMF (2003), 2002 Article IV consultation, Staff Report, IMF Country Report 3/99, April.

IMF (2011), Portugal: request for a three-year arrangement under the extended fund facility, IMF country report 11/127, June, Washington DC: International Monetary Fund.

IMF (2014), Portugal: Eleventh Review under the Extended Arrangement, and Request for Extension of the Arrangement and Waivers of Applicability of End-March Performance Criteria, IMF Country Report 14/102, April.

IMF (2015), First Post-Program Monitoring Discussions – Staff Report, IMF Country Report 15/21, January.

IMF (2016a), 2016 Article IV consultation, September.

IMF (2016b), Ex-post evaluation of exceptional access under the 2011 extended arrangement, September.

IMF (2017), "Fifth post-program monitoring discussions", February 2017.

IMF (2018), Portugal: Selected Issues – IMF Country Report 18/274, September.

Lebre de Freitas, Miguel, Luís C. Nunes, and Madalena S. Rodrigues (2017), "Euro Area membership and the probability of a sudden stop: an empirical assessment", *Journal of Common Market Studies*, 16, 4, 818–836.

Macedo, Jorge Braga de (2003), "Portugal's European integration: the limits of external pressure", in F. Monteiro, J. Tavares, M. Glatzer and A. Cardoso (eds), *Portugal: Strategic Options in a European Context*, Lanham, MD: Lexington Books, pp. 61–97.

Macedo, Jorge Braga de (2007), "Competitiveness and convergence in Portugal", GEE papers 4, Lisbon: Ministério da Economia e Inovação.

Macedo, Jorge Braga de (2017), "Reform complementarity and policy coordination in Europe: a view from Portugal", CIGI Papers No. 132 – June.

MFAP (2008), "Initiatives to Strengthen Financial Stability", Lisbon: Ministério das Finanças e da Administração Pública, 12 October.

MFAP (2009), "Stability and Growth Pact 2008–2011: January 2009 update", Lisbon: Ministério das Finanças e da Administração Pública.

Moury, Catherine and Adam Standring (2017), "Going beyond the Troika: power and discourse in Portuguese austerity politics", *European Journal of Political Research*. doi: 10.1111/1475-6765.12190.

OECD (2017), Economic survey, February.

Pereira Coutinho, Francisco (2017), "The Portuguese bailout, social rights and the rule of law", in A. Coli, B. Pacini and E. Stradella (eds), *Policy, Welfare and Financial Resources: The Impact of the Crisis on Territories*, Pisa: Pisa University Press, 57–92.

Perez, Sofia, Matsaganis, Manos (2018), "The political economy of austerity in Southern Europe", *New Political Economy*, 23, 2, 192–207.

Reis, Ricardo (2013), "The Portuguese slump and crash and the euro crisis", *Brookings Papers on Economic Activity*, 143–193, Spring.

Reis, Ricardo (2015), "Looking for a success in the euro crisis adjustment programs: the case of Portugal", *Brookings Papers on Economic Activity*, 433–447, Fall.

Soskice, David and David Hope (2016), "The Eurozone and political economic institutions", *Annual Review of Political Science*, 19, 163–185.

Torres, Francisco (1990), "Portugal, the EMS and 1992: stabilization and liberalization", in P. De Grauwe and L. Papademos (eds), *The EMS in the 1990s*, London: Longman, 225–246.

Torres, Francisco (1998), "Portugal towards EMU: a political economy perspective", in E. Jones, J. Frieden and F. Torres (eds), *Joining Europe's Monetary Club: The Challenges for Smaller Member States*, New York: St. Martin's Press and London: MacMillan, 171–202.

Torres, Francisco (2007), "A Convergência para a União Económica e Monetária: Objectivo Nacional ou Constrangimento Externo?", in P. Lains and M. Costa Lobo (eds), *Em Nome da Europa. Portugal em Mudança, 1986–2006*, Cascais: Principia (ICS), 97–120.

Torres, Francisco (2009), "Back to external pressure: policy responses to the financial crisis in Portugal", *South European Society and Politics*, 14, 1, 55–70.

Véron, Nicolas (2016), "The IMF's role in the euro area crisis: financial sector aspects", *IEO Background Paper 16–02/10*, Washington, D.C.: Independent Evaluation Office of the International Monetary Fund.

7 Using a sectoral bailout to make wide reforms

The case of Spain

Sebastián Royo and Federico Steinberg

Introduction

Between 2009 and 2013, Spain suffered its worst financial crisis in decades. Although successive governments implemented a number of gradual reforms, the restoration of the solvency and credibility of Spanish banks required a €42 billion bailout from the European authorities, which triggered a complete restructuring of the financial sector. Despite not having a full bailout program, structural policies were gradually introduced in virtually all areas of the economy. Spanish authorities made a strategic use of the external influence of the EU to implement economic reforms that they perceived as necessary but that faced important public resistance from different societal sectors. Strong economic growth, mainly export-led, resumed in 2014. Moreover, there is ample evidence that the reforms have somehow changed parts of the Spanish growth model, which now seems to be less dependent on domestic demand and construction. Nevertheless, important weaknesses remain. Unemployment (especially long-term and youth) remains stubbornly high, inequality and poverty have increased more than in other EU countries, the budget deficit is only being reduced slowly, and a number of economic reforms are still missing.

In the following pages, we will analyze the political economy of the Spanish bailout program and its subsequent reforms. By tracing the modernization of the Spanish economy since its accession to the Union, we will show that the government's decision to use the crisis to make substantial reforms with the support (and under the pressure) of European institutions is not a new phenomenon in Spanish politics. This time, however, given the severity of the crisis, the reforms encountered more domestic political resistance and produced results that were more mixed. They have disadvantaged the unemployed and those with precarious jobs (mostly young people and women), as well as the lower middle classes because their levels of protection were reduced. On the other hand, upper middle classes and pensioners did not experience substantial decreases in income during the crisis and benefited disproportionately when the recovery started.

We will also argue that the fact that Spain avoided a full bailout program contributed to eluding a sense of collective national failure that is observable in other program Mediterranean countries. This put less pressure on deeper and wider reforms and precluded an implosion of the political system as observed in other EU countries. In fact, despite the appearance of new political parties, the country has been able to include them in the political system without major problems. Moreover, there is no strong anti-EU or anti-Euro sentiment in Spain, which is a remarkable development given the severity of the crisis.

EMU membership and roots of the crisis: from boom to bust

Following Franco's death in 1975 and the restoration of democracy, Spain returned to the international arena, from which it had been relatively isolated during the dictatorship. In the 1980s, under the governments of the Socialist party, the country modernized, integrated into NATO (1982), and joined the European Community-EC (1986). The following two and a half decades were a period of phenomenal growth and modernization.

Indeed, before the global financial crisis the country had become one of Europe's most successful economies. While other European countries had been stuck in the mud, Spain performed much better. EU accession set in motion a complex and multifaceted process of reform. The country benefited extensively from the EU's "structural and cohesion funds", which were used to improve the physical infrastructure and capital stock of the country. Spanish trade with the Community expanded dramatically, as did inward investment, facilitating structural adjustment of the economy and rapid convergence with the EU average. The culmination of this process was the (largely unexpected) participation of the country as a founder of the European Monetary Union (EMU) in 1999.

European integration has had a profound effect on the country's economy and has served from the outset as a lever to implement structural reforms that were hindered by domestic political constraints. Under the terms of the accession agreement, Spain had to undertake significant steps to align its legislation on industrial, agriculture, economic, and financial policies to that of the European Community. Therefore, it is hard to contest that Spain has benefited immensely from accession. Since the last century, the obsession of Spanish reformists has been to make up the lost ground with modernized Europe. EU membership has been a critical step in this direction (see Royo and Manuel 2003). As Pagoulatos (2004: 57) puts it, during the 80s and the 90s, Spain, unlike Greece, was willing to let European policies influence its domestic economic and political dynamics due "to their extrovert ideological disposition, receptiveness towards developments in Western social democracy, ideational identification with Europe, and commitment to the European project".

Indeed, Spain has consistently used EU membership as a device to implement economic reforms (Molina 2013), and these structural reforms were one of the key drivers of the spectacular pre-2008 Spanish economic performance. Spain was (in 2008) in its 14th year of uninterrupted growth, and it was benefiting from the longest cycle of continuing expansion of the economy in modern history (only Ireland in the Eurozone has a better record). Indeed, in 20 years per capita income grew 20 points, to reach close to 90 percent of the

EU15 average. The country grew on average 1.4 percentage points more than the EU since 1996.

Unemployment fell from 20 percent in the mid-1990s to 8.2 percent in the first half of 2007 (the lowest level since 1978), as Spain became the second country in the EU (after Germany, with a much larger economy) in creating the most jobs (an average of 600,000 per year over the preceding decade). Economic growth contributed to per capita income growth and employment. The public deficit was also eliminated (the country had a *surplus* between 2005 and 2006, which reached 2.2 percent of GDP), and the public debt was reduced to 35.6 percent of GDP, one of the lower levels in the Eurozone.

The success of the financial sector was also notable. Between 2008 and 2010, the Spanish financial system, despite all its problems, was still one of the least affected by the crisis in Europe. In December 2010, Moody's ranked the Spanish banking system as the third strongest of the Eurozone, only behind Finland and France. Prior to the crisis, the Bank of Spain implemented a "dynamic provisioning system", which established a countercyclical capital regime for banks (Bank of Spain 2017: 60–63). On the basis of this regime, starting in 2000, banks had to make provisions for latent portfolio losses, which allowed for the creation of a buffer in the form of a reserve deducted from capital in good times and released in times of downturn. At the same time, the Central Bank also prevented the provision of dividend increases at times of growth that might undermine banks' solvency in the long term. Finally, the Central Bank prevented off-balance sheet activities. This framework provided Spanish banks with a countercyclical mechanism that was essential to overcome the first stage of the crisis. In the end, however, these provisions proved insufficient.

In sum, EMU served as a tool to implement a number of structural reforms and provided the basis for economic policy continuity. Despite changes in government, there were few economic policy shifts throughout the 1990s and early 2000s (Table 7.1).

Weaknesses of the pre-crisis growth model

The Spanish economic success was, however, marred by some glaring deficiencies that came to the fore in 2008 when the global financial crisis hit. It was, to a certain extent, a "miracle" based on bricks and mortar (Banco de España 2017: 27–36; Martinez-Mongay and Maza Lasierra 2009). The foundations of economic growth were fragile because the country had low productivity growth (total factor productivity contributed only 0.5 percentage points to GDP growth between 1998 and 2006) and deteriorating external competitiveness. Moreover, growth was largely based on labor-intensive economic sectors, such as services and construction, which were not exposed to international competition. For example, in 2006 most of the new jobs were created in low-productivity sectors such as construction (33 percent), services associated with housing such as sales and rentals (15 percent), and tourism and domestic service (30 percent). These sectors represented 75 percent of all the new jobs created in Spain in 2006 (new

Table 7.1 The boom years in Spain (2000–07)

Data	*2000*	*2001*	*2002*	*2003*	*2004*	*2005*	*2006*	*2007*
GDP growth at constant prices	5.3%	4.0%	2.9%	3.2%	3.2%	3.7%	4.2%	3.8%
GDP relative to EU 15	7.0%	7.3%	7.6%	8.0%	8.2%	8.6%	8.8%	9.0%
TFP growth (2010=100)	102.0	102.1	101.8	101.4	101.0	100.6	100.6	100.4
CPI inflation (% annual)	3.9%	2.7%	4.0%	2.6%	3.2%	3.7%	2.7%	4.2%
Unemployment rate (% of active population)	11.9%	10.6%	11.5%	11.5%	11.0%	9.2%	8.5%	8.2%
Real unit labor costs (2010=100)	100.6	99.8	98.8	98.1	97.2	96.6	96.1	96.9
Household and NPISH gross savings rate (% of disposable income)	10.5%	10.4%	10.4%	11.9%	10.6%	9.3%	7.9%	5.9%
Gross fixed capital formation (% of GDP)	25.4%	25.6%	26.1%	27.0%	27.5%	28.5%	29.4%	29.6%
General government deficit (% of GDP)	–1.1%	–0.5%	–0.4%	–0.4%	0.0%	1.2%	2.2%	1.9%
General government primary balance (cyclically adjusted; % of potential GDP)	0.8%	0.4%	0.5%	0.5%	0.7%	1.7%	2.2%	1.9%
Current account (% of GDP)	–4.1%	–4.1%	–3.8%	–3.9%	–5.6%	–7.6%	–9.0%	–9.6%
Exports of goods and services (% of GDP)	25.1%	25.1%	24.7%	24.7%	25.0%	24.5%	24.7%	25.8%
Government bond yields (yield curve)	1.1%	0.9%	1.6%	1.8%	2.0%	1.2%	0.7%	0.0%
Private sector debt (% of GDP)	103.0%	109.8%	116.4%	126.3%	137.6%	154.6%	177.6%	191.5%
Government gross debt (% of GDP)	58.0%	54.2%	51.3%	47.6%	45.3%	42.3%	38.9%	35.6%
Net International Investment position (% of GDP)	–34.8%	–38.2%	–44.7%	–48.2%	–55.7%	–58.9%	–67.9%	–79.6%

Source: AMECO and Eurostat.

manufacturing jobs, in contrast, represented only 5 percent). The labor temporary rate reached 33.3 percent in 2007, and inflation was a recurrent problem, which gradually eroded the price-competitiveness of Spanish exports.

As Fernández-Villaverde et al. (2013) have explained, joining the euro generated an acceleration of economic growth that made structural reforms seem less necessary precisely when losing monetary sovereignty would have required making labor and product markets more flexible to absorb shocks.

In the end, the long period of expansion had some unintended consequences, which materialized in an accumulation of excessive macroeconomic and financial imbalances, including excessive private indebtedness, speculative exuberance of the real estate market, external competitiveness losses, high dependence on external financing, and the mismanagement of part of the financial sector.

- *Excessive private indebtedness*. The entry to the EMU brought a significant reduction of interest rates in Spain, exacerbated by ECB's expansionary monetary policy prevalent during that period. Furthermore, consumer price inflation in Spain was well above that in the euro area. In this way, real interest rates in Spain were low compared to those that would have been required, given its cyclical position. The result was an extraordinary expansionary impulse in Spain, which favored increases in private spending financed by a sharp surge in the debt levels of households and companies. In terms of GDP, the indebtedness of the non-financial private sector rose by almost 100 pp to 191 percent between 2000 and 2007, household indebtedness reached a record 115 percent of disposable income in 2006, and the construction and housing sectors accounted for 18.5 percent of GDP (twice the Eurozone average).
- *Speculative exuberance of the real estate market.* Residential investment, as a percentage of GDP, almost doubled between 2000 and 2007, up to a maximum of 12 percent (over 5 pp higher than in the euro area), construction affiliates grew by more than a million people, and the number of new dwellings surpassed 600,000 units in 2007. House prices rose by 150 percent since 1998, and the average price of a square meter of residential property went up from €700 in 1997 to €2,000 at the end of 2006, even though the housing stock had doubled.
- *External competitiveness losses and high dependence on external financing.* External competitiveness losses were fueled by the recurrence of positive inflation differentials with the Eurozone since its inception (around 1 pp per year on average up to 2008), which in turn was explained by both higher dynamics of corporate margins and unit labor costs compared to the euro area. The latter expanded 25 percent more than those in the euro area as a whole, due to wage increases much higher than productivity ones. The strong impulse of demand and the loss of external competitiveness led to a high dependence on foreign savings.
- *The mismanagement of part of the financial sector.* The initial crisis was compounded by reckless bank investments and loans, particularly from the

> *cajas* (or savings and loans/building societies). When the economic crisis deepened, it led to a traditional banking crisis caused by the collapse of the real estate market, unemployment records, increasing government debt, and difficulties accessing credit in wholesale markets. The real estate boom-bust cycle, which materialized in particular in the *cajas* sector, exposed weaknesses in the policy and regulatory frameworks, as well as the sector's over-reliance on wholesale funding. In the end, the financial system could not decouple from the economic cycle and the huge macroeconomic crisis that has besieged the country.

A number of factors help account for the deteriorating performance of the Spanish banks after 2009, which led to the financial bailout. First, the deep recession and record-high unemployment triggered successive waves of loan losses in the Spanish mortgage market, which led to a rising share of non-performing loans when the real estate sector collapsed (the Bank of Spain classified €180 billion as troubled assets at the end of 2011). An additional factor was related to the country's sovereign debt: the sustainability of the Spanish government debt was affecting Spanish banks because they had been some of the biggest buyers of government debt in the wake of the ECB long-term refinancing operation liquidity infusions (the percentage of government bonds owned by domestic banks reached 30 percent in mid-2012). In the end, Spain fell into the "doom loop" caused by the close links between government finances and the banking system that had already afflicted Greece or Portugal and led to their bailout. Investors' concerns that the government would bail out weak banks caused sovereign bond yields to spike, while doubts over the country's fiscal health spilled over to the banks because they held too much government debt. A third factor was the dependence of Spanish financial institutions on wholesale funding for liquidity since the crisis started, and, in particular, their dependence on international wholesale financing, as 40 percent of their balance depended on funding from international markets. Once the crisis started this fund (with the notable exception of the ECB's) dried up and made them more vulnerable. Finally, the crisis also exposed weaknesses in the policy and regulatory framework. The Bank of Spain, whose policies had been widely praised prior to the crisis, bore also some responsibility because it chose the path of least resistance in alerting to the risks but failing to act decisively (Royo 2013; Steinberg, Otero Iglesias, and Royo 2017).

By the summer of 2008, the effects of the crisis were evident, and since then the country suffered one of the worst recessions in history, with unemployment reaching over 24 percent in 2012. This collapse was not fully unexpected. The global financial crisis and the surge in commodities, food, and energy prices brought to the fore the imbalances in the Spanish economy: the record current account deficit, persistent inflation, low productivity growth, dwindling competitiveness, increasing unit labor costs, excess consumption, and low savings had all set the stage for the devastating economic crisis (see Royo 2013).

In just a few months, the debt-fueled growth turned into a nightmare as the Spanish economy entered into recession in the second half of 2008, intensified by the tightening of global financing conditions, the decrease in private sector wealth (due to real estate and financial asset prices adjustment), the increased uncertainty, and the declining exports (because of the strong world trade contraction). Between mid-2008 and 2009, real GDP fell by almost 5 percent.

Reaction to crisis: reform and renewal

Initially, the government was reluctant to recognize the crisis because there were general elections in March 2008. Moreover, after the election, it was afraid to admit that it had not been entirely truthful during the campaign. As late as 17 August 2007, Finance Minister Solbes predicted that the crisis would have a relatively small effect on the Spanish economy.

When it became impossible to deny what was evident, the government's initial reluctance to recognize and address the crisis was rapidly replaced by frenetic activism and the introduction of a succession of plans and measures to try to confront it and to address the unprecedented dramatic surge of unemployment (see Royo 2013). Faced with this economic contraction, fiscal policy responded expansively. In 2008 and 2009, in addition to the activation of the automatic stabilizers, several discretionary measures were taken (in line with G-20 recommendations), while a significant decline in tax revenues occurred because of the real estate activity drop. As a result, a dramatic fiscal deterioration started.

However, financial tensions in the European sovereign debt markets after the Greek crisis, first, and the Irish, afterwards, significantly affected the Spanish economy. Thus, in line with the orientation set in the EU (see the chapter by Kincaid in this volume), fiscal policy reacted drastically, becoming contractive. At the beginning of 2010, the Spanish government approved the Fiscal Consolidation Plan 2010–13, in order to redirect the worsening of public finances during the first years of the crisis toward a sustainable path. This plan was essentially structural and based on reductions in public spending and on tax increases (rise in VAT and suspension of housing investment deductions). Subsequently, the government decided to bring forward an important part of the adjustment foreseen in that plan to 2010 and 2011.

Moreover, under intense pressure from European authorities and the ECB, Spain approved further reforms in 2010. This was just another instance in which the Spanish government made strategic use of EU pressures to implement structural reforms that had been hindered by domestic political constraints. The pension system was reformed with the gradual extension of the retirement age and of the period to calculate the pension. The labor market was made more flexible, public wages were cut an average of 5 percent, and a first timid round of financial reform was introduced (regulatory reform of savings banks and measures to increase transparency and capital requirements of credit institutions).

Despite all these efforts, the worsening of political problems in Greece in the first half of 2012 exacerbated tensions across the EMU as investors' concerns about euro reversibility increased. In this context, the recession of the Spanish economy intensified throughout 2012. The interaction of sovereign and banking risks in a recessive context and the acceleration of capital outflows led to the request for public recapitalization in May by one of the largest Spanish banks with a predominantly domestic exposure (BFA-Bankia).

Against this backdrop, in June 2012, the newly elected conservative Spanish government was forced to seek rescue amid growing fears that the financial crisis could drag down its entire economy and lead to a sovereign crisis that threatened the euro. Spain's borrowing costs had been increasing, with the country's interest rate on its 10-year bond rising to 6.18 percent on 7 June, a level that was seen potentially unsustainable at the time. On 9 June, the Eurogroup offered an aid package of up to €100 billion as a bailout for Spain's cash-starved banks. This decision made Spain the fourth and largest European country to agree to accept emergency assistance, which ended up totaling almost €41.3 billion.

The failure of BFA-Bankia validated concerns regarding insufficient regulatory oversight of the Spanish banking system, as well as the perception that Spanish banks and the Bank of Spain had downplayed the risk posed by real-estate loans in the run-up to the crisis. Since the inception of the crisis, Spain had adopted five financial reforms in three years and implemented three rounds of bank mergers, dropping the number of savings banks (known as *cajas*, in which most of the financial problems were concentrated) from 45 to nine (which by now are almost all banks) (Banco de España 2017).[1]

Box 7.1 Financial sector assistance program of Spain

Agreed: 23 July 2012.
Prime Minister: Mariano Rajoy (Partido Popular), until the end of the program.
Tenure: 18 months.
Size: ESM disburses €41.3 billion to Spain (€39.468 billion on 11/12/2012 and €1.865 billion on 05/02/2013). The rescue package was channeled through the FROB to the financial institutions concerned (half of the funds went to CAM, Bankia, Banco de Valencia, Catalunya Banc, and NCG Banco).
Contributors: European Stability Mechanism (ESM).
Objectives: Recapitalize and restructure troubled banks in Spain; increase the long-term resilience of the Spanish banking sector.

Main areas of intervention

Sector-specific objectives, based on three pillars:

- Remove doubts about the quality of the banks' balance sheets, allowing them to carry out their financial intermediation function;
- Facilitate an orderly downsizing of bank exposures to the real estate sector, restore market-based funding, and reduce bank's reliance on central bank liquidity support;
- Enhance risk identification and crisis management mechanisms pertaining to the Spanish banking sector so as to reduce the occurrence and severity of future financial crises.

To this aim, the Memorandum of Understanding (MOU) required the completion of a comprehensive asset quality review and bank-by-bank stress-test, required further strengthening of the operational independence of the Bank of Spain and its supervisory procedures, demanded strengthening consumer protection and securities legislation, suggested creating a bad bank (later called SAREB to purchase "toxic real estate assets" form the banking system), and also the completion of the reform of the savings banks.

Status: The strong implementation record culminated in a successful exit from the program on schedule, without any follow-up program.

More details on the Program and its assessment can be found at www.esm.europa.eu/assistance/spain.

In August 2012 a new financial reform was approved in response to the EU's financial rescue package (Banco de España 2017: 173–174). The Memorandum of Understanding (MOU) established the bail-in of some junior creditors (holders of the so-called *participaciones preferentes* – i.e., preferred shares) – which was significant because it was the first time that a bail-in was used in the crisis (there was no bail-in in the Irish rescue) and it was subsequently used in the Cyprus bail-out, incorporating it into the rules of the European Banking Union (see Box 7.1 for more details of the MOU).

As a result of the MOU, the Spanish government also created a "bad bank" (called SAREB), which absorbed the toxic assets from the real-estate sector and acquired the authority to buy and sell a variety of assets, as well as issue bonds. It also established a new process to restructure and liquidate financial institutions. Finally, the reform reduced the role of the regional governments in the restructuring and liquidation of the *cajas* (Banco de España 2017: 175–184).

The crisis and bailout were devastating for the centennial *cajas*, most of which were liquidated or transformed into banks, in most cases with public capital injections. In contrast, the large commercial banks (such as BBVA and Santander) proved resilient and performed comparatively well. In addition to their internationalization, they stood out for their low borrowing from outside the EU (i.e., non-Euro) and the relatively low rates of inter-bank borrowing (as compared to other European banks). Even where market-based borrowing was relatively high (as in the case of securitization), it had longer maturity than inter-bank borrowing, so the Spanish banks were not caught in the early waves of panic in the inter-bank market (Hardie and Howarth 2013). All these factors help explain why larger Spanish banks were not affected by the crisis as much as the *cajas*.

The Spanish government made strategic use of the bailout program to implement a number of important structural reforms, well beyond the financial system. In the fiscal sphere, the Organic Law of Budgetary Stability and Financial Sustainability was approved to strengthen budgetary discipline. In particular, budgetary balance objectives for all levels of public administrations, limits on public debt, requirements of transparency, and deviation corrections were set. On the labor front, the Law on Urgent Measures for Labor Reform entered into force in July 2012, which gave companies greater capacity to adapt prevalent labor market conditions to their specific situation (raising decentralization of collective bargaining, increasing the internal flexibility of companies, and rationalizing conditions for the elimination of permanent contracts). A Payment Scheme to Suppliers was also implemented, which contributed to alleviating the liquidity constraints of firms as a result of delays in payments by territorial administrations. At the same time, the government launched the Liquidity Fund to Autonomous Regions to ensure adequate financing of regional governments, which provide most of the social policies in Spain. Finally, a new pension reform which delinked pension revalorizations from inflation and capped pension increases at 0.25 percent per year was passed. Given that at that time Spain was experiencing deflation, the structural purchasing power reduction of the reform was partially hidden. However, as growth and inflation resumed, the reform was highly contested. Regardless, in the absence of the pressure exerted by the conditions established by the financial bailout program, the implementation of these reforms would have been much harder, if at all possible. Indeed, the bailout program provided political cover for the unpopular reforms, set a timeline that allowed for their rapid implementation, and helped to overcome domestic political constraints.

These domestic measures, together with those adopted at the European level (particularly strong were ECB's monetary policy actions of unlimited scope and renewed political momentum in the EMU with the proposal of establishment of the Single Supervisory Mechanism with ECB support), started to pay off. Since the end of the double-dip recession in mid-2013, the Spanish economy experienced a remarkable recovery. It completed five years of sustained expansion, with growth rates in activity and employment well above those in the other main euro area countries (in both macro-magnitudes about 1.5 points above the corresponding averages of Germany, France, and Italy).

This performance has led the Spanish economy to recover pre-crisis activity levels by mid-2017, although in terms of employment this convergence has been far less advanced. The reasons behind this successful recovery are both cyclical and structural (Banco de España 2017: 209–215). Among the transient factors are the expansionary impulses of demand policies (monetary and fiscal), the boom in tourism, the depreciation of the euro, and the fall in oil prices, which boosted real incomes and lowered production costs. For their part, permanent factors are partly associated with the effects of reforms (principally those in the labor market and the financial system), and include the reestablishment of external competitiveness, in terms of labor and financial costs. These factors also brought about a recovery in confidence of domestic agents and international investors, and the return of capital flows to the Spanish economy. Overall, the current growth model seems more balanced (less dependent on the construction sector, domestic consumption, and external financing and more on exports). In the end, the crises showed, yet again, the important role of European institutions in the country's process of economic reforms (Table 7.2).

Table 7.2 The economic crisis in Spain (2008–17)

Data	*2008*	*2009*	*2010*	*2011*	*2012*	*2013*	*2014*	*2015*	*2016*	*2017*
GDP growth at constant prices	1.1%	–3.6%	0.0%	–1.0%	–2.9%	–1.7%	1.4%	3.4%	3.3%	3.1%
GDP relative to EU 15	9.3%	9.5%	9.2%	8.8%	8.4%	8.2%	8.0%	7.9%	8.2%	8.3%
TFP growth (2010=100)	99.8	99.1	100.0	100.2	100.1	100.4	100.9	102.2	103.3	104.3
CPI inflation (% annual)	1.4%	0.8%	2.9%	2.4%	2.9%	0.25%	–1.0%	0.02%	1.6%	1.1%
Unemployment rate (% of active population)	11.3%	17.9%	19.9%	21.4%	24.8%	26.1%	24.5%	22.1%	19.6%	17.2%
Real unit labor costs (2010=100)	100.4	101.8	100.0	99.0	96.5	95.7	95.7	96.4	95.6	94.6
Household and NPISH gross savings rate (% of disposable income)	8.2%	13.4%	10.1%	10.8%	8.6%	9.6%	9.3%	8.6%	7.7%	5.7%
Gross fixed capital formation (% of GDP)	28.1%	24.2%	23.0%	21.7%	20.4%	20.0%	20.7%	21.3%	21.3%	21.7%
General government deficit (% of GDP)	–4.4%	–11.0%	–9.4%	–9.6%	–10.5%	–7.0%	–6.0%	–5.3%	–4.5%	–3.1%
General government primary balance (cyclically adjusted; % of potential GDP)	–3.5%	–7.5%	–5.1%	–4.0%	–3.2%	1.3%	1.6%	0.4%	–0.5%	–0.4%
Current account (% of GDP)	–9.2%	–4.3%	–3.9%	–3.3%	–0.4%	1.5%	1.0%	1.0%	1.9%	1.8%
Exports of goods and services (% of GDP)	25.3%	23.3%	25.5%	27.7%	28.8%	30.6%	31.5%	31.7%	32.1%	32.8%
Government bond yields (yield curve)	–0.3%	2.8%	3.4%	4.1%	5.3%	4.3%	2.5%	1.7%	1.7%	1.9%
Private sector debt (% of GDP)	195.9%	201.6%	200.6%	196.4%	188.0%	177.2%	165.8%	154.8%	146.8%	138.8%
Government gross debt (% of GDP)	39.5%	52.8%	60.1%	69.5%	85.7%	95.5%	100.4%	99.4%	99.0%	98.3%
Net International Investment position (% of GDP)	–80.2%	–93.5%	–88.6%	–91.9%	–89.9%	–95.2%	–98.0%	–89.5%	–85.3%	–83.8%

Source: AMECO and Eurostat.

Understanding support for reforms

As the previous section has shown, Spain went through an intense period of economic reform in the aftermath of the crisis. However, as opposed to other countries (like Greece), despite generating large groups of losers (more details below), these reforms, which have been perceived by the majority of the population as "imposed" by Brussels and the Troika, have not undermined the country's confidence in the EU and the euro (Fernandez Albertos and Kuo 2016).

In addition, the crisis and the reforms have transformed the political landscape but have not produced the collapse of the political system or the rise in anti-establishment, anti-EU parties that we have seen in other European countries. It is remarkable that Mariano Rajoy, the Prime Minister during the banking bailout, was able to remain in power after the 2015 and 2016 elections (he was the only sitting Prime Minister in the EU that won two consecutive elections in the aftermath crisis), while most of the other European leaders that governed during the crisis and reform period have lost power. Indeed, it was not the crisis but rather the accumulation of corruption scandals that finally led to his removal (and his conservative party's) from power in June 2018 after a successful no-confidence vote by the Socialist Pedro Sanchez.

Regardless, because of the economic crisis, the Spanish political system has experienced an intense transformation, just like those of other western democracies. However, the main two new parties that have emerged in the last decade, the leftwing Podemos and the liberal pro-reformist Ciudadanos, have not been able to replace (so far) the traditional parties (PSOE and PP), and there are notable differences between these two parties and the other populist and nationalist parties that have emerged in other European countries. Electoral support for Podemos seems to have a ceiling around 20 percent, and even this party is very careful in its messages. Unlike the M5S or the Lega in Italy or the National Front in France, they are anti-austerity but pro-euro, pro-EU, and even pro-reforms in a number of key economic areas (they are also pro-NATO, pro-refugees, and largely avoid making nationalist/protectionist proposals, which makes them different from other anti-establishment parties). Podemos has rapidly understood that an anti-EU message will never be popular in Spain for large segments of the electorate because there is a wide perception that EU membership has brought modernity and prosperity to the country and has historically helped Spanish institutions undertake complex economic reforms. If anything, the populist backlash in Spain has taken the form of the pro-independence movement in Catalonia.

Ciudadanos, on the other hand, is even more pro-European than the traditional parties, but also more rightwing/Spanish nationalist when it comes to the Catalan issue, which has been since 2017 the most divisive issue in Spanish politics. In economic policy, Ciudadanos has repeatedly argued that Spain should accelerate the path of economic reforms, accepting virtually all recommendations coming from the European Commission, form the establishment of a single contract in the labor market to the increase in VAT and the deregulation of the services sector.

Finally, for a long while it was remarkable that despite the increases in unemployment and the rise in inequality and immigration, there was no rightwing anti-EU party in Spain with the success of Golden Dawn in Greece, the National Front in France or the Lega in Italy. However, the recent success of the far-right Vox in the 2018 regional elections in Andalusia, where it obtained around 10 percent of the votes in the regional parliament (the first time it had won any representation at any level), may represent a turn in Spanish politics that will further align it with its European neighbors. In any case, Vox does not have a clear anti-European discourse and has not mentioned the euro at all in its electoral program.[2]

Yet, a key commonality among talk of these parties, with the exception of Vox, that stills differentiates Spain from other European countries (notably France, Italy, or Greece, but not Portugal), has been the very strong consensus and support around the EU. This consensus has been instrumental to legitimize and facilitate the implementation of unpopular reforms that emanated from Brussels. Indeed, the willingness of Spanish public opinion to accept reforms coming from the EU can only be understood through the lens of the idea of "Europe as Modernity" that is so entrenched in Spanish society. In fact, when comparing Spain with other Mediterranean countries that might also share this idea, there are some objective reasons why Spanish support for the EU and EU-sponsored reforms should be higher. First, during the first decade of the euro, no other country (except Ireland) has done better macro economically than Spain (Italy's GDP has stagnated, Portugal's has not grown spectacularly, and Greece grew accumulating unsustainable disequilibria). Second, during the crisis and post-crisis period, the collapse of Spanish GDP, while significant, has not been as severe as that of Greece, Portugal, or even Italy, and the recovery has been much faster. More importantly, the idea that Spain was able to avoid a full bailout program and that its economy could successfully be reformed within EMU is shared by a large majority of the electorate, even by groups that seriously contest the usefulness of austerity policies like Podemos.

In fact, as President Zapatero has argued in his memoirs (2013) and President Rajoy has publicly stated, the main guiding principle of Spanish economic policy from 2010 until 2015 has been to avoid a full bailout from the Troika. Both Presidents were convinced that the loss of economic sovereignty associated with a full rescue program would have sent them/their parties out of office, but, more importantly, they thought that avoiding a full bailout meant avoiding a sense of collective failure that could have had long-lasting negative consequences for the country. However, as Pascual Ramsay (2017) documents, most key economic advisors also understood the European pressure as an opportunity to implement reforms that were deemed as completely necessary after the period of unbalanced growth that the creation of the euro had generated.

However, it remains to be seen whether the recent success of Vox in Andalusia will have electoral and political implications at the national level and, if so, what the impact would be on the country's pre-European stance. The most recent spring 2018 Eurobarometer is worrisome. While 82 percent of Spaniards still consider themselves EU citizens (the sixth highest proportion among all member states), it shows that since autumn 2017, the proportion of respondents with a positive image of the EU has declined in 12 countries, most strikingly in Spain (33 percent, –6 points compared with the fall 2017 survey). Moreover, optimism about the future of the EU has decreased in eight EU member states, including Spain (60 percent, –6 points). Finally, while still strong, support for the single currency has also decreased in Spain (76 percent, –6).

The legacy of the crisis: winners, losers, and the transformation of the Spanish economic model

Overall, the performance of the Spanish economy has been improving since the 2014 recovery. Unemployment, inequality, and the risk of falling under the poverty line have been declining. The increase in employment has been undoubtedly one of the most satisfactory outcomes, but despite the reforms, progress has been both slow and uneven. Moreover, as the fog left by the long recession disappears, it is becoming increasingly clear that the mai n losers from the crisis have been young people (especially women), civil servants (whose wages have been frozen for almost a decade), and those who lost their jobs during the crisis and are re-entering the labor market with more precarious contracts (the so-called precariat). In addition, trade unions, whose role in collective bargaining has been seriously undermined by the labor market reforms, have also lost influence. Overall, while the middle classes and the pensioners experienced some loss in wealth and purchasing power because of the crisis, the main losers have been mainly those at the bottom of the income distribution (low-skilled young individuals in particular). In parallel, middle- and high-income groups have done quite well, especially by benefiting disproportionately of the recovery. Finally, the overall level of Spanish public debt, which increased dramatically during the crisis, remains stubbornly high, which reduces the margin of maneuver of the Spanish government and represents an important weakness for the economy. According to the Bank of Spain, total public debt was almost €950 billion at the end of 2018, slightly less than 100 percent of GDP (44 percent of the debt was in the hands of non-residents and around 30 percent was held by domestic banks and other financial institutions).[3]

Let's start with the unemployed. According to data from the Ministry of Labor, it took 10 years for the Social Security system to reach the 19 million affiliates that it had just before the start of the crisis. In September 2008 it had 19.02 million affiliates, and it reached this level again in June 2018 (the lowest level of affiliates during that decade was 16.17 million in January 2014). While this affiliation growth has been steady at a rate of 3 percent during the last 24 months, it has still to reach the record level of 19.5 million affiliates of July 2007, at the pinnacle of the real estate bubble.

Unemployment has also been declining sharply from a high of 5.04 million unemployed in February 2013, to 3.16 million in June 2018, the lowest level since December 2008. Since 2013, the worst employment year since the crisis, the unemployment rate has fallen a very robust 9 points (as a point of reference, during the recovery period that followed the crisis of the early 1990s, unemployment fell less than 6 points). However, the quality of jobs has fallen. Real wages in most new jobs have gone down and there is more precarious self-employment, both because of the labor market reform and technological change.

The recovery has had mixed results for women. In June 2018, for the fourth consecutive month, the country broke the record of women affiliated to the Social Security, reaching 8,779,129 women, which represents 46.19 percent of the employed population. However, according to EU data, while women still suffer from a significant pay gap (in 2016 women earned on average €414 less than men, down from €478 in 2015), the pay gap has been decreasing: 2.9pps between 2016 and 2018, one of the fastest rates in the EU. Yet, the unemployment rate among women is still higher: 18 percent versus 15 percent for men in 2017. Moreover, women are more likely than men to be in temporary contracts and, as a result, their wages tend to be lower (average hourly rate for workers with indefinite contracts is €15.6, while for those in temporary contracts is €11.97). They are also more likely to work part-time (out of 2.7 million part-time workers, two million are women, and salaries are even lower for those in part-time jobs: a full-time worker earns on average €15.6, while a part-time one earns €10.4 (Gómez 2017)) (Table 7.3).

Furthermore, on the negative side, one of the main challenges remains the high rate of temporary contracts, a problem that has not been resolved with the economic recovery or the economic reforms (Torres 2017; Gómez 2018). In 2017 alone, Spain broke its own record (established the prior year) with 21.5 million new contracts, 90 percent (or 19.6 million) of them temporary. Indeed, precariousness and employment instability still remain two important structural weaknesses of the country's labor market. The temporary rate remains stubbornly high at 27.4 percent, the highest rate in the EU. While there was a significant increase in the number of indefinite long-term contracts in 2017 (16.3 percent), temporary contracts still represented 90 percent of the labor contracts signed in the first half of 2018. In May and June 2018 (for the fifth time in history), there were two million labor contracts signed, which illustrates the very high rotation rate in employment. To compound the problem, the transition rates toward permanent contracts remain very low. When it happens, it takes even

Table 7.3 Inequality, poverty, and unemployment in Spain

	2008	*2013*	*2017*
Gini (disposable income, post taxes and transfers)	0.33	0.35	0.35
Gini coefficient of equivalent disposable income (scale from 0 to 100)	32.4	33.7	34.1
Poverty rate after taxes and transfers, poverty line 60%	0.21	0.23	0.16
Long-term unemployment rate (12 months or more)	2.0	13.0	7.7
Long-term unemployment as a percentage of total unemployment	12.8	45.4	44.5
Youth unemployment rate	24.5	55.5	38.6

Source: OECD and authors' calculations.

longer. Between 2008 and 2016 it took on average 94 months for a temporary contract to be converted into an indefinite one (in contrast between 2001 and 2007 it took 57 months); and the average length of the contracts is even shorter (according to data from the Public Service of Estate Employment – the SPEE – in 2017 the proportion of contracts that lasted five days or less was close to 26 percent of the total).[4] In sum, despite strong employment growth, the quality and stability of employment remains a problem and exacerbates inequality.

In addition, despite increases to the minimum wage (the government increased it by 4 percent in 2018), salaries have also stagnated. Purchasing capacity has barely improved between 2007 and 2017 because salaries have only grown between 1 and 2 percentage points over inflation during that period: The accumulated inflation between 2007 and 2017 was 14.2 percent, and salaries have only increased 15.1 percent for managers and 16.4 percent for regular workers during the same period (Sánchez-Silva 2018). Civil servants have seen their wages frozen for almost a decade.

One of the groups that remain severely affected by the crisis has been young people: At 38.6 percent, Spain still has the second highest (after Greece) youth unemployment rate of the EU. According to EU data, in spite of improving labor conditions, more than 70 percent of young workers in Spain are likely to be employed under non-standard and atypical form of employment including temporary jobs, involuntary part-time work, and lower-wage jobs. The high rotation prevents young people from accumulating experience and productivity at the companies that they work in, and hence increase their salaries and benefits. Finally, their salaries are very low: according to a recent study by *PeopleMatters* the entry salaries for young people with university degrees range between €21,000 and €32,000 a year, but the most typical average is €21,000.

There is, indeed, a financial generation gap that has been aggravated by the crises because Spain's welfare state is not particularly effective at helping the young or the neediest: the backbone of the Spanish welfare system is pensions, which average 80 percent of final salaries.[5] According to *The Economist* (2018),

> The average annual pre-tax income of households headed by 65- to 74-year-olds rose from €27,000 in 2008 to €29,700 in 2014, whereas for those under 35 it fell from €34,300 to €25,500. On present trends many of the baby-boom generation will retire on the maximum pension of €36,600 a year, in a country where 72 percent of the workforce earns less than €27,600.

Moreover, the employment crisis has not ended. The unemployment rate is still almost double what it was before the crisis, the number of unemployed is still far away from the lowest record of under two million unemployed before the crisis, and it is estimated that it will not go under 10 percent before 2020. At the same time, the crisis has also left a legacy of long-term unemployment that is more severe and persistent than during previous crises. Despite significant declines, at 7.7 percent, Spain is ranked next to last in the EU in long-term unemployment as a percentage of active population. Another negative consequence of the crisis has been the substitution of expensive workers (who have been laid off or early retired) for cheaper workers. Business benefits continue growing at a significantly faster pace than labor remunerations, and consequently the benefits of the economic recovery are still not felt by the less favored people.

Another negative consequence of the crisis has been the increasing levels of income inequality, which have risen above the OECD average, mainly because those at the bottom have become worse off. Indeed the costs of the crisis have been shared out unequally and so has the recovery. A recent EU report places Spain (in a group with Bulgaria, Greece, and Lithuania) last in that variable (European Commission 2018). While in the EU the richest 20 percent of households received an income share that was 5.2 times that of the poorest 20 percent, in Spain that proportion is a little over 6.5 times. Furthermore, the country has not yet re-stablished the levels of income equality that it had prior to the economic crisis. Despite the notable employment progress described above, its benefits have not been equitably distributed among the different segments of the population.[6] According to the European Commission in 2016, 28 percent of Spaniards were suffering, or were likely to suffer, from poverty and social exclusion.

The differences are particularly significant based on qualifications, with those less qualified having been particularly affected by lower employment rates, lower income, and by extension by widening income inequalities. According to the report, Spain faces "a critical situation" (p. 18) when it comes to early leavers from education and training. The persistence of income inequities is often connected to differentiated access to education, training, social protection, and jobs. The report also noted the negative impact of this development on equity, social inclusion, and sustainable growth. The reduction of working hours and wages that often follow the exit of the crisis has impacted more severely those who had lower incomes, particularly workers with low qualifications (58 percent of the jobs created during the recovery period have been in areas with high qualifications, and only 11 percent of the jobs created between 2014 and 2016 were filled by people with low qualifications), young workers, immigrants, and women (who have most of the temporary contracts and lower salaries).[7] The increasing number of temporary contracts is also having a negative impact on income because temporary contracts are also associated with lower salaries, as noted before. Finally, jobs are no longer a secure route out of poverty because starting pay for young people fell by about 35 percent in real terms between 2007 and 2014 (*The Economist*, 2018).

Indeed, despite improvements in the Gini coefficient, the economic recovery for people with low income has been too slow and has not helped to reduce inequalities between the top and bottom 20 percent of earners. Intermon (2018), using Eurostat data, documents that in the 2013–15 period (i.e., the first years of strong economic growth), the top 10 percent of the income distribution captured almost 30 percent of the increases in net income. Moreover, according to data from the National Institute of Statistics (INE), in 2016, 20 percent of the households with the highest income earned 6.6 times more than the bottom 20 percent households (before the crisis the difference was 5.6). In per capita income, in 2016 the 20 percent of bottom earners still received 15 percent less than in 2008, while the top 20 percent only lost 1 percent compared to 2008. Social Security contributions confirm this pattern: by 2018, the average base contributions in real terms were close to those from 2011, which suggests that salaries have recovered but with a more unequal distribution (Maqueda 2018). In sum, the recovery has been remarkably unequal and reforms have reduced the redistributive capacity of public policies, with the richest 10 percent receiving twice as much in transfers through public policies (mainly higher education and pensions) than any other income group in society (OECD 2017).

Further, according to data from the Bank of Spain, the level of indebtedness is still quite elevated among people with low income and young people. The intensive use of temporary and/or part-time contracts has been a key factor to account for the slower recovery for low-income people. As noted before, high rotation and/or fewer hours prevent these workers from gaining experience, and hence from improving their labor conditions and salaries.

At the same time, according to EU data, the depth and persistence of poverty remains high: the relative median at-risk-of-poverty gap is still close to 30 percent. Moreover, while the proportion of people at risk of poverty or social exclusion has improved, it remains high at close to 16 percent, and the impact of social policies reducing poverty has been limited: monetary poverty is only reduced by 25 percent after all social transfers, far from the 50 percent in the Nordic countries. In addition, the rate of quasi-joblessness remains worrisomely high at 14.9 percent, and the in-work at-risk-of-poverty rate is still one of the highest in the EU at 13.1 percent.

Finally, this economic cycle has reaffirmed the rollercoaster pattern from the previous crisis: the Spanish economy has a strong tendency to destroy employment very rapidly during periods of recession, and it creates employment at a very fast rate during periods of growth. This unfortunate pattern is quite unique in the EU, and it is possible because of temporary labor model that allows companies to hire workers with short-term contracts and eliminate those jobs whenever demands drops, which leads to sharp increases in unemployment. The cost of this model, however, is significant in terms of productivity, instability, and low salaries. This remains a key challenge for the Spanish economy.

Impact of the reforms on the economic model

It is still too early to claim how deep the structural transformation of the Spanish economy has been and to what extent the country's growth model can fit into a new category within the varieties of capitalism literature (see chapter by Marzinotto in this volume). According to Hall and Soskice (2001), the Mediterranean economies of Southern Europe used to display a distinctive variety of capitalism (different from the more stylized models of Liberal Market Economy (LME) and Coordinated Market Economy (CME) that predominate in the rest of western Europe). They featured some capacities for coordination in the sphere of corporate governance and limited capacities for strategic coordination in the sphere of labor relations because they lacked institutional capacities for the strategic coordination of wages, aside from periodic but short-lived social pacts. Hall (2012, 2014) also argued that the governments of southern European mixed market economies tended to be more inclined to pursue demand-led growth, based on the expansion of credit (an approach also characteristic of liberal market economies).

In this regard, Spain conformed to the so-called state capitalism model or a State-Influenced Mixed Market Economy (Royo 2013).[8] Indeed, Sapir included Spain (together with Greece, Italy, and Portugal) as part of the "Mediterranean Model", characterized by support for early retirement, regulated labor markets that protect employment, as well as provision of pensions (Sapir 2005).

Prior to the crisis, Royo (2013) showed that in Spain globalization and the euro had promoted rather than undermined coordination among economic actors. Unable to escape from economic interdependence, Spanish economic actors developed coordinating capacities at the macro and micro levels to address and resolve tensions between economic interdependence and political sovereignty. For instance, in the realm of industrial relations, and before the 2008 crisis, the trajectory of change in Spain paralleled development in the CMEs more closely than those in the LMEs.

Since the crisis, however, Spain has been moving toward the Anglo-Saxon model. As we have seen, the crisis imposed exigencies of increasing competitiveness on the Spanish economy (and firms), which compelled the country (under Brussels' insistence) to deregulate its labor market, welfare systems, and industrial relations. These reforms were largely based on deregulation and further liberalization, and have undermined coordinating capacity (see Table 7.4).

Table 7.4 Competitiveness indicators in Spain

	2008	*2013*	*2017*
Product market regulation (index scale 0–6; from least to most restrictive)	1.6	1.4	–
State control	2.2	1.9	–
Barriers to entrepreneurship	2.2	2.1	–
Barriers to trade and investment	0.4	0.4	–
Credit: strength of legal rights index	–	5.0	5.0
Cost to start a business (% of income per capita)	15.1	5.0	4.3
Minimum paid-in capital to start a business (% of income per capita)	13.7	13.2	12.9
Cost to enforce a contract (% claim)	17.2	17.2	18.5
Resolving insolvency: cost (% of state)	14.5	11.0	11.0
Time to resolve insolvency (years)	1.5	1.5	1.5
Labor tax and contributions (%)	35.5	35.6	35.6
Total tax rate (% of profit)	60.7	37.6	48.7
Political stability index (–2.5 weak; 2.5 strong)	–0.4	0.0	0.3

Source: OECD and authors' calculations.

Indeed, in Spain the deflation forced on the country by Brussels' policies and the financial bailout program was designed to lower unit labor costs and make its products more competitive. Moreover, the responses to the crisis included not only cuts to budget deficits, but also extensive structural reforms designed to reduce the role of the state in the economy and to make markets in products or labor more intensely competitive. In effect, the EU seemed to be trying to turn a mixed-market economy into a liberal market economy (Hall 2016). The PP labor reform, which established a more decentralized system of collective bargaining, clearly pointed in this direction.

It is still too early to extract firm conclusions. The recently elected Socialist government is already trying to change some of the more liberal policies implemented by its conservative predecessor. However, at the time of writing it is fair to conclude that one of the outcomes of the crisis has been the transformation of the Spanish economy into a more liberal market economy, in which inequality is higher and the overall role of the state and welfare policies is lower. At the same time, however, the new growth model seems more based on exports. However, it remains to be seen if current account surpluses can be sustained over time, especially once wages and oil prices start to grow.

Conclusions and lessons

Since the end of the double-dip recession in mid-2013, the Spanish economy has experienced a remarkable recovery, completing currently four years of sustained expansion, with growth rates in activity and employment well above those in the other main euro area countries. This performance has led the Spanish economy to recover pre-crisis activity levels by mid-2017, although in terms of employment, as we have seen, this convergence has been far less advanced.

The reasons for the successful recovery of the Spanish economy include both transitory elements as well as structural ones. Among the transient factors are the expansionary impulses of demand policies (monetary and fiscal), and the fall in oil prices in 2014 and 2015, which boosted real incomes and lowered production costs. For their part, structural factors are partly associated with the effects of reforms implemented in recent years in various fields and mentioned above (principally, labor market and financial system), which have contributed to the reestablishment of external competitiveness, in terms of labor and financial costs. These factors also brought about a recovery in confidence of domestic agents.

From a political standpoint, despite the painful consequences of the economic crisis, the increasing party fragmentation, and the relative political upheaval that culminated with the spring 2018 unexpected change in government, one of the notable outcomes that separates Spain from other European countries has been the fact that the country has not produced a radical anti-European party. In fact, Euroskepticism in Spain remains extremely low, reflecting the strong pro-European consensus that all major parties adhere to. This consensus helps explain why, despite running high budget deficits for the last ten years (often above the 3 percent of GDP benchmark established by the EU), Spain has largely avoided censure from the markets or Brussels. On the contrary, this leeway shows that the country has been credited for implementing structural reforms, cleaning up the banking sector, and generating high levels of growth.

Euro and EU membership is regarded in Spain as an anchor of political (and even economic) stability. Even though there is a significant debate in Spain about the necessary reforms the country has to undertake to increase its potential growth, reduce inequality, and raise its productivity level, few would argue that EU membership hampers those reforms. Business, trade unions, and civil society at large have different views about the distributional consequences of these reforms, but none of them claims that without the constraints imposed by EU and euro membership reforms would be better designed or implemented. The high levels of perceived corruption in Spain make most citizens afraid of eliminating the anchoring to transparency and rigor that EU membership provides. In fact, in areas like tax evasion in particular and corruption in general, there is a widespread sentiment that more pressure from the EU institutions would be beneficial. This is not the case for more consolidated democracies like the UK, Denmark, or even France, where citizens tend to trust more domestic institutions and politicians.

The Spanish experience serves as an important reminder that, in the context of a monetary union, countries only control fiscal policies and relative labor costs. Spain proved to be weak at both. It failed to develop an appropriate adjustment strategy to succeed within EMU, and it ignored the imperative that domestic policy choices have to be consistent with the international constraints imposed by EMU membership. On the contrary, in Spain domestic policies and EMU imperatives stood in uneasy relationship to one another. The crisis was the tipping point that brought this inconsistency to the fore, which led to the worst economic crisis in Spanish modern history. At the same time, it shows that, yet again, the Spanish government made strategic use of EU pressures and the bailout program to implement structural reforms that had been hindered by domestic political constraints.

In spite of these favorable developments, there are still challenges ahead to preserve the recent vigorous growth of the Spanish economy in the longer term, specifically: the need for fiscal consolidation, the impact on public finances of population ageing, the urgency of reducing high structural unemployment, and the necessity to invigorate productivity. Indeed, low productivity, inequalities, relative poor quality and stability of employment, as well as the duality of the labor market persist as structural problems that need to be addressed. The Spanish economy needs to continue developing its competitive capacity with knowledge-based investment that will contribute to faster productivity growth and address the persistent labor precariousness and social inequalities. This will require the consolidation of a different pattern of economic growth. Finally, the country needs to reform its welfare state, which is not very redistributive and is not particularly effective at helping the neediest; and it will need policies to promote a higher birth rate or immigration (or both).

Notes

1 The *cajas*, which were not listed on the stock market and accounted for half of the financial sector's assets. They did not have formal shareholders, did not distribute profits, and were governed by a broad range of private and public stakeholders. The *cajas* were peculiar credit institutions, a combination of a commercial bank and a foundation, which dedicated a significant portion of their profits (usually over 20 percent) to social causes: such as cultural activities, social assistance programs, and research-related activities.

2 The combination of the persisting social discontent with the austerity policies that followed the crisis, the corruption of the traditional parties, and the rise in immigration, together with regional factors such as the exhaustion of 36 years of Socialist rule, local corruption (two former Socialist regional premiers were on trial during the election), the disappointment with the Podemos-Izquierda Unida coalition, and a flat and overconfident campaign from the Socialists that failed to counter the aggressive campaign from the conservative parties, led to a record abstentionism and the overall victory of the right.

3 See General Secretariat of Treasury and International Financing of the Kingdom of Spain (2018) for details.

4 The Spanish government reached an agreement with the social partners in April 2017 to run recruitment competitions for 250,000 permanent public sector jobs over three years. This will contribute to reducing the high incidence of temporary workers in the public sector and tackling overall labor market segmentation (Gómez 2017).

5 This problem is compounded by the fact that the total fertility rate, at 1.3, is among the lowest in the EU, and the fact that Spain has the world's second-highest life expectancy after Japan. According to the OECD, by 2050, the number of pensioners will rise to 76 for every 100 workers (from 30-plus now). Furthermore, the pension system now depends on government funding to cover its annual deficit of €18 billion.

6 According to Goerlich (2016), unemployment explains up to 80 percent of the increases in inequality since the crisis: most of the people in the bottom 20 percent are unemployed or receive minimal income. In other words, the increases in inequality are not so much caused by higher incomes from the top earners, although they have benefited from the improved performance of their investments in the stock market, but rather by the fact that many in the bottom 20 percent do not have jobs, work fewer hours, experience high rotation, work part-time, or receive little or no income. This problem has been particularly severe for people with low qualifications who worked in the construction sector prior to the crisis.

7 The country's education and training system has long underperformed and has been failing many of its students, and the economic crisis has made things worse. According to recent data, almost one in five students drops out of school early, and many others stay on only until they can legally leave at 16. In the decade prior to the crisis young people took advantage of the construction boom (an unskilled construction worker could take home €1,000 a month, a salary higher than that of many skilled workers) and consequently the number of school dropouts surged further. This helps explain why around half of Spain's 3.3 million jobless never finished secondary school, and their lack of skills helps account for the fact that almost 2 million of those 3.3 million have been out of work for more than a year. The problem is also that many of them may never work again (Maqueda 2017).

8 This typology borrows from Schmidt (2012) and Hancké et al. (2007). Other European countries that have been included in this category are France, Portugal, Italy, and Greece.

References

Banco de España (2017), *Informe sobre la crisis financiera y bancaria en España, 2008–2014*. Madrid: Banco de España, May 2017.

Dellepiane, S. and N. Hardiman (2011), "Governing the Irish Economy". *UCD Geary Institute Discussion Series Papers*. Geary WP2011/03, 21 February.

The Economist (2018), Lessons from Spain's recovery after the euro crisis. 26 July.

European Commission (2018), *Joint Employment Report 2018*. Adopted by the EPSCO Council on 15 March 2018.

Fernandez Albertos, J. and A. Kuo (2016), "Economic Hardship and Policy Preferences in the Eurozone Periphery: Evidence from Spain", *Comparative Political Studies*, 49(7), 874–906.

Fernández-Villaverde, J., L. Garicano and T. Santos (2013), "Political Credit Cycles: The Case of the Eurozone", *Journal of Economic Perspectives*, 27(3), 145–166.

General Secretariat of Treasury and International Financing of the Kingdom of Spain (2018), *Treasury Bills: Distribution by Holders*. Retrieved from www.tesoro.es/sites/default/files/estadisticas/04.pdf.

Goerlich, F. J. (2016), "Crecimiento y distribución: Desigualdad, pobreza y condiciones de vida", in Ariño, A. and J. Romero (eds.): *Estructura Social Valenciana*. València: Ed. Alfons el Magnànim.

Gómez, M. V. (25 December 2017), "Menos recuperación para ellas", *El País*. Retrieved from https://elpais.com/economia/2017/12/24/actualidad/1514127250_287523.html. Last accessed 26 November 2018.

Gómez, M. V. (3 July 2018), "La Seguridad Social recupera la cota de los 19 millones de afiliados 10 años después", *El País*. Retrieved from https://elpais.com/economia/2018/07/03/actualidad/1530595889_757919.html. Last accessed on 26 November 2018.

Hall, P. (2012), "The Economics and Politics of the Euro Crisis", *German Politics*, 21, 355–381.

Hall, P. (2014), "Varieties of Capitalism and the Euro Crisis", *West European Politics*, 37, 1223–1243.

Hall, P. (2016), "Varieties of Capitalism in Light of the Euro Crisis". Paper presented at the 2016 Annual meeting of the *American Political Science Association*, Philadelphia.

Hall, P. and D. Soskice (2001), *Varieties of Capitalism*. New York: Oxford University Press.

Hancké, B., Rhodes, M. and Thatcher, M. (eds.) (2007), *Beyond Varieties of Capitalism: Conflict, Contradictions, and Complementarities in the European Economy*. Oxford: Oxford University Press.

Hardie, I. and Howarth, D. (2013), *Market-Based Banking and the International Financial Crisis*. Oxford: Oxford University Press.

Intermon (2018), "¿Realidad o ficción? La recuperación económica en manos de una minoría". Informe de Oxfam-Intermon 43. Madrid.

Maqueda, A. (10 December 2017), "Atrapados por la Desigualdad," *El País*. Retrieved from https://elpais.com/economia/2017/12/09/actualidad/1512844379_448525.html. Last accessed 26 November 2018.

Maqueda, A. (8 July 2018), "La recuperación económica no reduce la brecha entre las rentas altas y bajas", *El País*. Retrieved from https://elpais.com/economia/2018/07/08/actualidad/1531080236_187529.html. Last accessed 26 November 2018.

Martinez-Mongay, C. and L. A. Maza Lasierra (2009), "Competitiveness and Growth in the EU". *Economic Papers* 355. January, pp. 1–42.

Molina, I. (2013), "Una Nueva Política Europea después de Tocar Fondo", *Política Exterior* 152, Marzo/Abril.

OECD (2017), *2017 Economic Survey of Spain: Reforms for Inclusive Growth*, Paris: OECD.

Pagoulatos, G. (2004), "Believing in National Exceptionalism: Ideas and Economic Divergence in Southern Europe", *West European Politics*, 27(1), 45–70.

Pascual Ramsay, A. (2017), "The Management of the Economic Crisis in Spain by the PSOE Government: A Domestic Political Perspective", PhD Thesis, University of Cambridge, Cambridge.

Royo, S. (2013), *Lessons from the Economic Crises in Spain*, New York: Palgrave.

Royo S. and P. C. Manuel (2003), *Spain and Portugal in the European Union*, London: Frank Cass.

Sánchez-Silva, C. (13 January 2018), "Los salarios ganan solo dos puntos a la inflación en los últimos diez años", *El País*. Retrieved from https://elpais.com/economia/2018/01/13/actualidad/1515874590_492235.html. Last accessed 26 November 2018.

Sapir, A. (2005), "Globalisation and the Reform of European Social Models", *Bruegel*. Retrieved from http://bruegel.org/2005/09/globalisation-and-the-reform-of-european-social-models.

Schmidt, V. A. (2012), "What Happened to the State-Influenced Market Economies (SMEs)? France, Italy, and Spain Confront the Crisis as the Good, the Bad, and the Ugly", in W. Grant and G. K. Wilson (eds.): *The Consequences of the Global Financial Crisis: The Rhetoric of Reform and Regulation*, Oxford: Oxford University Press.

Steinberg, Federico, Miguel Otero Iglesias and Sebastián Royo (2017), *The Spanish Financial Crisis: Lessons for the European Banking Union.* Informe Elcano 20, Real Instituto Elcano, Madrid.

Torres, R. (4 August 2017), "La montaña rusa del empleo", *El País*. Retrieved from https://elpais.com/economia/2017/07/28/actualidad/1501251155_089117.html. Last accessed 26 November 2018.

Zapatero, J. L. (2013), *El Dilema: 600 dís de vertigo*, Madrid: Planeta.

8 Italy

Missed adjustments and political nemesis

Silvia Merler

Introduction

In March 2018, the Italian elections delivered the photograph of a political system that had become tri-polar. With the center-right gathering 37 percent of the votes, the populist Five Stars Movement (M5S) increasing its share to 32 percent, and the center-left down to 23 percent, none of the three major political forces had the majority needed to govern alone, and squaring the geometry of post-electoral coalition-making appeared impossible. After two months of negotiation, a government coalition was agreed between the two populist and (to different degrees) Euroskeptic parties. The League – formerly *Northern* League – had performed well in the north of the country, campaigning on a fiscal platform that implied redistribution toward the top and the elderly, underpinned by a revenue-reducing reform of the taxation system. The Five Stars Movement – a populist formation founded by former comedian Beppe Grillo – over-performed in the south of Italy, campaigning on redistribution toward the bottom and particularly the youth, through an expenditure-increasing expansion of the welfare state. These diametrically opposed conceptions of fiscal policy were combined into a 'government contract', and later into a budget for 2019–21 that projected a worsening of the Italian structural fiscal position and that opened up a heated confrontation with Brussels (Blanchard et al. 2018). In its open defiance of EU fiscal rules, Italy today finds itself alone, opposed not only – as one would logically expect – by the fiscal hawks in the Eurozone 'North', but also by those within the 'South' that Italy used to be able to count as friends or allies in the quest for Eurozone reform. The reason for this – I argue – is that Italy represents a case of missed adjustment. Before the crisis, Italy did not experience the kind of wide-ranging imbalances that Greece, Ireland, Portugal, and Spain developed. This notwithstanding, the country came under market pressure in 2011, but the appointment of the technocratic Monti government was enough for market pressure to subside and for Italy to avoid an EU/IMF macroeconomic adjustment program. This apparently positive solution, however, backfired in the longer term, because it delayed adjustment and slowed the recovery, with social repercussions that eventually would find their voice in the election of 2018. While the program countries have undergone a massive adjustment, Italy has remained stuck in a low-growth limbo. As a consequence, the country is now an outlier in the Eurozone: it retains an especially high public debt burden, competitiveness remains low, long-term nominal and real rates are rising due to perceived political risk, long-term youth unemployment remains stubbornly high and persistent, and standards of living have been stagnating for years with effects on inequality. The political repercussions of this idiosyncrasies for the future of Italy and the Eurozone are not yet clear, but their importance could hardly be overestimated.

The Italian economy before the crisis: between North and South

Within the current North vs. South debate on Eurozone reform, Italy belongs to the latter camp. From a purely macroeconomic standpoint, however, the Italian economy was in an intermediate position between North and South[1] prior to the Eurozone crisis. Differently from Greece, Ireland, Portugal, and Spain – which eventually had to undergo full or partial EU/IMF macroeconomic adjustment programs – Italy's pre-crisis growth model was not predominantly demand-driven. During the 1999–2007 period, domestic demand grew faster than GDP in all program countries (4.2 percent vs. 3.8 percent on average, respectively) and slower than GDP in the 'North' of the Eurozone (1.5 percent vs. 2 percent on average, respectively).[2] In Italy, GDP and demand grew at about the same pace, both before and after the introduction of the euro. Italy also did not share the bubble-like features that characterized program countries in the pre-crisis period, when the decline in nominal long-term interest rates coupled with persistent inflation differentials led to a strong decrease in real interest rates (Figure 8.1a) and to a credit boom (Figure 8.1b). In Italy, real rates remained slightly higher than in the program countries, and credit increased less, catching up with the North where credit growth had instead been stagnant for 40 years.

As a result, the accumulation of private debt in Italy was more modest than in the rest of the South. Private debt to GDP peaked at 125 percent in Italy in 2012 whereas in the program countries private debt to GDP was 194 percent the same year and, although declining, it was still 156 percent in 2017. That expansion of credit supply beyond banks' core liabilities was allowed by the unprecedented degree of financial integration and nominal convergence in the run-up to the introduction of the single currency. By removing the exchange rate risk, monetary unification then facilitated massive intra-Eurozone capital flows from north to south. The counterpart of these financial account dynamics was visible in the widening of intra-Eurozone current account imbalances, interpreted by observers at the time as a welcome sign that monetary unification had spurred a downhill flow of capital (Blanchard and Giavazzi 2002) (Figure 8.2a). The Italian current account also moved into a deficit position during the first decade after currency unification, but the deficit only reached 3.4 percent of GDP in 2010 (at its lowest). This was significantly smaller than the aggregate corresponding figure for the group of program countries, where the current account deficit reached 10 percent of total group GDP in 2008. Accordingly, the legacy

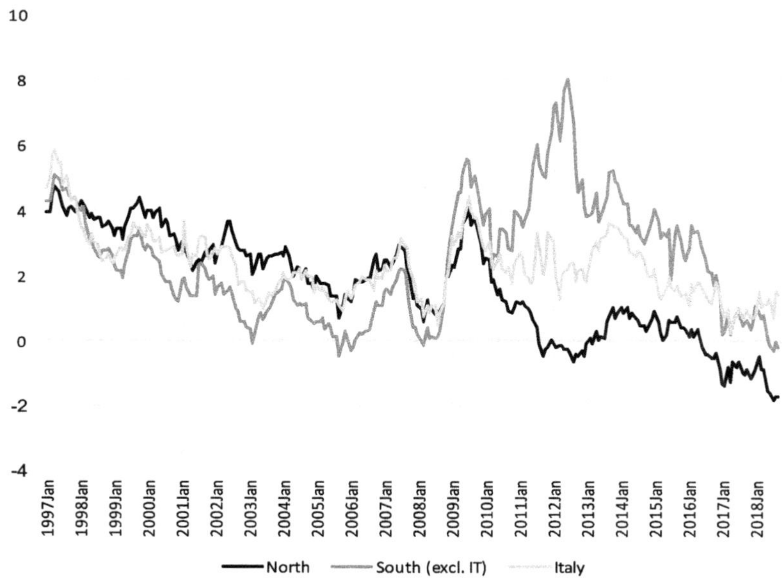

(a)

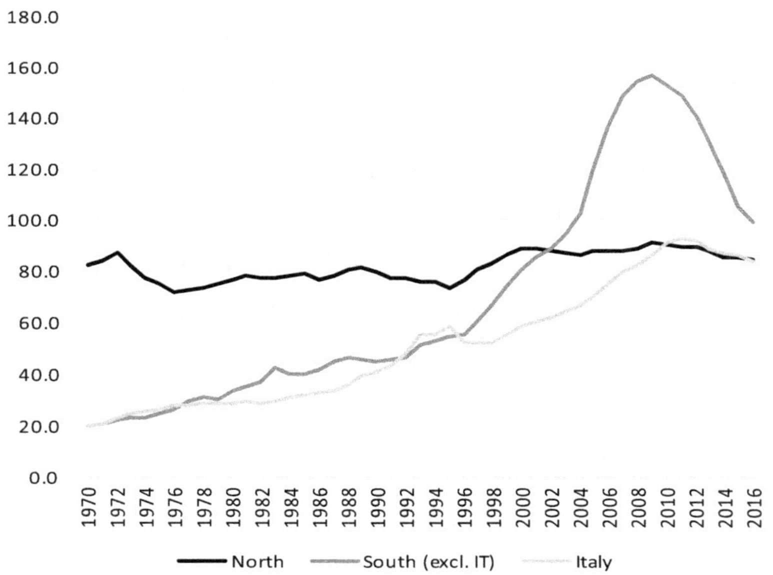

(b)

Figure 8.1 (a) Long-term real interest rates (%); (b) bank credit to private sector (% GDP) in Italy.

Source: author's calculations based on ECB and BIS data. Real rates are calculated as nominal rates minus inflation.

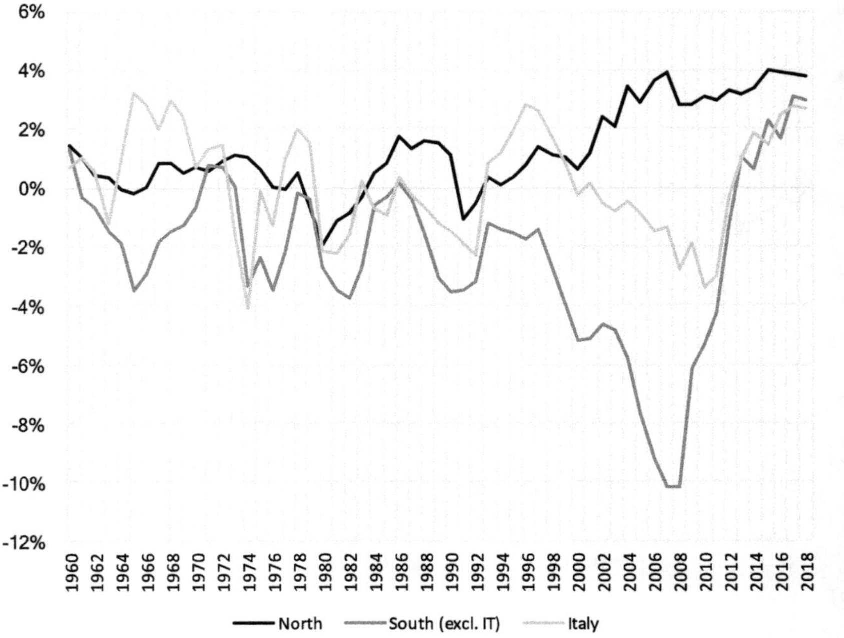

(a)

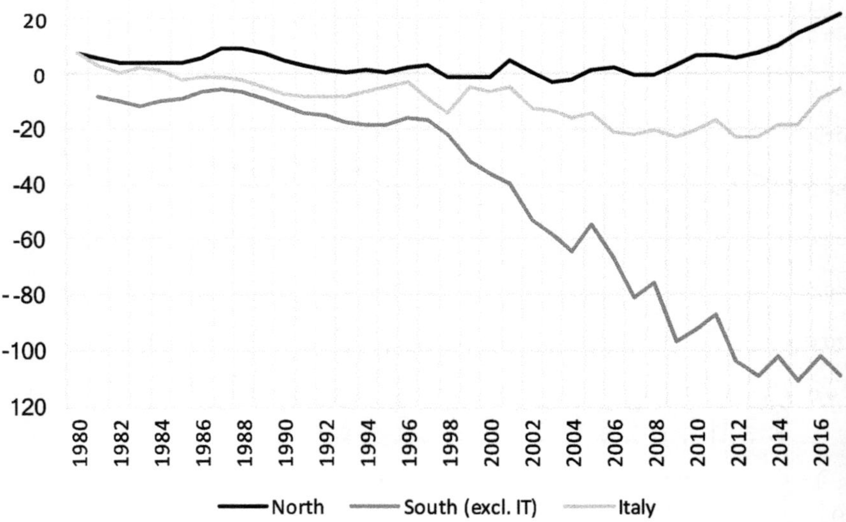

(b)

Figure 8.2 (a) Current account (% GDP); (b) bank credit to private sector (% GDP) in Italy.

Source: author's calculations based on AMECO and IMF data.

(a)

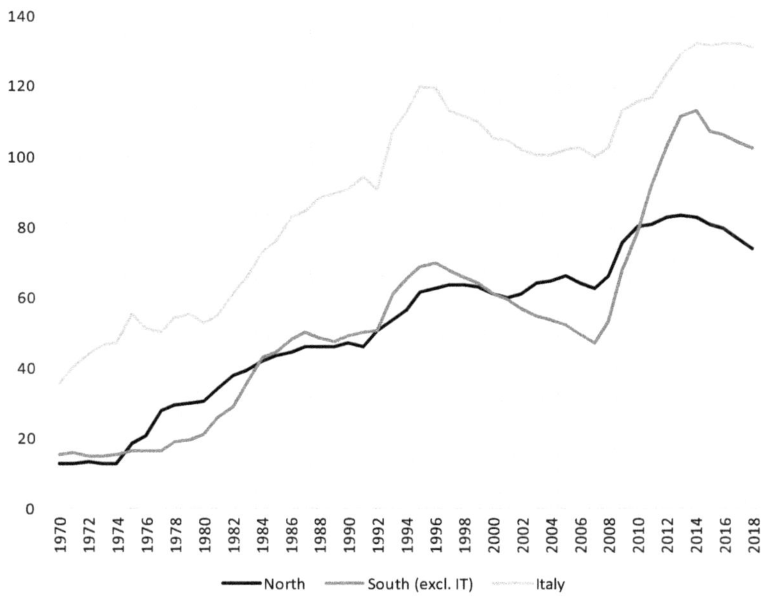

(b)

Figure 8.3 (a) Government deficit (% GDP); (b) government debt (% GDP) in Italy.

Source: author's calculations based on Eurostat and AMECO data.

of the crisis in terms of external debt – as reflected in the Net International Investment Position (NIIP) – is significantly less burdensome in Italy, which has almost entirely balanced its NIIP, compared to the program countries, where aggregate NIIP debt currently stands at around 100 percent of GDP.

On top of having a lower private debt, Italy also differs markedly from both the North and the rest of the South in its historically high public debt to GDP ratio (Figure 8.3b). During the pre-crisis period Italy kept its public finances in check, running modest headline deficits which allowed the country to keep a primary surplus for a long time (Figure 8.3a). As a consequence, public debt was on a declining trajectory between 1995 and 2007, when it touched 99.8 percent of GDP (the lowest in 14 years). Italy followed a 'northern path' during the global financial crisis, avoiding a large fiscal easing – a choice that would be central also to the political crisis of 2011, reviewed in the next section. Differently from the rest of the South – where the cost of expensive bank rescues weighed heavily on public finances during the crisis – the nominal growth of public debt in Italy did not increase significantly. Yet, the combination of still positive nominal debt growth and of zero nominal GDP growth led to an increase in the overall debt-to-GDP ratio, between 2008 and 2014. Since then, public debt has been hovering around 130 percent of GDP in Italy, whereas the aggregate public debt of program countries has been declining steadily, thanks to a stronger post-program rebound in growth.[3]

The Italian crisis of 2011

Although Italy did not resort to large fiscal easing in 2008–9, and although it did not spend as much as other countries on bank rescues, the high public debt and the significant home-bias in Italian banks' government debt holding left the country vulnerable to contagion during the Eurozone crisis (Merler and Pisani-Ferry 2012). In the summer and fall of 2011, Italy thus went through a full-blown economic, financial, and political crisis that resulted in the collapse of the fourth Berlusconi government and its replacement with a technocratic cabinet led by Mario Monti, economist and former European Commissioner.[4] After Greece, Ireland and Portugal had lost market access and asked for EU/IMF assistance, financial markets' pressure started to mount on Spain and Italy. The spread between the 10-year government bonds of Italy and Germany reached above 500 basis points at the end of the year, signaling a level of market stress that could call public debt sustainability into question. Market nervousness was partly due to a domestic political crisis that was slowly reaching its climax. On 30 July 2010, disagreement between PM Berlusconi and his long-term ally Gianfranco Fini[5] degenerated into an outright split within the majority. After constituting an autonomous political group within Parliament, the followers of Fini founded a new party (Future and Freedom, FF) that on 15 December 2010 formally distanced itself from the ruling majority. During the winter of 2010, the judicial investigations involving the PM entered a new phase, as more light was shed on the involvement of Berlusconi and some of his close collaborators in a sex scandal. The investigation was vastly covered by the media, and perceived as a blow to the credibility of the Italian government both at home and abroad. In the 2011 local elections, Berlusconi's party (People of Freedom, POF) underwent an historic defeat in Milan, where the candidate of the center-left prevailed. Milan and Lombardy had traditionally been strongholds of the center-right and the Northern League (NL) led by Umberto Bossi, an ally of Berlusconi who had proved problematic in the past. By withdrawing its support, the NL had in fact been responsible for the collapse of the first Berlusconi government in 1994, and the NL's votes had been key in the 2008 elections to ensure the center-right coalition led by Berlusconi could achieve a majority. The defeat of the center-right in Milan made the NL uncomfortable with the alliance. Another signal of the government's weakness came from the results of a referendum held in June 2011. Among the questions, Italians were asked whether the right of Prime Ministers and Ministers to invoke a 'legitimate impediment' as a justification for not being present at judicial court hearings should be abrogated. The law granting such a right had been approved by the Italian parliament in 2010, with the favorable votes of the POF and the NL only. It was perceived by public opinion as an ad hoc measure driven by Berlusconi's ongoing legal issues, and it had been declared partially unconstitutional by the Italian Constitutional Court. The majority of participants in the referendum voted for its abrogation.

This political turmoil constituted the background for the negotiation of the annual budget law, which spurred conflict within the majority party. Finance Minister Giulio Tremonti was in favor of an austerity budget, but the dismal result in the regional elections made his stance hardly appealing to the rest of the coalition. The medium-term budget law presented at the end of June 2011 was a political compromise in favor of delaying fiscal consolidation: of the €47 billion of fiscal tightening, only €7 billion were to be executed in 2011–12, and the rest was postponed to after the 2013 elections. The budget failed to reassure markets and during July 2011 the spread on Italian government bonds reached levels last seen before the introduction of the euro. On 15 July, the Italian parliament approved the austerity package,[6] but discontent was growing within the POF. In July 2011 a long-term investigation came to its conclusion, as the Milan court of appeal ruled that Berlusconi's Fininvest holding company should pay €560 million in damages to rival CIR. After public outcry, Berlusconi abandoned efforts to insert into the budget law an ad hoc clause that would have allowed Fininvest to delay these payments.[7] On 20 July, the Parliament authorized the arrest of Alfonso Papa,[8] an MP from Berlusconi's party. POF voted against the authorization but the NL abstained. At the end of July, the idea of a technocratic government started circulating as a possible solution in case of an outright government crisis. Mario Monti, economist and former European Commissioner, was rumored as a possible candidate to lead a non-partisan executive[9] – although he denied any interest in the position.

On 5 August, after the 10-year bonds spread reached 390 basis points, the Italian government received a letter from the European Central Bank (ECB). The letter asked Italy to 'urgently underpin the standing of its sovereign signature and its commitment to fiscal sustainability and structural reforms', detailing a number of measures that the ECB deemed 'essential' to this end. These included an exhortation to balance the fiscal budget in 2013 – one year ahead of the schedule set out in the budget law – and increase the fiscal adjustment foreseen for 2012.[10] On 13 August, the government approved an additional austerity package worth €45.5 billion, to achieve a balanced budget in 2013.[11] Meanwhile, the ECB started buying Spanish and Italian government bonds on the secondary market in the context of its Securities Market Program (SMP).[12] By the end of August, however, as the ECB's purchases had succeeded in temporarily lower government bond yields, Berlusconi announced a revision to the emergency austerity package, including the scrapping of a tax on high earners and a reduction in the planned cuts on local authorities' funds.[13] This was perceived as a backtrack on the commitment to fiscal consolidation, creating confusion among markets participants. At the urging of the President of the Republic, the emergency package was reinforced on 6 September and validated by the House of Deputies eight days later. Nonetheless, the rating agency Standard & Poor's downgraded Italian debt from A+ to A, stating that the 'government's tentative policy response to […] market pressures suggest[ed] continuing future political uncertainty about the means of addressing Italy's economic challenges'.[14]

On 1 November, the Greek government announced its intention to call a referendum on the austerity measures requested by its creditors. This triggered a generalized increase in the yields on government debt of the 'periphery' countries, and the spread on Italian debt reached 441 basis points. Three days later, at the G-20 Summit in Cannes, Italy came under pressure to accept EU/IMF's surveillance.[15] Despite claiming that he would remain in power because of the absence of eminent public figures 'able to represent the interests of the country internationally', Berlusconi was pressured to resign, including from within his own party (Benvenuti 2016). The political crisis reached its climax on 8 November, when the government was outvoted in Parliament on a budget document.[16] That same evening, Berlusconi announced its intention to resign after the vote on the budget law. On 12 November, once the budget law had been approved, Berlusconi effectively resigned. On 13 November, the President of the Republic conferred the task to form a new government to Mario Monti who, three days later, announced the composition of a new fully technocratic cabinet (Marangoni 2012) that would remain in office until December 2012.

The Monti interlude

The tenure of the Monti government was a defining moment in recent Italian history, and one which had lasting implications for the political discourse surrounding not only the 2013 but also the 2018 elections. Fabbrini (2013) sees Monti's tenure as an attempt at tackling the absence of four key political conditions necessary for the implementation of long-needed structural reforms,[17] against the backdrop of market pressure on one hand and the ECB's assertiveness on the other. This view sees the technocratic interlude as fitting within a long-standing Italian tradition of resorting to Europe as an *external constraint* (*vincolo esterno*) to achieve domestic objectives: a strategy that worked well in the run-up to monetary unification, but lost its charm after the Eurozone crisis (Jones 2018; Lucarelli 2016). Yet, the reaction of Italians to the appointment of the Monti government was – in the immediate short-term – very positive (Merler 2018). Albeit unelected, the government fully composed of non-partisan experts raised the hopes that the precarious Italian economic situation could be tackled without the need to resort to a macroeconomic adjustment program. As Bosco and McDonnell (2012) argue, the Italian financial crisis impacted on a party political system that was already debilitated and capable only of reacting slowly and poorly to events. In that context, it is unsurprising that Italian citizens had little faith in the ability of the country's politicians to tackle a major emergency such as the crisis, and welcomed a technocratic government of experts. This appears to chime with the view of the financial markets at the time. Studies of the impact of political announcements on the Italian sovereign bond spread find that announcements by members of the Monti cabinet had a significant effect in reducing the spread, while announcements made under both the preceding Berlusconi government and the following Letta government were ineffective (Falagiarda and Gregori 2015). The Monti government's program was indeed ambitious, involving four elements: revenue increases, spending cuts, rationalization of the state apparatus, and liberalization of protected sectors (Culpepper 2014). At least in the beginning, this program enjoyed wide parliamentary support and the government operated with considerable haste, showing a desire to 'force' Parliament to approve quickly the measures it had adopted (Marangoni 2012). This is evident also in the composition of the government's legislative activity: during its 13 months in power, the Monti government relied predominantly on legislative acts that could allow by-passing parliamentary negotiations, introducing 40 *decreti legge*, 88 *decreti legislativi*, and only 30 *disegni di legge* (Fabbrini 2013).

In December 2011, the government introduced the 'Save Italy Decree', a supplementary austerity package worth roughly €30 billion in fiscal adjustment, and aimed at balancing the budget by 2013.[18] The fiscal mix of the package was tilted toward tax increases rather than spending cuts,[19] and many of the most prominent revenue-raising measures came through regressive taxation (Culpepper 2014). Textual analysis of Monti's initial programmatic statement by Marangoni (2012) suggests an overwhelming focus on rationalizing the public administration, while the reform of welfare legislation was only the subject of a generic reference. And yet, the reform of the pension system would mark the tenure of the Monti government and have important political repercussions years ahead. The pension system has traditionally been a salient political and economic topic in Italy, due to the rapidly ageing population. In 2010, the general government devoted 13.3 percent of GDP to pension spending – the second-highest figure in the EU, after Greece, and higher than the EU average, which stood at 10 percent. The sustainability quandary was compounded by the fact that the Italian system offered generous early retirement options, and one of the highest replacement rates in Europe (Merler 2016a; Belloni et al. n.d.). These issues have been the focus of several successive waves of pension reform. The 1992 Dini reform increased retirement age gradually starting in 1994, to reach 65 years for men and 60 for women in 2000 (compared to 60 and 55, respectively, before the reform). The required years of contribution for old-age pensions were also increased, and indexation to wage growth was scrapped.[20] The 1995 Amato reform included a complete overhaul of the benefit computation methods for newly hired workers, who would receive their pension based on a notional defined contribution rather than a defined benefit calculation (whereas already hired workers with less than 18 years of contributions would be covered by a mixed system). The 2011 Fornero reform, bearing the name of Monti's Labor Minister, built on the Amato framework but reduced the transitional phase of the notional defined contribution rule starting in January 2012. It also tightened eligibility requirements for old-age pension and early retirement options: age requirements for old-age pensions were to be unified for men and women by 2018 and to increase to 69 years and nine months by 2050, whereas the years of contributions needed to access early retirement were increased (Belloni et al. n.d.). Indexation to inflation – which had been retained by the 1992 and 1995 reforms – was scrapped within the 2011 reform.[21] But the most politically damning aspect of the Fornero pension reform was the fact that by raising the retirement age, it created a group of workers (known as '*esodati*') who had opted for early retirement but were not allowed to receive their pension – thus being effectively deprived of a source of income. The way the reform had been pushed through would also turn out to be problematic. Culpepper (2014) rightly points out that unlike the pension reforms of the past, the 2011 one was not negotiated with social partners but was the product of pure government intervention in a political context which – because of the urgency of the economic crisis – had shifted toward 'unmediated democracy'. Because of its socially painful side-effect, the Fornero reform undermined people's confidence in the signaling effect of the technocratic government's expertise. At the same time, because of the way it was pushed through, the reform became a symbol for public opinion of the technocrats' lack of democratic accountability. Unsurprisingly, both the League and Five Stars Movement made it a centerpiece of their populist and/or Euroskeptic campaigns in the 2013 and 2018 elections.

The 'Save Italy' decree was successful in reducing market pressure on Italy. But with the easing of market pressure came an increased reluctance of the political parties to abide by the emergency and non-negotiation mode of governance. This started to surface in the context of the labor market reform discussion. In its intentions, the Monti labor market reform was ambitious and wide-ranging (Boeri and Garibaldi 2012), but the outcome was significantly less. The spirit of the reform was to address the dualism of the Italian labor market by raising protection for temporary and young workers and somewhat softening or restructuring the safety net for permanent workers (Cencig 2012). The parliamentary and public debate about the reform, however, focused on the proposed changes to the symbolic Article 18 of the Workers' Statute, which used to impose on small firms (with fewer than 15 employees) the mandatory reintegration of fired workers, if their dismissal had been ruled to be illegitimate by a labor court. The initial version of the Monti reform significantly modified the discipline of firings for economic reasons, proposing that if a dismissal were to be deemed unjustified, the firing firm would have been only obliged to pay compensation benefits to the worker but not to reintegrate him/her, unless the worker could demonstrate that the firing was, in fact, underpinned by a discriminatory or disciplinary intent (Banca d'Italia 2012). This change was strongly opposed by the unions, but the government tried to proceed without the agreement of the social partners. Following protests from the unions and a backlash with public opinion, the government changed course and softened the stance by partly reinstating the previously existing provisions (Cencig 2012; Culpepper 2014). The result was a reform that to many felt 'unfinished', marginal, and that potentially increased the uncertainty it aimed to reduce (Boeri and Garibaldi 2012; Tiraboschi 2012). An unelected government whose legitimacy came from the urgency to avoid a crisis and the signaling effect of its expertise, the Monti government suffered from its handling of the pension and labor market reform. The withdrawal of the center-right support led the Prime Minister to resign in December 2012, ahead of new elections.

The Renzi government

The key event in the 2013 elections was the rise of the Five Stars Movement (M5S), the first sign of what would become the shift in the Italian political landscape toward a tri-polar structure. The very good performance of the M5S on one hand, and the disappointing performance of the Democratic Party (PD) on the other, complicated the geometry of forming a government coalition. Agreement was eventually found between the PD, Berlusconi's party, and Monti's party. The government was to be headed by Enrico Letta (PD), who resigned after less than a year because of increasing disagreements both within the coalition and within PD itself. Letta was replaced as Prime Minister by Matteo Renzi, the then-secretary of PD who, at 47, became the youngest Prime Minister in Italian political history. His government was characterized by what has been defined as a 'personalistic' style, reflected in a rate of activism of the figure of the Prime Minister significantly above the one registered by the preceding governments (Marangoni 2012). The reform of the Italian labor market – which marked the end of the Monti government – would become a signature fight of the Renzi government, too. The 'Jobs Act',[22] introduced in 2014, represented a wide-ranging welfare state and labor market reform, including the introduction of a new open-ended contract, a reorganization of unemployment benefits and temporary lay-off benefit schemes, and more focus on Active Labor Market Policies. In the view of the proponents, the Act constituted a radical shift of focus compared to the strategy of 'flexibility at the margin' that had been characteristic of the reforms in previous decades (Nannicini 2015). In the view of critics, the Act significantly reduced workers' protection rights (Cirillo et al. 2017). A major change was the introduction of a new contract type for new hires (*contratto a tutele crescenti*), within which workers' protection would be increasing over time but without the right to be reinstated in case of economic dismissal. The Jobs Act thus succeeded where Monti's reform had failed, i.e., in significantly downsizing Article 18 of the Workers' Statute.[23] Overall, the Act seems to have had positive effects. Data point toward a rise in the share of new hiring by open-ended contracts and a significant increase in employed workers (Ichino 2015). Sestito and Viviano (2016) evaluate the impact of both the permanent hiring subsidy and the new regulations lowering cost and uncertainty of firing costs. They find that both contributed to double the monthly rate of conversion of fixed-term jobs into permanent positions and that the new firing rules appear to have made firms less reluctant to offer permanent job positions to yet untested workers. Boeri and Garibaldi (2018) find evidence of a causal increase in open-ended hirings by firms with more than 15 employees relative to smaller firms, an increase in the transformation from fixed-term to open-ended contracts, evidence of an increase in firing in larger firms relative to smaller firms, and a reduction in job-to-job flows for workers in firms with more than 15 employees. Pinelli et al. (2017) also notice that the Act has contributed to bringing Italian labor market institutions more closely into line with international benchmarks and with the principles of flexicurity. But there are also negative assessments, such as Cirillo et al. (2017) who highlight the existence of frictions in the distribution of new contracts by time structure (part- vs. full-time) and by age groups (young vs. old workers).

While succeeding in pushing through a significant labor market reform, the Renzi government was, however, defeated on its attempt to reform the Italian Constitution in a way that would have changed completely the structure and functioning of the Italian Parliament. The broad outline of what was to become Renzi's constitutional reform had been worked out already in April 2013 by a committee of knowledgeable people convened by President of the Republic Giorgio Napolitano in response to the inconclusive national elections that took place in February of the same year (Jones 2016). The recommendation from the committee was to reform the constitution by reducing the powers of the Senate, so that new governments would only require the confidence of the Chamber of Deputies. This reform was to be accompanied by a revised electoral law, which was supposed to ensure the existence of a working majority, and it would have needed to be validated by a popular referendum (as foreseen in Article 138 of the Italian Constitution for constitutional reforms that cannot be approved by a reinforced majority in Parliament). As Jones (2016) argues, building consensus in the public opinion around constitutional reform was always going to be challenging, but the Renzi government was in an especially weak position. The (indirect) involvement of the minister for reforming the constitution in a banking scandal that resulted in the bail-in of retail bondholders (see next section) caused a backlash in public opinion, and the major effort of adopting the Jobs Act – while successful – had imposed strains on the process of social concertation and cohesiveness (Vesan 2016). The government's strategy was therefore to delay the referendum vote, hoping that economic recovery would soothe the public opinion before the due date, but it proved unsuccessful. On Sunday, 4 December 2016, Italians headed to the polls and almost 60 percent of them decided against the constitutional reform proposed by the government. The geographical rejection rate is positively correlated with measures of 'economic malaise', such as unemployment and relative economic backwardness (Merler 2016b). Contrary to what was observed in the Brexit referendum vote, in Italy those areas with a higher share of young people tended to record a relatively higher share of rejection, and this appears to be linked to the incidence of youth unemployment at the province level. Contrary to the case of Brexit, the outcome of the Italian vote at the province level also does not appear to be driven by uneducated voters, or to be correlated to the share of foreign residents. These elements suggest that the referendum vote is best interpreted as an outburst of deep economic drivers (Renda 2016; Merler 2016b), the same that would then find expression in the context of the 2018 elections.

The banking crisis

Between 2015 and 2017, Italy also went through a banking crisis. This was a key event because it constituted the first test of the new EU rules for dealing with banking sector problems, and because it had significant domestic political repercussions. Two defining features characterize this crisis. First, there was a delay in addressing longstanding problems. The appointment of the Monti government in late 2011 kept Italy out of an EU/IMF adjustment program but it also sheltered the Italian banking system from the kind of deep monitoring and restructuring that was undertaken in the program countries. Although some problems – such those of the Tuscan bank Monte dei Paschi di Siena (MPS) – dated back to operations conducted in 2007/8,[24] Italian banks were generally quite resilient to the first wave of the global financial crisis, thanks to their low exposure to US subprime products and the absence of any housing bubble. But when the global crisis turned into a euro sovereign-banking crisis in 2010, the health of sector deteriorated due to the banks' significant exposure to Italian government debt. During summer 2011 – as market pressure on Italy intensified – MPS' liquidity position worsened, and the bank was forced to resort to the ECB's emergency lending toward the end of the year. In 2012 – while the Italian police had started searching the headquarters of the bank to establish whether it had misled regulators over operations conducted in 2007 – the European Banking Authority's (EBA's) stress tests identified a capital shortfall of €3.3 billion, attributable to the market valuation of €25 billion Italian government bonds held by the bank at that time. In December 2012, the European Commission approved a €3.9 billion recapitalization of MPS for reasons of financial stability. The injection took the form of hybrid capital instruments ('Monti bond', after the Prime Minister). But the troubles of MPS kept growing: in 2013 it posted a net loss of €1.44 billion and in summer 2014 the results of the ECB's stress tests singled out the bank as one of the weakest in the euro area – especially in light of its high non-performing loans (NPLs) ratio. In 2016, the ECB demanded a €10 billion reduction in MPS' net NPLs over the following three years and released a new round of stress tests showing that the bank's capital would be wiped out under the adverse scenario. At that point, a solution could no longer be delayed.

Meanwhile, the regulatory environment had undergone a major shift toward stricter rules on the use of public funds when dealing with banking crises. In particular, the EU framework included a requirement for (at least) shareholders and junior debtholders to bear losses before public funds could be used to recapitalize a bank. This requirement proved problematic in the Italian context because banks had been selling junior debt instrument to retail clients who often were unaware of the real risk of their investment (Merler 2016c). The second feature that characterizes the Italian banking crisis is, therefore, a consistent attempt at finding solutions that either prevented or compensated the losses of junior bondholders, in what can be described as an operation of 'political ring-fencing'. This feature is recurrent throughout all the episodes of banks' difficulties starting in July 2015 with the liquidation of Banca Romagna Cooperativa, whose junior debt holders were reimbursed by the Italian mutual sector's Institutional Guarantee Fund. In November 2015 – two months before the bail-in rules prescribed in BRRD entered into force – four small Italian banks were resolved.[25] The initial idea to use the Interbank Deposit Protection Fund (FITD) to shield subordinated creditors completely was ruled out due to conflicts with EU State Aid rules, and 10,500 subordinated bondholders were imposed losses for a total value of €789 million (Banca d'Italia 2016). After one of them committed suicide in December 2015, the government introduced a compensation scheme to reimburse some of the junior bondholders.[26]

In April 2016, two more banks (Banca Popolare di Vicenza and Veneto Banca) launched a capital raise to avoid resolution and the ensuing bail-in requirements. On 11 April, a new bank-funded fund – named *Atlas* – was created with the mission to act as a backstop and shore up confidence in the Italian banking sector (Merler 2016c). The fund was formally private – financed by Italian banks and privately held institutions – but there were rumors[27] that it was government-inspired. Atlas ended up becoming the majority shareholders in the two banks, with a share of 90 percent, but this did not end their problems. Both banks announced in 2017 that they would need an additional recapitalization, raising again the question of how to deal with subordinated retail bondholders. Eventually, the two banks were liquidated in 2017, and the entire equity stake held by Atlas – and through it, by other Italian banks in the system – was wiped out. By acting as a shareholder of last resort for those banks that were too weak to raise capital on the market, Atlas prevented bank resolution and subordinated debt's haircut in the short run, but at the cost of spreading risk onto the balance sheets of the rest of the banking system[28] and delaying a solution. MPS also faced a moment of reckoning in 2016, when it had to recapitalize following a disastrous performance in the ECB stress tests. The option considered was that of a 'precautionary recapitalization', an exception within EU rules in which extraordinary public financial support does not trigger resolution (Article 32(4.d) of BRRD).[29] This exception, however, remains subject to a burden-sharing requirement of equity and junior debt. In MPS, junior debt at the end of 2016 amounted to €5 billion, almost 65 percent of which had been sold to retail clients. This raised once again the conundrum of how to strengthen the bank's capital position without imposing losses onto the retail savers who had bought the bank's junior debt. From the perspective of the government – facing the delicate constitutional referendum in December 2016 – the timing was unfortunate. Imposing losses before the vote, even with ex-post compensation, would alienate voters. Eventually, it was decided that MPS would try to raise €5 billion of capital from private investors after the referendum. This private capital raise failed, and MPS eventually applied for precautionary recapitalization, which was granted by the European Commission subject to the bank's disposal of its entire NPL portfolio on market terms and a bail-in shareholders and junior bondholders (European Commission 2017). Retail clients who had been mis-sold junior bonds would, however, be reimbursed.

The missed adjustment and the political nemesis

The banking crisis of 2015–17 showed how the adjustment in the Italian financial sector had been significantly slower than it had been in countries subject to the EU/IMF macroeconomic adjustment programs. Rather than being tackled forcefully, banking problems in Italy lingered on, up to the point when addressing them had become more complex because of the changes in the EU regulatory framework. The implications of this missed adjustment for the banking sector are clearly visible. While the return on equity (ROE) for banks in the program countries has rebound strongly since 2014, the ROE of the Italian banking sector was still negative over the 2014–17 period, on average (Figure 8.4a). Loan-deposit margins – a measure of banks' ability to generate interest revenues – have also been lower for Italian banks after the crisis than for their peers in other Eurozone countries. The delayed adjustment in the banking sector had consequences on banks' ability to lend to the economy, which took a long time to recover. The problem was compounded by the lack of a major competitiveness adjustment. Compared to 1998 – just before currency unification – the Italian Real Effective Exchange Rate adjusted for Unit Labor Costs remains strongly overvalued vis-à-vis the rest of the EU 15 (Figure 8.4b).

It can be argued that the choice of 1998 as a base is problematic, because the Italian government was compressing wage growth to prepare for EMU and because Germany was experiencing the post-unification shock. But it is informative, because it defies one of the main arguments advanced by Italian Eurosceptics, i.e., that competitive adjustment cannot be achieved within the euro. Figure 8.4b shows clearly how the program countries – which share the same currency, and underwent a similar appreciation during the 1999–2010 period – were then able to achieve a remarkable real adjustment to the point that their competitiveness is now in line that of northern countries. Italy lacked such ability.

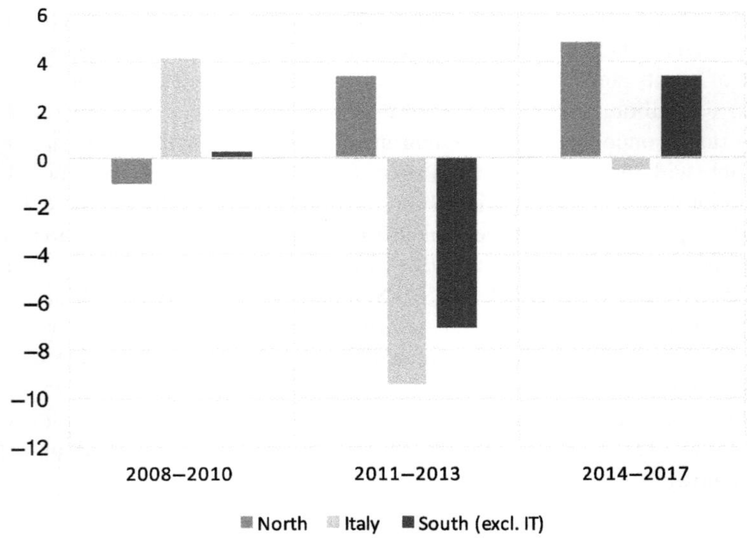

(a)

(b)

Figure 8.4 (a) Banks' return on equity (ROE); (b) REER unit labor costs (EU 15) in Italy.

Source: author's calculations based on ECB data.

Kangur (2018) finds that 45 percent of Italy's manufacturing ULC-gaps relative to Germany can be attributed to wage developments and 60 percent to lagging labor productivity (for which several explanations have been offered, including specialization into lower technology and labor-intensive products). Rather than translating into higher goods prices, the increase in ULC has weighed on profit margin, employment, and investment, imposing a drag on Italian exports.

Adjustment was slow on other fronts too, with painful social consequences. Total and youth unemployment – which had spiked during the crisis – are taking long to revert downwards. Youth unemployment in Italy was still 34.7 percent at the end of 2017, down 18 percent from its peak (Figure 8.5a). Youth unemployment in the program countries was on average slightly lower (33.6 percent) but it had declined more since the peak. Italy also stands out for the especially high share of youth unemployment which is long-term (longer than one year). In Italy, more than 50 percent of total youth unemployment was long-term at the end of 2017 – compared to below 30 percent on average across the program countries (Figure 8.5b). Part of this is historical, as Italy has traditionally recorded a higher share of long-term youth unemployment, which can also be related to the internal north–south economic divide. But some argue that the labor market reform contributed to the chronic sense of insecurity affecting some parts of the population. Cirillo et al. (2017), for example, argue that a relevant share of new open-ended positions created with the Jobs Act is characterized by part-time contracts, and that the increase in employment is concentrated among older workforce (over 50 years old). OECD data show that the share of involuntary part-time workers in total employment was 11 percent in 2017, but for young workers (15–24 years old) it was higher at 24 percent. Unsurprisingly, the socio-economic characteristics of the 'losers' of the labor reform are aligned with those who voted against the constitutional reform. The combination of stagnating growth and high unemployment has been reflected in a significant erosion of the standard of living. After remaining flat for two decades, real per capital GDP in 2017 was at the same level it had been in 1998. In comparison, real per capita GDP in the program countries did drop significantly during the crisis but it also rebounded rapidly after 2014 (Figure 8.6a). At the same time, inequality has been evolving differently in Italy than in the program countries. While the GINI coefficient increased significantly in the program countries during the crisis period, it then started to decrease again since 2012. In Italy, inequality instead kept widening (Figure 8.6b). The share of people at risk of poverty and social exclusion has increased from 25 percent before the crisis to 29 percent in 2017, but again with a significant regional and intergenerational gap. Individual relative poverty has increased significantly more in the south than in the north of the country, during the crisis. While the incidence poverty has decreased among Italians who are 65 or older, it has increased among all other younger cohorts and especially for those 15–24 years old. For this group, those at risk of poverty and social exclusion are 35 percent.[30]

These political economy dynamics help explain why Italy is unique also in its degree of Euroskepticism. The European Commission's Eurobarometer survey

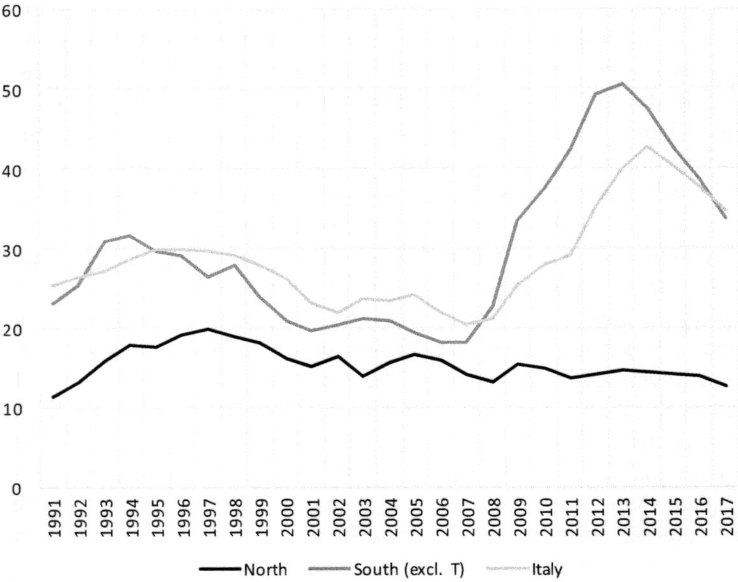

(a)

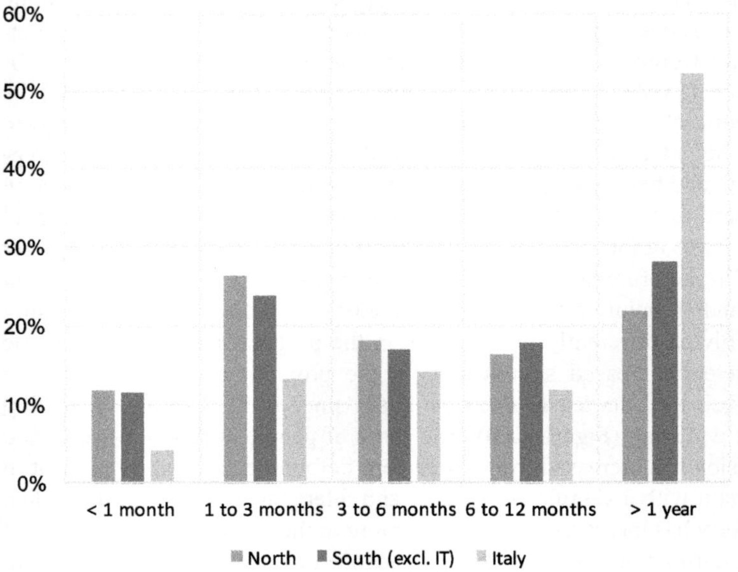

(b)

Figure 8.5 (a) Youth unemployment rate; (b) youth unemployment rate duration in Italy.

Source: author's calculations based on Eurostat.

(a)

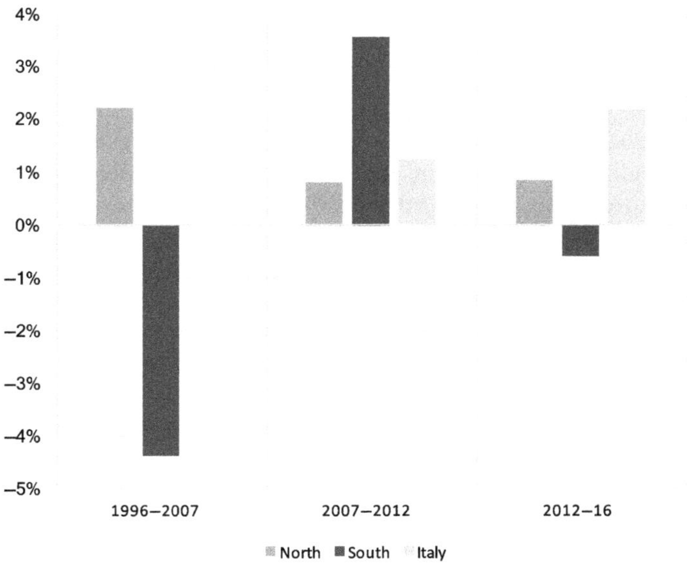

(b)

Figure 8.6 (a) Real per capita GDP ; (b) change in the GINI coefficient in Italy.

Source: author's calculations based on AMECO and World Bank.

Note

The change in GINI for Italy in the first period was zero.

contains a question asking respondents to state what the EU 'means to them personally', with a choice among a number of terms which include 'economic prosperity', 'unemployment', 'democracy', 'peace', etc. Before the crisis, the share of respondents who associated the EU with 'economic prosperity' was higher than the share of respondents associating the EU with 'unemployment'. This was true across all three geographical groups: north, program countries, and Italy. The situation completely reversed during the crisis, when the EU was predominantly associated with unemployment, everywhere. But in 2017 – after the crisis and the related adjustment – the EU is again associated with 'economic prosperity' more than 'unemployment' in the north and in the program countries, whereas Italians still see the EU as meaning 'unemployment'. In this context, the 2018 elections brought the rise of two populist parties who are (or at least have been in their past) openly Euroskeptic, and whose campaign pledges were very precisely targeted to the two most relevant constituencies of discontent in the country. Lega's core fiscal pledges implied a redistribution toward the top of the income distribution and the elderly, supported by a revenue-reducing reform of the taxation system. These pledges were mostly appealing to Lega's constituencies in the north. The Five Stars Movement's agenda was instead centered on a redistribution toward the bottom of the income distribution and particularly the youth, underpinned by an expenditure-increasing expansion of the welfare state. This was especially appealing to the weaker and younger constituencies mostly in the south.

Conclusion

In May 2018, Italy shocked the rest of Europe by putting in office a government coalition of two populist and (to different degrees) Euroskeptic parties, whose initial policy actions are setting them in open confrontation with Brussels. This chapter reviewed briefly the experience of Italy before and during the Eurozone crisis, in order to draw a link between this past and the recent political dynamics. We have argued that the Italian economy was in an intermediate place between north and south of the Eurozone before the crisis: Italy did not run external imbalances comparable to those that became common in the program countries, nor it did experience any private credit bubble, but it nevertheless came under market pressure in 2011 as a casualty of perceived fiscal irresponsibility and weakened government credibility. The hurried appointment of an unelected technocratic government headed by a former European Commissioner avoided the loss of market access as well as the need for Italy to request a macroeconomic adjustment program. In that, however, it planted the seeds of the missed adjustment that would be so important for the future economic and political dynamics. While both the Monti and the Renzi government were very active in the field of pension and labor market reforms, problems in the Italian banking sector were allowed to linger on well into 2015. This had two consequences. First, it imposed a drag on the economic recovery – which was compounded by the fact that long-term Italian competitiveness issues were not addressed in a way that could spur growth. Second, when the moment of reckoning finally came, those problems had to be addressed within a new regulatory framework that was stricter on the use of public money – with the consequence that losses (even though compensated ex post) had to be imposed on retail investors often unaware of the risk they had bought. These factors combined into eroding the political support of the Monti government first, and of the Renzi government later, and found expression in the voting pattern observed during the 2018 elections. The implication of the missed adjustment is that Italy today stands out from both north and south of the Eurozone, as a special case. Program countries have become significantly more similar to the core ones – after the crisis-related adjustment. Italy retains an especially high public debt burden, has achieved no major improvement in competitiveness, faces rising long-term nominal and real rates (due to political risk), fights with stubbornly high long-term youth unemployment, stagnating standards of living and rising inequality, and displays a unique loss of faith in the 'meaning' of the EU as a prosperity project. The use of 'Europe' as a 'transformative force' – once seen as a useful 'external constraint' – is now hardly tenable politically. The consequences of this major shift for both Italy and the rest of the Eurozone are yet unclear, but the importance of it cannot be overestimated. Italy's unique political dynamics and challenge to Brussels have resulted in the loss of support even from those countries in the south that could once be counted as friends and which – having undergone the painful adjustment that Italy has avoided – are not willing to accommodate. Writing in 1978, Adam Posner observed that in terms of its interaction with the international political economy one of Italy's main bargaining devices had traditionally been the fact that 'its creditors could not afford to see it go bankrupt'.[31] While this is probably still true today from a purely financial standpoint, the data surveyed in this chapter suggest that north and south are today much closer than they have been since 1999. In such an environment, the path that Italy is currently on could easily result in its isolation while the rest of the club moves on to a more closely integrated union.

Notes

1 Throughout the rest of this chapter, north and south are defined as follows. South comprises the program countries: Greece, Ireland, Portugal, Spain. North comprises Austria, Belgium, Finland, France, Germany, Netherlands.

2 Author's calculations based on data from the European Commission's AMECO database. Figures for 'north' and 'south' are obtained as compounded annual growth rates for the total demand and GDP of the two groups.

3 Compounded annual growth of real GDP growth in the program countries averaged 4 percent over the 2014–18 period, compared to 1 percent in Italy.

4 An extensive account of the events in Italy is available in Benvenuti (2016); Jones (2014) complements it with a recount of events in the euro area. See Merler (2018) for a more detailed discussion of the effects of the appointment of the Monti government.

5 Fini was formerly secretary the 'National Alliance', a right-wing party traditionally allied with the center-right that eventually merged with Berlusconi's 'People of Freedom' party in 2009.

6 The law was passed with 161 votes in favor and 135 against in the Senate; 316 in favor and 284 against in the Lower House.

7 An inserted comma in article 37, which if approved would have modified article 283 of the Code of Civil Procedure: www.repubblica.it/politica/2011/07/04/news/nella_manovra_un_comma_per_bloccare_il_risarcimento-18652993.

8 www.corriere.it/politica/11_luglio_20/arresto-papa-voto-in-aula_fd7c395e-b2d1-11e0-97dd-09b07ad852d4.shtml.

9 See Benvenuti (2016) for an account of the early contacts between Monti and the President of the Republic, as well as journalistic sources.

10 The text of the letter can be found at: www.corriere.it/economia/11_settembre_29/trichet_draghi_inglese_304a5f1e-ea59-11e0-ae06-4da866778017.shtml?refresh_ce-cp.

11 www.corriere.it/economia/11_settembre_29/sensini_documento_bce_e68f29d6-ea58-11e0-ae06-4da866778017.shtml.

12 See Jones (2014) for an account of the euro area crisis during this period.

13 https://next.ft.com/content/d5a93728-d2e4-11e0-9aae-00144feab49a.

14 Full text: www.telegraph.co.uk/finance/financialcrisis/8775616/SandP-downgrades-Italy-the-full-text.html; Moody's followed on 4 October, and Fitch on 7 October.

15 www.theguardian.com/world/2011/nov/04/g20-italy-imf-checks-cuts; see also Benvenuti (2016).

16 Rendiconto Generale del Bilancio dello Stato.

17 The four conditions are non-defensibility of the status quo, bi-partisan support, acceptance by citizens of reforms as part of a larger clear and coherent vision, and a global understanding of reforms as expression of supra-national strategy.

18 See Benvenuti (2016) for a discussion.

19 See Cencig (2012) and also the assessment by the Italian Court of Auditors: www.corteconti.it/export/sites/portalecdc/_documenti/chi_siamo/audizioni/audizione_23_aprile_2012.pdf.

20 See Belloni et al. (n.d.) for a detailed discussion of successive reforms.

21 Although it was later reinstated by the Constitutional Court, see Merler (2016a).

22 More formally, Law 183 of 2014 plus eight legislative decrees implementing it. See Ichino (2015) for a discussion of the provisions in the eight decrees.

23 Since then, various provisions of the Jobs Act have been altered both by decisions of the Constitutional Court and by the so-called 'Dignity Decree', recently legislated by the Lega-M5S government that came to power in 2018. See Ichino (2018a, 2018b) for a discussion of the latest developments.

24 See Merler (2016c) for a detailed discussion.

25 Banca Marche, Cassa di risparmio di Ferrara, Banca Etruria, and CariChieti.

26 Law decree no. 59 of May 2016 stated that junior bondholders who had bought the bonds before 12 June 2014 could ask for a reimbursement of 80 percent of the principal without having to go through arbitration, provided that their wealth was less than 100,000 euros and their 2014 annual income was less than 35,000 euros.

27 FT: www.ft.com/content/f52f1ca6-02ec-11e6-af1d-c47326021344.

28 This became evident as participating banks significantly wrote down the value of their investment in Atlas, in late 2016 and 2017. Reuters: www.reuters.com/article/us-eurozone-banks-italy-insight-idUSKBN15I2BW.

29 The conditions are that the extraordinary public support shall be of a precautionary and temporary nature, and not be used to offset losses that the institution has incurred or is likely to incur in the near future. Moreover, the extraordinary injections are limited to the amount necessary to address a capital shortfall established in a stress test, asset quality reviews, or equivalent exercises.

30 Author's calculations using Eurostat and ISTAT data.

31 Page 837.

References

Banca d'Italia (2012) – 'Relazione annuale. Presentata all'Assemblea Ordinaria dei Partecipanti Roma, 31 maggio 2012, anno 2011'.

Belloni, M., Brugiavini, A., Buia, E., and G. Pasini (n.d.) – 'Social Security Wealth in Italy: 20 Years of Pension Reforms', working paper.

Benvenuti, A. (2016) – 'Italy, the Monti government and the euro crisis (2011–12)', *Australia and New Zealand Journal of European Studies*, 8 (2).

Blanchard, O. and F. Giavazzi (2002) – 'Current Account Deficits in the Euro Area: The End of the Feldstein Horioka Puzzle?', Brookings Papers on Economic Activity, Economic Studies Program, The Brookings Institution, 33(2), 147–210.

Blanchard, O., Leandro, A., Merler, S. and J. Zettelmeyer (2018) – 'Impact of Italy's Draft Budget on Growth and Fiscal Solvency', PIIE Policy Brief 18–24.

Boeri, T. and P. Garibaldi (2012) – 'Politiche del Lavoro', in 'Bilancio del Governo Monti', lavoce.info, December 2012.

Boeri, T. and P. Garibaldi (2018) – 'Graded Security and Labor Market Mobility: Clean Evidence from the Italian Jobs Act', INPS Working Papers, available at: www.inps.it/docallegatiNP/Mig/InpsComunica/WorkInps_Papers/10_WorkINPS_Papers_19febbraio_2018.pdf.

Bosco, A. and D. McDonnell (2012) – 'Introduction: The Monti Government and the Downgrade of Italian Parties'. *Italian Politics: From Berlusconi to Monti 27* (2012), 37–56. Berghahn Books.

Cencig, E. (2012) – 'Italy's Economy in the Euro Zone Crisis and Monti's Reform Agenda'. Working Paper FG 1, 2012/05, September 2012 SWP Berlin.

Cirillo, V., Fana, M., and D. Guarascio (2017) – 'Labour Market Reform in Italy: Evaluating the Effects of the Jobs Act'. *Economia Politica: Journal of Analytical and Institutional Economics*, Springer; Fondazione Edison, vol. 34(2), 211–232.

Culpepper, P. D. (2014) – 'The Political Economy of Unmediated Democracy: Italian Austerity under Mario Monti', *West European Politics*, 37(6), 1264–1281.

European Commission (2017) – 'State Aid: Commission Authorises Precautionary Recapitalisation of Italian Monte dei Paschi di Siena', Press release, 4 July.

Fabbrini, S. (2013) – 'Political and Institutional Constraints on Structural Reforms: Interpreting the Italian Experience'. *Modern Italy*, 18(4), 423–436.

Falagiarda M. and W. D. Gregori (2015) – 'The Impact of Fiscal Policy Announcements by the Italian Government on the Sovereign Spread: A Comparative Analysis'. *European Journal of Political Economy*, 39(2015), 288–304.

Ichino, P. (2015) – 'Labour Reforms in Italy: Structure, Main Content and First Results'. Available at: www.pietroichino.it/wp-content/uploads/2015/11/Milano.BCCI_.6XI15_EN.pdf.

Ichino, P. (2018a) – 'La sentenza della consulta non scalfisce l'impianto del Jobs Act', available at: www.pietroichino.it/?p=50555.

Ichino, P. (2018b) – 'Lavoro: l'Italia ritorna in mezzo al guado', available at: www.pietroichino.it/?p=50580.

Jones, E. (2014) – *The Year the Crisis Ended*, Palgrave Macmillan.

Jones, E. (2016) – 'Renzi's Gamble', available at: https://erikjones.net/2016/12/08/renzis-gamble.

Jones, E. (2018) – 'Italy and the completion of the euro area'. Sieps European Policy Analysis, February, Issue 2018:1.

Jones, G. (2012) – 'Monti's Labour Reform Rejected by Those It Aims to Help', *Reuters*, 27 March.

Kangur, Alvar (2018) – 'Competitiveness and Wage Bargaining Reform in Italy'. IMF Working Paper WP/18/61.

Lucarelli, S. (2016) – 'Italy and the EU: From True Love to Disenchantment', *Journal of Common Market Studies*, 53(1), 40–60.

Marangoni, F. (2012) – 'Technocrats in Government: The Composition and Legislative Initiatives of the Monti Government Eight Months into Its Term of Office'. *Bulletin of Italian Politics*, 4(1), 135–149.

Merler, S. and J. Pisani-Ferry (2012) – 'Who's Afraid of Sovereign Bonds?', Bruegel Policy Contribution 2012(2).

Merler, S. (2016a) – 'Dura Lex, Sed Lex (?)', Bruegel blog, available at: http://bruegel.org/2015/05/dura-lex-sed-lex.

Merler, S. (2016b) – 'Socio-Economic Determinants of the Italian Vote', Bruegel blog, available at: http://bruegel.org/2016/12/socio-economic-determinants-of-the-italian-vote.

Merler, S. (2016c) – 'Italy', chapter in 'Bank Resolution and Bail-In in the EU: Selected Case Studies Pre and Post BRRD', World Bank FinSAC report.

Merler, S. (2018) – 'Technocracy, Trust, and Democracy: Evidence from a Natural Experiment in Italy'. Paper presented at the 2018 annual meetings of the American Political Science Association.

Nannicini, T. (2015) – www.tommasonannicini.eu/en/works/il-contratto-tutele-crescenti.

Pasquino, Gianfranco and Marco Valbruzzi (2012) – 'Non-Partisan Governments Italian-Style: Decision-Making and Accountability', *Journal of Modern Italian Studies*, 17(5), 612–629.

Pinelli, D., Torre, R., Pace, L., Cassio, L., and A. Arpaia (2017). 'The Recent Reform of the Labour Market in Italy: A Review', European Commission, European Economy Discussion Paper 072.

Posner, A. (1977) – 'Italy: Dependence and Political Fragmentation', in ed. P. Katzenstein, *Between Power and Plenty: Foreign Economic Policies of Advanced Industrial States*, International Organization, 31(4).

Renda, A. (2016) – 'Renzi's Defeat Is Not Another Victory of Populism', CEPS commentary, December 2016. Available at http://aei.pitt.edu/82501/1/AR_Renzi_final.pdf.

Sestito, P. and E. Viviano (2016) – 'Hiring Incentives and/or Firing Cost Reduction? Evaluating the Impact of the 2015 Policies on the Italian Labour Market', Bank of Italy Occasional Papers no. 3625.

Tiraboschi, M. (2012) – 'I paradossi di una riforma sbagliata (e che si farà, anche se non piace a nessuno)', in 'Lavoro: una riforma sbagliata. Ulteriori osservazioni sul DDL n. 5256/2012, Disposizioni in materia di riforma del mercato del lavoro in una prospettiva di crescita', ed. P. Rausei and M. Tiraboschi, Adapt Labour Series ebook no. 2.

Vesan, P. (2016) – 'Young Workers and the Labor Market Policies of Renzi's Government', *Italian Politics*, 31(1).

Part III

National growth models and the political economy of adjustment

9 Unity in diversity?

Varieties of capitalism before and after the euro crisis

Benedicta Marzinotto

Introduction

This chapter explores the dualism in macroeconomic performance in the European Monetary Union (EMU) before and after the Euro crisis from the perspective of the Varieties of Capitalism (VoC) literature. It focuses on euro area countries that fell under stress, including those that received formal financial assistance (Greece, Ireland, and Portugal) as well as those that obtained assistance from other euro area partners under special conditions (Spain). To better understand the specificity of this group of countries – which are similar albeit not identical along a number of significant dimensions – their performance is juxtaposed to that of Continental member countries that were not under stress (Austria, Belgium, Finland, Germany, and the Netherlands).[1]

The divergence in macroeconomic performance across the two groups of countries is epitomized by the evolution of macroeconomic imbalances. Stressed countries had, on average, significant and persistent current account deficits, signaling that they were consuming above the value of their production and getting indebted to the outside in order to finance the excess consumption. During the crisis, they were forced to cut back on consumption as foreign credit stopped flowing in, earlier in Ireland and Greece, and later on in the other stressed countries (see, for example, Lane 2012; Lane and Milesi-Ferretti 2012; Baldwin and Giavazzi 2015; chapters by Pagoulatos and Cardiff in this book). By contrast, continental euro area countries enjoyed large current account surpluses, indicating that part of the national income was saved and indeed invested abroad. Most of them, and Germany in particular, continued to preserve strong external positions in the midst of the Euro debt crisis. The correction of macroeconomic imbalances since crisis times has thus been, at least partially, asymmetric (Lane and Milesi-Ferretti 2014), a piece of evidence that is possibly indicative of the fact that the drivers of current account deficits may not necessarily be identical to those of surpluses.

There is a now well-established strand of comparative-political-economy (CPE) research that attributes this dichotomy to the fact that stressed and non-stressed euro area countries represent different VoC or, in fact, opposing growth models (see Chapter 1 of this volume as well as Hall 2012, 2014, 2018; Iversen and

Soskice 2012; Johnston, Hancké, and Pant 2014; Baccaro and Pontusson 2016; Johnston and Regan 2016; Hope and Soskice 2016; Iversen, Soskice, and Hope 2016).[2] The mixed-market economies (MMEs) of the South of Europe (i.e., Greece, Spain, and Portugal) embody demand-driven growth models, where consumption provides for the largest contribution to GDP growth, as evident from the fact that these countries suffer from persistent current account deficits, a situation typical of countries that consume more than they produce. A liberal market economy (LME) such as Ireland is equally classified as a demand-driven economy. Coordinated market economies (CMEs) of Continental Europe (i.e., Austria, Belgium, Finland, Germany, and the Netherlands) are characterized by domestic institutions ranging from wage-setting systems to education and training that rather support an export-led growth model. The EMU and the completion of the single market that preceded it were functional to the export-led model, allowing these countries to maximize returns in a highly integrated market and to rapidly accumulate current account surpluses. The same conditions were ill-adapted to the demand-driven model. These countries were deprived of the devaluation option, which in the past allowed them to offset the price consequences of their excessive consumption, sustaining exports at least temporarily. The widening of their current account deficits would thus signal deteriorating cost competitiveness in the absence of the option of altering the nominal exchange rate in a discretionary fashion.

That euro area macroeconomic imbalances and the related euro crisis have an institutional origin comes with important implications in the context of the so-called Future-of-Europe debate. If entrenched institutions mediate the response of each country to cyclical conditions, then business cycle synchronization might be a necessary but not sufficient condition for the proper functioning of the monetary union and will have to be associated with at least some institutional convergence. Absent some convergence in growth models, the correction of future imbalances will impose a burden only on countries with a demand-driven growth model because they will have no choice but to restrain consumption in the bust, as happened in the recent crisis, whilst countries with a current account surplus may well continue to refuse inflating their own economy, as it would make them loose market shares. This asymmetry would threaten over time the political sustainability of the Euro project.

This chapter takes stock of the institutions and institutional complementarities that underpin the two opposing growth models sketched above, explaining how they might have contributed to the build-up and subsequent asymmetric unwinding of macroeconomic imbalances. It further elaborates on whether the crisis experience has fundamentally altered institutional settings in the South of Europe and Ireland or whether measures undertaken in response to it were necessary in the circumstances but not bound to have persistent effects that have altered or will alter these countries' growth model in the years ahead. It remains an open question whether new EU institutions and procedures such as the Macroeconomic Imbalance Procedure (MIP) are sufficient to prevent future imbalances in the euro area, either by promoting a process of structural convergence or by accommodating frictions across persistently divergent growth models.

EMU and the fate of institutional complementarities

The comparative-capitalism literature builds on the idea that growth models rest on different, more or less efficient, institutional complementarities. The strongest interaction identified by the literature is the one between wage-setting systems and the macroeconomic regime. CMEs such as Germany and all the countries of the former DM-block are described as having intermediate wage bargaining centralization. Intermediate centralization refers to the fact that wages are mostly set at the sectoral level and then possibly extended to all firms in the same sector. This implies that there are a small number of wage-setters in the economy, which could theoretically impose their own wage conditions. Nevertheless, this does not happen because the national central bank stands ready to punish inflationary wage settlements with a contraction of nominal money supply. The few wage bargainers that populate CMEs tend to opt for wage moderation so as to prevent unemployment, supporting therewith their country's export-led model (Hall and Soskice 2001; Soskice 2007; Carlin 2013; Hancké 2013). They also enjoy high levels of wage bargaining coordination, meaning that one sector tends to act as wage leader for all the others, which implies wage moderation across all sectors. The efficient institutional complementarity between intermediate centralization and a rigid aggregate demand management regime was preserved under the EMU because the new macroeconomic setting was equally rigid with an inflation-avert common central bank.[3] By contrast, in MMEs, the macroeconomic regime had been relatively loose prior to the EMU and wage bargaining neither centralized nor coordinated (Amable 2003; Molina and Rhodes 2007; Hancké 2013), which contributed in the years before monetary unification to wage-price spirals and the recurrent use of devaluation to recoup cost competitiveness. Ultimately, devaluation allowed them to offset the consequences of their demand-driven growth model with fewer costs than would have been the case if domestic consumption came to a halt. It is generally argued that the same was not possible under the rigid EMU regime, with the result that cost competitiveness deteriorated and the current account generated significant deficits.

When peripheral countries came under stress, the European Union (EU) offered them financial assistance. The problems that each peripheral country faced were quite diverse (Marzinotto, Pisani-Ferry, and Sapir 2010). There was first the extraordinary package designed specifically for Greece, a country with an over-expanded public sector that had borrowed from outside to finance government consumption. At the same time, at the May 2010 European Council, EU governments agreed on the creation of two special purpose vehicles to convey funds to countries that would subsequently follow under pressure. Those original two funds were the European Financial Stabilization Mechanism (EFSM) guaranteed by the EU Budget and with a lending capacity of €60 billion and the European Financial Stability Facility (EFSF) guaranteed on an intergovernmental basis by all euro area members and with a lending capacity of €500 billion. The latter was then transformed into a permanent crisis management tool under the name of European Stability Mechanism (ESM). For a description of the political economy of financial assistance during the Euro crisis see Marzinotto (2016). Ireland was the first country for which those two funds were activated together with assistance from the International Monetary Fund (IMF) and from non-euro area individual countries. Portugal followed suit. Their underlying problems were but not primarily fiscal in nature. Ireland had a large, highly leveraged financial sector that was at risk of imploding, whilst Portugal suffered from poor cost- and non-cost competitiveness. These weaknesses were sufficient to scare international credit markets. Formal assistance to Greece, Ireland, and Portugal was offered only in exchange for a severe adjustment program that included lower public consumption and lower domestic prices in an effort to make them internationally competitive, allowing for some economic growth to be generated by stronger exports (see the chapters by Pagoulatos, Cardiff, and Torres and de Freitas in this volume). The liberalization of product and labor markets was believed to generate the required drop in relative prices. Spain obtained special assistance later on, with the specific purpose of recapitalizing the domestic banking system but not subject to an adjustment program. Nevertheless, the country received economy policy recommendations in the framework of the European Semester that equally focused on fiscal consolidation and structural reforms to make product and labor markets more competitive (see chapter by Steinberg and Royo in this volume) and possibly mimic the performance of Continental euro area countries. Even if the origins of the crisis and vulnerabilities differed from country to country, economic policy prescriptions were identical, including those concerning the ideal structure and operation of markets. The Five Presidents' Report refers unequivocally to the need to achieve structural convergence, which may indeed imply some harmonization or even full convergence towards an export-oriented growth model.

While building on the idea that distinctive growth models are at the roots of the build-up of macroeconomic imbalances, this chapter adds to the above-mentioned literature in a number of ways. First, it provides for a broader definition of the macroeconomic regime that takes account of the role of financial intermediaries rather than just of the operation of the reference central bank. The new European Central Bank (ECB) has been indeed designed as a non-accommodating monetary policy authority, but the parallel emergence of a vast European inter-bank market and the fact that, at the same time, bank lending was increasingly market-based explains why the ultimate degree of monetary accommodation has been a function, in each country, of the extent to which domestic commercial banks were exploring international sources of funding alternative to deposits, which tend to be domestic. The available CPE literature has invoked a role for finance but has been relying for decades on the static dichotomy between bank-based and capital-based financial systems (Zysman 1983). As is well argued in Hardie and Howarth (2013), such a characterization of financial systems is useless when accounting for the fact that, in recent times, banks have moved beyond collecting savings in the form of deposits. They have significantly expanded their funding sources that now range from capital to short-term debt collected on the inter-bank market and engaged in securitization, whereby illiquid financial claims (i.e., loans) are being transformed into tradable one (i.e., loans are sold to investors). These activities have made bank-based financial systems more similar to market-based financial systems. So, for example, credit institutions in MMEs and Ireland compensated for EMU's formally rigid macroeconomic regime by providing large credit supply to the domestic economy (see also Fernandez-Villaverde, Garicano, and Santos 2013), with the growth in credit reliant on increasing short-term wholesale funding, as international credit markets were becoming increasingly integrated following the completion of the single market and the subsequent adoption of the single currency. The deterioration of the current account would thus signal capital inflows as commercial banks continued to contract debt on the international inter-bank market. Such behavior was specific to the periphery because commercial banks here had been more constrained than those in the core, given relatively more significant capital controls prior to the completion of the single market. Moreover, banks in the periphery were mostly public in the early 1990s. It follows that the rapid and significant privatization starting from the mid-1990s onwards can well explain excessive risk-taking by new or privatized old banks that were suddenly exposed to the rules of the market. Bank-financed debt accumulation allowed peripheral countries to preserve their demand-driven model, even in the presence of an inflation-averse common central bank (and of stringent top-down fiscal rules). That they could not make use of competitive devaluations is a fact, but it is too simplistic an explanation of deteriorating current account imbalances that takes account only of the supply-side.

Second, this chapter goes beyond the distinction between a demand- and an export-driven model to suggest that macroeconomic imbalances are not only driven by the level of consumption relative to income but also by how income is distributed (see also Baccaro and Pontusson 2016, 2018). It is no mere coincidence that stressed countries had above-average levels of income inequality when they accessed the EMU, and that the unequal distribution of income is one of the few dimensions that MMEs and LMEs have in common. Building on existing empirical research, it is argued that excess consumption is mostly pronounced in unequal societies where low-/middle-income agents either try to "catch-up with their neighbors" or are optimistic about their future income, and that this became possible when liquidity constraints were eliminated after the abolition of capital controls and the rapid integration of euro area interbank money markets.

Third, the chapter accounts for the fact that institutional settings, especially those concerning the operation of labor markets, were reformed in most euro area countries during the EMU period, and that the hypothesis of no-regime-change of some of the available CPE literature (e.g., Johnston, Hancké, and Pant 2014; Johnston and Regan 2016) rests on weak empirical foundations. Labor market reforms in CMEs resulted in a significant decentralization in wage bargaining. By contrast, wage bargaining centralization rose in MMEs and more significantly so in Ireland. This did not come with the efficient institutional complementarity between wage setting and the underlying aggregate demand management regime that underpins CMEs. The reason is that EMU's macroeconomic regime has not been for them as rigid as normally portrayed. As alluded to earlier, the periphery witnessed a significant rise in credit supply coming from both foreign investors and domestic banks, which made the new independent and inflation-avert central bank much less of a threat to demand conditions than suggested by the received wisdom.

Macro-financial systems and varieties of capitalism

The European Central Bank (ECB) has an inflation target defined in its Statute and is bound to manage nominal money supply with care, with the primary objective of avoiding an acceleration in price growth. *Prima facie*, the beginning of EMU would appear to be associated, in MMEs, with a shift away from the rather accommodating macroeconomic regime they had prior to the Euro, whilst in CMEs, it implied simply a continuation of a relatively rigid non-accommodating regime. This narrative would be appropriate if one sticks to the assumption of exogenous nominal money supply that is embedded in some of the most recent macroeconomic models (see, for example, Iversen and Soskice 1998), the same that form the theoretical context against which the VoC literature has been setting the discussion about the strategic interaction between wage setters and monetary authorities (Soskice 2007). The assumption implies that the amount of money supply is exogenously determined by the reference central bank and thus fixed in the eyes of domestic economic agents. This is not necessarily true in advanced financial systems, where financial intermediaries not only shift resources from savers to borrowers but also raise capital on the market and borrow from other banks, including those sitting abroad, and engage in innovative lending activities that can increase the value of loans to the real economy well above that of deposits. As the composition of commercial banks' balance sheets changes, so does the standard transmission of monetary policy. It follows that the monetary policy decisions of a central bank may not reach the real economy if banks are not responsive to money market conditions (e.g., securitization may imply that a drop in short-term nominal interest rates does not come with a fall in the price of the assets that commercial banks own). Ultimately, financial intermediaries contribute to supporting demand conditions beyond the degree of monetary accommodation set by the reference central bank, and the more they do so, the less reliant they become on standard sources of funding such as deposits.

The VoC/CPE literature has not been inattentive to finance, but it has treated it mostly as a microeconomic supply-side phenomenon, for which credit is transferred to the real economy by two types of institutions, either banks or markets, but has per se no macroeconomic impact. This led to the standard classification of financial systems into bank- or market-based (Zysman 1983). CMEs are said to have bank-based systems, with firms obtaining "patient" capital that allow them to initiate processes of incremental innovation, whilst LMEs have market-based financial systems in which firms can finance themselves on the market to support risky radical innovation (Hall and Soskice 2001). It is implicit that households in CMEs access bank credit just like firms, even if the literature on household behavior is extremely thin, and even if there is rising academic interest in the factors that might explain cross-country differences in the extent and modalities through which households access credit (see, for example, Fuller 2015). Vitols (2001) documents, for example, that societies in CMEs consist of risk-averse savers that take advantage of available financial instruments to make better use of their savings, which often flow into conservative private pension schemes. By contrast, households in LMEs should be risk-takers borrowing to finance innovative or hazardous investment activities; or greedy consumers that get indebted for further consumption; or hand-to-mouth consumers typically defined as those that use their entire income for consumption (Hall and Soskice 2001; Crouch 2012). At the same time, there is no clear-cut categorization of financial systems in MMEs, where but one common trait seems to be that a significant share of commercial banks is publicly owned. The usefulness of such a dichotomized view of financial regimes has been criticized recently in Hardie and Howarth (2013). To our knowledge, they have been the first CPE scholars that have persuasively questioned Zysman's paradigm. They argue that, in recent times, banks in advanced economies have become as reliant on markets as capital. Their "market-based banking model" refers to the fact that commercial banks have engaged since the 1990s in business activities that have taken them away from the mere collection of household deposits and made them strong market players endowed with the capacity to set the price of loans.

In the euro area context, though, the interesting aspect is not so much the emergence of a market-based banking model per se but the fact that this has been truer of the periphery than of the core. Whilst MMEs and Ireland have been progressively resorting to non-deposit funding, CMEs retrenched back into safe household deposits after the introduction of the single currency. This is well evident in the evolution of the so-called funding gap. The funding gap – defined as the difference between loans to the non-financial private sector and deposits – started rising since the 1990s to reach on average a peak of 40 percent of GDP in the periphery immediately prior to the Euro debt crisis and then fell slightly in the midst of the Euro crisis, as commercial banks stopped lending to the real economy. In the core, as of the late 1990s, the funding gap was on a downward trend from 20 down to about 10 percent of GDP on average at the outbreak of the crisis. Lane and McQuade (2014) show persuasively that the main source of funding for banks in the euro area periphery was represented by other banks in the core. These countries' current account deficits would thus simply signal the fact that the real economy was contracting debt with foreigners to finance consumption and investment, and that such debt was fully intermediated by the domestic banking system. The opposite happened in the export-oriented CMEs, where credit institutions were more and more financed by abundantly available deposits, as evident from a declining funding gap. It should also be noted that the integration of retail markets was relatively less dramatic. Loans to the real economy provided by non-resident banks doubled in Greece, Portugal, and

Spain, with their size never exceeding that of the domestic economy. Ireland is the exception, as loans by non-resident banks rose from 30 percent of GDP in 2000 up to 220 percent of GDP in 2009 immediately prior to the crisis and back down to 120 percent in 2015.

One can hardly overstate the role of banks in the Euro crisis. One other channel through which they impacted on macroeconomic conditions is the so-called bank-sovereign negative feedback loop. EU banks detained large amounts of government bonds, which made them highly vulnerable to stress on government bond markets. As banks themselves came under stress, governments in MMEs and Ireland intervened through recapitalization and nationalization respectively (Acharya et al. 2014; Mody and Sandri 2012), thereby contributing to deteriorating fiscal outcomes. The International Monetary Fund (IMF) estimates that the rise in public debt attributable to the restructuring of the financial sector over 2008–2012 amounted to 44.5 percent of GDP in Greece, 72.8 percent in Ireland, 33.6 percent in Portugal, and 30.7 in Spain (Laeven and Valencia 2018).

A persuasive explanation of why commercial banks in MMEs and Ireland relied on non-deposit funding more than CMEs is that they might have attempted to catch up with more liberal neighboring markets (Abiad and Mody 2005). When looking at the broad institutional context against which domestic financial intermediaries operated immediately prior to the introduction of the single currency, it is noteworthy that the periphery and the core differed significantly across two important regulatory macro-features of finance: *de jure* capital account openness and domestic credit market regulation. Even if institutionally determined and hugely important from an economic perspective, these dimensions have not gone under much scrutiny by the CPE literature. To differentiate the analysis from that of the traditional institutionalist literature that has divided financial systems into bank- and market-based, as well as from more recent research on varieties of financial capitalism (see Chapter 1 of this book), this section refers to macro-financial systems to describe the extent to which a country is open, *de jure*, to foreign capital, and the extent to which domestic banks are free to act – including by taking advantage of international funding, either because they are privately owned or because no interest rate control is in place, which would imply that they can engage in profit-maximization.

The core element of the regime change associated with EMU was the complete elimination of capital controls in the early 1990s, as part of the completion of the single market. Yet, this level playing field was imposed on countries that started from different levels of financial openness. There is a plausible link between financial openness and the relative strength and the volatility of the nominal exchange rate. Hard-currency countries can afford a more open capital account, whilst soft-currency countries that have a poor reputation on foreign exchange markets because of repeated devaluations would have to "hide" behind a less open capital account. Different degrees of financial openness between CMEs and MMEs prior to EMU reflect the fact that the former were hard-currency and the latter soft-currency regimes, but the implications of having an open capital account go well beyond exchange rate issues. The economics research has persuasively shown that the degree to which the capital account is open is an independent determinant of liquidity constraints (Lewis 1997). High financial openness implies that a relatively high share of households and firms has easy access to credit. Low financial openness signifies that there is a low share of the real economy that has access to credit.

Capital mobility is a necessary regulatory condition to the build-up of euro area macroeconomic imbalances because it explains why debtors in the stressed periphery could gain access to foreign savings in the core. Yet, it is per se not a sufficient condition. Domestic credit market regulation is likely to affect the incentives under which domestic banks may want to channel capital inflows to the real economy and how. The extent to which banks can decide on whether to provide loans to the real economy, including by using foreign resources, and at what costs – given the central bank's monetary policy stance – is a function of institutional features of the domestic financial system such as, for example, the ratio of private to public banks and the presence or not of interest rate controls. It is the dynamic evolution of these institutional features in interaction with the macro-financial environment that explains cross-country differences in bank lending behavior. So, for example, the privatization of banks in the periphery coincided with the sudden and full integration of European credit markets, and it is potentially the combination of these two elements that explains why resident banks did not refrain from making use of the new larger international inter-bank market, once this became accessible, to provide abundant (risky) loans to the domestic economy.

Figure 9.1 provides evidence on *de jure* capital account openness as measured by the Chinn-Ito index and on domestic credit market regulation, here described by the ratio of private to public banks and the presence and magnitude of interest rate controls. The data capture median levels for each of the two indexes over the period 1980–2015 for Austria, Belgium, Finland, Germany, and the Netherlands (CMEs), on the one hand, and for Greece, Spain, Portugal (MMEs), and Ireland (LME), on the other. Historically, MMEs and Ireland have been much less financially open economies than the countries belonging to the former DM-bloc. The formal abolition of capital controls in the early 1990s enhanced by the elimination of exchange rate risks as of 1999 altered dramatically their macro-financial landscape – although this is much truer for MMEs than for Ireland. As foreign capital could easily flow into these countries, a high share of domestic agents that had once been credit-constrained finally obtained access to credit to finance investment in the non-traded sector or excess consumption. Capital account liberalization was accompanied by a softening of domestic credit market regulation in formerly highly regulated economies. This was mostly marked by the progressive privatization of domestic banking systems in MMEs, much less so in Ireland. Interest rate controls were instead not biting in the early 1990s either in CMEs or in MMEs or Ireland. Banks on the periphery suddenly enjoyed access to international credit markets and newly privatized banks have been faster in

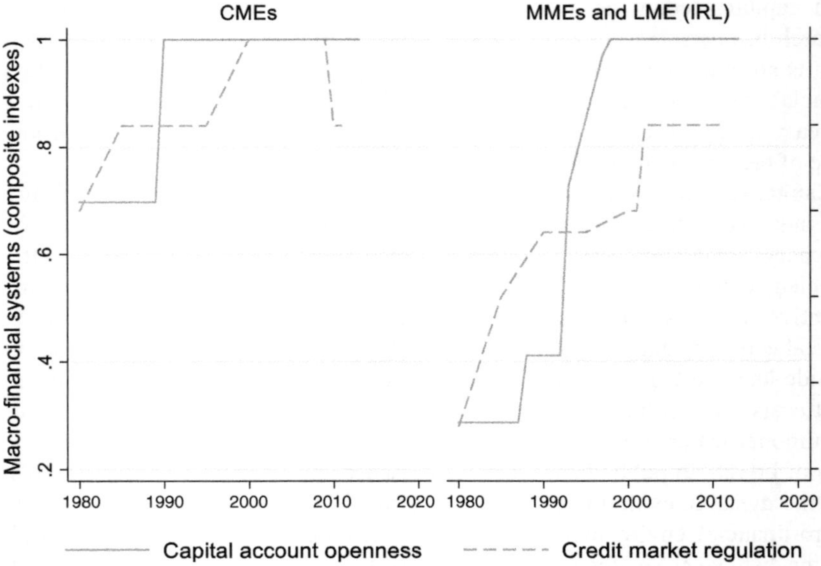

Figure 9.1 Macro-financial systems and varieties of capitalism, 1980–2015.

Source: Own elaboration based on Chinn and Ito (2008) and Fraser Institute.

Key: The Chinn-Ito index captures all restrictions on cross-border financial transactions. The credit market regulation index refers to the ratio of private to public banks and the presence of interest rate controls. The values of the index rise for higher levels of financial openness and for a lower share of public relatively to private banks and a relatively moderate presence of interest rate controls, respectively. "CMEs" include Austria, Belgium, Finland, Germany, and the Netherlands. "MMEs and LME (IRL)" include Greece, Ireland, Portugal, and Spain.

taking advantage of the opportunity than private banks in CMEs. Peripheral banks' catching-up with their most liberal neighbors resulted in strong credit growth, which was followed by a dramatic credit crunch as the crisis hit.

The massive capital inflows received in the periphery created a loose macroeconomic landscape. The inability to use the exchange rate to foster foreign demand as well as legal constraints on the stimulus that could come from the government sector did not compromise aggregate demand conditions, which remained well supported by the aggressive lending behavior of domestic banks (see also Fernandez-Villaverde, Garicano, and Santos 2013). Moreover, peripheral banks that had opted for securitization ended up being less dependent upon the ECB's monetary policy rates when deciding on loan supply (Estrella 2002; Loutskina and Strahan 2006; Altunbas, Gambacorta, and Marques-Ibanez 2009). Capital net debt inflows sowed the seeds of their sudden reversal as market perception and macroeconomic conditions worsened (Merler and Pisani-Ferry 2012), forcing MMEs to cut back on consumption abruptly, a circumstance that allowed a significant correction of their current account deficits, yet at the costs of rising unemployment.

Income inequality and varieties of capitalism

Varieties of capitalism or growth models display important differences in the way in which income is distributed (Wallerstein 1999; Rueda and Pontusson 2000; Hall and Soskice 2001; Sapir 2006; Baccaro and Pontusson 2016). CMEs tend to be egalitarian societies, whilst both MMEs and LMEs are typically plagued with high income inequality. A multiplicity of factors explains this outcome. The high centralization in wage bargaining that is characteristic of CMEs is often associated with low dispersion in earnings, whilst the opposite is true of individual wage bargaining in LMEs (Wallerstein 1999; Rueda and Pontusson 2000; Koeniger, Leonardi, and Nunziata 2007). MMEs are generally quite different from each other in their wage-setting institutions and outcomes, but they all tend to score low when it comes to income equality. Fiscal policy is the other obvious candidate explanation for developments in income inequality, as a redistributive welfare state may well be able to revert a market-driven rise in income inequality.

Existing research recognizes a relationship between income inequality and current account positions. The link is little explored in the CPE literature, with the exception of Iversen and Soskice (2012, 2016), Hope and Soskice (2016), and Baccaro and Pontusson (2016). Interest has been stronger in the economics profession. Kumhof et al. (2012) have shown that greater inequality induces those that are negatively affected to borrow because of habit persistence, including from the outside, which generates current account deficits. Al-Hussami and Remesal (2012) argue that rising inequality is associated with worse external positions because of the behavior of low-/middle-income groups, who borrow to emulate the consumption patterns of high-income groups. These arguments are at odds with the fact that non-stressed euro area countries have all seen rising inequality in pre-crisis times at the same time that the current account was delivering significant surpluses. A possible explanation is provided in Marzinotto (2017), where the author argues that the financial reform that was associated with EMU had a differentiated effect on aggregate consumption and hence on the current account, depending on the initial country-specific income distribution. The process of financial liberalization that preceded and then accompanied the monetary-union project came with a relaxation of liquidity constraints specifically for low-/middle-income groups that started to engage in debt-financed consumption. As the share of low-/middle-income groups is higher in more unequal than in less unequal societies, it follows that aggregate consumption rose faster in MMEs and Ireland than in CMEs, leading to the accumulation of current account deficits and to surpluses in CMEs, where the share of the low-/middle-income group that finally got access to credit was modest to start with or, to put it differently, not large enough to bear an impact on aggregate consumption. The data provided in Marzinotto (2017) indeed show that, in the periphery, low-income groups were on average more indebted than low-income groups in the core.

Thinking in terms of social rather than growth models, there is an established tradition of classifying social models based on outcomes, that is to say on how they score in terms of equity (i.e., income distribution) and efficiency (i.e., employment rate) (Sapir 2005). CMEs are able to deliver both on equity and efficiency. LMEs are efficient but not equitable. Finally, MMEs countries underperform in terms of both efficiency and equity. Figure 9.2 shows median levels of income inequality and median employment rates across stressed and non-stressed countries from 1980 to 2015. As in the received wisdom, CMEs enjoy a more equitable distribution of income than MMEs and Ireland but these countries' track record has been worsening in the late 1990s and early 2000s, partly due to reforms to the wage-setting system (see next section) that reverted during the crisis when the boom burst in the periphery. Inequality remains high in MMEs and Ireland but has been decreasing during the boom to start rising again in the recession.

Matthijs (2016) explains this inequality puzzle, alluding to the fact that during good times, CMEs reduced wages, which allowed them to be competitive on international markets at the cost of rising inequality; during the same period, inequality was decreasing in MMEs and Ireland as wages grew during the boom and the return on capital fell. In the recession, however, in CMEs, there was room for inflating wages, so that the rise in inequality reversed, whereas MMEs and Ireland saw wages falling with the result that income inequality started rising again.

The evidence in Figure 9.2 would provide additional granularity to a possible explanation of the income-inequality puzzle. It does show that in MMEs and

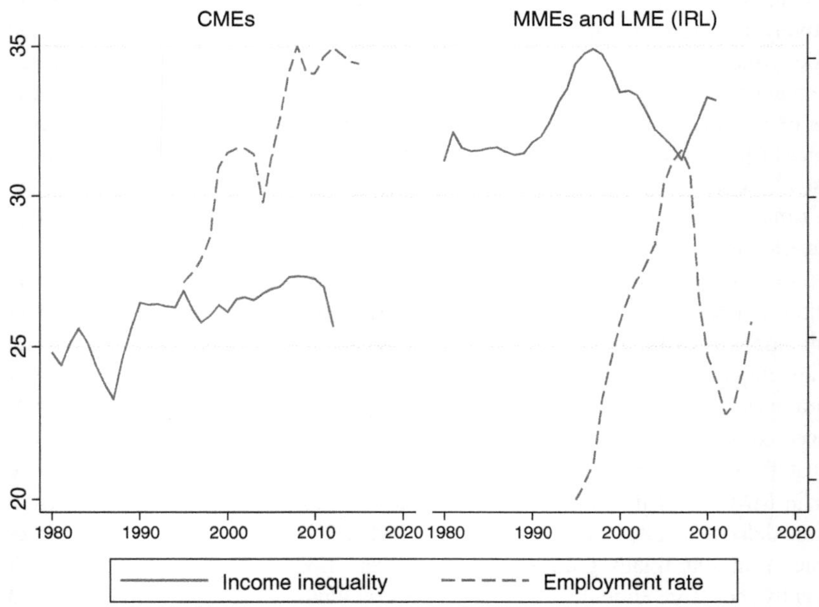

Figure 9.2 Income inequality and varieties of capitalism, 1980–2015.

Source: Own elaboration based on Solt (2009) and Eurostat.

Key: Income inequality is captured by the standardized post-taxes-and-transfers Gini coefficient. Higher values indicate rising inequality. The employment rate is the share of employees to the working-age population (15–64 years). "CMEs" include Austria, Belgium, Finland, Germany, and the Netherlands. "MMEs and LME (IRL)" include Greece, Ireland, Portugal, and Spain.

Ireland, inequality trends are very much linked to employment dynamics, and that it is access to the labor market that significantly contributes to the dynamic evolution of income inequality. Here, falling income inequality has been accompanied by a strengthening of efficiency, with higher shares of the population accessing the labor market, whilst rising inequality has been associated with the fact that numerous workers are pulled out of the labor market. The over-the-cycle correlation between income inequality and employment is, however, less evident in CMEs, where visual inspection suggests that rising inequality comes with a higher employment rate possibly because lower (inequality-enhancing) wages support labor demand. Nevertheless, falling inequality is not necessarily linked to labor market dynamics but rather to availability or lack of financial investment opportunities for owners of capital, at constant employment.

Varieties of capitalism and institutional change

An implicit hypothesis in the VoC literature is that models of production are institutionally entrenched and, as such, resilient. Different varieties can thus co-exist in open global markets because their respective institutions promote different competitive advantages (Hall and Soskice 2001). The analyses that look at how EMU affected the nature of this co-existence tend to be rather static in that they do not recognize that, together with the macroeconomic regime, other key institutions such as wage-bargaining systems have been reformed in the majority of the euro area countries. Intense reform efforts in the area of labor markets under EMU are justified in relation to the Optimum Currency Area (OCA) theory, for which wage-setting systems that allow for some wage flexibility empower members of a monetary union with shock-absorbing capacity in the absence of the nominal exchange rate. It should not come as a surprise that most of the adjustment programs devised for assisted countries (Greece, Portugal, and Ireland), as well as the EU's country-specific recommendations delivered to Spain and the others under the European Semester, advocate the reform of national wage-setting systems through a process of wage-bargaining decentralization that brings wage-setting closer to the firm-level to make sure that wage growth is aligned with productivity developments. It should be noted that the wage moderation that the VoC literature attributes to CMEs is equal, in macroeconomic terms, to a situation in which nominal wages grow in line with productivity developments. In the same direction goes the initiative to create independent National Productivity Boards (NPBs) tasked with the objective of analyzing competitiveness developments in each euro area member, with the ultimate objective of fostering convergence (EU Council Recommendations 349/01, 2016).[4]

The economic argument is that certain wage-setting systems are self-adjusting because they are populated by rational forward-looking wage setters that are able to observe cyclical conditions and adjust wage demands in ways that allow the real exchange rate to return to its equilibrium level (Carlin 2013). Two features make wage-setters rational and forward-looking. First, they should be large enough to internalize the consequences of their actions, which is a function of the level of wage-bargaining centralization. Second, they should coordinate wage increases at least to some extent, with adjustment capacity maximized when bargaining coordination takes place via pattern-setting by the exposed sector, as the latter has a specific interest in making sure that the real exchange rate adjusts enough to sustain export growth (Hancké 2013).

Visser (2013) identifies four possible levels of wage-bargaining centralization: absence of collective bargaining; firm-level; sector-level; and national collective bargaining. The standard characterization of CMEs is that of systems that have intermediate levels of centralization, in that wages are mostly determined at the sectoral level, with strong coordination as wage settlements in the export-oriented sectors set the pattern for all the others, including the public sector (Hall and Soskice 2001; Johnston, Hanckè, and Pant 2014). LMEs have normally individual wage bargaining, with wages being disciplined by the markets (Hall and Soskice 2001). Ireland is an exception; starting from the late 1980s and until the Euro crisis, a number of successive tripartite agreements between the government and the social partners on wage restraint were signed that functioned almost as a national wage norm. Much more diverse is the situation in MMEs, where levels of wage centralization and coordination vary significantly from one country to the other but labor markets are strongly unionized (Amable 2003; Molina and Rhodes 2007).

Figure 9.3 provides evidence on median levels of bargaining centralization across CMEs, MMEs, and Ireland over 1980–2015. Formal centralization is defined as the level at which bargaining takes place, including the articulation of multi-level bargaining that would indirectly contain some information on the level of coordination. De facto centralization incorporates also the use and variation of opening clauses, which may well allow for significant deviations from agreements taken at a higher level (Visser 2013). The data suggest a dramatic transformation to the operation of labor markets in CMEs where the extensive use of opening clauses ended up significantly decentralizing wage bargaining, an aspect that is not formally captured by standard measures of centralization. The trend goes in the opposite direction in MMEs and Ireland, where formal centralization has been rising over time but there is significant cross-country variation as concerns the relative importance of opening clauses, which remain much less common here than in CMEs. Still, the post-crisis reforms have created conditions for a larger use of derogations. So, for example, the Spanish government approved in 2010 a law widening the circumstances under which pay clauses at the company level can be lower than sectoral minima. In Ireland, after the crisis, temporary derogations from sectoral agreements were introduced in cases in which employers would prove unable to pay, a measure that was implicitly addressing the problems of the construction sector. The adjustment program for Portugal advocated more negotiating powers for works councils with the aim of strengthening lower levels of bargaining, whilst the Greek government was pressured by the Troika to change the hierarchy across bargaining levels, giving greater weight to the company – relatively to the sector – level of bargaining (Visser 2013).

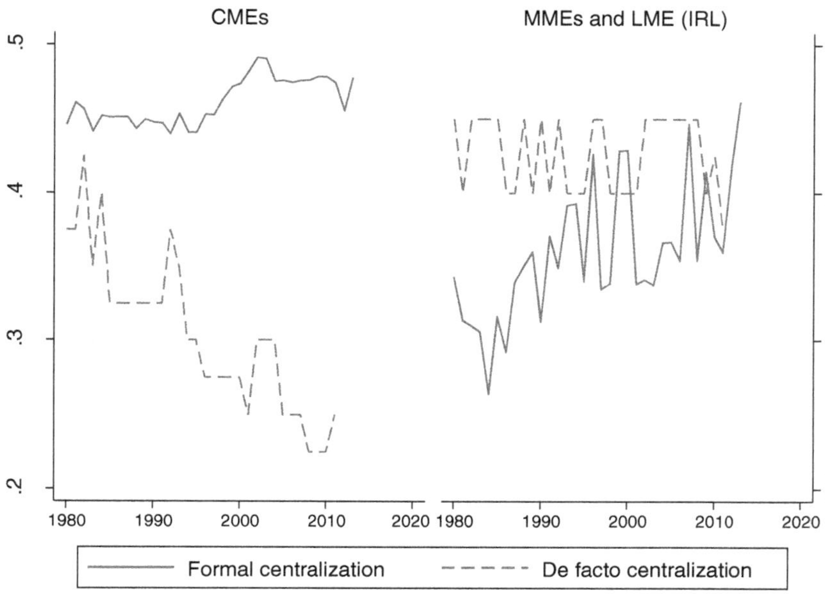

Figure 9.3 Wage-setting systems and varieties of capitalism, 1980–2015.

Source: Own elaboration based on Visser (2013, 2016).

Key: Formal centralization is a summary measure of centralization of wage bargaining, taking into account both union authority and union concentration at multiple levels. De facto centralization refers to the level of bargaining, the articulation or governance of multi-level bargaining, and the relative importance of opening clauses. The values of the index rise for higher levels of wage-bargaining centralization, whether formal or de facto. "CMEs" include Austria, Belgium, Finland, Germany, and the Netherlands. "MMEs and LME (IRL)" include Greece, Ireland, Portugal, and Spain.

The de facto decentralization of bargaining in CMEs has not compromised the efficient institutional complementarity between labor markets and the underlying macroeconomic regime, just because wage coordination remained high with the export-oriented sector still acting as wage leader for all the others. It has, however, dramatically altered the distribution of income, as wages of low-skilled workers that have progressively become more responsive to productivity developments inevitably grew much less than those of medium-to-high-skill workers (Dustmann et al. 2014). Moreover, some of the labor market reforms implemented in Germany in the early years of EMU created uncertainty, enhancing precautionary saving and making a society of risk-averse households even more risk-averse (Carlin and Soskice 2008), enhancing the distance of the country's export-led model from the demand-driven model of the periphery. This also confirms the suggestion made earlier of a complex relationship between income inequality and current account positions. Such a relation is non-linear, with rising inequality from low levels leading to precautionary saving, hence stronger external positions, and falling inequality from high levels leading to higher aggregate consumption, hence weaker external positions.

Summing-up and policy implications

Table 9.1 summarizes institutional changes across CMEs, MMEs, and Ireland under EMU along the dimensions here identified. It provides for an assessment of the extent to which varieties of capitalism are converging or not and whether the dynamics at play is enhancing or preventing the future build-up of macroeconomic imbalances.

The accumulation of euro area macroeconomic imbalances reflects the fact that member countries represent opposing growth models. Non-stressed countries embody an export-oriented growth model that flourished in rising market integration following the introduction of the single currency. Stressed countries are demand-driven economies, whose survival appeared endangered by the euro, and the ensuing incapacity to make use of competitive devaluations forced their respective governments to put in place significant structural reforms. Demand-driven economies neither perished nor reformed (Fernandez-Villaverde, Garicano, and Santos 2013). This chapter adds to the existing VoC literature in some important ways.

First, EMU does not come with a single monetary regime. Bank lending strategies bear an important impact on the degree of monetary accommodation above and beyond the monetary base set by the new central bank. The once-financially repressed MMEs and to a smaller extent Ireland obtained access to the international wholesale markets, and public banks were privatized. To catch up with their neighbors, Southern and Irish could afford supplying credit well above the value of domestic deposits at the same time as banks in CMEs seemed to be retrenching back into traditional patterns of bank-related savings and borrowings. Relaxed credit conditions allowed these countries to preserve their demand-driven model, albeit at the cost of increasing financial instability.

Second, the distribution of income is relevant to the evolution of macroeconomic imbalances. In the more unequal societies of MMEs and Ireland, formerly credit-constrained agents finally engage in inter-temporal consumption following financial liberalization, with the result that aggregate consumption grew above the value of production, leading to deteriorated current account positions. In CMEs, the credit-constrained group that eventually had access to credit following the completion of the single market and the elimination of exchange rate risk was too small to drive aggregate consumption, but rising inequality in the society starting from a relatively equal distribution of income is likely to have pushed numerous agents into precautionary saving, thereby strengthening initial current account surpluses.

Third, the hypothesis that labor market institutions are static is relaxed. In the core, de facto centralization has been decreasing following the extensive use of opening clauses, but coordination remains relatively high and wage discipline generally important in a context in which bank lending is deposit-based and

Table 9.1 Varieties of capitalism before and after the crisis

	CMEs	*MMEs*	*LMEs (vs IRL)*	*ASSESSMENT*
Capital account openness	High	Low > Rising	High (Low > Rising)	***Converged (worsening imbalances)
Interest rate controls	Low	Low	Low (Low)	Converged (theoretically neutral to imbalances)
Bank ownership	Private	Public < Decreasing	Private (Private)	Converging (theoretically neutral to imbalances)
Type of households	Risk-averse savers > Rising to more risk-averse savers	Risk-averse savers and hand-to-mouth < > Decreasing to less risk-averse savers and rising to indebted hand-to-mouth	Risk-takers and hand-to-mouth (risk-takers and hand-to-mouth > rising to indebted hand-to-mouth)	***Diverging (worsening imbalances)
Income inequality	Low > Increasing	High > becoming volatile	High (High > becoming volatile)	***Diverging idiosyncratically (worsening imbalances in good times)
Employment	High	Low > becoming volatile	High (low > becoming volatile)	Diverging (theoretically neutral/ irrelevant to imbalances)
Wage-bargaining centralization	Sector < Decreasing	Firm and sector > Rising	Firm (Sector)	Diverging (theoretically neutral/ irrelevant to imbalances)
Wage-bargaining coordination	High	Low-to-medium > Rising	Low (High)	Moderately converging (theoretically neutral/irrelevant to imbalances)

Source: author's own elaboration.

Notes
Text underlined indicates regime change; *** signals potential risk of future macroeconomic imbalances.

strongly related to the degree of monetary accommodation set by the new reference central bank.

EU institutions have not been inattentive to the risks posed by macroeconomic imbalances and launched in 2011 the Macroeconomic Imbalance Procedure (MIP) with the aim of preventing and correcting imbalances especially related to the operation of the private sector. This can provide for a useful "early warning" in the eyes of national authorities, but the implementation record of MIP-related country-specific recommendations is poor and, in fact, declining over time (Estathiou and Wolff 2018). Inside EU institutions, there is an increasing consensus that some degree of institutional convergence is required to prevent the build-up of excessive macroeconomic imbalances. Wage-setting institutions receive the greatest attention. The Five Presidents' Report recommends the creation of Competitiveness Authorities, whose objective should be to exchange best practices. Whilst not harmful, this initiative may be missing the target.

The narrative proposed in this chapter has important implications for how one understands the origins and the cure of macroeconomic imbalances. The resilience of Continental European countries inside the monetary union should not be solely attributed to a well-developed capacity of delivering wage moderation in support of exports but also to historical high levels of financial depth (i.e., households' access to credit) and to the effect of increasing income inequality on consumption/saving behavior. Symmetrically, the poor performance of Southern European countries goes beyond the incapacity to use the exchange rate to recoup competitiveness. Their poor performance is also related to the dramatic one-off switch from a repressed to a liberal financial system as well as to historical high levels of inequality that induced the poorest households to borrow for consumption. It follows that, to prevent future imbalances, macro-prudential policies should be jointly managed by the ECB and national authorities to tame the potential impact of full capital mobility on external positions in a heterogeneous union. A convergence in growth models, not visible at present, might also not be necessary for the political viability of the euro project.

Notes

1 Italy did not receive bailout loans but was nonetheless perceived by financial markets as weak. Still, it is not included in the group of stressed countries as it represents, in many respects, a special case (see the chapter by Merler in this volume). Equally, even if France could access credit at relatively favorable conditions during the crisis, it is not included amongst the non-stressed countries because the country's institutional structures differ significantly from those of the other Continental euro area members.

2 The terms "varieties of capitalism" and "growth models" are here used interchangeably. It should be noted, however, that they are treated separately in the literature. The standard VoC literature classifies countries based on the way in which the production system is organized (see, for example, Hall and Soskice 2001; Amable 2003; Hancké, Thatcher, and Rhodes 2007). Instead, the literature on growth models is rather concerned with the demand side and classifies countries based on whether exports or domestic demand provide for the largest contribution to GDP growth (Baccaro and

Pontusson 2016, 2018). The distinction, though, leads to the same country clustering for all European countries but those in Scandinavia, which is why the two terms are used interchangeably without losing sight of the fact that each is concerned with a different "side" of the economic system.

3 Irrespective of the monetary regime, though, CMEs have a strong export orientation supported over the years not only by the wage-setting system but also by a system of vocational training that keeps high the supply of high-skill workers, allowing for a high-value-added export model (Hall and Soskice 2001; Iversen, Soskice, and Hope 2016).

4 As of the end of 2018, the following euro area countries had appointed a National Productivity Board: Cyprus, France, Ireland, Lithuania, Luxembourg, the Netherlands, and Slovenia. The same Council recommendation encourages also non-euro area members to set up similar bodies. The following non-euro area countries had one such body at the end of 2018: Denmark, Hungary, and Romania.

References

Abiad, Abdul and Mody, Ashoka (2005), "Financial reform: what shakes it? what shapes it?", in: *The American Economic Review*, 95(1), 66–88.

Al-Hussami, Fares and Remesal, Alvaro Martin (2012), "Current account imbalances and income inequality: theory and evidence", Kiel Advanced Studies Working Papers 459.

Altunbas, Yener, Gambacorta, Leonardo and Marques-Ibanez, David (2009), "Securitisation and the bank lending channel", in: *European Economic Review*, 53(8), 996–1009.

Amable, Bruno (2003), *The Diversity of Modern Capitalism*. Oxford University Press: Oxford, UK.

Acharya, Viral, Drechsler, Itamar and Schnabl, Philipp (2014), "A pyrrhic victory? Bank bailouts and sovereign credit risk", in: *The Journal of Finance*, 69, 2689–2739.

Baccaro, Lucio and Pontusson, Jonas (2016), "Rethinking comparative political economy: the growth model perspective", in: *Politics and Society*, 44(2), 175–207.

Baccaro, Lucio and Pontusson, Jonas (2018), "Comparative political economy and varieties of macroeconomics", MPIfG Discussion Paper 18/10.

Baldwin, Richard and Giavazzi, Francesco (2015), "The eurozone crisis: a consensus view of the causes and a few possible solutions". VoxEU.org.

Carlin, Wendy (2013), "Real exchange rate adjustment, wage-setting institutions, and fiscal stabilization policy: lessons of the eurozone's first decade", in: *CESifo Economic Studies*, 59(3), 489–519.

Carlin, Wendy and Soskice, David (2008), "Reforms macroeconomic policy and economic performance in Germany", in: Schettkat, Ronald and Langkau, Jochem (eds.) *Economic Policy Proposals for Germany and Europe*, 72–118, Routledge: Abingdon, UK.

Chinn, Menzie, and Ito, Hiro (2006), "What matter for financial development? Capital controls, institutions, and interactions", in: *Journal of Development Economics*, 81(1), 163–192.

Crouch, Colin (2012), "Employment, consumption, debt, and European industrial relations systems", in: *Industrial Relations*, 51, 389–412.

Dustmann, Christian, Fitzenberger, Bernd, Schönberg, Uta and Spitz-Oener, Alexandra (2014), "From sick man of Europe to economic superstar: Germany's resurgent economy", in: *Journal of Economic Perspectives*, 28(1), 167–188.

Estathiou, Konstantinos and Wolff, Guntram (2018), "Is the European semester effective and useful?", Bruegel Policy Contribution, 9.

Estrella Arturo (2002), "Securitization and the efficacy of monetary policy", in: *FRBNY Economic Policy Review*, May, 243–255.

European Commission (2015), "Completing Europe's Economic and Monetary Union – report by Jean-Claude Juncker in close cooperation with Donald Tusk, Jeroen Dijsselbloem, Mario Draghi and Martin Schultz", Brussels.

Fernandez-Villaverde, Jesus, Garicano, Luis and Santos, Tano (2013), "Political credit cycles: the case of the euro zone", in: *Journal of Economic Perspectives*, 27(3), 1–44.

Fuller, Gregory (2015), "Who's borrowing? Credit encouragement vs. credit mitigation in national financial systems", in: *Politics & Society*, 43(2), 241–268.

Fuller, Gregory (2018), 'Exporting assets: EMU and the financial drivers of European macroeconomic imbalances", in: *New Political Economy*, 23(2), 174–191.

Gabrisch, Hubert, and Staehr, Karsten (2015), "The euro plus pact: competitiveness and external capital flows in the EU countries", in: *Journal of Common Market Studies*, 53(3), 558–576.

Hall Peter (2012), "The economics and politics of the euro crisis", in: *German Politics*, 21(4), 355–371.

Hall, Peter (2014), "Varieties of capitalism and the euro crisis", in: *West European Politics*, 37(6), 1223–1243.

Hall, Peter (2018), "Varieties of capitalism in light of the euro crisis", in: *Journal of European Public Policy*, 25(1), 7–30.

Hall, Peter and Soskice, David (eds) (2001), *Varieties of Capitalism: The Institutional Foundations of Comparative Advantage*, Oxford University Press: Oxford.

Hancké, Bob (2013), *Unions, Central Banks, and EMU: Labor Market Institutions and Monetary Integration in Europe*, Oxford: Oxford University Press.

Hardie, Iain and Howarth, David (2013), *Marked-Based Banking and the International Financial Crisis*, Oxford: Oxford University Press.

Hope, David and Soskice, David (2016), "Growth models, varieties of capitalism, and macroeconomics", in: *Politics and Society*, 44(2), 209–226.

Iversen, Torben and Soskice, David (1998), "Multiple wage bargaining systems in the single European currency area", in: *Oxford Review of Economic Policy*, 14(3), 110–124.

Iversen, Torben and Soskice, David (2012), "Modern capitalism and the advanced nation state: understanding the causes of the crisis", in: Bermeo, Nancy and Pontusson, Jonas (eds), *Coping with the Crisis: Government Reactions to the Great Recession*, Russel Sage: New York, 35–64.

Iversen, Torben, Soskice, David and Hope, David (2016), "The eurozone and political economic institutions", in: *Annual Review of Political Science*, 19, 163–185.

Johnston, Alison and Regan, Aidan (2016), "European monetary integration and the incompatibility of national varieties of capitalism", in: *JCMS: Journal of Common Market Studies*, 54(2), 318–336.

Johnston, Alison, Hancké, Bob and Pant, Suman (2014), "Comparative institutional advantage in the European sovereign debt crisis", *Comparative Political Studies*, 47(13), 1771–1800.

Jones, Erik (2015), "Forgotten financial union", in Matthijs, Matthias and Blyth, Mark (eds), *The Future of the Euro*, Oxford: Oxford University Press, 44–69.

Koeniger, Winfried, Leonardi, Marco and Nunziata, Luca (2007), "Labour market institutions and wage inequality", in: *Industrial and Labour Relations Review*, 60, 340–356.

Kumhof, Michael, Lebarz, Claire, Ranciere, Roman, Richter, Alexander and Throckmorton, Nathaniel (2012), "Income inequality and current account imbalances", IMF Working Paper 08.

Laeven, Luc and Valencia, Fabian (2018), "Systemic banking crises revisited", IMF Working Paper 206.
Lane, Philip R. (2012), "The European sovereign debt crisis", in: *Journal of Economic Perspectives*, 26(3), 49–68.
Lane, Philip R. and Milesi-Ferretti, Gian Maria (2012), "External adjustment and the global crisis", in: *Journal of International Economics*, 88(2), 252–265.
Lane, Philip and McQuade, Peter (2014), "Domestic credit growth and international capital flows", in: *Scandinavian Journal of Economics*, 116(1), 218–252.
Lewis, Karen (1997), "Are countries with official international restrictions liquidity-constrained?", in: *European Economic Review*, 41(6), 1079–1109.
Loutskina Elena and Strahan Philip (2006), "Securitization and the declining impact of bank finance on loan supply: evidence from mortgage acceptance rate", NBER Working Paper Series, 11983.
Marzinotto, Benedicta (2016), "United we fall: the Eurozone's silent balance of payment crisis in comparison with previous ones", in: Caporaso, James and Rhodes, Martin (eds), *Political and Economic Dynamics of the Eurozone Crisis*, Oxford: Oxford University Press, 100–121.
Marzinotto, Benedicta (2017), "Euro area macroeconomic imbalances and their asymmetric reversal: the link between financial integration and income inequality", in: *Economia Politica*, 34(1), 83–104.
Marzinotto, Benedicta, Pisani-Ferry, Jean and Sapir, André (2010), "Two crises, two responses", Bruegel Policy Brief.
Matthijs, Matthias (2016), "The euro's winner-take-all political economy: institutional choices, policy drift, and diverging patterns of inequality", in: *Politics & Society*, 44(3), 393–422.
Merler, Silvia and Pisani-Ferry, Jean (2012), "Sudden stops in the euro area", Bruegel Policy Contribution.
Mody, Ashoka and Sandri, Damiano (2012), "The eurozone crisis: how banks and sovereigns came to be joined at the hip", in: *Economic Policy*, 27(70), 199–230.
Molina, Oscar and Rhodes, Martin (2007), "The political economy of adjustment in mixed market economies: a study of Spain and Italy", in Hancké, Bob, Thatcher, Mark and Rhodes, Martin (eds), *Beyond Varieties of Capitalism: Conflict, Contradictions and Complementarities in the European Economy*, Oxford: Oxford University Press, 223–252.
Pontusson, Jonas and Swenson, Peter (1996), "Labor markets, production strategies and wage-bargaining institutions: the Swedish employers' offensive in comparative perspective", in: *Comparative Political Studies*, 29(2), 223–250.
Rueda, David and Pontusson, Jonas (2000), "Wage inequality and varieties of capitalism", in: *World Politics*, 52, 350–383.
Sapir, André (2006), "Globalization and the reform of European social models", in: *JCMS: Journal of Common Market Studies*, 44, 369–390.
Schelkle, Waltraud (2017), *The Political Economy of Monetary Solidarity: Understanding the Euro Experiment*, Oxford: Oxford University Press.
Solt, Frederick (2009), Standardised World Income Inequality Database.
Soskice, David (2007), "Macroeconomics and varieties of capitalism", in Hancké, Bob, Thatcher, Mark and Rhodes, Martin (eds), *Beyond Varieties of Capitalism: Conflict, Contradictions and Complementarities in the European Economy*, Oxford: Oxford University Press, 89–121.
Visser, Jelle (2013), "Wage bargaining institutions – from crisis to crisis", Economic Papers 488, European Economy.

Visser, Jelle (2016), Database on Institutional Characteristics of Trade Unions, Wage Setting, State Intervention and Social Pacts in 34 countries between 1960 and 2014, AIAS.

Vitols, Sigurt (2001), "The origins of bank-based and market-based financial systems: Japan, Germany, and the US", in: Streeck, Wolfgang and Yamamura, Kozo (eds), *The Origins of Non-Liberal Capitalism*, Cornell University Press: Ithaca, NY.

Wallerstein, Michael (1999), "Wage-setting institutions and pay inequality in advanced societies", in: *American Journal of Political Science*, 43(3), 649–680.

Zysman, John (1983), *Governments, Markets and Growth: Financial Systems and the Politics of Industrial Change*, Cornell University Press: Ithaca, NY.

10 Conclusion

The political economy of adjustment

Michele Chang, Federico Steinberg and Francisco Torres

Introduction

The euro is now 20 years old. It enjoyed a first decade of relative success (and tranquility), while its teenage years have been rather turbulent. Since the outbreak of the global financial and economic crisis in 2008, it faced and subsequently had to confront what became an existential crisis. This threatened its very survival, forced deep institutional reforms in its governance structure, involved exceptional actions by the ECB and required complex programs of financial assistance for five of its members.

During EMU's first decade, there was an absence of market pressure, as financial markets failed to differentiate between the sustainability of public debt and external imbalances among participants, and some member states did not implement needed national reforms. The Stability and Growth Pact has never applied its excessive deficit procedure, despite the repeated failure of Eurozone governments (including Germany) to adhere to the fiscal rules. At the same time, the announced objectives of the Lisbon Strategy for economic coordination were poorly implemented, and its informal peer-review process "did not bite". The lack of enforcement of the SGP and the Lisbon Strategy, combined with the economic boom that the introduction of the euro generated, reduced governments' incentives for economic reforms, especially in the periphery (Fernández-Villaverde et al., 2013).

EMU's institutional incompleteness rendered it incapable of dealing with the cumulative effects of the financial and sovereign debt crises. The EU did move toward increased coordinated financial supervision in response to the global financial crisis, but this was insufficient given the absence of financial backstops for stressed sovereigns or strained banks. This made it impossible to counter sudden stops in financial flows (Mongelli et al., 2016), and the global financial crisis segued into a Eurozone crisis

However, the single currency survived. In fact, it proved more resilient than had been anticipated. The process of creating new institutions and mechanisms displayed significant political and institutional resilience in the face of the crisis. The crisis triggered advances in economic governance that took place through a multitude of successive steps, driven by market pressure and motivated by the need to ensure the survival of EMU. Most academics and commentators who repeatedly anticipated the euro's demise tended to overlook that EMU is part of that wider political project whose viability cannot be assessed merely on the grounds of the Optimum Currency Area (OCA) theory (Otero-Iglesias, 2015). In fact, and despite being perceived by some as a golden straitjacket or as an unhappy marriage with an unbearable divorce cost (Tsoukalis, 2016), recent Eurobarometer data indicate that support for the common currency reached its highest level ever in 2017 and 2018. Today, the euro area has more member states than at the beginning of the crisis, and most of its citizens seem to acknowledge that, despite economic hardship, life is even more difficult outside the single currency.

But if the crisis demonstrated that leaving the euro is no easy task, it also made plain that its institutional design is still incomplete (De Grauwe and Ji, 2016). Moreover, it now seems clear that the management of the global financial crisis and the euro zone sovereign debt crisis was far from optimal (Pickford et al., 2014; Jones and Torres, 2016). The handling of the crisis exposed a deep split between northern (creditor) countries and southern (debtor) countries. This divide, far from being resolved, has intensified with the social and political fractures generated by the crisis and the subsequent rescue programs. This has made it even more difficult to agree on the institutional reforms needed to ensure the sustainability of the single currency in the long run, namely a full banking union, a fiscal union and some sort of political union to legitimize the transfer of sovereignty from member states to the center.

On the one hand, appropriate structural reforms are growth enhancing in the long run, yet they often fail to bring about immediate benefits (IMF, 2015). They come with a high political cost when they collide with entrenched interest groups or affect vulnerable social groups. With the sovereign debt crisis, the common objectives to which member states committed under the Europe 2020 Strategy have come to encompass increasingly salient political and distributional issues, not only in but also between member states. Since competencies and instruments have remained national, the enforcement (under market and peer pressure and conditionality of the various bailout programs) of reform objectives to which the member states had previously committed would always risk being perceived as intrusive, unless the government in question assumed ownership of reforms (Bongardt and Torres, 2018). On the other hand, there has been resistance to creating Eurozone-wide risk sharing for Europe-wide shocks, which implies increased fiscal integration, for fear that it may lead to structural rather than temporary fiscal transfers between member states.

As a result, the euro continues to be work in progress. At the same time, as the chapters in this volume show, peripheral countries that required bailout programs (including Italy, which was not obliged to adopt one) went through deep changes. They suffered a lost decade in terms of growth and had to implement painful austerity programs and a variety of structural reforms. Most of them witnessed the transformation of their political systems, some of which are now exhibiting populist anti-establishment parties critical of the EU and the single currency. That said, the emergence of populist parties was not confined to those countries, but they also made an appearance in other Eurozone (e.g., France or Germany) and non-Euro area (e.g., Denmark or the UK) countries.

Still, with the benefit of hindsight, we can now see that those countries' economic models have only been partially modified or modernized. Using the Varieties of Capitalism (VoC) analytical framework, the case studies in this volume show that there has only been limited convergence in economic models across the Eurozone. This is because each of the program countries started from different positions and faced different problems, while the political coalitions behind the policies that they implemented were also diverse and, in some cases, changed during the process. Moreover, the troika also behaved differently in each of the country cases, both because of its growing internal divisions and because some countries had more leverage than others when dealing with it. Therefore, neither the problems nor the solutions were one-size-fits-all, and the Eurozone periphery still exhibits diversity.

Main findings

This book started from the basic observation that the countries that received a bailout handled their programs differently and their subsequent growth trajectories have also been divergent. Moreover, the troika behaved differently in the different cases; as noted in the chapter by Lütz et al., the three actors in the troika had different interests, and their relative influence varied from case to case. The reforms implemented, both at the Eurozone level and in the rescued countries (plus Italy), have not been able to fully address the underlying economic imbalances or to fully prepare countries for the next crisis. In addition, the social and political implications of the economic policies that they adopted have also been different in terms of inequality, poverty, unemployment, financial system health or sustainability of pension systems and public finances.

In particular, each case study has addressed the following questions:

- What was the national growth model before the crisis?
- What were the primary causes of the crisis?
- What problems did the EU/troika identify?
- What were the major reforms undertaken by the government?
- What remains to be done?

The answers to these questions are summarized in Table 10.1.

Besides the governance failures of the Eurozone architecture that exacerbated the crisis and made it more difficult to timely address at its outset (identified by Kincaid in his chapter), the primary causes of the crisis in each country also differed. The creation of the euro in 1999 substantially reduced financing costs for the euro countries in the periphery, allowing banks, governments and households to increase their debt and maintain their demand-driven growth models. This destabilized financial systems, fueled a real estate bubble (and therefore private

Table 10.1 Summary of case studies

	Ireland	*Portugal*	*Spain*	*Greece*
Pre-crisis national growth model	• recent shift toward demand-led • FDI • construction	• demand-led via public sector and current account deficits • capital inflows • expansion of non-tradable sector	• demand-led via current account deficits • construction	• demand-led via public sector and current account deficits • expansion of credit construction
Primary cause of crisis	• real estate bubble • overleveraged banking sector • collapse of government revenues	• high public deficit and debt • declining competitiveness and high current account deficits • "sudden stop" of capital inflows	• real estate bubble • high private debt levels • declining competitiveness and high current account deficit	• high public deficit and debt • declining competitiveness and high current account deficits • "sudden stop" of capital inflows
Major problems indicated by EU/ troika	• housing bubble • banking sector • structural adjustments in fiscal mix and in the economy (fiscal and banking adjustments already well underway before the program started)	• banking sector • weak fiscal institutions and high government spending • loss of competitiveness: current account deficit, high unit labor costs and labor market segmentation • stalled product market reforms	• housing bubble • banking sector, particularly for the *cajas* • high private debt • loss of competitiveness: current account deficit, high unit labor costs and labor market segmentation	• weak fiscal institutions and high government spending • loss of competitiveness: current account deficit, high unit labor costs • pension and health system deficits

Major reforms undertaken by government	• fiscal consolidation and reduction of public sector • financial system reforms, including losses for private sector • social programs adjusted, with measures to support competitiveness • flexible bankruptcy arrangements	• financial system reforms, including bank recapitalization • budgetary institutions • privatizations • labor market reforms, including easier access to professions • licensing, enhanced competition in medicines and in the housing market	• financial system reforms • pension system reforms (partially reversed) • labor market reforms	• fiscal consolidation and pension reform • labor market reforms, including reduction of minimum wage and liberalization of professions • state sector reform • reform of product and services markets
Remaining areas for reform post-crisis	• high levels of debt • reduce NPLs in the banking sector	• high levels of debt • product market reform • labor market • public administration reform • health system reforms	• high levels of debt • labor market • pension system • high unemployment and inequality	• high levels of debt • high unemployment and inequality • public administration reform • streamlining of justice system • reduce NPLs in the banking sector • privatizations

debt) in Ireland and Spain and contributed to a dramatic increase in government debt in Greece. Capital inflows, higher wages and a demand-led growth model in Greece, Portugal and Spain accelerated inflation and unit labor costs (vis-à-vis Germany and other northern trading partners), which, in turn, generated losses in competitiveness that resulted in large current account deficits that required ongoing external financing (see Chapter 1). While Portugal, Spain and Greece conformed to VOC models of demand-led economies, the classification of the Irish and Italian growth models did not conform as neatly to VOC expectations. Ireland's pre-crisis growth model did not rely heavily on imports until 2005, contrary to LME expectations that demand-led growth would be more entrenched (see Cardiff's chapter). As Merler noted in her chapter, Italy's pre-crisis growth model was not primarily demand driven, and it did not experience a post-euro/pre-crisis economic boom.

Starting in 2009, the crisis and the redenomination risk precipitated a sudden stop. The pre-crisis complacency of financial markets gave way to focused attention on euro area economies in the periphery that had a questionable ability to fulfill public debt obligations, albeit for a variety of reasons. While Greece and to a lesser extent Portugal suffered from high levels of public and private debt, the debt in Spain and Ireland was fueled by private debt that became public and government revenues related to the construction boom that collapsed. Italy, on the other hand, carried a high level of public debt over several decades that potentially became unsustainable in a low economic growth environment. These domestic economic issues were exacerbated by the absence of a banking union and a true lender of last resort that would have reduced the capital flows from the periphery to the center by helping to break the doom loop between banks and sovereigns. Higher-risk premia in sovereign debt, combined with the fact that the traditional option of devaluing the currency to regain competitiveness was absent, led Greece, Ireland and Portugal to require external financial assistance. Spain, which was too large for a full bailout from the ESM, later requested a credit line to recapitalize its financial sector. And in July 2012 ECB President Mario Draghi made his now famous *whatever it takes* statement, which calmed the markets, eliminated the redenomination risk and allowed Italy to escape from a bailout program.

Diagnosing the specific reforms that each country needed was not difficult. They were well known. The problem had more to do with implementation, sequencing and the domestic political economy dynamics in each of the countries. Moreover, there were differences in the treatment that each country received. For example, the troika decided that Ireland had to bail out all the creditors of its banking system, while Spain introduced a bail-in principle that the rules of the European Banking Union generalized in 2014 with the Bank Recovery and Resolution Directive. Similarly, the balance between structural reforms and fiscal austerity was different in each program. The first Greek program focused more on fiscal sustainability, while Portugal's emphasized more structural reforms. Ireland's dealt mainly with recapitalizing the banking system and in reducing the budget deficit, and its economy responded faster to the troika reforms than in the other cases. In Spain, the Memorandum of Understanding that the government signed only included measures to reform the financial system and ensure its sustainability. However, the government also passed labor market, tax, education and pension reforms, taking advantage of the external pressure coming from Brussels. There was also a difference in the type of fiscal consolidation adopted, with Spain's featuring a larger share of tax hikes and not resulting in a decline in the debt ratio, and Ireland's based on spending cuts with lower output costs and a sharp decline in debt (Alesina et al., 2019). Finally, in Italy, reforms have been very limited. Powerful domestic interest groups, combined with the fact that the country did not have a rescue program, managed to resist reforms. Italy was too big to fail but too big to be rescued.

Overall, as the chapters in this volume make clear, the higher the degree of national ownership of rescue programs and reforms that each country had, the more successful the program was. In the cases of Ireland and Spain, and to a lesser extent Portugal, national governments had a reform agenda that the troika helped to implement, overcoming parts of the domestic opposition to change. In Greece, however, the perception of "lost economic sovereignty to the troika" was much higher. In Italy, there was little domestic consensus for reforms, so absent a formal program, economic policy changes were minor.

As we have argued, there was no substantial change in national growth models because of the Troika programs. Given that the main goal of an adjustment program was to reestablish market access and ensure long-term financial sustainability (and only indirectly to increase potential growth and make the peripheral economies converge structurally with those at the center), one can regard the programs as relatively successful, especially in the cases of Ireland and Spain. Nevertheless, if creditor countries' elites dreamed that the bailouts would lead to an overall convergence in European economic models toward the coordinated market economies of the north, this has not been the case. It is true that the Eurozone has exhibited in the last years a substantial current account surplus (which is now the largest in the world), but it remains to be seen if peripheral countries can sustain these surpluses once their domestic demands recover, oil prices rise and their unemployment levels fall.

A decade after the start of the crisis, the Eurozone periphery would benefit from further reform. Needed reforms have been delayed because of the new fractures that emerged from the economic hardship of the last decades, mainly increases in poverty and inequality. Indeed, the level of income inequality, something that had not been emphasized by the Troika, plays an important role in understanding the robustness of VOC models, as argued in the chapter by Marzinotto. Moreover, Italy, Greece, Portugal and to a certain extent Ireland still have problems in their financial systems. Spain, Greece and Portugal still need to reform their labor markets. and all countries need new strategies to reduce high public debt levels and to make their pensions systems sustainable.

Finally, the last decade has seen the collapse of the centrist parties in Europe and the rise of the extremes. This phenomenon has happened across the continent, but the intensity of the crisis and the domestic perception of the troika's policies played a role in their ascendance in the bailed-out countries. However, it is remarkable that Ireland and Portugal (and to a lesser extent Spain), which were violently hit by the crisis, have not exhibited so far the rise of a clear extreme anti-euro party. On the other hand, in Greece, Syriza has been transforming itself into a social-democratic pro-euro party (at least tactically) while in Italy, which had no rescue program, two anti-euro and Euroskeptic parties (*La Lega* and *Movimento 5 Stelle*) have formed a coalition government (much like what had happened before in Greece). The long-term impact of these parties on the respective growth models of their countries remains to be seen.

The political economy of adjustment and completing EMU

Efforts to create a "genuine EMU", however, have only made limited progress. Fiscal integration has progressed little since 2011; states like Portugal, Spain, France and Italy fell foul of the new fiscal rules but still escaped sanctioning, and French President Emmanuel Macron's attempt to establish a euro area budget ran into substantial opposition from the new Hanseatic League countries in northern Europe. Although financial integration (banking union) progressed substantially, one of its three pillars (namely, the common insurance deposit scheme) is still missing.

On the other hand, EMU depends not only on the completion of EMU governance but also on the creation of sufficient adjustment capacity and ownership of reforms at the member state level. Here, preferences have been slow to converge and member states continue, to different extents, to resort to a negative narrative in national debates about the EU. Yet, EMU's resilience depends on both EU and national reforms, as they are mutually reinforcing, contributing to a stronger EU identity built around its core, the Eurozone.

In the sovereign debt crisis, market pressure and conditionality have provided additional de facto enforcement mechanisms for softly coordinated economic reforms. For those countries whose bailout programs are analyzed in this volume, the new crisis-enacted mechanisms and the conditionality-linked availability of funds have positively affected the implementation of some structural reforms.

All in all, the eurozone crisis triggered important (but insufficient) reforms in both EMU governance and member state economies. However, as has been the case since the inception of the EU, this is a gradual and slow process that still needs to continue.

References

Alesina, A., Favero, C. & Giavazzi, F. 2019. *Austerity: When It Works and When It Doesn't*. Princeton, NJ: Princeton University Press.

Bongardt, A. & Torres, F. 2018. Completing EMU, Deepening the EU. In: Caetano, J. & Sousa, M. (eds), *Challenges and Opportunities for Eurozone Governance*. New York: Novapublishers, pp. 165–182.

De Grauwe, P. & Ji, Y. 2016. Correcting for the Eurozone Design Failures: The Role of the ECB. In: Jones, E. & Torres, F. (eds), *Governance of the European Monetary Union*. London and New York: Routledge, pp. 739–754.

Fernández-Villaverde, J., Garicano, L. & Santos, T. 2013. "Political Credit Cycles: The Case of the Eurozone", *Journal of Economic Perspectives*, 27 (3): 145–166.

International Monetary Fund. 2015. Where Are We Headed? Perspectives on Potential Output. Chapter 3 in *World Economic Outlook: Uneven Growth – Short- and Long-Term Factors*. Washington DC: IMF, April.

Jones, Erik & Torres, Francisco (eds). 2016. *Governance of the European Monetary Union: Recasting Political, Fiscal and Financial Integration*. London: Routledge.

Mongelli, F., Dorrucci, E., Ioannou, D. & Terzi, A. 2016. Responses to the Euro Area Crisis: Measuring the Path of European Institutional Integration In: Jones, E. & Torres, F. (eds), *Governance of the European Monetary Union*. London and New York: Routledge, pp. 769–786.

Otero-Iglesias, M. 2015. "Stateless Euro: The Euro Crisis and the Revenge of the Chartalist Theory of Money", *Journal of Common Market Studies*, 53 (2): 349–364.

Pickford, S. et al. 2014. "How to Fix the Euro: Strengthening Economic Governance in Europe", Chatham House, Elcano and Arel Report, Chatham House, London, March.

Tsoukalis, L. 2016. *In Defence of Europe: Can the European Project Be Saved?* Oxford: Oxford University Press.

Index

Page numbers in **bold** denote tables, those in *italics* denote figures.

For Product Safety Concerns and Information please contact our EU
representative GPSR@taylorandfrancis.com
Taylor & Francis Verlag GmbH, Kaufingerstraße 24, 80331 München, Germany

www.ingramcontent.com/pod-product-compliance
Ingram Content Group UK Ltd.
Pitfield, Milton Keynes, MK11 3LW, UK
UKHW020012200926
475702UK00014B/1843
* 9 7 8 0 3 6 7 7 8 4 4 6 1 *